An Empire of Facts

An Empire of Facts presents a fascinating account of the formation of French conceptions of Islam in France's largest and most important colony. During the period from 1870–1914, travelers, bureaucrats, scholars, and writers formed influential and long-lasting misconceptions about Islam that determined the imperial cultural politics of Algeria and its interactions with republican France. Narratives of Islamic mysticism, rituals, gender relations, and sensational crimes brought unfamiliar cultural forms and practices to popular attention in France, but also constructed Algerian Muslims as objects for colonial intervention. Personal lives and interactions between Algerian and French men and women inflected these texts, determining their style, content, and consequences. Drawing on sources in Arabic and French, this book places such personal moments at the heart of the production of colonial knowledge, emphasizing the indeterminacy of ethnography, and its political context in the unfolding of France's empire and its relations with Muslim North Africa.

GEORGE R. TRUMBULL IV is Assistant Professor of History at Dartmouth College, New Hampshire.

Critical Perspectives on Empire

Editors

Professor Catherine Hall
University College London

Professor Mrinalini Sinha
Pennsylvania State University

Professor Kathleen Wilson
State University of New York, Stony Brook

Critical Perspectives on Empire is a major new series of ambitious, cross-disciplinary works in the emerging field of critical imperial studies. Books in the series will explore the connections, exchanges and mediations at the heart of national and global histories, the contributions of local as well as metropolitan knowledge, and the flows of people, ideas and identities facilitated by colonial contact. To that end, the series will not only offer a space for outstanding scholars working at the intersection of several disciplines to bring to wider attention the impact of their work; it will also take a leading role in reconfiguring contemporary historical and critical knowledge, of the past and of ourselves.

An Empire of Facts

Colonial Power, Cultural Knowledge, and Islam in Algeria, 1870–1914

George R. Trumbull IV

Dartmouth College

CAMBRIDGE
UNIVERSITY PRESS

CAMBRIDGE UNIVERSITY PRESS
Cambridge, New York, Melbourne, Madrid, Cape Town, Singapore, São Paulo, Delhi

Cambridge University Press
The Edinburgh Building, Cambridge CB2 8RU, UK

Published in the United States of America by Cambridge University Press, New York

www.cambridge.org
Information on this title: www.cambridge.org/9780521734349

First published 2009

Printed in the United Kingdom at the University Press, Cambridge

A catalogue record for this publication is available from the British Library

Library of Congress Cataloguing in Publication data
Trumbull, George R., 1977–
An empire of facts : colonial power, cultural knowledge, and Islam in Algeria, 1870–1914 / George R. Trumbull IV.
p. cm. – (Critical perspectives on empire)
Includes bibliographical references and index.
ISBN 978-0-521-51654-9 (hbk.) – ISBN 978-0-521-73434-9 (pbk.)
1. Algeria – Foreign public opinion, French. 2. Islam – Public opinion – History. 3. Public opinion – France – History. 4. Ethnology – Political aspects – France – History. 5. Islam – Algeria – Historiography. 6. Algeria – Colonial influence – Historiography. 7. Algeria – Ethnic relations – Historiography. 8. Political culture – Algeria – Historiography. 9. Algeria – Relations – France – Historiography. 10. France – Relations – Algeria – Historiography. I. Title. II. Series.
DT287.5.F8T78 2009
965′.03–dc22 2009028173

ISBN 978-0-521-51654-9 Hardback
ISBN 978-0-521-73434-9 Paperback

For my parents,
George R. Trumbull III and Lynda M. Trumbull,
and my sister, Melissa I. Trumbull,
for their love and support.

Contents

Illustrations

Acknowledgments

The years I spent on this book, I passed in a series of places new and old. The streets of New Haven, New Orleans, and New York framed this book, and in these places I incurred many intellectual debts. I wrote most of the dissertation, and much of the book, in Old Saybrook, where the debts I incurred were more personal but no less important. As I write these words, I embark on another new destination, in New Hampshire, and I greatly appreciate the confidence of my new colleagues in my work.

My dissertation committee enthusiastically and supportively oversaw a dissertation whose scope at times seemed daunting, and which forms the basis of this book. I owe a particular debt to John Merriman, who, in advising this dissertation, allowed me the freedom to develop it after my own fashion. His guidance preserved me from errors, both great and small, in interpretation and in methodology, and I learned much from the example of his diligent commitment to archival research. At Yale, I benefited greatly from the intellectual community of historians of the Francophone world that he fostered, and I remain in his debt for my six years under his tutelage.

Abbas Amanat's insistence on both the commonalities and the historical specificities of various parts of the Islamic world ensured that I kept both local and regional perspectives in balance. His interest in religion, politics, and cultural exchange across the Islamic world proved invaluable in the elaboration of my own thoughts throughout my graduate career. I thank him for his support for the project and for my development as a scholar of the Islamic world.

Christopher L. Miller's theoretical and meticulous scholarship provided the intellectual inspiration for this project. His devotion to truly interdisciplinary work in Francophone studies remains the model to which I look for my own work. Equally importantly, without his cogent critiques and kind words of encouragement, my dissertation would have proved a far more arduous task, and probably an impossible one. I am most grateful for his commitment to theory, for his belief in my project, and for the rigorous and considerate feedback he gave me from its very inception.

Julia Clancy-Smith proved the most present long-distance committee member I could ever have hoped to find. Her challenging queries and enthusiastic comments helped to mold this book. In particular, I thank her for helping me avoid gross errors of bibliographic omission, for her belief in the relevance of this project to Middle Eastern Studies, and for the high standards her scholarship has set for all who work in French colonial studies. She understood my attempts to make this a dissertation as relevant to North Africa as to France, and consistently pointed out ways I could do so more fruitfully.

Jay Winter, Stuart Schwartz, Jon Butler, Glenda Gilmore, Valerie Hansen, Paul Kennedy, Ben Kiernan, Stuart Schwartz, Frank Turner, and Jay Winter all freely shared their time and guidance in New Haven and beyond, and I thank them for their efforts.

I have benefited from an intellectual community of mutually supportive and brilliant scholars. I owe the greatest debt to Charles P. Keith, who read the majority of the words here (often from many time zones away), and discussed virtually all of these ideas with me over the past several years. His intellectual commitment to a sustained, critical scholarship of French colonialism and his never-flagging good cheer have inspired me at difficult moments. I thank him for his intellectual camaraderie, and I look forward to reading his own book in the near future. Kate Cambor provided companionship in New Haven, France, and New York, sharing her keen sense of humor and offering the shining example of her brilliance. Without her, graduate school and life after would have seemed far darker and far more difficult. I read more widely, wrote more fluently, and spoke more knowledgeably because of her example and her constant encouragement. My writing group, Katherine Mellen Charron, Claire Nee Nelson, and Adriane D. Lentz-Smith, provided me with critical ears, supportive words, and more intellectual companionship than any scholar has a right to expect in his entire career, let alone over a few years in graduate school.

I have found outstanding colleagues at many places in my academic career, among them Jennifer Boittin, Geraldo Cadava, Janet Chen, Rachel Chrastil, Catherine Dunlop, the Faillard family, Elizabeth Foster, Gretchen Heefner, Tammy Ingram, Caroline Kelly, Leah Mancina Khaghani, James Lundberg, Kenneth Loiselle, Julia Ott, John Warne Monroe, Jocelyn Olcott, Rebecca Rix, Katherine Scharf, Rebecca L. Slitt, and Helen Veit in New Haven and beyond; Rosanne Adderley, Victoria Allison, George Bernstein, Donna Denneen, Kenneth Harl,

Dick Latner, Tom Luongo, Colin MacLachlan, Jennifer Neighbors, Alisa Plant, Larry Powell, Sam Ramer, Susan Schroeder, Rich Watts, Eric Wedig, and especially Jim Boyden and Neeti Nair (to whom I remain most grateful for her friendship and good cheer), in New Orleans. At New York University, Edward Berenson, Jane Burbank, Herrick Chapman, Frederick Cooper, Michael Dash, Stéphane Gerson, Michael Gilsenan, Zachary Lockman, Judith Miller, and Frédéric Viguier gave freely of their time and advice. As an undergraduate at Princeton, I reaped the benefits of the greatest collegiate education in the world, with the best colleagues imaginable, at the hands of many of the greatest scholars and teachers, among them David Bellos, Robert Darnton, Raymond Fogelson, Norman Itzkowitz, Jonathan Lamb, Margaret Larkin, Rena Lederman, and Suzanne Marchand. My formative intellectual experiences occurred under their tutelage and by their example. I am also grateful to new colleagues at Dartmouth College, in whose congenial and stimulating company I completed this book.

The greater community of French colonial and North African historians have provided welcoming, challenging, and immensely helpful comments. Deborah Neil and I have discussed and debated the history of empire on two continents, always with great utility and joy. Patricia Lorcin offered much valuable advice, in Aix-en-Provence, subsequently, and, along with Paula Sanders, for a special issue of *French Historical Studies*. I also thank Alice L. Conklin, Matthew Connelly, Eric Jennings, and, in particular, Edmund "Terry" Burke III for sharing their experiences and invaluable perspective on many occasions. At Cambridge University Press, I am most grateful to Michael Watson and Helen Waterhouse for their hard work and faith in this project. Two readers' reports and series editors Catherine Hall, Mrinalini Sinha, and Kathleen Wilson provided many useful suggestions.

The generous support of many institutions and fellowships enabled the research and completion of this project, including the Mrs. Giles Whiting Foundation, the Yale Center for International and Area Studies and International Security Studies, the Smith Richardson Foundation, the Bourse Chateaubriand, a Fulbright–Hays dissertation research grant, and the Social Science Research Council's International Dissertation Field Research Fellowship. The last three grants allowed me to conduct research in Aix-en-Provence, Paris, Rabat, and Tunis, and without them this project would not have been possible. Madame Françoise Aujogue, archivist at the Archives nationales de France, generously shared her time and the breadth of her knowledge of Henri Duveyrier. Every effort has been made to secure necessary permissions to reproduce copyright material in this work, though in some cases it has proved impossible to trace copyright holders. If any omissions are brought to my notice, I will be happy to include appropriate acknowledgments on reprinting.

I thank multiple friends outside the academy for their forbearance when I returned calls with much delay, begged off on social occasions, or spoke too readily or at too much length about the book, especially Brian Bergstein, Alexis Newbrand Cooke, Krista C. Dobi, E. Bruce McEvoy IV, Thomas B. Nath, Sonia W. Nath, Rebecca Stewart, and Elizabeth C. Trumbull. Bill, Betty, and Mary Conner provided welcome refuge in Houston and support during my evacuation from New Orleans during Hurricane Katrina.

My greatest debt and most fervent thanks I owe to my family. My parents, George and Lyn Trumbull, and my sister, Melissa, offered never-failing support, good cheer, a boundless belief in my abilities, and ceaseless encouragement during the most difficult period. I cannot begin to express my gratitude.

I wrote the acknowledgments to the dissertation upon which I based this book in the aftermath of the greatest natural disaster in American history. I feel especially keenly the weight of my debt to the people listed in these pages. Any errors in the work, or omissions in these pages, reflect not a lack of gratitude, but rather the enormity of the task of properly acknowledging all those who have aided me in this process.

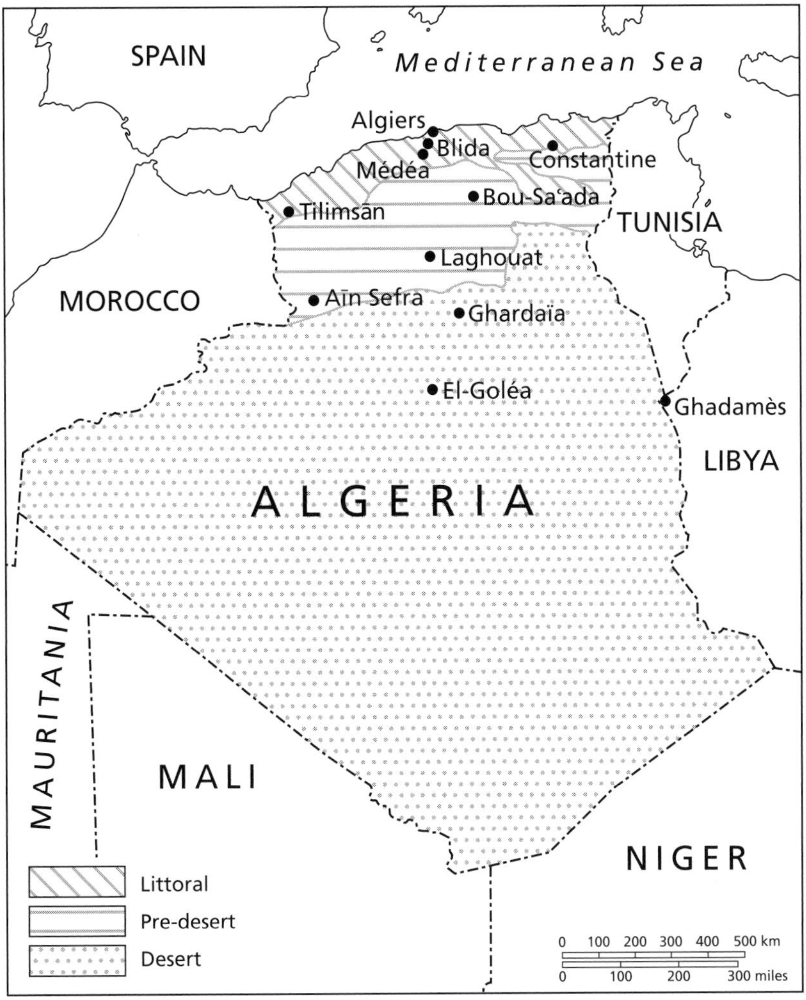

Ecological regions of Algeria

Settlement patterns in late nineteenth-century Algeria

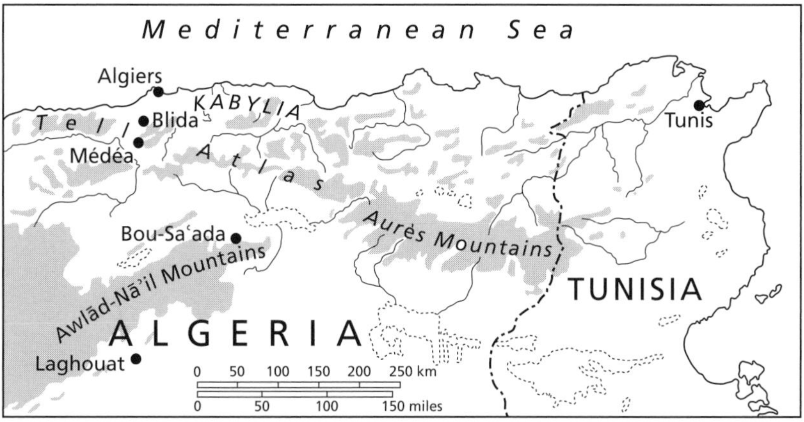

Kabylia, the Aurès and the mountains of the Awlād-Nā'il

Introduction: "sa vie étrange autour de nous"

Writing in 1891, Louis Rinn, French colonial administrator, ethnographer, and self-promoter, claimed in retrospect that on "July 13th, 1871, despite our reverses, despite the faults or the failings of several of our agents, we remained still, in the eyes of the natives, the uncontested sovereigns and recognized friends of the political or religious lords of the Sahara," and, he implied, of Algeria as a whole, despite the insurrection of 1870–1.[1] These words would have rung false, in 1870 or in 1871 or in 1891, to most Algerians, for whom colonial administrative failures loomed far more significant than any assertions of amity. Notwithstanding Rinn's assertions to the contrary, there remained, in 1871 and in 1914, nothing "uncontested" about empire in Algeria. The massive insurrection of 1871, initiated by the Raḥmāniyya in Kabylia, had threatened French control over Algeria.[2] Even on July 13, 1871, few administrators would have hazarded Rinn's later assertion. After such a demonstration of the precariousness of the colonial project in Algeria, administrators, scholars, and others struggled to prevent the constant, if often localized, forms of contestation of empire from again erupting into full-scale rebellion.

Indeed, these very contestations of sovereignty, the persistent and often violent rejection of colonial claims, resulted, in the aftermath of 1870, in a proliferation of texts that recorded the interests, anxieties, and errors of a colonial state stubbornly attempting to assert its power. The history of such texts, of their methodologies, narratives, and analyses, reveals the methods French colonial administrators, scholars, travelers, and politicians used to gather information about Algerians. These writers gathered, above all, potentially useful information, narrating cultural forms in an attempt to facilitate control. As J. P. Daughton contends, "French colonialism took shape according to the exigencies of limited colonial

[1] Louis Rinn, *Histoire de l'insurrection de 1871 en Algérie* (Algiers: Adolphe Jourdan, 1891), 503.

[2] Edmond Doutté, *L'Islam algérien en l'an 1900* (Algiers: Giralt, 1900), 75–7.

manpower and budgets, as well as fears over indigenous unrest."[3] Between the end of the insurrection of 1871 and the (illusory) rise of the specter of Pan-Islamism in the 1910s, cultural descriptions articulated with an eye toward the maintenance of power represented the fundamental means through which agents of French colonialism conceived of Algerians and analyzed potential unrest. Comprehending the history of Algeria in the late nineteenth century requires teasing out these strands of politically interested narratives, and demands a critical understanding of the relationship between the production of cultural knowledge and attempts to sustain colonial control.

These narratives, analyses, and descriptions represented the fundamental means through which administrators and others interested in empire came to terms with Algeria and with Algerian Islam. In essence, personal interactions enshrined in texts governed how French administrators governed, producing generalizations and explanations that determined practices. These texts reveal the ways in which their authors recognized difference in an attempt to limit its political impact. "Each time that [he] had the occasion of the details of Arab life," Achille Robert, ethnographer and colonial administrator, had "but one desire, that of lifting a bit more the veil that yet hides from our eyes the native people."[4] In tellingly gendered language, Robert presented his role as one of uncovering, exposing, laying bare. The gift he made of his book to the governor general's chief of staff leaves little room for doubt about the ultimate purpose of such revelation. The exposure of cultural elements of Algeria aimed at providing a corpus of handbooks for the colonial project and its administrators.

Many of these texts took the form of what I call here "ethnography," cultural narratives drawn from participant observation and research in vernacular languages, in this case largely Arabic, though also various Berber languages. Ethnography is a pervasive style of culture writing simultaneously resulting from and valorizing participant observation as a method of knowing about others. During its formative years, ethnography bolstered colonial authority by codifying identity as a discrete realm for colonial intervention. It includes "a characteristic attitude of participant observation among the artifacts of a defamiliarized cultural reality."[5]

3 J. P. Daughton, *An Empire Divided: Religion, Republicanism, and the Making of French Colonialism, 1880–1914* (Oxford: Oxford University Press, 2006), 261.

4 Achille Robert, *L'Arabe tel qu'il est: études algériennes et tunisiennes* (Algiers: Imprimerie Joseph Angelini, 1900), 5.

5 James Clifford, *The Predicament of Culture: Twentieth-Century Ethnography, Literature, and Art* (Cambridge, Mass.: Harvard University Press, 1988), 121; Herman Lebovics, *True France: The Wars over Cultural Identity, 1900–1945* (Ithaca, NY: Cornell University Press,

Though long the preserve of anthropologists or ethnologists, ethnography itself represents not a discipline, and assuredly not a "science,"[6] but a genre, a specific kind of non-fiction writing with attendant narrative conventions and set pieces in prose. However, "ethnography, a hybrid activity," in the words of James Clifford, "appears as writing, as collecting, as modernist collage, as imperial power, as subversive critique."[7] Moreover, in colonial Algeria, various other forms of texts consciously mimicked ethnographies based on participant observation. In an attempt to bolster their own narrative and analytical authority, travelers, novelists, and political figures imitated ethnographies, creating not ethnographies of their own, but rather ethnographic texts, narratives that intentionally resembled other forms of ethnography, and largely participated in the same discursive debates. The genre's recent rediscovery by non-anthropologists returns ethnography to its roots in manifold disciplines, highlighting its multiplicity of voices. Neither the twentieth century, nor any particular discipline, gave birth to ethnography. This book represents not a history of the discipline of ethnology, but rather of ethno*graphy*, of narrative writing about culture that took place in part, and often largely, outside of disciplines. The history of ethnography traces not a disciplinary history, but a literary one.

Defined through relations of participant observation enmeshed in unequal power relations, colonial ethnographies trace the histories, above all, of interactions. The behaviors and beliefs of many Algerians remained occluded, outside the purview of ethnographers. Hence, colonial ethnographies, like all administrative archives, perhaps overemphasize zones of contact and interaction.[8] The Algerians who had closest contact with ethnographers manifested various intentions, personal and political,

1992), 15. Cf. Emmanuelle Sibeud, *Une Science impériale pour l'Afrique?: La construction des savoirs africanistes en France 1878–1930* (Paris: Éditions de l'École des hautes études en sciences sociales, 2002), 35–40, 244.

6 Stephen A. Tyler, "Post-Modern Ethnography: From Document of the Occult to Occult Document," in James Clifford and George E. Marcus, eds., *Writing Culture: The Poetics and Politics of Ethnography* (Berkeley, Calif.: University of California Press, 1986), 130.

7 Clifford, *Predicament*, 13; James Clifford, "Introduction: Partial Truths," in Clifford and Marcus, *Writing Culture*, 2.

8 Allan Christelow, *Muslim Law Courts and the French Colonial State in Algeria* (Princeton, NJ: Princeton University Press, 1985), 83–4; David A. Robinson, *Paths of Accommodation: Muslim Societies and French Colonial Authorities in Senegal and Mauritania, 1880–1920*, Western African Studies (Athens, OH: Ohio University Press, 2000), 2–4, 37–8, 50. Julia Clancy-Smith correctly identifies "bet hedging, revolt, shifting trade strategies, migration, withdrawal [and] avoidance protest" as "the main motors of historical change" in nineteenth-century Algeria; only some of these "kinds of sociopolitical action" show up in ethnographic texts, though all such ethnographies arose out of such a context. Julia Clancy-Smith, *Rebel and Saint: Muslim Notables, Populist Protest, Colonial Encounters (Algeria and Tunisia, 1800–1904)* (Berkeley, Calif.: University of California Press, 1994),

through the information or misinformation they provided to administrators and other writers.[9] Nevertheless, colonial administrators and other ethnographers *interpreted* such intentional interactions as *typical*; each informant served as the presumed archetype for the multitude of Algerians who refused to countenance such ties, who may or may not have shared such intentions, and about whose beliefs the archive often remains silent.

Moreover, such interactions arose out of specific political and intellectual formations on the part of bureaucrats, as well. French engagement with Islam and with Algeria by no means began in 1870 (or, for that matter, 1871). The scant few weeks between Charles X's 1830 invasion of Algeria and the rise of the July Monarchy demonstrate a fundamental continuity in France's colonial policy in North Africa. Despite the often violent transitions from the Restoration, to the July Monarchy, to the Second Republic, to the Second Empire, to the Third Republic, no nineteenth-century French regime attempted to roll back France's empire in Algeria. Although the challenges, responses, policies, and commitment of these various regimes differed, they ultimately all shared the pursuit of the extension of French control over the Maghrib. Nevertheless, Algerians contested the colonial project, at times violently and episodically, and at others times in more covert, if more deeply entrenched, ways.[10]

Moments of violent resistance often occurred simultaneously with, or in response to, French attempts at closer domination. The 1830s and 1840s witnessed the efflorescence of ʿAbd al-Qādir's attempts to purge Algeria of the French and the concomitant expansion of French use of violence, the despoliation of *ḥubus* land (land bequests for specific religious purposes), and the creation of the *bureaux arabes*, the first French attempts to codify knowledge about Algerians. Intelligence officers and Arabic speakers, the agents of the *bureaux arabes* formed much of the policy directed at Algerians, in the process alienating Algerians and settlers alike, yet also providing a template for the emergence of a codified body of knowledge and purported expertise.[11]

4. On theorizing power gradients in the contact zone, see Mary Louise Pratt, *Imperial Eyes: Travel Writing and Transculturation* (London: Routledge, 1992), 1–11.

[9] See, broadly, James C. Scott, *Domination and the Arts of Resistance: Hidden Transcripts* (New Haven, Conn.: Yale University Press, 1990).

[10] Clancy-Smith, *Rebel and Saint*, 4; Charles-André Julien, *Histoire de l'Algérie contemporaine*, vol II: *La Conquête et les débuts de la colonization (1827–1871)* (Paris: Presses universitaires de France, 1964), 427–9.

[11] Patricia Lorcin, *Imperial Identities: Stereotyping, Prejudice and Race in Colonial Algeria* (London: I. B. Tauris, 1999), 78–81, 91; John Ruedy, *Modern Algeria: The Origins and Development of a Nation*, 2nd edn (Bloomington, Ind.: Indiana University Press, 2005), 72–3.

The turmoil of the Second Republic at home mirrored turmoil in Algeria. France's affirmation of Algeria as inalienable, French territory in 1848 fooled none of the Algerians who rose up in the Aurès, Zaʿatsha, Kabylia, or Laghouat between 1850 and 1852. Though discontinuous in their armed contestation, Algerians never acquiesced to French bureaucratic and military impositions. Indeed, Napoleon III's 1860 introduction of the concept of a French "Arab Kingdom" may, in fact, have reflected less the emperor's affinities for Algerians than a belated recognition of the precariousness, eventual if not immediate, of France's empire in North Africa.[12] The continued legalized and extralegal confiscations of communally held lands throughout the 1860s attested, however, to the continuation of colonial policies favoring the increasingly large and increasingly strident settler population of Algeria. Whatever its rhetoric, during the Second Empire Napoleon III's "Arab Kingdom" shrank both as a political idea and in terms of the area of land under Algerian control. Similarly, as Patricia Lorcin has ably demonstrated, the emergence of the "Kabyle Myth" reflected the assimilationist and discriminatory cultural logic of colonial power.[13] Token policies, such as the ability for Algerians to request naturalization as French citizens, came with such severe strictures as to render their application nearly moot, and the French "Arab Kingdom" did little or nothing to mitigate the effects of the massive 1865 famine.[14]

The fall of the Second Empire dramatically changed the relationship among the colonial government, settlers, and Algerians. Both the 1870 Crémieux Decree, which granted French citizenship to Algerian Jews, and the major Raḥmāniyya insurrection of the same year, which nearly ousted French control, ushered in a new era of cultural and administrative politics. The Ṣūfī-organized insurrection, in particular, threatened to destabilize the foundations of the colonial regime.[15] Administrative changes in the 1880s both bound the colony more tightly to France politically and augmented the settlers' role in governance. Increased settler participation in colonial governance exacerbated colonial tensions and worsened conditions for many Algerians.[16] By 1914, compulsory

[12] On the *Royaume arabe*, see Julien, *Histoire de l'Algérie* 425; Lorcin, *Imperial Identities*, 76–97; Ruedy, *Modern Algeria*, 75–7; Benjamin Stora, *Algeria 1830–2000*, trans. Jane Marie Todd (Ithaca, NY: Cornell University Press, 2001), 5.

[13] Lorcin, *Imperial Identities*; Charles-Robert Ageron, *Histoire de l'Algérie contemporaine*, vol. II: *De l'insurrection de 1871 au déclenchement de la guerre de libération (1954)* (Paris: Presses universitaires de France, 1979), 137–51.

[14] On the Second Empire more broadly, see Julien, *Histoire de l'Algérie*, 387–452.

[15] Clancy-Smith, *Rebel and Saint*; Julien, *Histoire de l'Algérie*, 453–500.

[16] Ageron, *Histoire de l'Algérie*, 10, 19, 66; Julien, *Histoire de l'Algérie*; 495–500; Ruedy, *Modern Algeria*, 81–6; Stora, *Algeria*, 6–7.

military participation meant that almost 200,000 Algerians fought as soldiers in World War I, yet the imminent disintegration of the Ottoman Empire raised Pan-Islamism as a looming specter in French, if not Algerian, eyes.

The period between the Raḥmāniyya insurrection and the largely illusory Pan-Islamist "threat" corresponded to administrative and political change in France and Algeria that reoriented scholarship produced on Islam. The period 1870–1914 witnessed modifications in both policies and representations, contestations, and experiences, in the religious and cultural politics of empire. The concatenation of debates about French republicanism, the aftermath of the Raḥmāniyya insurrection, the emergence of the social sciences, changes in governance practices in Algeria, and debates about religion make 1870–1914 a particularly fruitful period to examine the production of ethnographic texts, before the advent of World War I and the potential threat of Pan-Islamism fundamentally altered interpretations of Islam. As a form of narrative associated with fieldwork practices, ethnography took on greater importance in the early Third Republic.

Republicanism among colonial bureaucrats and ethnographers assuredly did not represent any kind of transcendent, unitary political ideology. Rather, ethnographers and administrators in Algeria embodied the republic in ways similar to those of French people in the metropole: discontinuously, ambivalently, contradictorily, if at all. "We need," notes Frederick Cooper, "to take seriously what it meant for a polity to *think like an empire*."[17] If, in Algeria, writers and officials paid a certain attention to republican political questions, it may have represented more an adherence to bureaucratic form than to any ideology. When I describe texts as "republican," I refer to their reception in ambiguously republican France, not to any evanescent political intent of the author. Colonial ethnography was "republican," when it was, through its engagement with ambivalent debates *about* republicanism.[18] Writing from a wide variety of political perspectives, and explicitly specifying them only rarely, ethnographers did not embody any of the divergent "republican ideologies." Instead, they helped form their parameters. Ethnography did not reflect

[17] Frederick Cooper, *Colonialism in Question: Theory, Knowledge, History* (Berkeley, Calif.: University of California Press, 2005), 200. Such thinking, Cooper argues, did not involve thinking like a nation-state, but rather like an empire-state (153, 156, 182); Daughton, *An Empire Divided*, 21. See especially James McDougall on the dangers of projecting the Algerian nation backward through time: James McDougall, *History and the Culture of Nationalism in Algeria* (Cambridge: Cambridge University Press, 2006), 5, 10, 225–38.

[18] Daughton, *An Empire Divided*, 23, notes "how fragmented and diverse republican opinion about colonization . . . was."

French republicanism but articulated different positions about what that republicanism might look like.

From the perspective of colonial ethnography, republicanism frequently remained a practical or bureaucratic question, rather than an ideological one. Algeria in the early Third Republic formed part of a republican empire-state, but debates about ideology played out differently. "Republicanism" often served as a discursive strategy, utilized for promotion within the bureaucratic ranks or mobilized as an ideological counter-construction to a reified Islamic Algeria. French colonialism relied on and exploited the fluid process of defining the meanings of a republican empire.[19] For the most part, colonial ethnographers manifested an interest in republican ideology only to the extent to which their professional or intellectual formation required it of them in specific contexts, as in their dealings with the politics of religion. As Allan Christelow has written of earlier administrators, "[t]hough the French . . . were not exalted revolutionaries, they did have an egalitarian revolutionary heritage – which occasionally came to the fore . . . and which strongly influenced the values of at least some sectors of the colonial regime."[20] That foregrounding of France's "revolutionary heritage" arose sporadically in colonial ethnography, not as part of a clear, ideological project, but in relation to some aspects of Algeria rather than others. Ethnographic interest in Islam indicates less the triumph of republican secularism or the civilizing mission than anxieties about challenges to both; political ethnography focused on Islam out of concern for its potentially disruptive nature.

Moreover, ethnographers did not actually have to believe in republican values for their texts to serve the purposes of the Third Republic's empire; the political allegiances of authors, varied though they were, scarcely determined the state's readings of ethnographies. As a result, ethnography of Algeria was "republican" only insofar as it enacted a series of discursive practices benefiting from the force – often literal – of power. These practices in turn reinforced the attempted domination of the Third Republic over Algerians. Algerian ethnography illuminates the ways in which the colonial project, fundamentally opposed to many

19 On meaning-making in the republican empire, see Alice L. Conklin, *A Mission to Civilize: The Republican Idea of Empire in France and West Africa, 1895–1930* (Stanford, Calif.: Stanford University Press, 1997); Cooper, *Colonialism in Question*, 171–7; Herman Lebovics, *True France: Wars Over Cultural Identity, 1900–1945* (Ithaca, NY: Cornell University Press, 1992); Gary Wilder, *The French Imperial Nation-State: Negritude and Colonial Humanism between the Two World Wars* (Chicago: University of Chicago Press, 2005).

20 Allan Christelow, *Muslim Law Courts and the French Colonial State in Algeria* (Princeton, NJ: Princeton University Press, 1985), 109.

aspects of the republic, subsumed and incorporated divergent political views in pursuit of domination.

Colonial ethnographies created cultural representations enforced through assertions of authenticity, generating "facts," descriptions with the force of claims to truth. However, these signs posing as facts have no easily ascertainable relationship to the underlying phenomena they purport to describe. Pierre Martino, a colonial commentator, wrote of contemporary ethnography, "one will never know the true value of these books – what they contain of spontaneous impressions, and of literary procedure, true admiration and official enthusiasm – but in meeting the author," a possibility definitively denied to historians.[21] As James Clifford notes, ethnography has never offered a privileged scientific register for the depiction of cultures.

> There is no way definitely, surgically, to separate the factual from the allegorical in cultural accounts. The data of ethnography make sense only within patterned . . . narratives, and these are conventional, political, and meaningful in a more than referential sense. Cultural facts are not true and cultural allegories false . . . [T]he relation of fact to allegory is a domain of struggle. The meanings of an ethnographic account are uncontrollable,[22]

uncontrollable in the double sense, both escaping hegemonic fixation and lacking a scientific, experimental "control." Specifying particular ethnographic allegories, as with the reading of any other literary texts, in no way forecloses other possible readings. These texts, polysemic and narratively rich, give rise to multiple possible readings, of which I can address only a few.

Chapter 1 introduces the mechanisms and practices of colonial ethnographic writing. Focusing on the emergence of participant-observation methodology and the articulation of concomitant narrative forms, the chapter focuses on the political contexts that gave rise to specific ways of writing about culture.

The second chapter traces the lives and worlds of various ethnographers. Their trajectories within institutions, across Algeria, and both inside and outside of organized power structures reveal the diverse opportunities and constrictions that women and men in colonial Algeria faced in writing ethnography. Drawing on theoretical works on reflexive ethnographic narrative, the chapter emphasizes the personal experiences,

21 Pierre Martino, "L'Œuvre algérienne d'Ernest Feydeau," *Revue africaine* 274 (1909:3), 134–5.

22 James Clifford, "On Ethnographic Allegory," in Clifford and Marcus, eds., *Writing Culture*, 119–20.

at times occluded and only gestured at, that construct ethnographic authority.

Chapter 3 analyzes representations of religious sociability. Ṣūfī orders provided the primary means of organizing religious life in nineteenth-century Algeria, at times playing a major role in organizing revolt and providing foyers for cultural, intellectual, and social continuities. In the context of debates over religion and republicanism in France, colonial ethnographies depicted various Ṣūfī orders as politically oriented in various ways. Nevertheless, ethnographic descriptions reached no conclusions about individual orders; rather, such texts often portrayed individual Ṣūfī orders as simultaneously threatening and anodyne, useful and potentially dangerous.

Addressing popular forms of religious belief, chapter 4 investigates the political generalizations and the creation of primitivist ethnography. Beliefs in genies and rituals to end drought reveal specific tropes in the colonial denigration of Algerians' intellectual capacities. The civilizing mission required an object on which to act, an object furnished by ethnographers and their generation of primitivist interpretations of popular beliefs.

Chapter 5 illustrates the moral context under which ethnography operated. Colonial ethnographers reconfigured gender relations among Algerians as the central moral problem, as both empire's obstacle and the means to overcome it. The civilizing mission in Algeria functioned, as well, as a moralizing one revolving around interventions on gendered bodies.

Finally, chapter 6 reveals the ultimate consequences of representations rooted in violence. The deaths of three explorers, their sensationalized coverage in print media and in ethnographies, and their commemorations revolved around configuring entire ethnic groups of the Sahara as inescapably criminal, as culturally predestined to murder and violence. The imbrication of colonial ethnography with the political interests of empire created representations that equated cultural identities with crime.

Colonial ethnography served avowedly political ends. Participants in and observers of the daily lives of Algerians from the Mediterranean to the Sahara, administrators, authors, scholars, and others intended, ultimately, to produce usable texts. The explorer Fernand Foureau addressed one military ethnographer in the introduction to Captain Métois's *La Soumission des Touareg du Nord* (1906). "You have now to surround yourself with serious and sure informants, and you have, by a rigorous control and a meticulous selection, constituted a sort of memo on the political . . . state of the tribes," wrote Foureau, "information that, alone, permitted you to direct them easily and without clashes towards the goals that seemed the best for the interest of France and for the future of the country itself."[23] Nevertheless, within politicized ethnography emerged other, more narrative impulses both advancing and restraining such aims. Magali-Boisnard, in her ethnography of the Aurès, wrote a poem in rhyme as an ode to her experiences in the region. "Nous voulons voir sa vie étrange autour de nous / Ses gestes de Barbare aux yeux larges et doux";[24] aesthetic experiences of the exotic attracted ethnographers as much as any political project of empire. Direction always remained difficult, goals conflicting, lives strange, clashes numerous and violent. This empire of facts emerged out of contestation and strife, out of narratives and politics.

[23] Fernand Foureau, "Préface," Captain Métois, *La Soumission des Touareg du Nord* (Paris: Augustin Challamel, 1906), 6.

[24] "We want to see its [i.e., the Aurès's] strange life around us / Its gestures of Barbary with large, soft eyes"; Magali-Boisnard, "L'Aurès barbare," *Bulletin de la Société de Géographie d'Alger et de l'Afrique du Nord* 13 (1908:1): 45.

1 Writing like a state: the question of anthropology and the colonial origins of politicized ethnography

"The Algerian question," wrote Camille Sabatier, senator, administrator, colonist, and ethnographer, "is in part a question of anthropology."[1] In 1883, when Sabatier penned these words, France stood in the middle of the long period historians have erroneously referred to as the "pacification" of Algeria. Not coincidentally, the period corresponds precisely to the attempts of the early Third Republic (1871–1914) to consolidate republican government in metropolitan France. The "Algerian question," the problem of how to integrate a hostile, perplexingly different territory into France, seems more a question of politics than anthropology.

In fact, the two were inseparable. Creating the fiction of French Algeria required not only political machinations, but also intellectual sleight of hand. Nascent social science disciplines generated the intellectual bases of empire. At the same time, "there never was," Philippe Lucas and Jean-Claude Vatin declared, "an *anthropology* of Algeria. The struggle for national liberation proved it: the chimeras had never been accepted."[2] The Algerian question was only partly a question of anthropology. Administrators,[3] scholars, and travel writers[4] relied upon particular forms of methodology and narrative to codify information about

[1] Camille Sabatier, "La Femme kabyle," *Bulletin de la Société de Géographie et d'Archéologie d'Oran* [*BSGAO*] 16 (1883): 136.

[2] Philippe Lucas and Jean-Claude Vatin, *L'Algérie des anthropologues* (Paris: François Maspéro, 1975), 7.

[3] Patricia M. E. Lorcin, *Imperial Identities: Stereotyping, Prejudice and Race in Colonial Algeria* (London: I. B. Tauris, 1999), 130–6; Emmanuelle Sibeud, *Une Science impériale pour l'Afrique? La construction des savoirs africanistes en France, 1878–1930* (Paris: Éditions de l'École des hautes études en sciences sociales, 2002), 85. On the administration, see Charles-Robert Ageron, *Les Algériens musulmans et la France (1871–1919)*, vol. II: (Paris: Presses universitaires de France, 1968), 631–706; Charles-Robert Ageron, *Histoire de l'Algérie contemporaine*, vol. II: *De l'insurrection de 1871 au déclenchement de la guerre de libération (1954)* (Paris: Presses universitaires de France, 1979), 19–68, 183–200, 227–53.

[4] Cf. James Clifford, *Routes: Travel Writing and Transculturation in the Late Twentieth Century* (Cambridge, Mass.: Harvard University Press, 1997), 2, 3, 53.

Algerians. Arising from technologies of authoritarian control, participant observation demonstrated its utility by providing practical knowledge about Algerians.[5] The colonial administration exerted selective pressure on narrative *styles*, rewarding its functionaries and scholars for producing useful texts. Ethnography proved the most effective means of presenting, communicating, and, perhaps most importantly, perpetuating French conceptions of Algerian identity.

An analysis of genre, narrative strategies, and the creation of authority circumvents two methodological problems. First, a narrow focus on academic social science omits travelers, administrators, settlers, and scholars who wrote ethnographies outside of academic restrictions, to say nothing of the Algerian informants. Methodological innovation caused and resulted from dissociation from academic institutions. Moreover, Stephen A. Tyler contends that "the history of ethnographic writing . . . implicate[s] different *uses* of ethnography"[6] arising from political necessities. As James Clifford notes, "the development of ethnographic science cannot ultimately be understood in isolation from more general political-epistemological debates about . . . otherness."[7] Focusing on ethnographic discourses reintegrates such narratives with other, larger strands in the intellectual, cultural, and political history of the Third Republic.

Secondly, a disciplinary history risks reinscribing that discipline's intellectual trajectory. Twentieth-century ethnographers played central roles in the development of the social sciences and the study of Islam.[8]

[5] Lorcin, *Imperial Identities*, 165; Edward Said, *Culture and Imperialism* (New York: Alfred A. Knopf, 1994), xiv; Abdellah Hammoudi, *Master and Disciple: The Cultural Foundations of Moroccan Authoritarianism* (Chicago: University of Chicago Press, 1997), 107; cf. Peter Dunwoodie, *Writing French Algeria* (Oxford: Clarendon Press, 1998), 39; cf. Nicholas B. Dirks, *Castes of Mind: Colonialism and the Making of Modern India* (Princeton, NJ: Princeton University Press, 2001), 191 on India. Emmanuelle Sibeud's contention that imperial participant observation did not occur because of colonial power gradients misunderstands the impossibility of fieldwork outside of a context of narrative authority and power relations; see Sibeud, *Une Science impériale pour l'Afrique*, 167–8. Moreover, her approach renders Africa as an alarmingly homogenized discursive field.

[6] Stephen A. Tyler, "Post-Modern Ethnography: From Document of the Occult to Occult Document," in James Clifford and George E. Marcus, eds., *Writing Culture: The Poetics and Politics of Ethnography* (Berkeley, Calif.: University of California Press, 1986), 127.

[7] James Clifford, *The Predicament of Culture: Twentieth-Century Ethnography, Literature, and Art* (Cambridge, Mass.: Harvard University Press, 1988), 24.

[8] On Durkheim: Manfred Halpern, "Emile Durkheim: Analyst of Solidarity but Not of Transformation," in *Connaissances du Maghreb: sciences sociales et colonization*, Recherches sur les sociétés méditerranéennes (Paris: Éditions du Centre national de la recherche scientifique, 1984), 245, and Lucette Valensi, "Le Maghreb vu du centre: sa place dans l'école sociologique française," in *Connaissances du Maghreb*, 227–44; George W. Stocking, Jr., *Delimiting Anthropology: Occasional Essays and Reflections* (Madison, Wisc.: University of Wisconsin Press, 2001), 216. On Frazer: Edmond Doutté, *Magie*

Nevertheless, they emerged out of a dialogue with the lesser-known ethnographers whose texts form the basis of this study. Moreover, Lucas errs in positing "a progressive detachment of ethnological knowledge from the element of colonial *command*."[9] Just as Nicholas Dirks argues for India, in Algeria "ethnography became the primary colonial modality of representation, linking politics and epistemology in a tight embrace."[10] The historical notion of the development of ethnology into value-free description of other cultures, a notion that has rapidly imploded as anthropologists have turned their analytical gaze inward, minimizes ethnology's origins in colonial racial science[11] and must not obfuscate the collusion of early *ethnographers* with colonialism's physical and epistemic violence. Historians cannot assume that the intellectual development of any discipline was a foregone conclusion and instead must resurrect forgotten texts to understand how that evolution occurred.[12] In focusing this study not on disciplinary boundaries, but rather on their transgression, enacted through ethnographies, I will avoid the reinscription of an intellectual pre-history of the social sciences

et religion dans l'Afrique du Nord: la société musulmane du Maghrib (Algiers: Adolphe Jourdan, 1909), 511 and *passim*; see Alfred Bel, "Sidi Bou Medyan et son maître Ed-Daqqâq à Fès", *Mélanges René Basset: études nord-africaines et orientales* I (1923), 38; Alfred Bel, "Survivance d'une fête du printemps à Tunis signalée aux XIe siècle de l'h. (XVIIe de J.-C.[)] par l'historien musulman Ibn Abî Dînâr al-Qaîrawânî," *Revue tunisienne*, nos. 19–20 (1934): 343; Edmond Doutté, *Merrâkech* (Paris: Comité du Maroc, 1905), 73–8, 89. Abdellah Hammoudi, *The Victim and its Masks: An Essay on Sacrifice and Masquerade in the Maghreb*, trans. Paula Wissing (Chicago: University of Chicago Press, 1993), 25. On Mauss: Doutté, *Magie et religion*, 67; Doutté, *Merrâkech*, 103; Clifford, *Predicament*, 123–5. On Tylor: Alfred Bel, *La Population musulmane de Tlemcen* (Paris: Libraire Paul Geuthner, 1908), 57; Alfred Bel, review of "A. van GENNEP: la formation des légendes," *BSGAO* 31 (March 1911): 81. On Gellner: Talal Asad, "The Concept of Cultural Translation in British Social Anthropology," in Clifford and Marcus, eds., *Writing Culture*, 141–64.

9 Philippe Lucas, "Structures dialogiques dans les ethnologies françaises de l'Algérie: hypothèses de travail," in *Connaissances du Maghreb*, 251. Emphasis in the original. See Clifford, "Introduction: Partial Truths," in Clifford and Marcus, eds., *Writing Culture*, 11, on the need for "noncelebratory histories" of ethnography.

10 Dirks, *Castes of Mind*, 123.

11 See Lorcin, *Imperial Identities*.

12 On the dangers of a history of disciplines: Michel Foucault, *The Archeology of Knowledge and the Discourse on Language*, trans. A. M. Sheridan Smith (New York: Pantheon Books, 1972), 137–40, and 162. Lorcin, *Imperial Identities*, offers the perfect example of how to write the history of a concept (race) enacted through both disciplines and institutions. Also on race: Gilles Boëtsch and Jean-Noël Ferrié, "L'Impossible Objet de la raciologie: prologue à une anthropologie physique du Nord de l'Afrique"; Noël Coye, "Préhistoire et protohistoire en Algérie au XIXe siècle: les significations du document archéologique"; Jean-Noël Ferrié, "La Naissance de l'aire culturelle méditerranéenne dans l'anthropologie physique de l'Afrique du Nord"; Karim Haoui, "Classifications linguistiques et anthropologiques de la Société d'anthropologie de Paris au XIXe siècle"; and Ann Thomson, "La Classification raciale de l'Afrique du Nord au début du XIXe siècle"; all in *Cahiers d'études africaines* 129, no. 33 (1993:1).

in the hope of explicating the close links between colonial politics and ethnography.

A genre history reveals two fundamental elements in the French colonial ethnography of Algeria. As a methodology, participant observation arose out of the power politics of empire. Ethnography, as its concomitant form of narrative, marshaled that methodology to make authoritative statements, enabling the oppressive political interests of the colonial state to appear less obtrusive. Hence, the history of colonial Algerian ethnography must reconcile the history of discursive, rhetorical, and epistemic violence with the history of physical, political, and ontological violence by revealing the implication of the latter in the use of the former. It must aim at what Herman Lebovics calls "cultural history with the state not only left in but with a commanding presence,"[13] at demystifying the construction of what Michel Foucault has called power-knowledge.[14] As Talal Asad has noted, empire "made possible the kind of human intimacy on which anthropological fieldwork is based, but ensured that that intimacy should be one-sided and provisional."[15] The authority of words, representations, and knowledge did not exist separately from the authority of bullets, actions, and technologies; they form an epistemological and historical whole. The colonial state, as Dirks asserts, is an ethnographic state.[16]

Sherry B. Ortner elaborates a role for cultural history that provides the underpinning methodological orientation for my work. She emphasizes "the issue of meaning-*making*" and the need to focus on "the culture of the ethnographer," not as a normative form, but rather as an object of study.[17]

> There is always a story to be told, a story of struggle and change, a story in which actors are differentially situated with respect to power and have differential intentions. "Culture" is the means of understanding . . . the forms of power and agency [people] are able to construct . . . embedding cultural interpretation within larger (represented or implied) narratives of social and political existence – of people both gripped by circumstances and transforming them – is another way of . . . illuminating the complex motives and complex debates that are the stuff of real lives and struggles.[18]

[13] Herman Lebovics, *True France: The Wars over Cultural Identity, 1900–1945* (Ithaca, NY: Cornell University Press, 1992), xvi. See also Hammoudi, *Master and Disciple*, xiv.

[14] Michel Foucault, *The Foucault Reader*, ed. Paul Rabinow (New York: Pantheon Books, 1984), 175.

[15] Talal Asad, "Introduction," in Talal Asad, ed., *Anthropology and the Colonial Encounter* (New York: Humanities Press, 1973), 17.

[16] Dirks, *Castes of Mind*, 53, 60, 123.

[17] Sherry B. Ortner, "Introduction," in *The Fate of "Culture": Geertz and Beyond* (Berkeley, Calif: University of California Press, 1998), 8–9. Emphasis in the original.

[18] Ortner, "Introduction," 9–11.

Ortner reconciles sociopolitical processes with individual lives by analyzing culture as a means by which people represent those processes to themselves. Moreover, as Christopher L. Miller contends, "if we confront and analyze the degree to which hegemonic forces tried to be monolithic, we are not in any way foreclosing a reading of resistances . . . or hybridities that happened to confound them."[19] Embedding the study of culture in relation to hegemonic forces facilitates the study of contestation.

Ethnography resembles James Scott's "state simplifications," which are "*interested,* utilitarian . . . documentary . . . aggregate . . . [and] *standardized.*"[20] Participant observation assisted the colonial state in reading Algerian cultures and lent its authority to ethnography as state simplification, but with a diverse and at times contradictory variety of legible forms.[21] Ethnography embodies how the French colonial state in Algeria wrote. "Legibility," Scott contends, "is a condition of manipulation."[22] Equally importantly, however, it is an *effect* of manipulation; the creation of manifold identity effects through politicized ethnography facilitated French control. Like Scott's "state simplifications," ethnographic texts "represented only that slice of [society] that interested the official observer,"[23] but those representations took many shapes.

State simplifications respond to particular circumstances. Ethnographic authority depends on detailed knowledge of a circumscribed space, the field.[24] Despite recent re-examinations of disciplinary assumptions about the field, fieldwork remains at the heart of ethnography's identity.[25] Ethnographers used fieldwork to construct authority and render colonial societies legible. Thus, the study of colonial ethnography

19 Christopher L. Miller, *Nationalists and Nomads: Essays on Francophone African Literature and Culture* (Chicago: University of Chicago Press, 1998), 4.

20 James C. Scott, *Seeing Like a State: How Certain Schemes to Improve the Human Condition Have Failed* (New Haven, Conn.: Yale University Press, 1998), 80. Emphasis in the original. See also 4, 91, 97.

21 Frederick Cooper notes that "grandiose" attempts at legibility arose out of many political forms other than nation-states and questions the utility of the category of "high modernism" in favor of emphasizing the discontinuities and critiques embedded within "the modern"; Frederick Cooper, *Colonialism in Question: Theory, Knowledge, History* (Berkeley, Calif.: University of California Press, 2005), 140–2.

22 Scott, *Seeing Like a State,* 183. See also 2, 78, 186. See also David A. Robinson, *Paths of Accommodation: Muslim Societies and French Colonial Authorities in Senegal and Mauritania, 1880–1920,* Western African Studies (Athens, OH: Ohio University Press, 2000), 2–4, 50.

23 Scott, *Seeing Like a State,* 3, 24, 77. Note the parallels between Dirks's "ethnographic state" and Scott's "state simplifications"; Dirks, *Castes of Mind,* 43, 60.

24 Akhil Gupta and James Ferguson, "Discipline and Practice: 'The Field' as Site, Method, and Location in Anthropology," in Akhil Gupta and James Ferguson, eds., *Anthropological Locations: Boundaries and Grounds of a Field Science* (Berkeley, Calif.: University of California Press, 1997), 8. See also Clifford, *Routes,* 8, 20–2, 64–5.

25 Gupta and Ferguson, "Discipline and Practice," 5.

demands grounding not just in larger discursive trends of Orientalism,[26] but also in the politically localized[27] environment of the field; although "the field is not conceived of as already filled with texts,"[28] Edward Said reminds us that, in fact, it is. A history of ethnography must embed the field in the locally specific authoritarianism of empire, in the process historicizing Orientalist representations in discrete moments of power. Ethnography's attachment to the field perforce associates experiential cultural representation with a specific political context; no ethnographer conducts research in a field denuded of power relations. Hence, participant observation did not provide any kind of unmediated information about Algerians to French ethnographers. The historicization of Orientalism and ethnography requires making both local; it compels the integration of the field with the history of the exercise of power within that delineated boundary.

Political delineations and ethnographic field sites rarely were coterminous. The division of the Maghrib into discrete colonial units made more sense to European states than to mobile North Africans. Moreover, Algeria functioned as part of Islamic, African, Middle Eastern, and Pan-Mediterranean worlds. Metropolitan French remained more familiar with Algeria than with any other colony; its large settler population, tourist infrastructure, and administrative status as three *départements* made it politically and discursively unique.

Hence, I have concentrated the analytical gaze of this study not on Orientalist ethnography as a whole, but instead on its elaboration in the context of France's largest, closest, most symbolically important, and best-known colony. The question remains of *how* colonial ethnography related to Orientalism, through what practices and representations. As Mary Des Chene has observed, "from the point of view of a person doing historical research, 'the field' may be neither a self-evident site nor a compelling metaphor for conceptualizing the terrain of study," particularly for multi-sited objects of research such as "colonial district officers [and] academics."[29] Colonial Algeria does not represent *the* or

26 Edward W. Said, *Orientalism* (New York: Vintage Books, 1979), 13.

27 Paul Rabinow, "Representations are Social Facts: Modernity and Postmodernity in Anthropology," in Clifford and Marcus, eds., *Writing Culture*, 251; Donald C. Holsinger, "Islam and State Expansion in Algeria: Nineteenth-Century Saharan Frontiers," in John Ruedy, ed., *Islamism and Secularism in North Africa*. Center for Contemporary Arab Studies, Georgetown University (New York: St. Martin's Press, 1994), 12.

28 Clifford, "On Ethnographic Allegory," 117.

29 Mary Des Chene, "Locating the Past," in Akhil and Gupta, eds., *Anthropological Locations*, 71; see also John Comaroff and Jean Comaroff, *Ethnography and the Historical Imagination* (Boulder, Colo.: Westview Press, 1992), 34–5; Dirks, *Castes of Mind*, 107, 195.

even *a* field for ethnographers, but rather formed a set of manifold field sites unified by the colonial power dynamic specific to Algeria.

Thus, methodology and narrative, as mutually reinforcing technologies of colonial domination, require a common analytical frame. This chapter analyzes methodology and narrative as forms of control, paying particular attention to the manner in which participant observation and ethnography developed as a unitary response to the challenges of empire.

Watching, listening, and the maintenance of order

A tool of political authority, participant observation arose out of the situation of fluent Arabic-, Tamahaq-, or Tamazight-speaking administrators in specific communities for the purposes of inculcating in them detailed knowledge of Algerian life. As administrators, they maintained order but also documented events and identities useful to the colonial state. Thus, the brief of administrators expanded to include Algerian culture; the religious beliefs and behaviors, gender relations, or criminal activity of Algerians became politically significant. In Algeria, administrators participating in local life – favoring collaborators, punishing the intransigent, but also manipulated by Algerians with political motivations of their own – observed the cultural realms of the Algerian communities in which they lived.[30]

Surveillance documentation functioned as the basic means through which participant observation served political interests. Innumerable forms, surveys, and administrative documents attest to government attempts at the codification of surveillance.[31] Jules Cambon's widely disseminated *Instruction sur la surveillance politique* (1895) codified procedures developed largely since the fall of Napoleon III's "royaume arabe." Wrote Governor General Cambon, "in protecting Arab society against itself, . . . we can, with time, destroy little by little its prejudices, attenuate, if not extinguish completely, its spirit of independence and fuse its interests . . . with ours, to which they are intimately linked."[32] Through surveillance, political control became the pretext for social rejuvenation. Furthermore, *Instruction* delineated cultural elements that required

30 Cf. Dirks, *Castes of Mind.*

31 Archives du Gouvernement général de l'Algérie (AGGA), 1H/84, 9H/8, 11H/21, 16H/5, 16H/11, 16H/13, 16H/25, 16H/29, 16H/30, 16H/31, 16H/56; Archives du Département d'Alger (ADA), 2U/20; Archives du Département d'Oran (ADO), 2U/8b; Louis Rinn, *Régime pénal de l'indigénat en Algérie: les commissions disciplinaires* (Algiers: Adolphe Jourdan, 1885), appendix; Dale Eickelman, "New Directions in Interpreting North African Society," in *Connaissances du Maghreb*, 281.

32 Jules Cambon, *Instruction sur la surveillance politique et administrative des indigènes algériens et des musulmans étrangers* (Algiers: Pierre Fontana, 1895), 8–9, in AGGA, 9X/118.

surveillance, such as specific Ṣūfī orders.[33] The governor general himself linked processes of domination with the cultural politics of the colonial state. According to Cambon, the orders contested French political and economic domination and provided a reservoir of fanaticism. "Under the pretext of a religious or political mission," Ṣūfī leaders "criticize the acts of our Administration and try to create difficulties for us."[34] Cambon offered regulations on how to observe and police family relations, religious figures, itinerant traders, even snake charmers.[35] An exercise in colonial power, surveillance rapidly expanded the penetrating gaze of French authority into areas of Algerian society, such as religion and the family, that formed the locus of colonial ethnographies.

In his ethnography of Ṣūfism, Marcel Simian portrayed religious culture as an administrative issue best solved through political means.

> We must thus strictly survey all these religious groups. This task, delicate and difficult, falls above all upon the administrators . . . in constant contact with the Muslim populations, of which they know deeply the language and mores, and are very current with all the details of their religious organization, they exercise on the Islamic orders an effective surveillance.[36]

Simian emphasized methodologies central to ethnography, whether administrative or scholarly. Ethnographers evinced linguistic and cultural fluency that enabled them, in theory at least, to penetrate the mysteries of the cultural milieu in which they lived. In Algeria, participant observation represented not an intensification of surveillance methodology, but rather its constituent element.

Colonial administrators argued for the utility of their embedding in indigenous society, claiming their close association facilitated detailed knowledge. Many relied upon their experience to make authoritative statements about Algerians. In the words of the mayor of one town,

> Wherever military or civil authority extends itself it is possible . . . to know what happens in the heart of the [religious] assemblies . . . one can keep the religious societies [in a state of] wakefulness against any hostile tendency and [can] obtain a relative security[.][37]

The mayor, then, linked the spread of European influence with the detailed knowledge of such rivals. Surveillance knowledge based on

33 Cambon, *Instruction*, 23. 34 Cambon, *Instruction*, 23–8.

35 Cambon, *Instruction*, 9–10, 23–8, 38–40.

36 Marcel Simian, *Les Confréries islamiques en Algérie (Rahmanya-Tidjanya)* (Algiers: Adolphe Jourdan, 1910), 88.

37 AGGA, 16H/8, Mayor of Rouiba to the Prefect of the Department of Algiers, no. 260, Rouiba, June 14, 1895.

intimate contact proved, he argued, the easiest means of asserting French control.

In particular, projects for the governance of the Sahara elaborated participant observation as a means of acquiring knowledge. In the early 1870s, military officers' studies of sites' defensive characteristics provided an early template for the inclusion of ethnographic detail.[38] Later reports on the Sahara followed suit; General Hubert Lyautey praised one report for its "summary of intelligence collected and verified by the Lieutenant Tommy Martin during his stay of more than a year at Bou Anan" and for its "useful and interesting details . . . on populations still little known."[39] Martin's year-long sojourn among the Awlād al-Nāṣr provided, not merely picturesque details, but useful information.

A. Le Chatelier's "Étude sur les Chaamba" (1906) demonstrated the imbrication of political control and the creation of knowledge. Focusing on Shaʿamba political organization, Le Chatelier drew upon a network of Shaʿamba informants who provided him with information on Saharan power structures.[40] At the same time, the Shaʿamba also instructed Le Chatelier more largely in their ways of life.

> Ample and generous manners, a brilliant hospitality, an imposing bearing, a certain Oriental cachet, the appeal of the mysterious and of the unknown, have brought, to these chiefs of the South, sympathies more lively than reasoned, more numerous than merited, to which they have often owed a liberty greater than would have permitted the interests of service.[41]

To misunderstand the role of "manners" and "bearing" in the construction of such relationships, Le Chatelier argued, undermined the larger project of gaining the adherence of the Shaʿamba.[42] Thus, he linked the improving view of the French in the Sahara with the moral and cultural characteristics of Shaʿamba customs. For Le Chatelier, detailed surveillance, "the examination of the current situation" in the region, "serve[d]

[38] Archives militaires de Vincennes (AMV), Service historique de l'Armée de la Terre (SHAT), 1M/2260, Lt. E. Martin, "Mémoire sur l'étude d'une position militaire située à El Kantour (Province de Constantine)," November 13–14, 1873; Capt. A. Chevalme, "Mémoire sur une position militaire située à l'Est de Tlemcen," 1874; Capt. Léonce Bach, "Mémoire sur la position militaire de Dely-Ibrahim (Div[on] d'Alger)," Algiers, November 27, 1874; Lt. Hugot-Deville, untitled, Blida, October 1, 1875; Maurice Joppé, "Étude de la position militaire de Bizot," December 7, 1875.

[39] AGGA, 22H/79, General Lyautey commanding the Division of Oran to Governor General of Algeria, Oran, May 14, 1910.

[40] AGGA, 22H/72, A. Le Chatelier, "Étude sur les Chaamba," Algiers, August 10, 1906, 25.

[41] Le Chatelier, "Étude," 75. See also 8X/330, E. Laquière, untitled treatise on Aïn Chair, Aïn Chair, November 22, 1909.

[42] Le Chatelier, "Étude," 88–9.

as the basis for the determination of methods by which" French dominion "could be the most surely obtained."[43]

The governor general emphasized the political need to account for differences of temperament. In 1913, he composed a lengthy document to "giv[e] more coordination to the efforts of our different police forces." He elucidated one abiding rule to which the French experience in the Sahara had given rise: "the geographic unity [of the Sahara] imposes the unity of the means of material actions; moral diversity, the variety of political methods."[44] Similarly, Military Commander Payn, of the Territory of the Oases, gave a series of "directives and instructions" requiring the "thorough study of the country from a topographic, geological, botanic, [and] ethnographic point of view."[45] Such research, he contended, must result from a significant investment of time in gathering relevant knowledge: "to do a bit, and very well, every day, suffices for the task."[46] "If our task" of gathering knowledge, he admonished, "is less brilliant than that of" conquest, "it is nevertheless beautiful and useful."[47] By World War I, cultural knowledge had become central to French *political* policy in desert Algeria. Military officials turned their attention to the difficulties of governing a hostile population, who daily contested "pacification." Through participant observation, attention to differing "moral" characteristics became an integral part of French colonialism in Algeria.

"Une étrange saveur du terroir"

Administrators penned some of the most significant ethnographic works on Algeria. Participant-observation surveillance provided a methodological framework for bureaucrats to apply their expertise in more scholarly formats. The voluminous correspondence of the colonial regime provided background material for aspiring ethnographers; one low-level bureaucrat demonstrated the imbrication of the archive and ethnography, noting that, "not having found anything" "in the archives on the subject of this question, I have had, to draw up this record, to collect intelligence from indigenous agents."[48] The combination of ready access

43 Le Chatelier, "Étude," 2.
44 AGGA, 22H/79, Governor General of Algeria to the Military commanders of the Territories of Aïn-Sefra, Laghouat, In-Salah, and Biskra, August 29, 1913, and AGGA, 22H/79, Governor General of Algeria, "Pénétration Saharienne," June 2, 1913.
45 AGGA, Archives des Oasis 46, Chef d'Escadron Payn, Military Commander of the Territory of the Oases, to the Captain, Head of the Annex, In-Salah, May 7, 1912, 3.
46 Oasis//46, Payn to Head of the Annex, In-Salah, May 7, 1912, 38.
47 Oasis//46, Payn to Head of the Annex, In-Salah, May 7, 1912, 38.
48 ADA, 2U/20, Assistant for the Administrator on Leave to the Prefect of Algiers, Department and Arrondissement of Algiers, Commune mixte de Gouraya (Résidence à Cherchel), Cherchel, September 30, 1882.

to both informants and archives transformed many bureaucrats into ethnographers.

One particular administrator's work served as a model for administrative ethnography. In 1884, Louis Rinn, the chief of the Native Affairs service in Algeria and later named Conseiller d'état, published his monumental work on the Ṣūfī orders of Algeria, *Marabouts et khouan*, the greatest contribution of Algerian administrative scholarship to the development of ethnography. Other administrators had written similar, limited, texts on Islam, to which Rinn made recourse.[49] None, however, had the access or experience that Rinn's high position gave him. A monumental feat of research, *Marabouts et khouan* drew upon administrative archives and included details on nearly every religious group in Algeria. More importantly, it utilized Rinn's extensive network of personal contacts among Algerians.

Born of surveillance work, *Marabouts et khouan* organized French knowledge about Islam. Rinn's desire to synthesize information about Algerian Ṣūfism into an encyclopedic text required a broader approach than a mere literature review. Despite his open access, the resources of the colonial archives did not suffice, precisely *because* the colonial state required a text such as *Marabouts et khouan.*

> Even in Algeria, this question of religious orders is not known as would be necessary for good surveillance . . . The few publications that have been done . . . are very rare, already ancient, or lost . . . ; most are no longer to be found in the library.[50] . . . [T]his book will still facilitate . . . the research and studies of workers, as it also will furnish precious indications to all the French agents who, with whatever title, in Algeria or abroad, have the delicate and difficult mission of monitoring the religious or political machinations of Muslims.[51]

Hence, Rinn intended his work to complete the intellectual preparation of colonial administrators. Although Rinn referred to previous

[49] Louis Rinn, *Marabouts et khouan: étude sur l'Islam en Algérie* (Algiers: Adolphe Jourdan, 1884), viii. All citations of *Marabouts et khouan* are from Rinn's personal copy (AGGA, 16H/2), which includes his emendations and additions. *Marabout* (in French and English; in Arabic usually *murābiṭ*, "one who resides in or is affiliated with a garrison or redoubt") refers to a learned Islamic holy figure, often Ṣūfīs, though also at times unaffiliated. Their roles can involve local healing practices, the provision of amulets, or providing more general religious services, and their locations often served as sites of local pilgrimage. *Khouan* represents a common French transliteration of the Algerian colloquial pronunciation of the *fuṣḥa ikhwān*, brothers or siblings, the term used to refer to members of a Ṣūfī order.

[50] E. de Neveu, *Les Khouan: ordres religieux* (Algiers: n.p., 1862), and A. Hanoteau and A. Letourneux, *La Kabylie et les coutumes kabyles*, vol. II (Paris, 1873), in Rinn, *Marabouts et khouan*, vii.

[51] Rinn, *Marabouts et khouan*, vii.

administrators' conclusions about Ṣūfism,[52] he rejected them as the basis of his study.

A useful text on Algerian religion required a different set of methodological imperatives. The insufficiency of the colonial archives prevented effective policing of the Algerian population. In one monograph, Rinn included an 1880 memorandum on effective surveillance.

> There does exist, almost always, in the archives of the bureaux, documents that could be usefully consulted, but they are not always established in a practical manner, a rather long period of time passes, in which the new administrator, already struggling with the other difficulties inherent in any installation, remains perforce at the mercy of the intelligence that he receives from his French or indigenous subordinates: the first may be incomplete, the second are always suspect or interested.[53]

While one possible solution lay in the strict supervision of every individual Muslim in the circumscription, Rinn drew another conclusion; the "interested" and "suspect" information of the Algerians furnished crucial source material for *Marabouts et khouan*.

Rinn juxtaposed the colonial archives with knowledge from informants, utilizing Algerians to verify archival texts. In essence, he relied on the fieldwork reports of previous administrators and on his own contact with Algerians.

> [W]e have had all the desirable opportunities to draw our information from the most authoritative sources; our personal relations with several religious notables, such as Si Ahmed Tedjini, Cheikh El-Missoum, Ali ben Otsman [*sic*], permitted us to verify and complete [this] information.[54]

Rinn's lifetime of experience living with and surveying Algerians provided a network of informants to buttress the authority of the text. He drew his conclusions "according to intelligence furnished directly by the chiefs of the orders" and their followers.[55] In noting the sources

52 Rinn, *Marabouts et khouan*, ix; though Rinn spoke Arabic as well as Tamazight; see p. 69 for a discussion of his linguistic work. See also AGGA, 16H/7, division of Oran, subdivision of Tlemcen, Colas, *Notice sur les ordres religieux* (1884). Jean-Louis Triaud, *La Légende noire de la Sanûsiyya: une confrére musulmane saharienne sous le regard français (1840–1930)*, vol. I (Paris: Éditions de la Maison des sciences de l'homme, 1995), 172, 185, 227, 332; Charles Brosselard, *Les Khouans: de la constitution des ordres religieux musulmans en Algérie* (Paris: Challamel Aîné, and Algiers: Tissier, 1859); E. de Neveu, *Les Khouan: ordres religieux*. 3rd edn (Algiers: Adolphe Jourdan, 1913).

53 "Circulaire," in Rinn, *Régime pénal de l'indigénat en Algérie*.

54 Rinn, *Marabouts et khouan*, viii, 340 n.2. On al-Misūm, see also chapter 3.

55 Rinn, *Marabouts et khouan*, 101.

for one section, he cited other ethnographers,[56] but also acknowledged "the verbal intelligence collected directly from the moqaddem or affiliates of the order; among other those given me by Hassein-ben-Brihmat, director of the Mèderça [*sic*: *madrasa*] of Algiers;"[57] one Ṣūfī leader even provided Rinn with crucial ritual phrases and texts.[58] For Rinn, religion replaced the ethnologist's category of race as the operative category of difference; hence, he relied on information culled from his network of contacts. His text revolved around informants such as "a learned Muslim, intelligent and enlightened, that [Rinn] interrogated about the doctrines" of the religious orders.[59] As Clifford remarked, "at the close of the nineteenth century nothing guaranteed, a priori, the ethnographer's status as the best interpreter of native life – as opposed to the traveler, and especially the missionary and administrator, some of whom," like Louis Rinn, "had been in the field far longer and had better research contexts and linguistic skills."[60] The administrators *were* ethnographers. *Marabouts et khouan* contributed to the emergence of a politicized ethnography by juxtaposing information gathered through surveillance with administrative texts; Rinn connected the authoritative texts of administrators with informants and the experience of surveillance fieldwork.

"All [this] information" in *Marabouts et khouan*, Rinn noted ruefully, "[is] not easy to procure," given the secrecy of the religious groups and the facility with which they discerned French motives.[61] Despite his acknowledgment of their aid, Rinn rarely attributed his information to specific individuals. He spoke eloquently about the leadership characteristics sought after among the heads of the religious orders but provided no indication of whence such information came.[62] Some of his reticence probably resulted from the difficulty of writing for a public audience while maintaining his position as a high government official privy to detailed knowledge of governance. More broadly, however, it constructed *Marabouts et khouan* as a seamless narrative posing, not as political intervention, but rather as an accurate description of Algerian Islam. "A student, too ingenious, gave us, for the word djelala [*sic*: *jalāla*, majesty, sublimity] another etymology that, if not true, shows at least how the ignorant natives are little embarrassed to furnish an explanation

56 On Neveu, see Julia Clancy-Smith, "In the Eye of the Beholder: Sufi and Saint in North Africa and the Colonial Production fo Knowledge, 1830–1900," *Africana Studies* 15 (1990): 226–30; Lorcin, *Imperial Identities*, 55–8.

57 Rinn, *Marabouts et khouan*, 174 n.∗.

58 Rinn, *Marabouts et khouan*, 231 n.1, 251–2, 263.

59 Rinn, *Marabouts et khouan*, 308.

60 Clifford, *Predicament*, 26.

61 Rinn, *Marabouts et khouan*, vii.

62 Rinn, *Marabouts et khouan*, 81.

of that which they do not comprehend."[63] Through his reticent narration, Rinn subordinated the anonymous informant to his own expertise; the present absence of the informant served only to bolster Rinn's authority.

Copious reviews of *Marabouts et khouan* indicated Rinn's emerging reputation for expertise on Islam. Not only did the work increase Rinn's visibility within the administrative elite of colonial Algeria, it opened him up to attack. An anonymous reviewer in *Le Républicain* of Constantine referred to him as the "*alter ego* of" the governor general and voiced suspicions that both bureaucrats evinced entirely too much sympathy for Algerian Muslims.[64] *L'Indépendant* of Constantine and *La Solidarité* of Algiers denounced Rinn's call for salaried Muslim clergy, a suggestion with which some colleagues demurred.[65] Similarly, *Le Radical algérien* excoriated Rinn's failure to acknowledge that religions in general, particularly Islam, "are a stumbling block to progress and liberty."[66] Ethnographers such as Émile Masqueray and popular journalists alike praised or condemned Rinn's work, or, more frequently, Rinn himself, for his attempt at synthesizing Algerian Islam into a usable form for the colonial state.[67] Hence, through texts such as *Marabouts et khouan*, the cultural politics of the colonial administration entered into political debate. *Marabouts et khouan* not only provided administrators with invaluable information on Islam; it brought religious politics to public awareness.

Some reviews emphasized Rinn's methodology as providing unique value. *Le Chélif* contended that Rinn's "official position . . . , connections with the chiefs of local power, his knowledge of Muslims, his long practice of . . . political administration, give to this book an exceptional importance[.]"[68] Rinn's verification of textual sources through recourse to Algerian Muslim experts both bolstered his authority and established a new methodology for the study of Islam. Using his personal connections

[63] Rinn, *Marabouts et khouan*, 84–5.

[64] AGGA, 3X/1 (Personal Papers of Louis Rinn), unattributed review of *Marabouts et khouan*, *Le Républicain* (Constantine), August 5, 1884. Italics in the original.

[65] AGGA, 3X/1, E. Zeys, "Bibliographie," *Bulletin de la Société de Géographie de Constantine* April–May–June 1884; AGGA, 3X/1, review of *Marabouts et khouan*, *L'Indépendant* (Constantine), August 23, 1884; AGGA, 3X/1, "Le Clergé musulman official," August 28, 1884.

[66] AGGA, 3X/1, Ahmed ben Rihmat, "*Marabouts et khouan* par M. le commandant Rinn," *Le Radical algérien*, September 10, 1884.

[67] AGGA, 3X/1, Émile Masqueray, review of *Marabouts et khouan*, *Journal des Débats* (Algiers?), August 9, 1884; AGGA, 3X/1, Émile Masqueray, review of *Marabouts et khouan*, *Bulletin de Correspondance africaine* 4 (1885): 178–83; AGGA 3X/1, Belkassem ben Sedira, *Marabouts et khouan*, no source given.

[68] AGGA, 3X/1, "*Marabouts et khouan*," *Le Chélif* (Orléansville?), September 4, 1884.

among Algerians and his unprecedented access to government sources, Rinn integrated administrative texts and details from informants into a larger, synthetic text, thus paving the way for the emergence of an ethnography firmly grounded in the quotidian exigencies of colonial rule.

Edouard Cat, a prominent academic contemporary of Rinn, offered the most incisive analysis of Rinn's innovations. Disparaging cursory studies of Algerian culture carried out by metropolitan dilettantes, Cat grounded cultural expertise in fieldwork.

> The authors who write on Algeria belong to two principal categories: those come from France . . . , passing rapidly through our beautiful country, carrying with them a more or less exact, more or less good idea; then, having returned, . . . writing their memories and their impressions. These books are often worth what the authors are themselves, some are good, some are bad, many are mediocre, many are very bad. The second category comprises men who have lived in Algeria, who have handled affairs, who have seen up close and even into the intimate things of this indigenous society so profoundly different from ours. Their books are never mediocre nor bad, for they do not take their entire worth from the worth of the man who has written them; they always contain a good portion of truth, exact observations, portraits taken from life and they are like a strange taste of the land.[69]

Despite Cat's ignorance of women ethnographers, his review differentiated superficial studies from nascent ethnography. Moreover, valorizing experiential knowledge over the vagaries of armchair theorizing, he offered *Marbouts et khouan* as an example of the scrupulous research methods he endorsed.

> It is a work of a decade of observations and laborious research . . . its author had at his disposition all sorts of documents that a private citizen would lack . . . when certain facts seemed incomplete to him, M. Rinn could have recourse to his comrades . . . or yet to religious notables like Si Hammed Tedjini and the cheikh El Missoum [*sic*]. It is thus a particularly exact and serious work.[70]

The review presciently underlined *Marabouts et khouan*'s most significant contribution, its multifaceted methodology. Cat's bibliographic essay represented a research agenda for later scholars as much as at did a review of Rinn's work.

69 AGGA, 3X/1, Edouard Cat, "Bibliographie," *Bulletin de la Société de Géographie de Constantine*, April–May–June 1884, 81–2.

70 Cat, "Bibliographie," 83–4. See also AGGA, 3X/1, A. C. Barbier de Maynard, clipping from *Journal des Savants*.

The bureaucrats' ethnography

In 1897, Governor General Cambon commissioned two administrators to continue the work of Rinn.[71] Octave Depont, an administrator in the Native Affairs Service, collaborated with Xavier Coppolani,[72] a secretary in a commune mixte, on the work. By the 1890s, *Marabouts et khouan* had begun to seem dated; expansion into the Sahara altered the religious politics of colonial Algeria. As a result, Cambon commissioned the two young bureaucrats to write not merely an authoritative text to supplement or replace Rinn, but also one with a larger scope, to address what seemed the rising tide of Pan-Islamism.[73] Reviews of Depont and Coppolani's work (in Rinn's scrapbook) indicate that *Les Confréries religieuses musulmanes* garnered a somewhat uneven reception.[74]

The methodology of Depont and Coppolani differed significantly from that of Rinn. While Rinn conducted most of his research personally, Depont and Coppolani relied on the results of an 1895 survey on religious orders in Algeria, though Rinn lauded their "absolute competence" resulting from "hav[ing] lived in the midst of native populations."[75] Jules Cambon ordered the survey in preparation for *Confréries religieuses* to fill a void in French knowledge. The apparent expansion of Ṣūfī orders in Tunisia and Tripolitania underscored the stagnation of useful French scholarship on Ṣūfism and alarming bureaucratic ignorance of popular Islam.[76] Depont and Coppolani meticulously pored over the surveys, culling relevant information for *Confréries religieuses.* Depont and Coppolani, as armchair anthropologists (though fluent in Arabic

[71] Christopher Harrison, *France and Islam in West Africa, 1860–1960* (Cambridge: Cambridge University Press, 1988), 19–20.

[72] On Coppolani: *Bulletin du Comité de l'Afrique française*, Organe du Comité du Maroc, 15 (Paris: Comité de l'Afrique Française, 1905), 210–1; Harrison, *France and Islam in West Africa*, 20–2, 27, 43–4; Robinson, *Paths of Accommodation, passim.*

[73] Octave Depont and Xavier Coppolani, *Les Confréries religieuses musulmanes: publié sous le patronage de M. Jules Cambon, Gouverneur général de l'Algérie* (Algiers: Adolphe Jourdan, 1897), 291. Lucas and Vatin, *L'Algérie des anthropologues*, 24; Clancy-Smith, "In the Eye of the Beholder," 246–8.

[74] E.g., AGGA, 3X/1, J.-B. Chabot, review of Depont and Coppolani, *Les Confréries religieuses musulmanes*, *Revue critique d'histoire et de literature* 32, no. 11 (March 14, 1898).

[75] AGGA, 3X/1, Rinn's note, "Chambre des deputes. Séance du 14 juin 1901. Page 1378."

[76] ADA, 2U/20, Governor General Jules Cambon to the Prefect of the Department of Algiers, Paris, February 16, 1895; ADA, 2U/20, "Circulaire à MM. les Sous-Préfets, Administrateurs et Maires du Département," March 12, 1895. See also AGGA, 16H/8, "Minute de la lettre écrite à M. le gouverneur général," November 11, 1894. See Fanny Colonna, "Présence des ordres mystique dans l'Aurès aux XIXe et XXe siècles: contribution à une histoire sociale des forces religieuses en Algérie," in A. Popovic and G. Veinstein, *Les Ordres mystiques dans l'Islam: Cheminements et situation actuelle* (Paris, Éditions de l'École des hautes études en sciences sociales, 1982), 260.

and probably Tamazight), put forth a research question, relying on the local knowledge of hundreds of fieldworkers throughout Algeria. Hence, *Confréries religieuses* added yet another layer to the complex narrative genres that were becoming ethnography; just as armchair anthropology's emphasis on fieldwork eventually paved the way for the subsequent unification of narrator and local expert into one person, so, too, did the project of Depont and Coppolani contribute to the establishment of fieldwork and of participant observation as the dominant paradigm of ethnographic authority.

The administrators who furnished field reports for Depont and Coppolani framed their own work in terms of Rinn's. *Marabouts et khouan* had become the normative model to which information on Algerian Ṣūfism conformed. A letter to the prefect from Tizi-Ouzou even bore the title "Marabouts et khouan," as if the work had become a category of knowledge, like "surveillance."[77] Not all administrators, however, proved capable of providing information. Like surveillance itself, some adminstrators proved more adept than others.

Therefore, Depont and Coppolani faced a difficult task; the fieldwork reports that formed the basis of their work proved of varying quality. While Depont occupied himself in the archives in Paris, Coppolani analyzed the results of the inquiry of 1895.[78] Mayors of settler towns spoke little Arabic and had few contacts within the Algerian community. Depont and Coppolani perforce relied on administrators' authoritative statements drawn from participant observation to distinguish a text's utility; originally a technology of surveillance, participant observation attested to authoritative knowledge. In ordering the 1895 survey, Cambon had established clear indications of required information. Each administrator had to submit statistical information, general descriptions, and, if possible, photographs, for each Ṣūfī order.[79] In collating the reports, administrators emphasized the attributes of successful description. General Rogny, Commander of the Division in Constantine,

[77] AGGA, 16H/8, Secretary of the Sub-Prefecture to the Prefect of Tizi-Ouzou, Tizi-Ouzou, June 25, 1895. 16H/8–10 contain the administrative records that Depont and Coppolani used for *Confréries* – including margin notes of Coppolani himself. The documents are frequently mutilated, with pictures missing and *silsilāt* modified or removed.

[78] AGGA, 16H/8, Assistant Director of the Cabinet, of Personnel, and of the Secretariat, for the Minister of Colonies and by order, to M. Depont, the administrator attached to the Service of Native Affairs of the Government general of Algeria, Paris, September 25, 1895; Octave Depont to Governor General Jules Cambon, Paris, September 28, 1895.

[79] ADA, 2U/20, Cambon to Prefect of Department of Algiers, February 16, 1895; ADA, 2U/20, "Circulaire," March 12, 1895; Depont and Coppolani, *Confréries religieuses*, 211–17.

singled out three "notices . . . [as] documented, methodical, well edited and [which] constitute in sum most interesting works." In addition, he highlighted photographs and drawings adorning other reports.[80] The Commandant Supérieure in Boghar praised one report for "meticulous and patient research . . . and . . . discrete zeal."[81] Thus, the 1895 inquiry valued orderly, methodical research over more slapdash, impressionistic, or vague descriptions. Detailed, meticulous, ethnographic research based on participant observation formed the backbone of *Confréries religieuses*.

The report from one particular Saharan backwater, Berrouaghia, proved influential. A low-level administrator developed a particularly close relationship with one informant, Ṭayyib bin al-Ḥājj Bāshir, who provided the majority of information for the report. Aside from the numerous photographs that decorated the text, the author also related his informant's contributions to Rinn's understanding; "the preceding details" on one Ṣūfī order, "although erroneous on many points, if one refers to the work of M. Rinn, are those, however, that serve as the basis of instruction" within the order. Despite his familiarity with *Marabouts et khouan*, the administrator constructed his text "according to the statement of the natives."[82] He conformed to the project that Cambon had set out, correcting the 1884 work with the knowledge of Algerians. A participant in colonial life in Berrouaghia, the administrator called upon informants to verify knowledge about Algerians.

The Berrouaghia report did not differ greatly from other reports. Indeed, its methodology became the dominant way of acquiring the information for the 1895 inquiry. Although some administrators in Europeanized areas relied less on Algerian informants, Depont and Coppolani depended on those who manifested a methodological commitment to participant observation. Even Coppolani, often an armchair anthropologist, marked information from a Laghouat report "to verify with the mufti."[83] Algerians' verification of information allowed administrators to generalize about Muslims on the basis of the authoritative statements of

[80] AGGA, 16H/10, General Rogny commanding the Division of Constantine to the Governor General of Algeria, Constantine, June 14, 1895; see also AGGA, 16H/10, "Division de Constantine, Subdivision de Batna, Cercle de Touggourth, Annexe d'El Oued. Notice sur les Confréries religieuses musulmanes de l'Annexe," Touggourt, [1895].

[81] AGGA, 16H/8, Lt. Rodet, "Notice détaillée sur les confréries religieuses dans le Cercle de Bohar (année 1895)," Boghar, June 6, 1895.

[82] AGGA, 16H/8, [illeg.], "Études sur les confréries religieuses musulmanes de la commune mixte de Berrouaghia. 1895," Berrouaghia, February 17, 1896, 13, 16–17, 28, 39.

[83] AGGA, 16H/8, "État des confréries religieuses musulmanes au 15 juin 1895," Laghouat, June 15, 1895.

individuals. In utilizing participant observation to control the accuracy of their reports, colonial bureaucrats synthesized authoritative statements about cultures through reference to the superior knowledge of informants.

Nevertheless, the extent to which administrators participated in Algerian life varied across geographical regions. In certain communes mixtes, the mayors frequently neither read nor spoke Arabic, and the comparatively large number of Europeans limited the social sphere of mayors to settler society. While isolated administrators might come to know Algerians well, mayors often had neither the inclination nor the ability to cultivate a network of indigenous informants. Although most mayors used the official government questionnaire in their responses to the 1895 inquiry, many had difficulty providing even the basic information, while rural administrators almost universally wrote voluminous, detailed reports, abandoning the official questionnaire in favor of narrative. In a letter to Jules Cambon, the prefect of Oran plaintively disparaged his mayors' lack of participant-observation skills.

> I have recommended to the administrators and mayors to take more care in undertaking this work . . . the latter . . . have been able to produce absolutely nothing . . . the mayors are both ill prepared and ill equipped for a work of this nature, that the administrators themselves already have much difficulty to bring to a good end.[84]

The demands of the 1895 inquiry proved beyond the capabilities of urban mayors.[85] While even rural administrators occasionally struggled with conforming to the survey's imperatives, mayors lacked the basic ability to carry out field research. Continued the prefect, "there are . . . few administrators who combine both a sufficient practice of Native Affairs and above all a serious enough knowledge of the Arab language to study in depth such a question, without being more or less obliged to rely blindly on the information furnished by some indigenous agent."[86]

[84] AGGA, 16H/9, Prefect of Oran to Governor Jules Cambon, Oran, December 6, 1895.

[85] AGGA, 16H/8, Mayor of Affreville to the Sub-Prefect of Milianah, June 12, 1895; AGGA, 16H/9, Sub-Prefect of Bougie to the Prefect of Constantine, June 12, 1895; AGGA, 16H/8, Administrator of the Commune mixte of Azeffoun to the Sub-Prefect of Tizi-Ouzou, June 12, 1895. AGGA, 16H/9, "Rapport sur les confréries religieuses, mosquées, Zaouïa de la Commune-Mixte," Department of Constantine, Arrondissement of Constantine, Commune mixte of Sedrata, December 31, 1895. See AGGA, 16H/8, Administrator of the Commune mixte of Aumale to the Prefect of the Department of Algiers, June 14, 1895. See also AGGA, 16H/8, Mayor of Miliana to the Sub-Prefect of Miliana in the Department of Algiers, June 19, 1895. AGGA, 16H/10, anonymous military interpreter, "Notice sur l'état des Confréries religieuses dans le cercle de Géryvile au 15 juin 1895," May 20, 1895.

[86] AGGA, 16H/9, Prefect of Oran to Governor Jules Cambon, Oran, December 6, 1895.

The prefect met with the fundamental methodological stumbling block of armchair anthropology: the editing anthropologist has no means of controlling the utility of the fieldwork. Coppolani read through hundreds of administrative reports yet only drew upon several dozen in writing *Confréries religieuses*. He relied on the discriminating power of other administrators, and on their evaluations of the methodological rigor of various reports. The prefect of Oran singled out several administrators' reports as particularly useful due to their "serious and most personal study" of Algerian cultural politics.[87] Only through personal contact with informants could ethnographer-administrators provide useful information. Through projects such as the 1895 inquiry and *Confréries religieuses*, ethnographic methodology served as the fundamental basis for the acquisition of cultural knowledge.

The creation of ethnographic authority

Not all colonial writers limited themselves to collating texts, instead undertaking their own fieldwork to construct ethnographies. Most prominent among them, Edmond Doutté wrote extensively about Islam. A confident Arabic speaker, Doutté, in his *Notes sur l'Islâm* (1900), emphasized interaction with Algerians in the vernacular to acquire information. Attempting to ascertain the name of a buried holy man, Doutté encountered some resistance. "Interrogating the natives of Tlemcen [*sic*]" on the issue, "we could not manage to have the name, when finally, one of our interlocutors, pressed by us," relented, and "we took careful note of the name of this pious character."[88] Doutté blithely ignored the coercive overtones of the passage, instead using it to buttress the authority of his generalizations. He drew much of his information from "oral traditions," contending that "old women . . . are the most useful informants."[89] For Doutté, only participant observation furnished essential information about Algerian Islam.[90] Whereas Depont and Coppolani mostly relied upon others' fieldwork, the narrative authority of *Notes sur l'Islâm* arose out of references to Doutté's own fieldwork.

Moreover, he situated his own ethnographic generalizations in the context of previous work by Rinn and Depont and Coppolani. According to Doutté, ethnographic scholarship played an important role in the work of colonial governance.

87 AGGA, 16H/9, Prefect of Oran to Governor Jules Cambon, Oran, December 6, 1895.
88 Edmond Doutté, *Notes sur l'Islâm maghribin: les Marabouts* (Paris: Ernest Leroux, 1900), 54; see also Doutté, *Missions au Maroc: en tribu* (Paris: Paul Geuthner, 1914), v–vii, x.
89 Doutté, *Notes*, 96–7. 90 Doutté, *Notes*, 115–16.

Important works of the Algerian administrative school, in first rank of which are placed the considerable works of Messieurs Rinn, Depont and Coppolani, have cleared the terrain . . . It behooves this Algerian school to put itself to work submitting to the wisdom of our governors the results of its [i.e., the "school's"] works; we would not dare flatter ourselves that these several notes collected here could be a useful contribution to these studies; at least we will perhaps have succeeded in showing by which method of patient analysis of facts it appears to us that it would be indispensable to proceed.[91]

Doutté's tortuous syntax aside, he expressly couched his own contribution as methodological. Depicting his own work as a "patient analysis of facts," Doutté created a tidy position of authority in *Notes sur l'Islâm*. To use Doutté's own words, his "analysis" of "facts" from his "informants" formed a "useful contribution" to colonial governance. He understood his role as ethnographer as synthesizing information, analyzing it, and rendering it useful for the government.

Indeed, Doutté scrutizined contemporary methodology. Rinn, Doutté maintained, "almost never cites his sources . . . one never knows if his statements come from oral intelligence, Arabic writings or administrative reports." Although he praised Depont and Coppolani for their acknowledgment of sources, in an uncharacteristically scathing remark Doutté argued that "the first part of the book . . . must be completely revised in our opinion: it contains no materials of study and is consecrated to the personal views of the authors." In contrast, in Charles de Foucauld's *Reconnaissance au Maroc*, "direct observation . . . is carefully separated from oral information." Finally, Doutté praised Auguste Mouliéras's *Le Maroc inconnu* for "rely[ing] solely upon oral information . . . His oral intelligence is all the more precious because he himself speaks the Arabic and Berber dialects with as much ease and purity as the natives themselves."[92] Thus, Doutté established a methodological hierarchy, evaluating disparate authors according to adherence to methodological imperatives Doutté himself assembled. For Doutté, useful, rigorous scholarship openly disclosed its sources. Moreover, its information came from oral sources, from interviews and interrogations conducted by fluent speakers of Algerian languages, from "direct observations." Doutté scrupulously policed the boundaries of the ethnographer's professional identity. In *Notes sur l'Islâm*, the ethnographic expert appeared as a fluent Arabic or Tamazight speaker and a rigorously analytical scientist.

Doutté merely codified a longstanding administrative tradition of collecting information and analyzing it in narrative form. The geographer

[91] Doutté, *Notes*, 116.
[92] Doutté, *Notes*, 4–5 n.1; on Mouliéras: Hammoudi, *Victim and its Masks*, 17–19.

and ethnographer Augustin Bernard lauded "that remarkable aptitude at collecting, coordinating, and interpreting native intelligence that has always been one of the specialties of the *bureaux arabes*."[93] As early as 1882, one author offered a collection of stories from Kabylia, highlighting that he "had lived several years in direct contact with Berber populations" and hence that "these stories collected from the mouths of natives" offered an accurate portrayal of the Kabyle language.[94] Such methodology did not arise out of metropolitan social science, but rather the systemization of colonial administrative statecraft. Participant observation dominated the methodological and rhetorical devices of colonial studies of Algerian culture.

The intimate familiarity with Algerians that participant observation presumed bound ethnographic knowledge to discourses of authority. In "Contribution au folk-lore des indigènes de l'Algérie" (1905), Achille Robert classified cultural knowledge as a necessary aspect of colonial control. Though comparatively few settlers bothered to learn the languages, the Algerian administrative corps hardly suffered from a lack of Arabic or Tamazight speakers. What Robert decried among administrators, however, was a lack of *cultural* fluency. "To appreciate truly the mentality of a people, it is necessary not only to know its language, but also to study its mores, customs, beliefs, traditions. Nothing must be neglected in the authentication of minute sociological facts." He continued, "there is no detail, however small it may be, that should not be recorded; such a fact that at first view seems insignificant, of an entirely secondary order, can have a correlation with a more important manifestation of the life of the people that one studies, and can thus cause greater understanding of the said manifestation."[95] The microscopic worlds of the field site became magnified as a way of capturing the colonial subject in text. Through the universalizing gaze of the ethnographer, the generalizing voice of ethnographic narrative rendered the insignificant essential.

To this conception of expertise Robert yoked social scientific positivism. "Desiring that our work include but facts capable of being

[93] Augustin Bernard, "Préface," in Gen. E. Daumas, *La Femme arabe* (Algiers: Adolphe Jourdan, 1912), viii. On the *bureaux*: Jacques Frémeaux, *Les Bureaux arabes dans l'Algérie de la conquête* (Paris: Denoël, 1993).

[94] J. Rivière, *Recueil de contes populaires de la Kabylie du Djurdjura recueillis et traduits par J. Rivière*, Collection de contes et de chansons populaires, 4 (Paris: Ernest Leroux, 1882), iii–iv.

[95] Achille Robert, "Contribution au folk-lore des indigènes de l'Algérie," in *Actes du XIVe Congrès internationale des Orientalistes. Alger, 1905*, vol. III (Paris: Ernest Leroux, 1907), 561. See also A. de Boisroger, *Le Sahara algérien illustré: souvenirs de voyage: notes et croquis, 1886–1887* (Paris: G. Rolla, 1887), iii–iv.

scrupulously controlled, we have applied ourselves to relate only the result of our authentications, eliminating all that which we could not verify or that appeared to us exaggerated or inspired by the fancy of the natives."[96] Whereas Doutté's ethnographer functioned as the scientific brake on the excesses of informants, Robert offered an even more significant role for the ethnographer. In a discursive turn that is nothing short of astonishing, Robert robbed Algerians of the capacity to make authoritative statements about Algerian culture and vested that authority in ethnographers. Robert served as the arbiter of authenticity, silencing certain facts altogether by exiling them to the realm of native fantasy. Ethnographers did not "go native"; they simply assumed for themselves the ability to speak *for* "natives." The development of participant observation and the idea of the "native informant" engendered precisely that authoritative, ethnographic voice that allowed an author to censor informants' testimonies.

Other ethnographers crafted their texts to suit particular political ends. Like Robert, Arthur Girault categorized ethnographic knowledge as essential to the colonial project. In particular, he reiterated that "studying indigenous customs . . . is indispensable from the scientific and political points of view. In many cases, in Algeria notably, we would have avoided certain mistakes, if we had better known the native institutions." He maintained that "to study indigenous customs, one must have recourse to specialists. Only a specialist will understand certain institutions, will seize certain nuances, will know [how] to make useful parallels."[97] Girault, Robert, Doutté, and others classified ethnographic knowledge as *applied* cultural knowledge generative of insights for colonial domination. As a methodology, participant observation allowed ethnographers to adopt the authoritative narrative tone that enabled them to speak effectively to power.

The development of fieldwork expertise to underpin colonial ethnography constructed a politicized, colonizing narrative authority.[98] The ability of the ethnographer to create such illusions about Algerian culture required precisely such a narrative logic. Thus, the informants of colonial ethnographers function as "sources," as dehumanized pieces of evidence buttressing the authority of the ethnographer, who arrogates the hegemonic voice of generalization.

[96] Robert, "Contribution au folk-lore," 561.

[97] Congrès internationale de sociologie coloniale. *Rapports et procès-verbaux des séances* (Paris: Arthur Rousseau, 1901), 205.

[98] Tyler, "Post-Modern Ethnography," 131; Rabinow, "Representations are Social Facts," 245.

Fieldwork-spectacle and ethnographer-tourist

Ethnography developed a corpus of narrative strategies to correspond to its politicized methodological imperatives. Without reifying binary differences, colonial administrators and scholarly ethnographers elucidated different *categories* of others. A third category of writers also contributed significantly to the emergence of these narrative forms of difference. Tourists,[99] however, traveled to Algeria with the express purpose of experiencing the dramatically different. They came, in droves, to Algeria for its exoticism. The vast preponderance of tourists spoke no Arabic or Tamazight.[100] Hence, few could participate in or observe Algerian cultural life. Nevertheless, tourists sought out what, in their narratives, they deemed "authentic" cultural experiences. Through prepackaged experiences of ostensible authenticity, tourists mimicked the voyeurism of the ethnographic. For tourists and ethnographers alike, the concept of home always remained normative. Tourist narrative relied on comparisons with a normative France.[101] Unable to communicate with most Algerians, tourists settled for commodified cultural performances tailored to an ethnographic tourist aesthetic that packaged Algerian culture into discrete, knowable units. Moreover, tourist literature itself mimetically parroted the conclusions of ethnographers. Drawing upon these texts and upon their own commodified experiences, many tourists situated their narratives in relation to discourses of authenticity constructed through ethnographic methodology.

Scholars have far too blithely separated ethnographic narrative and tourist literature as diametrically opposed, fundamentally irreconcilable genres. Relying on insufficiently deconstructed notions of ethnographic authenticity, they demean tourist writing as somehow inefficacious or of little import.[102] In *Writing French Algeria*, Peter Dunwoodie inadvertently echoes colonialist discourses of the impenetrable other: "The European traveler during this period inevitably remained outside, a simple spectator responding initially to . . . superficial orientalism . . . a touch of excitement." Dunwoodie divides the world of the tourist too neatly into binary

99 Journalism, too, mimicked ethnography; see, for example, Denise Brahimi, ed., *Maupassant au Maghreb: au soleil, la vie errante d'Alger à Tunis, vers Kairouan* (Paris: Le Sycomore, 1982).

100 Comte V. d'Adhémar, *Mirages algériens: Le voyage pratique* (Toulouse: Édouard Privat, 1900), 39, 65–6; Ernest Fallot, *Par delà la Méditerranée: Kabylie, Aurès, Kroumirie* (Paris: Plon, Nourrit, 1887), 287.

101 E.g., M.-J. Baudel, *Un An à Alger: excursions et souvenirs* (Paris: Ch. Delagrave, 1887), 206.

102 See the critique in Mary Louise Pratt, "Fieldwork in Common Places," in Clifford and Marcus, eds., *Writing Culture*, 27.

categories of inside or outside. After all, travel, in the words of one voyager, "is a sure means of instructing oneself."[103] Or, as J.-J. Clamageran, senator and tourist, contended, "an excursion to Algeria would be for a Frenchman the natural complement to a liberal and patriotic education."[104] Emerging ethnographic texts and travel writing occupied the same discursive space. Whether or not tourists progressed beyond "superficial orientalism," they nevertheless sought out experiences of colonial culture that they would come to deem "authentic." Tourism in Algeria was fundamentally *ethnographic* tourism: visitors from France, Britain, and elsewhere wanted, not just "a touch of excitement," but voyeuristic experiences that emphasized difference. Even Augustin Bernard wistfully recalled the writings of Pierre Loti and wrote briefly of his own experience as a tourist in Tilimsān.[105] Alfred Bel expressly acknowledged the "research" of tourists on Tilimsān.[106] Like ethnography, much colonial tourist literature enunciated operative categories of cultural difference. Tourist narrative echoed ethnographic generalizations, elucidating, for a largely metropolitan readership, the basis of the discriminatory logic of the colonial state.

The instability of genre labels arbitrarily attached to tourist narratives may distinguish them from other types of colonial writing. Incorporating elements of ethnography, nonfiction, fiction,[107] personal writing, and natural historical writing, the term "travel writing" refers to a corpus of narrative techniques and authorial styles, rather than any specific body of literature. Ethnographic generalization emerged as an authorizing set of discourses *within* travel writing: explicit references to participation in and observation of colonial life conveyed, with immediacy, the sense of the author having been "there." Ethnographic narratives emerged, not merely out of administrators' documents or scholarly texts, but also out of popular writing.

The abbot Edmond Lambert's *À travers l'Algérie* (1884) recounted the author's voyage to Algeria, an attempted reconciliation of his diverse interests in history, religion, and folklore studies. What emerged closely

103 Baudel, *Un An à Alger*, 1; Charles Desprez, *L'Hiver à Alger*, 5th edn (Paris: Augustin Challamel, 1898), 167.

104 J.-J. Clamageran, *L'Algérie: impressions de voyage (17 mars – 4 juin 1873; 14–29 avril 1881)* (Paris: Germer Baillière, 1883), 231–2.

105 Augustin Bernard, *En Oranie* (Oran: L. Fouque, 1901), 5.

106 Bel, *Population musulmane de Tlemcen*, 1.

107 J. de Fontanes, *Deux Touristes en Algérie: Nedjéma* (Paris: Calmann Lévy, 1879); Ernest Feydeau, *Souna: mœurs arabes* (Paris: Calmann Lévy, 1876); Sakina Messaadi, *Les Romancières coloniales et la femme colonisée: contribution à une étude de la littérature coloniale en Algérie dans la première moitié du XXe siècle* (Algiers: Entreprise nationale du livre, 1900), 295.

resembles a travelogue; each chapter commenced with a new place, a new exotic anecdote. At the same time, however, Lambert not only posited alterity, but also offered explanations. *À travers l'Algérie* juxtaposed the structure of travel writing with the cultural and intellectual interests of the author.

Lambert's visit to Oran revealed his complicated analytical rubric. He visited what he called the "black quarter" to witness life in an Algerian city. In the zeal of historical analysis, we must not take the cursory wanderings of a peripatetic abbot for ethnographic fieldwork. However, Lambert's running commentary on this visit manifested a sophisticated relation of the experience to dominant intellectual trends within anthropological thought of the time.

> Seeing the miserable state of these *nègres* and these *négresses*: "It would truly be difficult to prove to M. Darwin that man is the masterpiece of creation, and not the descendant of the ape, and to M. Huxley that man is not a degenerate ape." Pardon me for this reflection, which was suggested to me by the study I am currently making of the theory of the English author [i.e., Huxley].[108]

In other words, Lambert expressly related his travel experience – a fairly typical one, at that – in Oran to larger strands in the emerging human sciences. Most significantly, Lambert did not merely present an exoticized anecdote but rather analyzed it as an intellectual generalization. At a time when many French anthropologists remained both avowedly Lamarckian and firmly ensconced in (arm)chairs at French universities, the Catholic abbot both traveled as a tourist and read Darwin.

Moreover, Lambert voyaged in Algeria precisely *for* such experiences. He hoped to draw cultural generalizations from his observation. "Arab society," he claimed, "rests upon three general characters," which resulted "from reasons drawn from culture and the nature of the country that these people inhabit."[109] In the anecdotes that begin each section, Lambert used participatory observations to make cultural generalizations. The abbot with a penchant for citing Lafontaine remained thoroughly imbued with the narrative style of ethnographic authority. "I will stick," he assured the reader, "solely to reporting to you the interesting things that I have seen and heard."[110] He came, he saw, he published.

Three Gouvernement général publications demonstrated the packaging of ethnographic experiences for tourist consumption. G. Guiauchain's *Winter in Algeria* marketed ethnographic tourism in Algeria to English-speaking tourists. For Guiauchain, the charm of Algeria lay in its exotic difference. Depicting a convenient Orientalism,

[108] Abbé Edmond Lambert, *À travers l'Algérie: Histoires, mœurs et légendes des Arabes* (Paris: René Haton, 1884), 34; also 48, 323–4.
[109] Lambert, *À travers l'Algérie*, 40. [110] Lambert, *À travers l'Algérie*, 265.

accessible from London in two days' time, or from New York "by . . . fast and comfortable steamers,"[111] he sold Algeria for its novelty, its easily accessed experiences of the exotic. Indeed, the colonial government established institutions to package "authentic" Algerian cultural experiences for tourists.

> The Algerian Winter Committee, n° 1, rue Combes, Algiers, is most happy to give the information its members have collected on Algeria, and does all in its power to render a visit more agreeable by organising excursions, Arab spectacles, concerts and other entertainments.[112]

As a marketing tool, *Winter in Algeria* targeted the tourist's desire for comfortable difference experienced through "spectacles."

Guiauchain's section on Algiers emphasized the ease of experiencing "native" Algeria. Contrasting the Europeanized city with the exotic, Arab city, he valorized the first as thoroughly modern, while depicting the latter as imprisoned by its past. While "the modern town has all the facilities of an [*sic*] European one for obtaining both necessities and luxuries," "the old town . . . has remained exactly as it was in the time of the Pirates."[113] In winter Algeria, a tourist could escape sooty London or snowy New York and visit people and places frozen in time, thoughtfully preserved for the tourist's possessive gaze by the Algerian Winter Committee (1, rue Combes, Algiers). "Shadowy and mysterious," in Algiers, "streets take on [*sic*] into an unfamiliar world."[114] In addition, the itinerary included a visit to "an Arab town of the most primitive type," situated amidst "the weird effects of the boundless desert spaces."[115] A theater of the picturesque, tourism in Algeria strung together striking scenes to provide an ethnographic narrative of weird effects and primitive types. In *Winter in Algeria*, Guiauchain depicted Algeria as simultaneously Europeanized and colonized *and* exotic and colonial. Sharing with Lambert the conception of tourism as a means of accessing another culture, *Winter in Algeria* reinscribed ethnographic generalizations in tourist literature.

Five years later, the colonial government published another work aimed at popularizing Algeria as a tourist destination. Pierre Batail's *Le Tourisme en Algérie* (1906) cited Guiauchain's work but made explicit the connections between the tourist and the ethnographer. Batail understood tourism as a search for an authentic, Orientalist other. Structuring the work as an itinerary, the author conceived of the order of travel as an entrance further into exotic Algeria, culminating in the desert south.

[111] G. Guiauchain, *Winter in Algeria* (Algiers: Imprimerie algérienne, 1901), 1.
[112] Guiauchain, *Winter in Algeria*, 2
[113] Guiauchain, *Winter in Algeria*, 10.
[114] Guiauchian, *Winter in Algeria*, 10.
[115] Guiauchain, *Winter in Algeria*, 34.

Toward the beginning, he remarked that "Blida [a city close to Algiers] is no longer . . . what it was formerly . . . Long ago the numerous *houris* tasked with giving to the sons of the Prophet a foretaste of paradise have ceased to come there."[116] The narrative itinerary continues to deeper, more exoticized regions. By the time Batail arrives at Tilimsān, the reader has seen places and spectacles representative of Algerian culture. For Batail, however, "it is vainly that the tourist would seek out, after what he has already seen since his arrival in Algeria, something unheard-of."[117] Paradoxically, the Algerian spectacles most familiar to tourists become, according to Batail, trivialized as they become commodified, known. The phantasmogorical houris depart Blida and leave it to be trod by the countless feet of the tourist hordes. "That [Algeria] has its theatrical side, we remain in agreement. It is that, moreover, which seduces the tourists."[118]

Morever, the newspaper *L'Algérie hivernale*, published by the Comité d'Hivernage Algérien, used prominent scholars to entice tourists. Shortly before World War I, the weekly included an article by a law professor in Algiers.[119] Interspersed with historical and ethnographic analysis of Islamic practices were advertisements in French and English. The official newspaper of the Algierian Winter Committee introduced elements of Algerian culture to tourists in prepackaged and simplified form.

The ethnographic generalizations of tourists came under direct assault from other ethnographers. In particular, tourist pretensions to universal knowledge provoked scorn from scholars. Moreover, such writers singled out for disapprobation tourists' claims of having participated in and observed Algerians' daily lives. As the scholar Ernest Mercier contended, the traveler "convinces himself of the experience he has acquired."[120] Césaire Fabre, in his ethnography *Grande Kabylie* (1901), emphasized the superficial knowledge of many writers. "All the real literature that concerns Africa is there," in Africa. "You would seek in vain a different note, unless you take as literature the exotic harangues" of tourists, "or the verses written by some publicists who seem to have thought of Paris and who have sent their essays to daily broadsheets or periodicals."[121] Deftly Fabre set up Paris in opposition to Africa, exoticism aimed at vulgarization and "true literature." Excluding cursory studies of Kabylia, Fabre reserved veracity for works such as his own.

[116] Pierre Batail, *Le Tourisme en Algérie* (Algiers: Imprimerie algérienne, 1906), 15.

[117] Batail, *Le Tourisme en Algérie*, 18. [118] Batail, *Le Tourisme en Algérie*, 28.

[119] AGGA, 14X/8, Émile Chauvin, "Les Marabouts," *L'Algérie hivernale*, December 22, 1913, 2–3.

[120] Ernest Mercier, *L'Algérie en 1880: le cinquantenaire d'une colonie* (Paris: Challamel Aîné, 1880), 5.

[121] Césaire Fabre, *Grande Kabylie: légendes et souvenirs* (Paris: Léon Vanier, 1901), 37.

At the 1903 Congrès national des Sociétés de géographie, Th. Monbrun disparaged tourists' affectations of scientific description. "The time has passed, in effect, where a voyage to Algeria – even a voyage of study or research! – consisted of seeing the Arab and steed," or, he continued, of "attending *fantasias*, . . . attending the belly dance and making from this coast of the water simple descriptions of our enchanting country."[122] Eschewing "simple description" in favor of "practical works,"[123] Monbrun had had "enough of [the] orientalism, sometimes theatrical," of tourists who traveled south of the Mediterranean, only to write in France on the exotic wonders of Algerian culture. Monbrun, like Fabre, could not tolerate tourist literature's aspirations to ethnographic authority and its deployment of participant observation as a paradigm of "study or research." Authoritative generalizations about Algerian culture drawn from participant observation, it seems, remained a jealously guarded preserve for some social scientists.

Moreover, other ethnographers responded to prevalent views disseminated through ethnographic tourist literature. Germain Sabatier, the Arabic-speaking mayor of Tilimsān, enhanced his claims to textual authority by limiting their scope in comparison with the universality travel writers purported. "I know of Algeria only the province of Oran. The tribes in the midst of whom I lived were of Arab origin, or, if they were of Kabyle origin, have been so penetrated by the Arab element that they have conserved but slight traces of their primitive character."[124] Thus establishing his close ties to Algerian daily life, Sabatier used the authority of participant observation to criticize superficial travel writing. "I have visited Kabylia, as a tourist. I have interrogated much and listened much, but this rapid study would not give me the right to speak about Kabylia and the Kabyles. It is above all in Algeria that it is wise to scorn appearances and the notions that one acquires only at the gallop."[125] Although he ostensibly diminished his time in Kabylia, Sabatier, with no little lack of humility, mentioned the extent of his experience, in comparison to statements drawn from research "at the gallop." These passages offer a peculiar kind of arrogance, a false modesty whereby the renunciation of the ability to generalize about *all* Algerians legitimated statements about a smaller subgroup, a smaller field. The foil of illicitly generalizing texts

122 Th. Monbrun, *Conférence sur l'Algérie* (Oran: Imprimerie typographique et lithographique L. Fouque, 1904), 6. One tourist made a similar claim: Desprez, *L'Hiver à Alger*, 5.

123 Monbrun, *Conférence*, 6.

124 Germain Sabatier, *Études sur les réformes algériennes* (Oran: Imprimerie Paul Perrier, 1891), 8; cf. Fallot, *Par delà la Méditerrané*, i–iii.

125 Sabatier, *Études . . . algériennes*, 8.

allowed Sabatier to entitle a section "The Organization of the Muslim Family." Through the repudiation of universal knowledge, he created for himself a position of total, if limited, authority.

In brief, ethnographers criticized tourists for trying to write like ethnographers. The voices of ethnographic authority proved sites of contestation between scholar and artist. The 1880s and 1890s in particular witnessed the increasingly zealous policing of the narrative boundaries of colonial cultural studies, a sign pointing toward the imminent professionalization of ethnographic writing as the exclusive preserve of the scholar. Georges Viollier expressed it best in *Les Deux Algérie* (1899). "The two Algerias, here they are: the one picturesque, the Algeria of the tourist, of the vaguely consumptive *snob*, of the artist... That Algeria, oh! It is charming, vibrant."[126] But, he continued, "as soon as it is too hot, one abandons it for more clement countries." In contrast to the tourism of the Algierian Winter Committee, at 1, rue Combes, Viollier placed "the colonial Algeria, that which one does not leave in the summer, a country rich in grains and vines, but also in deceptions, in sorrow, in trickeries of all sorts. These two Algerias, so different," he concluded, "I have seen them both, the one with the eye of the artist, the other with the eye of the observer."[127] Viollier practiced participant observation in a hall of mirrors. Watching Europeans "look[in]g at these 'barbarians' with compassion,... [he] had at that instant shame for [his] compatriot*s*," shame for their obvious intrusion and their pretensions to voyeurism. "They were ugly, ignoble, in their unaesthetic European rags," feet bare and "keeping on the head, according to the prescription of the Muslim rite, their soft, formless felt hats or their greasy derbies." He witnessed "two drunk hoodlums staggering and elbowing while laughing." Far from the Algeria of observation, he had stumbled upon the Algeria of the "artist," of the voyeur, of the tourist. "In front of this contrast, was it not permitted to ask myself on which side was civilization, who were the barbarians?"[128]

The indeterminacy of ethnographic narrative rendered it a site of contestation. Administrators, scholars, and tourists made recourse to discourses of methodological authority, while sometimes trying to preserve that narrative power for themselves. The genre history of ethnography requires not just the deconstruction of political power, but also of narrative power, and of petty power. The more trivial critiques launched against Depont and Coppolani, or the false modesty of Germain Sabatier,

[126] Georges Viollier, *Les Deux Algérie*, new edn (Paris: Paul Dupont, 1899), 7. Italics in the original

[127] Viollier, *Deux Algérie*, 7; cf. AGGA, 3X/2, Louis Rinn, "La Question des Ouled Sidi Cheikh en 1885," *al-Akhbar*, July 22–29, 1885.

[128] Viollier, *Deux Algérie*, 21; cf. Doutté, *Magie et religion*, 501.

demonstrate the overlapping struggles of political and disciplinary power.

Power and publication

The colonial state exerted selective pressure on the narrative forms that scholars, tourists, and administrators developed. Through the provision of subventions, logistical aid, and information, and through the influence exerted directly on the publishing industry, the Gouvernement général de l'Algérie encouraged ethnographic scholarship. Although ethnographic studies of Algeria emerged out of varied texts, they benefited from a colonial state committed to perpetuating useful knowledge. Ethnographic narrative and methodology dominated colonial cultural studies in part due to concerted efforts to facilitate the publication of ethnography.

One of the first ethnographers to utilize government resources was Henri Duveyrier. At seventeen, Duveyrier became the youngest European traveler in the Sahara, in the late 1850s and early 1860s. His *Les Touareg du Nord*, the central text in the study of the Sahara for decades, synthesized his experiences living among the Tuareg. In the fall of 1859, his father requested Algerian government funding for Henri's "work of scientific exploration. He merits for his character and his special knowledge, as well as for the utility of [his] work . . . , the confidence and interest of your administration."[129] Only two days later, Henri's patron made a similar request. On November 30, General de Martinprey expedited official letters of introduction for Henri, offering any logistical help the government could provide.[130] In the spring of 1862, Henri Duveyrier himself, noting the financial and logistical aid already received, requested permission to publish *Les Touareg du Nord*, perhaps because of the 8000F he had received from the colonial government of Algeria.[131] Indeed, the very nature of his research arose out of an 1860 order to "inquire . . . of the different peoples that he will visit; of their religions, mores, and customs, their degree of civilization."[132] That permission, duly granted, reflected a recognition on the part of both state and ethnographer of the deference to political utility that the stipend implied. Duveyrier researched the

[129] AGGA, 6X/20 (Papiers Henri Duveyrier, 1859–1909), Charles Duveyrier to Comte de Chaneloupe-Laubat, Governor General of Algeria, Paris, November 26, 1859.

[130] AGGA, 6X/20, A. Warnier to Gen. de Martinprey, Commandant de la Terre & Mer, Algiers, November 28, 1859.

[131] AGGA, 6X/20, Henri Duveyrier to the Marshall Duke of Malakof, Governor General of Algeria, [1862?].

[132] Archives privées des Archives nationales de la France (AP), 47/AP:9 (Papiers privés Duveyrier), "Instructions particulières du Général Commmandant Supérieur pour M. Duveyrier," April 12, 1860.

Tuareg, thanks to the support of the state, and published his ethnography only with its acquiescence.

The networks of patronage of the Second Empire differed from those of the Third Republic, operating in a manner more conducive to a well-connected, promising, if slightly naïf, explorer. Nevertheless, Duveyrier, canny and diligent, leveraged *Les Touareg du Nord* into later government connections, as well.[133] Duveyrier negotiated the transition from empire to republic without alienating his bureaucratic backers. Not surprisingly, the Algerian colonial government funded numerous other explorations of the cultural terrain of Algeria.[134]

The reach of the Algiers government extended to the publishing industry itself.[135] Even a cursory glance at the bibliography reveals the close association of Adolphe Jourdan's publishing company with Algerian ethnography. Tantalizing glimpses hint at a close, if perhaps informal, relationship between the colonial government and the nearby Imprimerie Adolphe Jourdan. In 1891, when Henri Bissuel, formerly of the *bureaux arabes*, published a series of lectures on the Sahara he had given to a garrison, he turned, not to the official government printing company, but to Jourdan.[136] Moreover, for Depont and Coppolani's *Confréries religieuses*, the governor general himself signed the publication contract with Adolphe Jourdan's firm.[137] A government-directed project from the start, the government laid claim to the intellectual property of Depont and Coppolani, and arranged for its publication. Perhaps the anonymous reviewer in the October 30, 1890 issue of *La Vigie algérienne* of Algiers summarized it best: "Jourdan took the task of making of his publishing

133 "Extraits des Procès-Verbaux des Séances, Séance du 6 janvier 1875," *Bulletin de la Société de Géographie* (Paris) 9 (January–June 1875): 213.

134 AGGA, 4H/33, Minister of Public Education and Fine Arts to the Governor General of Algeria, December 27, 1899; Auguste Mouliéras, *Fez* (Paris: Augustin Challamel, 1902), 80; 4H/22, Director of Higher Education to the Governor General of Algeria, Paris, January 24, 1906, and February 28, 1906; Maurice Benhazera, *Six Mois chez les Touareg du Ahaggar* (Algiers: Adolphe Jourdan, 1908); AGGA, 22H/72, Maurice Benhazera to Governor General of Algeria, Bou-Medfa, June 19, 1907; Aymard, "Note pour Monsieur de Saint-Germain," Algiers, July 18, 1908. Auguste Castéran, *L'Algérie d'aujourd'hui* (Algiers: Imprimerie algérienne, 1905); Edmond Doutté, *L'Islam algérien en l'an 1900*, Exposition Universelle de 1900 (Algiers-Mustapha: Giralt, 1900), 169–70.

135 On Orientalist publishing: Said, *Orientalism*, 221.

136 H. Bissuel, *Le Sahara français: conférence sur les questions sahariennes faite les 21 et 31 mars 1891 à MM. les officiers de la garnison de Médéa* (Algiers: Adolphe Jourdan, 1891). More broadly: René Basset, "Mission scientifique en Algérie et au Maroc," *Bulletin de la Société de Géographie de l'Est* (Nancy: 1883); Augustin Bernard, "Documents pour Servir à l'Étude du Nord-Ouest Africain," *BSGAO* 17 (1897); Sibeud, *Science impériale*, 90.

137 AGGA, 16H/8, draft of a contract between Adolphe Jourdan, Publisher-bookseller, Algiers, and the Governor General of Algeria.

house an Algerian library . . . [H]e aids those who, like himself, love Algeria," the Algeria of the colonial administration.[138]

Additionally, the colonial government of Algeria facilitated the dissemination of ethnography through colonial societies. Scholarly societies by no means represented any sort of free intellectual discourse about empire. To the contrary, arms of the colonial state closely controlled their content. The president of the Société de Géographie de l'Est (Nancy) in 1894 apologized abjectly to the Colonial Ministry for errors deemed harmful.[139] In 1900, the president of the Société de Géographie d'Alger requested a modest stipend, and the colonial ministry expedited books of interest or special speakers to geographic societies on several occasions.[140] The colonial ministry even offered book prizes for works "judged of urgent relevance."[141] Not only did administrators contribute to emerging cultural discourses about Algerians, Algiers offered fiduciary incentives for publication. Just as the state encouraged the development of participant observation and ethnographic narrative, it also facilitated the institutionalization of ethnographic publishing.

The colonial libraries represented the most significant institutional factor linking state and scholar. Nearly every administrative district in Algeria possessed some library, however rudimentary. From the Moroccan border to Constantine, administrators pointedly complained about the paucity of relevant books, depicting such holdings as something of a cross between a necessity and an entitlement.[142] Their purchasing

138 AGGA, 3X/1 (Personal Papers of Louis Rinn), anonymous [Rinn identified him as "de Sambœuf[,]Avocat"], "Un Livre," *La Vigie algérienne* (Algiers), Octobre 30, 1890. AGGA, 3X/1, de Loizillon, review of *Marabouts et khouans*, *Moniteur de l'Algérie* (Algiers), July 28, 1884; AGGA, 3X/1, anonymous review of *Marabouts et khouan*, *La Solidarité*, August 17, 1884; AGGA, 3X/1, anonymous review of *Marabouts et khouan*, *al-Akhbar:* (Algiers) August 18–19, 1884; Desprez, *L'Hiver à Alger*, 223. Jourdan published all of Rinn's works.

139 Fonds ministériels, Généralités 304 (1997) [FM GEN 304(1997)], [illeg.] to M. J. L. Deloncle, Sub-Director to the Minister of the Colonies, Nancy, Septembre 28, 1894. On learned societies: Lorcin, *Imperial Identities*, 146–66; Stocking, *Delimiting Anthropology*, 211.

140 FM GEN 304(1997), President of the Société de Géographie d'Alger, to the Minister of the Colonies, Algiers, March 29, 1900; Minister of the Colonies, General Secretary, Paris, January 30, 1900; Minister of the Colonies, 3rd Direction, 2nd Bureau, "Approvisionnements, etc., Transports de livres pour la Société géographique de Boulogne-sur-Mer," July 4, 1896;

141 FM GEN 305(2001), Lt.-Col. Berrie, President of la Société de Géographie et d'Archéologie de la province d'Oran, to the Minister of the Colonies in Paris, Oran, May 13, 1902.

142 AGGA, 10H/74, Général Gillet, Commander of the Division of Constantine, to the Governor General, Constantine, January 22, 1908; Hubert Lyautey, Commander of the Division of Oran to the Governor General of Algeria, Oran, May 25, 1908; Governor General to the Commander of the Division [of Oran], Algiers, June 2, 1908; Lyautey to Governor General, October 21, 1908.

records illuminate the priorities of the state, preferring certain works over others. A 1904 book order from the Annex of Beni-Ounif evinced a distinct preponderance of ethnographic texts, including such familiar names as Bernard, Cat, and Depont and Coppolani.[143] Revelatory of the small world of Algerian publishing, large book orders arrived directly from the Imprimerie Adolphe Jourdan.[144] As to whether or not administrators actually *read* these books, the archive remains silent. Nevertheless, the government manifestly preferred to stock colonial libraries with ethnographies.

Hence, administrators organized purchases around utilitarian ends. Certain works proved, if not best-sellers, then at the very least widely circulated. First among them was Rinn's *Marabouts et khouan.* Indeed, the 1895 survey of religious practice operated under the assumption that all administrators had ready access to *Marabouts et khouan.*[145] Perhaps due in part to Rinn's success, Depont and Coppolani's work itself proved so popular with senators that Louis Favre, the librarian for the senatorial library, requested the regular dispatch of similar works.[146]

Exchanging books cemented informal ties between ethnographers and the administration. While the *Revue coloniale* provided free subscriptions in 1899 for the President of the Republic, the Governor General of Algiers, various chambers of commerce, and the Prefect of Oran,[147] colonial authorities, too, used texts to foster a common intellectual world. Not only did the governor general fund Maurice Benhazera's fieldwork for *Six Mois chez les Touareg du Ahaggar*, he authorized the purchase of dozens of

[143] Only two of the twenty books had no ethnographic content: a book on drainage, and an atlas; AGGA, 10H/74, General Herson, Commander of the Division of Oran, to Governor General, "Demande de'ouvrages pour la bibliothèque de Beni Ounif," February 24, 1904; General O'Connor, Commander of the Division of Oran to Governor General, "Demande de livres," November 25, 1903; O'Connor to Governor General, "Demande d'ouvrages," November 25, 1903; "Liste des ouvrages et cartes envoyés aux Bibliothèque de l'annexe de Timmemoun, Touat, d'Insalah."

[144] AGGA, 10H/74, General Servière, Commander of the Division of Alger, to Governor General, "Ouvrages destinés à la bibliothèque des Oasis Sahariennes," March 7, 1902; 10H/80, Minute of the letter written by the Head of the Bureau to the Head of the 6th Bureau, December 30, 1889; AGGA, 10H/81, Adolphe Jourdan to the Head of the Service of Native Officers, August 18, 1896.

[145] AGGA, 16H/9, Administrator of the Commune mixte of Fedj-M'zala to the Prefect of the Department of Constantine, Fadj-Mzala, May 9, 1895.

[146] AGGA, 10H/80, Louis Favre, Chief Librarian, Sénat, Bibliothèque, to Governor General of Algeria, December 7, 1897.

[147] FM GEN 246(1726), "Liste du Service gratuit de la Revue Coloniale 1899." In 1897, the *Revue coloniale* sent out approximately 57,500 copies; FM GEN 236(1688), "Bon pour le transport à Paris, à l'adresse de M. le Ministre des Colonies, Secrétariat Général, Service géographique et Missions au Pavillon de Flore, Palais de Tuileries, de deux colis pesant ensemble 106 kilos, à livrer à domicile par le messager Galbrun au compte de la Maison centrale," Melun, March 23, 1897.

copies for various libraries. More significantly, he also sent examples to ethnographers, including Le Châtelier, Bernard, and Doutté. To these, Benhazera added geographic societies and various additional government officials.[148] Algiers purchased one hundred copies of Rinn's *Histoire de l'Insurrection de 1871*, reflecting Rinn's status both as authority and as second-highest ranking government official in Algiers.[149] Such purchases ensured that Algerian ethnography remained vibrant, that Doutté remained as knowledgeable about the Sahara as he did about Morocco and the Oranais, that an administrator could look to others who had used their time in outposts for the intellectual profit of the state. The common intellectual milieu in which ethnographers moved owed much to the vigilance of a colonial government committed to the perpetuation of useful knowledge about Algerians.

In addition, the Algerian colonial government commissioned projects to familiarize metropolitan French people with Algerians. Expositions provided opportunities to market the colonial project. Self-styled experts, colonial ethnographers seemed the logical choice to author such texts. As early as 1878, colonial expositions provided an opportunity for governments to convince a popular audience that colonization represented something nobler and richer than a mere drain on resources.[150] Often held in conjunction with expositions, colonial conferences fostered lively scholarly debates on a wide variety of colonial and international questions.[151]

Ethnography and politics came together as students of Algerian culture familiarized exposition-goers with colonial cultures to popularize empire. Drawing on his fieldwork, Doutté wrote his detailed *L'Islam algérien en l'an 1900* for the Exposition Universelle. He interpreted his text as a contribution to the European understanding of Islam in the new century. "We have not hesitated," he explained, "to give our personal opinions,

148 AGGA, 22H/72, Minute of the letter written regarding the work of M. Benhazera. *Six Mois chez les Touaregs de Ahaggar*, n.d.; Maurice Benhazera to "Mon Commandant," Bou Medfa, June 5, 1908.

149 AGGA, 3X/1, Secretary-General of the Government for the Governer General, to Louis Rinn, Conseiller d'État, Algiers, March 6, 1891.

150 E.g., C. Allan, *Conférence sur l'Algérie par M. C. Allan, publiciste. 17 septembre 1878* (Paris: Imprimerie nationale, 1879); *Coup d'œil sur l'histoire de la colonisation en Algérie* (Algiers: A. Bouyer, 1878); AGGA, 20H/6, "Dossier: Correspondance relative aux Chefs indigènes se rendant à l'exposition: 1878." 1G (Exposition universelle de Paris de 1878 et la création du Musée d'Ethnographie du Trocadéro; les débuts de son administration). 1a (Exposition universelle de 1878; projet d'un Musée des provinces de France) (2AM/1G/1a), *Exposition universelle de 1878: description complète et détaillée des Palais [du] Champs du Mars et du Trocadéro* (Paris: Le Bailly, 1878).

151 *Congrès colonial français de 1908* (Paris: Au Secrétariat général des Congrès coloniaux français, 1909).

convinced that, if they may at times express provisional truths, they will also often be completed and rectified: "that, he continued, was his greatest hope, "as the progress of our knowledge [comes] but at that price."[152] Doutté utilized his personal experiences to popularize a particular view of Algerian Islam through the medium of the Universal Exposition. The 1908 exposition witnessed no less than the establishment of a Tuareg community in Paris, so that Parisians and others could observe Tuaregs in a facsimile of their home environment. Dr. Atgier, a Parisian anthropologist, wrote his bizarre *Les Touareg à Paris* as an ethnography of Saharan Algerians with the corner of the boulevard de Clichy and the rue Blanche as his field site.[153] Colonial expositions literally transposed the ethnographic model of participant-observation methodology from Algeria to the streets of Paris and Chicago.

Moreover, the French government commissioned exposition texts *in Arabic*. Such texts reenacted, in the vernacular, the choices and silences of French-language ethnographic texts: the government disseminated them to propagate politically useful interpretations of Arabic-speaking cultures. Just as ethnographers consciously emphasized or downplayed various aspects, so, too, the Arabic authors of these documents made strategic narrative choices. The authors became speaking ethnographic objects on display. In his *Muḥāḍarāt bi-maʿriḍ Bārīs al-ʿām, sana 1900, al-mumārisa al-ūlā* (Lectures for the Paris General Exposition of 1900, First Conference) (1901),[154] Shaykh Abū Naẓẓāra discussed the lectures he gave at the Musée de l'homme. "When the French government learned of the aims of the shaykh, they listened to his words at the Trocadéro museum [which] was under the patronage of the governor[155] of the provinces and

[152] Doutté, *Islam algérien*, avant-propos. See also E. Lacanaud, *L'Algérie au point de vue de l'économie sociale* (Algiers–Mustapha: Giralt, 1900), similarly published for the 1900 Exposition.

[153] Dr. Atgier, *Les Touareg à Paris* (Paris: Société d'Anthropologie de Paris, 1910). On the Chicago Exposition of 1893: Hippolyte Giraud, *Exposition internationale de Chicago: section algérienne. Rapport.* (Algiers: Pierre Fontana, 1893); Erik Larson, *The Devil in the White City: Murder, Magic, and Madness at the Fair that Changed America* (New York: Vintage Books, 2003), *passim*; FM GEN 282(1878); FM GEN 282(1879); FM GEN 308(2014).

[154] All translations from Arabic are my own unless otherwise noted. The French published the text in Arabic but printed along with it a cover in French, labelled: "Abou Naddara [a translation approximating the pronunciation of his name in Algerian Colloquial Arabic, which frequently reads a ḍ for a ẓ], *Les Conférences du Cheikh Abou Naddara: Chaër-El-Molk, à l'Exposition de 1900. 1re Conférence* (Paris: [Imprimerie nationale?], January 1902. For the sake of simplicity, I will cite Abū Naẓẓāra as *Muḥāḍarāt*. On Abū Naẓẓāra's request for a subvention, see FM GEN 305(2001), "Note au Secrét^{at} G^{al} (S^{e} géographique), Paris, October 26, 1901.

[155] Abū Naẓẓāra uses *mudīr* (Egyptian and Levantine: governor); Abū Naẓẓāra, *Muḥāḍarāt*, 5.

colonies and nations and protectorates."[156] The shaykh knew of the significance of his appearance at the Trocadéro and took no small amount of pride that, at the secular temple to empire, the French government came to listen – and that the Parisian press took note.[157] Abū Naẓẓāra parroted official French propaganda about North Africa, affirming that the region had a long history of amicable ties with Europe dating back to the time of Carlos V and Hārūn al-Rashīd. Among these nations, "France is the first," he continued, noting "the friendship . . . of the current President of the Republic and His Majesty the Sultan Abdelhamid" of the Ottoman Empire.[158] Indeed, Abū Naẓẓāra spent pages on the splendor of the exhibition, its opulence, and that of the President of the Republic himself.[159]

Abū Naẓẓāra did not stray from the broad narrative, the script, the French had provided for him. If nothing else, his exhaustive list of French colonial possessions[160] situated the text within the totalizing, universalizing gaze of colonial exposition politics. In an introduction, Henri Malo thanked Abū Naẓẓāra for "addressing the Oriental natives of the Exposition, in their language," which "proved that here, in France, we interest ourselves in them and that we have made efforts to make their stay in the capital agreeable." Malo, the secretary for the Minister of the Colonies, interpreted Abū Naẓẓāra's speech as a critical piece of propaganda for "our Algerians, our Tunisians, the Egyptians, the Moroccans, all those who understand Arabic."[161] Those who did, however, seemed to Abū Naẓẓāra himself to have interpreted it differently. "Besides," he plaintively chastised his audience, in Arabic, at the

156 Abū Naẓẓāra, *Muḥāḍarāt*, 5. He uses two words, *maḥmiyya* and *kila'*. Abū Naẓẓāra carefully rendered in Arabic the juridically separate forms of French colonialism: Algeria was a province or *département* [*qism*]; he used other terms for other colonies.

157 Abū Naẓẓāra, *Muḥāḍarāt*, 5.

158 Abū Naẓẓāra, *Muḥāḍarāt*, 6. Another Arabic text specifically addressed French fears of religious revival in their Arabic-speaking, Muslim colonies. Shaykh Sīdī Muḥammad bin Muṣṭafā bin al-Khūja al-Jazā'irī wrote that "religious fanaticism [*ta'aṣṣub*] is forbidden in munificent [*samḥa*, which can also mean "permitted," a meaning not allowed by its use as a modifier of "Sharī'a," which by definition is licit] Sharī'a [Islamic law]." See Shaykh Sīdī Muḥammad bin Muṣṭafā bin al-Khūja al-Jazā'irī, *Iqāmat al-Brāhīn al-'Aẓīm 'alā nafī al-ta'aṣṣub al-dīnī fi-l Islām* [Great Liturgical Proof of the Rejection of Religious Fanaticism in Islam] (Paris: Imprimerie Pierre Fontana, 1906), 4. The author taught at a mosque in Algiers; FM GEN 305(1998), Governor General Grévy to the Minister of the Colonies, March 6, 1902, noted bin al-Khouja al-Jazā'irī's text with approval.

159 Abū Naẓẓāra, *Muḥāḍarāt*, 8–10. Page 8 even commented on the personal presence of the President of the Republic himself.

160 Abū Naẓẓāra, *Muḥāḍarāt*, 30–1. He even detailed each of France's Polynesian island possessions by name, in Arabic.

161 Abū Naẓẓāra, *Muḥāḍarāt*, introduction.

Exposition, "when I read to one of [my] colleagues, you [plural] did not pay me the respect of your attention to my address."[162] In response, one of them demurred, and "said to me, 'Sī [a term of respect] Shaykh, your words were excellent.' "[163] Not merely excellent: they were *mlīḥ*. In a departure from his habitually formal *fuṣḥa*, Abū Naẓẓāra rendered the riposte in Algerian Colloquial Arabic. He left no doubt as to the nationality of those who did not heed his words.

In text, French ethnographers could make informants such as Abū Naẓẓāra espouse the virtues of French colonization, and could put words in informants' mouths attesting to the righteousness of the political order of empire. The presence of the "native" informant only served, for French readers, to establish the veracity of the ethnographer's generalizations. In the colonial expositions and the ethnographic museum, however, Abū Naẓẓāra's spoken words at the Exposition rang hollow for Arabic speakers. Such generalizations seemed authoritative only to French politicians and ethnographers. Many Algerians, it seems, simply refused to listen.

The French colonial system developed methods of codifying and perpetuating politically interested cultural knowledge about Algerians. In establishing participant observation as the dominant means of acquiring knowledge, many administrators, scholars, and tourists reinforced the hegemonic intellectual power of the colonial state. Ethnography, as a system of narratives associated with certain methodological forms, both arose out of and contributed to the most basic political imperatives of colonialism. As a system of ruthless, authoritarian policing of difference, French rule required the organization of knowledge into discrete, utilitarian facts. It created cultural "facts" to render the processes of control simpler. These intellectual artifacts took on lives of their own, perpetuating themselves both discursively and politically. The ethnographic facts that arose out of French colonial Algeria created an empire of their own; they attempted total, hegemonic control of cultural discourse about Algerians, and, at times, succeeded. From Constantine to Chicago, ethnographers, basing their expertise on discourses of participant observation, inscribed authoritative statements about Algerians, rendered as facts, in effect, the politically oriented concerns and conclusions of their analyses. From 1, rue Combes in Algiers to the boulevard de Clichy in Paris, this was an empire of facts.

[162] Abū Naẓẓāra, *Muḥāḍarāt*, 8. [163] Abū Naẓẓāra, *Muḥāḍarāt*, 8.

2 The lies that empire tells itself when times are easy

I am the lie that empire tells itself when times are easy.[1]

J. M. Coetzee, *Waiting for the Barbarians*

Sometime in 1911 or 1912, Arnold Van Gennep visited a disreputable little café in the Algerian city of Tilimsān. Van Gennep himself never achieved renown at a major French university, relegated to marginality. In this dingy café, however, Van Gennep would learn a more important lesson than any bruited in the Sorbonne. That café witnessed the exchange of notions of expertise and ethnographic authority between an isolated, prolific schoolteacher and Van Gennep himself.

Van Gennep's description of the café reveals his apprehension about his visit. On this trip to Tilimsān, Van Gennep began interaction with Algerians. "There is in Tlemcen," he wrote in *En Algérie*, in 1914, "a Moorish café at the corner of the rue de Mascara and a little square on which empty several commercial streets."[2] Surrounded by *fanādiq*, hostels, "[t]he square . . . is shaded by enormous trees against which rest . . . benches where perch . . . the idle of the village, town criers, . . . native peasants from the four corners of North Africa." They must have gaped when Van Gennep visited. "However," he continued, "in front of these benches there are round, iron tables like one sees in the cafés of our [French] villages, although for the clients of mark, Europeans or Frankified shaykhs, there are cane chairs that are put more or less in equilibrium on the round stones and the muddy hollows of the little square, changing their place with the movement of the shadows, no indeed, *ce café maure n'est pas chic du tout.*"[3]

To most of the inhabitants of Tilimsān, that café seemed more than démodé or rustic. It was downright disreputable. Van Gennep perceived

[1] J. M. Coetzee, *Waiting for the Barbarians* (Johannesburg: Ravan Press, 1981), 135.

[2] Arnold Van Gennep, *En Algérie* (Paris: Mercure de France, 1914), 19. On Van Gennep's 1911–12 voyage to Algeria, see Emmanuelle Sibeud, *Une Science impériale pour l'Afrique? La construction des savoirs africanistes en France, 1878–1930* (Paris: Éditions de l'École des hautes études en sciences sociales, 2002), 242; also 161, 213, *passim*.

[3] Van Gennep, *En Algérie*, 19–20.

that "in installing myself there, I debased myself from the first day in the estimation of the real people of Tilimsān, natives as much as Europeans, who, functionaries or colonists, for nothing in the world would let themselves be seen there, even to accompany some stranger curious about local mores: 'The natives, Monsieur, we don't associate with them except for the work that we can extract from them, and the money that they bring,'" one inhabitant informed him.[4] What, then, led Van Gennep to violate this unspoken colonial taboo? What drew the polymath to this dismal, disagreeable little café, its muddy pavement and its rickety chairs, that welcomed him with no warmth?

Van Gennep went to the dingy café to talk to Algerians. Colonial ethnographers moved in individual arcs across an intellectual space bounded as much discursively, by narratives, as socially, by relationships. No armchair theorists, these women and men sat in dimly lit cafés and wrote in dusty Saharan outposts. The personal mattered; the personal was political. The intellectual world of colonial Algeria created texts bound by personal relations with informants and with power. Concealed within authoritative statements about culture lie personal ties. As constitutive experiences, personal trajectories played a fundamental role in determining the direction and analytical scope of texts.

Hence, an understanding of the production and use of colonial ethnography demands a critical engagement with choices available and options foreclosed. Their names represent trajectories across a shared, if diffuse, world; their life stories exemplified the entire range of opportunities and exclusions of colonial Algeria, yet the stories of ethnographers themselves tell something of empire's exploitation of diverse, even contradictory, strands of intellectual production.

Anthropologists, literary critics, and, to a lesser extent, historians have focused on the creation of ethnographies as self-consciously literary texts. "The writing and reading of ethnography," writes James Clifford, "are overdetermined by forces ultimately beyond the control of either an author or an interpretive community. These contingencies – of language, rhetoric, power, and history . . . can no longer be evaded."[5] Moreover, early ethnographers concealed the traces of the rectification of the

4 Van Gennep, *En Algérie*, 20.

5 James Clifford, "Introduction," in James Clifford and George E. Marcus, eds., *Writing Culture: The Poetics and Politics of Ethnography* (Berkeley, Calif.: University of California Press, 1986), 3–4, 13–15, 25. See also Charlotte Aull Davies, *Reflexive Ethnography: A Guide to Researching Selves and Others* (London: Routledge, 1999), 5; James Clifford, *The Predicament of Culture: Twentieth-Century Ethnography, Literature, and Art* (Cambridge, Mass.: Harvard University Press, 1988), 41; Mary Louise Pratt, "Fieldwork in Common Places," in Clifford and Marcus, eds., *Writing Culture*, 32.

personal with language, power, history within the texts themselves. Ethnographers rooted narrative in personal contact.

As anthropologists have explicitly acknowledged their own role in the creation of statements about culture(s), some have taken into account personal presence and the power of writing. More experimental ethnographic writing juxtaposes cultural analysis with personal explication illustrative of the power exerted through writing. As Ruth Behar phrased it, most ethnographers "act as a participant, but don't forget to keep your eyes open . . . But when the grant money runs out . . . please stand up, dust yourself off, go to your desk, and write down what you saw and heard. Relate it to something you've read by Marx, Weber, Gramsci, or Geertz, and you're on your way to doing anthropology."[6] Behar, nevertheless, found that formula deeply unsatisfying. "I found myself resisting the 'I' of the ethnographer as a privileged eye, a voyeuristic eye, an all-powerful eye. Every ethnography, I knew, depended on some form of ethnographic authority," and she not only questions her own formulation of such authority but incorporates her doubts into ethnography.[7]

However, Behar appears to disavow history in favor of a personal mode of writing. In response to the critiques of ethnographic authority mooted by Clifford and others, some, "as [Behar] once did, have retreated" from fieldwork-based anthropology "to history, to the quiet of the archives and the study of the past, where presumably the observer can do less damage, not have to be quite so disturbingly present."[8] Yet, as Michel Foucault, Alain Corbin, Ann Laura Stoler, Natalie Zemon Davis, Robert Darnton, Arlette Farge, and countless others have shown us, the silence of the archive rapidly dissolves into a cacophony of voices. The observers, though archived and dead, who wrote the ethnographic texts about which I in turn write remain present – and damaging. To read ethnographic texts historically requires a willingness to engage with questions raised by Clifford and others, to read colonial ethnographies for their reflexivity, for the interactions authoritative voices conceal.

Reading and writing texts reflexively relates the personal to the textual, the psychological to the analytical, through a careful winnowing of (auto)biographical detail. It does not aim to replace scholarly analysis

6 Ruth Behar, *The Vulnerable Observer: Anthropology that Breaks Your Heart* (Boston: Beacon Press, 1996), 5. See also James Clifford, *Routes: Travel and Translation in the Late Twentieth Century* (Cambridge, Mass.: Harvard University Press, 1997), 88–9; Vincent Crapanzano *The Hamadsha: A Study in Moroccan Ethnopsychiatry* (Berkeley, Calif.: University of California Press, 1973); Renato Rosaldo, *Culture and Truth: The Remaking of Social Analysis* (Boston: Beacon Press, 1993); Aull Davies, *Reflexive Ethnography*, 21.

7 Behar, *The Vulnerable Observer*, 21.

8 Behar, *The Vulnerable Observer*, 25. See also Pratt, "Fieldwork in Common Places," 31–5.

with personal detail; it merely acknowledges their inseparability within the ethnographic moment. "The meanings," clarifies Clifford, "of an ethnographic account are uncontrollable. Neither an author's intention, nor disciplinary training, nor the rules of genre can limit the readings of a text that will emerge with new historical, scientific, or political projects."[9] I use the reflexive critique of ethnographic narrative and method as a means of examining the production of cultural knowledge. Reflexive moments situate ethnography within the social, political, and historical context of its production, while destabilizing the omniscience of narrative authority. At the same time, such reading must remain wary of psychological determinism. "I am not," writes Michael M. J. Fischer, "advocating a reductive reading of ethnographies in terms of the biographies of their authors." Biography "makes reading richer and more informed."[10] The richest biographical readings unify the microscopic stories of a life with the collective processes of change.

Behar narrates the emotions that contribute to her analyses; colonial ethnographers rarely did. What remains is an archive, the text. Behar maintains that "[t]he ethnography serves as the only proof of the anthropologist's voyage."[11] Hence, a reading of reflexivity inscribed in colonial ethnographies becomes at once literary and historical, theoretical and archival. The ethnographer imprints narrative choices on thick description. "And so begins," writes Behar, "our work, our hardest work – to bring the ethnographic moment back, to resurrect it . . . [F]ieldnotes become palimpsests, useless unless plumbed for forgotten revelatory moments."[12] No historians can perform Lazarus-like miracles on the body of dead text. In these grave representations, however, lie revelations, desires, regrets. In the detritus we find the archive of a lost world, and it proves revelatory. Reading reflexivity in historical ethnographies demands the evocation of an interpersonal world and series of interactions best conveyed with techniques drawn equally from textual analysis and social history.[13] The history of ethnography demands a lens at once

9 James Clifford, "On Ethnographic Allegory," in Clifford and Marcus, eds., *Writing Culture*, 120; see also Paul Rabinow, "Representations are Social Facts: Modernity and Post-Modernity in Anthropology", in Clifford and Marcus, eds., *Writing Culture*, 242.

10 Michael M. J. Fischer, "Ethnicity and the Post-Modern Arts of Memory," in Clifford and Marcus, eds., *Writing Culture*, 200; John Comaroff and Jean Comaroff, *Ethnography and the Historical Imagination* (Boulder, Colo.: Westview Press, 1992), 25.

11 Behar, *The Vulnerable Observer*, 7. On personal voices in Orientalism, see Edward W. Said, *Orientalism* (New York: Vintage Books, 1979), 157–8, 197.

12 Behar, *The Vulnerable Observer*, 8–9.

13 Aull Davies, *Reflexive Ethnography*, 5; Abdelhamid Hannoum, "L'Auteur comme authorité en ethnographie coloniale: le cas de Robert Montagne," in François Pouillon and Daniel Rivet, eds., *La Sociologie musulmane de Robert Montagne* (Paris: Maisonneuve et Larose, 2000), 249.

tele- and microscopic, capable of containing biography, narrative, and context within one analytical frame.

In the context of colonial Algeria, this optic must disentangle the Third Republic and the hegemonic impulses of the colonial project. The republic required the imperial object for its self-fashioning. As Philip Nord notes, "[t]he culture of the republic generated some strange intellectual hybrids – a scientific racism, a scientific misogyny – that flew in the face of the regime's more fundamental democratic strivings."[14] The trajectories of these ethnographers across the intellectual world of colonial Algeria simultaneously represented movements through the world of the republic. The lives sketched in this chapter flourished in what Nord calls "the rot of imperialism."[15] Moreover, by the end of the Third Republic, they and intellectuals like them had *already* contributed to the transformation of the moralizing of the civilizing mission into the panoptic, oppressive mechanisms of colonial power. Though they moved across particular intellectual spaces, they remained embedded, too, in a collective, political one. The "solid institutional and associational foundations" of civil society that Nord sees as the basis of republican strength at home[16] provided in Algeria the very structure of imperial hegemony. The lies – about politics, about power, about the danger of the state's willingness to discriminate on the basis of identity – that returned to haunt France in 1940 had their roots in empire, embodied in individuals and agents. Some of them, like Alfred Bel and Edmond Doutté, led lives of scholarly influence, their reports and texts turning up repeatedly in citations, in administrative libraries, and purchase orders.[17] Some, like Henri Duveyrier and Juliette Salmon, confessed deeply personal experiences and misgivings in lavishly written narratives or in revelatory asides. Others, like Simone Bernard d'Attanoux, worked in close partnership with the colonial administration's intentions and parroted its goals. And one, Louis Rinn, did all of this, and more. Figures important to the disciplinary history of French sociology or European physical anthropology, despite their use of texts *produced* in Algeria, had relatively little impact on early debates emerging out of the *field*, except through footnotes and reading patterns. Other ethnographers, administrators, and writers exemplified different trajectories, or told the same stories in less compelling ways, or figure only as names attached to texts, without personal biographies. These trajectories here offer but a glimpse of how ethnographers moved, intellectually and personally, in a politically charged world, with no pretension to

[14] Philip Nord, *The Republican Moment: Struggles for Democracy in Nineteenth-Century France* (Cambridge, Mass.: Harvard University Press, 1998), 32.

[15] Nord, *The Republican Moment*, 246. [16] Nord, *The Republican Moment*, 253.

[17] See, broadly, AGGA, 10H/73 and 10H/74.

completion and no gesture at uniformity. The lives that people this chapter, contradictory and polyvalent though they were, were also the lies that empire told itself when times were easy.

"The self is detestable, but one must at times excuse it"

French colonial ethnographers in Algeria furnished a wealth of personally inflected writings. In the years before the attachment of ethnography to disciplinary anthropology, the prohibitions on the intrusion of personal narrative into analytical texts had not yet crystallized. Indeed, for Jean Le Roy, a judge who spent two years in Kabylia, the personal voice buttressed the authority of participant observation. Quite simply, he acknowledged the central role that the difficulties of fieldwork played in his understanding of Kabyle culture.

> I found myself every day in contact with its inhabitants, in the middle of the conflict of their passions . . . I could at least detect in them several essential traits; I try here to retrace them. I do not want to make a book, but simply to bring the deposition of a witness, a sort of minutes of that which I saw, heard, and understood. I expose myself thus in saying often: "I have seen, one told me, I know." The self is detestable; but one must at times excuse it; a traveler, a witness is well obliged to repeat endlessly: "I was there, such a thing happened to me."[18]

Only four years later, Bronislaw Malinowski would save such confessions for his diary. Le Roy offered with a perhaps telling defensiveness his use of the first person as part of the justificatory edifice of narrative authority. Personal voices attested to personal experience and explained interpretive choices.

Similarly, the bureaucrat Achille Robert, in his *L'Arabe tel qu'il est* (1900), proffered his personal frustrations and thwarted investigations to explain flaws in his text. Personal narratives of fieldwork amounted to both *authorizing* discourse *and* a deflection of criticism. They enhanced the authority of the text. Robert's explanation emphasized methodological difficulty.

> To write on Algeria is not always easy, for the native does not deliver himself; when one interrogates him, he seeks first of all to know the goal pursued and it is but with the greatest restrictions that he consents to respond to the questions that are formulated to him. Often his mistrust vis-à-vis the Christian pushes him to mislead him and he gives himself at times a malign pleasure in misleading him.
>
> If one wants to proceed methodically and penetrate the little secrets of Arab life, one always experiences many difficulties; the intimate details of this life escape

[18] Jean Le Roy, *Deux Ans de séjour en petite Kabylie: un peuple de Barbares en territoire française* (Paris: Augustin Challamel, 1911), 9.

us for reason of the care that the natives put in hiding them from us. Thus must one seize them in passage each time they present themselves.

It is this last manner of proceeding that obliged me to relate what I have seen and heard, from day to day, without framing or coordination.[19]

This strange passage, itself related largely not in the first person, but with that most useful and most French third person *on*, nevertheless served primarily to exculpate Robert from accusations that his text, far from offering an account of "the Arab as he is," merely listed daily personal interactions, like a diary or memoir. In this apologetic, Robert demonstrated his fear of attacks for lack of methodological rigor, for the use of the personal voice. The difficulty of fieldwork, he maintained, necessitated his seemingly haphazard analysis.

Although numerous ethnographers evinced a tension between the personal experiences of participant observation and resistance to reflexivity, many portrayed such reflexive moments as threatening to subsume an analytical text in emotion. Though not yet totalizing, limitations on personal voice started to emerge during the Third Republic. Camille Sabatier, ethnographer, colonist, and bureaucrat, openly mourned the death of his informant, Sīdī ʿAbd al-Qādir bin Milūd, killed for his ties with French administrators. "I need to recall," he wrote, "that the pain that I have felt again from the sad end of my friend must not make me go beyond the limits I have imposed to myself. This is a book of cold discussion. I do not want to remonstrate with anyone and I need to remember . . ."[20] Sabatier's ellipsis left open the question of what, exactly, he needed to remember. Perhaps Sabatier hoped to remind himself that emotions detracted from the expressly political purpose of his ethnography. Perhaps, however, he offered such reflection as testimony for his impetus to write in the first place. Despite the evident strength of his emotional attachment to bin Milūd, Sabatier could only interpret its revelation in text as potentially destabilizing.

Personal voices functioned differently in different texts. Le Roy and Robert displayed emotion defensively and out of necessity, illuminating the text's import while attesting to its veracity. For some ethnographers, reflexive writing *enhanced* claims to authority. Nevertheless, Camille Sabatier presented his personal struggle as an incursion that ultimately could only subvert the authority of his text. Personal revelation played a vital role in the establishment of an authoritative ethnographic

[19] Achille Robert, *L'Arabe tel qu'il est: études algériennes et tunisiennes* (Algiers: Imprimerie Joseph Angelini, 1900), 6. See also Ernest Mercier, *La Condition de la femme musulmane dans l'Afrique septentrionale* (Algiers: Adolphe Jourdan, 1895), 5–12.

[20] Camille Sabatier, *La Question du Sud-Ouest* (Algiers: Adolphe Jourdan, 1881), 36–7.

register. Contemporary anthropologists hold no monopoly over debates about intimate writing.

Rereading the actions of his youth

For twenty-nine months, starting in 1859, a young man of nineteen traveled across the Sahara, alone. His experience and the personal connections he forged served as a pattern for colonial ethnography. A lone voyager, at once completely isolated from and intimately connected to the Tuareg among whom he traveled, Henri Duveyrier explicated his intimate interactions with the people of the Sahara. His interest in other cultures started even earlier than his voyages. At fourteen, Henri departed Paris for boarding school in Germany. His brother's journal inspired the incipient explorer to "begin [his] journal, at the moment when my career as a man will unwind."[21] René Pottier, Duveyrier's eccentric biographer, remarked that "this *Journal* unveils so completely what the man would be that I think it good to stop on it a moment."[22] While his father intended him for a career in commerce, Henri paid particular attention to the customs of his new home.[23] By March of 1855, Henri met another student with a similar interest in folklore and culture. "At dinner we spoke of the legends of the Bretons and of those of the Germans," which aroused the interest of the budding ethnographer. "At the end of dinner we had to change places and I found myself now very far from him, that pained me, as we were talking together of things that others do not know, like history, linguistics, etc.... I had even undertaken to make him recount to me all the legends that he knows."[24] Though his impulse for ethnographic interrogation may have made him a tiresome dinner companion, Duveyrier had found in another boy an intellectual companion with whom to discuss all that fascinated Henri as boy and man: language, history, culture.

Indeed, Henri demonstrated a useful facility with languages, peppering his journals with passages in German, English, and Greek and earning his prefect's praise.[25] Even at fourteen, however, Duveyrier acknowledged the defamiliarization of the foreign. The May 1855 assassination attempt on Napoleon III created friction; "the Germans... are calling

[21] Archives nationales de France, Archives privées, 47AP/1 (Fonds Duveyrier), "Journal depuis le 1 août 1854 jusqu'au 22 août 1855 continué jusqu'au 1er Janvier 1857. Henri Duveyrier. Paris, Genève, Lautrach" (hereafter Journal 1854–5), 1–2.

[22] René Pottier, "Un Seigneur du désert: Duveyrier," *Sahara de demain* 2 (October 1958): 19.

[23] Journal 1854–5, 1, 16–7. [24] Journal 1854–5, 31. Ellipses are in the original.

[25] Journal 1854–5, 44, 53, 64; René Pottier, "Hommage à Henry [sic] Duveyrier," *Comptes-Rendus mensuels des séances de l'Académie des sciences d'Outre-Mer* 19 (March 6, 20, April 17, 1959): 139.

me *Königsmördur* (murderer of the king) . . . because of that as if it were my fault," perhaps because of his father's affinity for Saint-Simonianism.[26] Such difficulties humanize the child's perspicacious journal.

Another tale of the discomfort of the foreign indicated a menacing sense of isolation. Duveyrier took interest in the suffering of his British friend Scott. Henri related Scott's story in halting English in his journal, to conceal its details from prying readers or out of loyalty. "I have spoken with Scott," he wrote,

> and he has tolet me that he kann not lives more here, I have told him that he must think a little before than ask to the Direcer to go back in England, bu he has told me that it was impossible that he lives more here, and that he have think before to a suicide. I have told him there that he could do wath he want. He has give a letter to sir Sheridan (le maître d'Anglais) to give it to the director. [*sic*][27]

Duveyrier's broken English leaves the text open to doubt; did he mean to tell the troubled Scott that in England he would be free to act as he pleased, or did he, with a telling and chilling indifference to the threats of suicide, advise the boy to do as he wished? Their friendship presented more than a mere insight into the diverse circle of Duveyrier's childhood friends. It introduced, not for the last time, the specter of suicide. He wrote "so that when I am older, I can reread the actions of my youth."[28]

Henri Duveyrier's 1859 voyage called upon his language skills, his intense interest in other cultures, and his ability to form personal connections with others. Naively, fortuitously, he made recourse to the goodwill of those he met along the way. His major work, *Les Touareg du Nord* (1864), undertaken with the support of the colonial government, revealed the depth of his relationships in the Sahara.[29] No mere explorer, Henri

[26] 47AP/1, Journal 1854–5, 53. On Saint-Simonianism, see Patricia M. E. Lorcin, *Imperial Identities: Stereotyping, Prejudice and Race in Colonial Algeria* (London: I. B. Tauris, 1995), 99–117; Michael Heffernan, "The Limits of Utopia: Henri Duveyrier and the Exploration of the Sahara in the Nineteenth Century," *The Geographical Journal* 155, no. 3 (November 1989): 342–52; René Pottier, *Un Prince saharien méconnu: Henri Duveyrier* (Paris: Plon, 1938), 1–11. M. Emerit, *Les Saint-Simoniens en Algérie* (Paris: Les Belles Lettres, 1941), 219–55, cited in Paul Pandolfi, "Imaginaire colonial et litterature: Jules Verne chez les Touaregs," *Ethnologies compares* 5 (Autumn 2002): 9–10; René Pottier, "A propos d'un Centenaire . . . Henri Duveyrier," *Notre Sahara* 3, no. 15 (25 October 1960): 42; Jean-Louis Triaud, *La Légende noire de la Sanûsiyya: une confrérie musulmane saharienne sous le regard français (1840–1930)*, vol. I (Aix-en-Provence: Institut de recherches et d'études sur le monde arabe et musulmane, and Paris: Éditions de la Maison des sciences de l'homme, 1995), 13–15 (especially n.12), 105.

[27] Journal 1854–5, 35.

[28] From Duveyrier's journal, an unattributed quotation in Pottier, "Seigneur," 19.

[29] On Duveyrier and the government: AGGA, 4H/5, "Instructions particulières du Géneral commandant Supérieur pour M. Duveyier"; AN, 47AP/9, Prefect Levert to unnamed general, April 12, 1860 (copy); AGGA, 6X/20, Henri Duveyrier to General de

traveled for personal as well as academic reasons. He found the voyage, like the dinner only five years earlier, emotionally and intellectually satisfying. Acknowledging his debts to Muslims he met along the way, Duveyrier named his friends, informants, and helpers. In *Les Touareg du Nord*, he noted the particular aid of Sīdī Ḥamza, Sīdī Muḥammad al-ʿĪd, Shaykh ʿUthmān, and Sīdī Muḥammad al-Bakkay in the preparation of his section on Tuareg religion.[30] Unlike Camille Sabatier or others, Duveyrier expressed no doubts about sharing his affection for them. The presence of named informants contributed to the authority of his text. Duveyrier's relationships with his informants were no less coercive than any other imperial ties. Despite his situation in the oppressive politics of empire, Duveyrier evinced a sophisticated conception of authority and expertise. "I have had the happy chance to travel with [the Tuareg] tribe[s], to observe the life of the Tuareg people; I can thus try to recount it, which has not been done," Duveyrier explained.[31] In an intellectual world still dominated by armchair theorists, the personal dimensions of his fieldwork experience stand out.

In the posthumous *Sahara algérien et tunisien: journal de route de Henri Duveyrier* (1905), Duveyrier more fully expounded on the personal experience of his voyages, not surprising in a journal not intended for publication. He made no secret of his Christianity (such as it was), dressed as an Arab, and studied the Qur'ān for relevant passages on tolerance.[32] This preparation, indicative of an unusually open mind for a colonial explorer, outfitted Henri for the difficulties of sustained cultural study. He attended weddings, received gifts and hospitality from various Algerians, including "a civilized and learned man, who gave me good pieces of historical information."[33] The *Journal de route* clarified that the warp and weft of quotidian interactions provided the cloth of Duveyrier's knowledge,

Martinsprey, High Commander of the Forces of Land and Sea in Algeria, Tripoli, October 11, 1860; AGGA, 6X/20, note, "Non datée. Sans doute Mars 1862"; AGGA, 4H/5, "Direction Général des Services Civils. 3me Division, 1ère Section, N– 859. Transmission d'une quittance en double expédition, à faire signés à M. Henri Duveyrier. Note pour Monsieur le Général de Division, Sous-Gouverneur"; AN, 47AP/1, Henri Duveyrier to Charles Duveyrier, Constantine, January 1, 1860; Duveyrier, *Notes sur les Touareg et leur pays* (Paris: Imprimerie de L. Martinet, 1863); Triaud, *Légende noire*, 166, and *passim*.

30 Henri Duveyrier, *Les Touareg du Nord: exploration du Sahara* (Paris: Challamel Aîné, 1864), 315.

31 Duveyrier, *Touareg du Nord*, 403.

32 Duveyrier, *Sahara algérien et tunisien: journal de route de Henri Duveyrier*, ed. Ch. Maunoir and H. Schirmer (Paris: Augustin Challamel, 1905), xxii–xxiii.

33 Duveyrier, *Journal de route*, 13–4, 37, 38; Duveyrier, "De Telemsan à Melila en 1886," *Bulletin de la Société de Geographie* [*BSGP*], 7th ser., 14 (1893: 2): 207.

much as his assorted diaries and notebooks from his schooldays told of knowledge of folk tales gleaned from chance friendships.

In the Jarīd, Duveyrier "went at night to see the marabout Sidi Moustapha ben Azouûz [*sic*: Muṣṭafā bin ʿAzzūz], who received me in a most civil fashion, and tried hard to make me understand that all, Muslims, Christians and Jews, are His children, all are those whom God has created . . . he approved of my studies" in religion and language. The cleric blessed Duveyrier, invited him to stay, though the young traveler "was obliged to give long details on electricity, steam, and many other such things." Students at the shrine harassed Duveyrier, until bin ʿAzzūz offered him an escort.[34] He mentioned hostility, cold welcome, derision; he interpreted an eclipse as a happy augury for a rainy and fertile winter; he listened to complaints about a *qā'id*.[35] Most importantly, Duveyrier made a fast friend of Ikhenoukhen, an influential leader of the Tuareg Ajjer.[36] Above all, he traveled in vulnerability and privilege, simultaneously completely alone and the subject of an aggressive and expanding empire.

His language lessons embodied this ambiguity. Studying Tifinagh from two Tuareg women, Duveyrier begged them to remove their veils and allow him to see their faces. Of course, they refused.[37] After two weeks of lessons, however, Duveyrier's relations with them changed. On September 14, his last night in Ghadamès on the Libyan-Tunisian-Algerian border before his departure for Tripoli, he offered this as his last journal entry:

I had a language lesson . . . with Mala and Ihemma. Mala is quite young, without malice or biases and very pretty. During the lesson, I amused myself with her little foot, and, after the lesson, when Ihemma left, I exchanged several kisses

34 Duveyrier, *Journal de route*, 49, in Julia Clancy-Smith, *Rebel and Saint: Muslim Notables, Populist Protest, Colonial Encounters (Algeria and Tunisia, 1800–1904*, ed. Barbara D. Metcalf (Berkeley, Calif.: University of California Press, 1997), 153; Duveyrier, *Journal de route*, 144; E[mile] M[asqueray], "Henri Duveyrier," *l'Expansion coloniale*, May 23, 1892, 246–8; AN, 47AP/2, "Carnet No. 7. 4 sept. 1859 – 15 sept. 1859," 74, 80; AN, 47AP/2, "Carnet No. 2. 13 déc – ? 27 déc 1874"; and Henri Schirmer, *Le Sahara* (Paris: Hachette, 1893), 381.

35 Duveyrier, *Journal de route*, 71, 137, 138.

36 AGGA, 4H/5, Henri Duveyrier to Auguste Warnier, Rhat [*sic*: Ghat], March 25, 1861; AGGA, 6X/20, E[mile] M[asqueray], "Henri Duveyrier." The estimations of Pottier, "Centenaire," 42–3, on Ikhenoukhen (Akhnoukhen) are assuredly too harsh; cf. Pottier, "Hommage," 140–1; Pottier, "Seigneur," 23, and Lionel Galand, ed., *Lettres au Marabout: messages touaregs au Père du Foucauld* (Paris: Belin, 1999), 12–14. On Ikhenoukhen and Duveyrier, see also Fernand Foureau, *Rapport sur ma mission au Sahara et chez les Touaregs Azdjer, octobre 1893–mars 1894* (Paris: Augustin Challamel, 1894), 103, 107.

37 Duveyrier, *Journal de route*, 188; cf. AN, 47AP/2, "Carnet No. 19.2 juin 1860 – 18 juin 1860," 13.

with her. We are thus very good friends. She promised to come back upon my return and to play for me here the rabazâ.[38]

It is the most intimate passage in Algerian ethnography. It remains impossible to unpack or deconstruct. Whether coercive or transgressive or violent or genuine, their relationship altered Duveyrier's relationship to the Tuareg. For him, they remained very good friends. Their relationship attested, moreover, to his "career as a man."[39] Duveyrier overlaid his discourses of exploration and ethnographic description with a personal narrative positing his voyages as a journey to manhood. Such accounts offered a window onto the world in which Duveyrier moved, an unequal world of gendered power gradients, but also of exchanging stories about God and gas lamps, and in the *Journal de route* he never hesitated to offer up such stories as illustrative – as *important*. The names matter, the voices matter, the connections matter. Ethnography is writing about people.

Another set of relationships illustrates the seminal importance of personal narrative in ethnography. A *muqaddim* (local leader) of the Tijāniyya Ṣūfī order had given Henri letters of introduction for his Saharan voyage, and the young explorer retained an affinity with the order throughout his life. During his 1885 voyage to Morocco, Duveyrier relied on his connections among the Tijāniyya as an entrance into the social world of Fez and as a means of procuring informants.[40] Twenty-six years earlier, Duveyrier contended, the Tijāniyya had publicly initiated him into the order. The *zāwiya* that had initiated Duveyrier, in Timmasīn, advised their sibling organization in Fez that Duveyrier and Charles Feraud would arrive; a muezzin from the *zāwiya* arrived at Duveyrier's lodging to collect him for a meeting with the local *muqaddim*.[41] In the *muqaddim*'s house, they shared mint tea and cakes; the holy man blessed him and the explorer narrated his travels and answered questions about politics in Algeria, Britain, Russia, Istanbul.[42] His ties with the Tijāniyya opened up an entirely different world. The links of friendship and intimacy marked him, at least for the *muqaddim* of Fez, as a different kind of man.

[38] Duveyrier, *Journal de route*, 204. AN, 47AP/2, "Carnet No. 2. 13 déc – ? 27 déc 1874," 142–3, described Duveyrier's intrusion onto the flirtations of some young Awlād ʿUmar. On the same trip to the Shaṭṭ, he narrated, in Arabic, the story of a woman walking in on him at the *ḥammām al-muslimīn*.

[39] Journal 1854–5, 1–2; Pottier, "Seigneur," 19.

[40] Henri Duveyrier, *Les "Chemins des ambassades" de Tanger à Fâs et Meknâs, en 1885* (Paris: Société de géographie de Paris, 1886), 344, 357. See also Pottier, *Un Prince saharien méconnu*, 42; Marcel Simian, *Les Confréries islamiques en Algérie (Rahmanya-Tidjanya)* (Algiers: Adolphe Jourdan, 1910), 84.

[41] Duveyrier, *Chemin des ambassades*, 357–8. It remains difficult to ascertain whether Duveyrier belonged to the Tijāniyya.

[42] Duveyrier, *Chemin des Ambassades*, 359–60.

The Tijāniyya accorded Duveyrier a rare opportunity, one that Duveyrier comprehended entirely. Whatever the peculiar context, he depicted a scene of genuine intimacy; an encounter merely acquiescing to the coercions of French power would not have involved the contact with women that Duveyrier claimed to have experienced:

> [T]he wives and daughters of the grand master stood, without veil, in the doorway of a room, . . . as if I were their close relative. After all was I not . . . their brother and a bit the son of their lord and master? They could thus show their faces without infringing on the rules of Muslim decency.

Duveyrier recognized the boundaries of fictive kinship, referring to members of the Tijāniyya as "*frères*" (presumably *ikhwān*).[43] This account, if true, manifested Duveyrier's intimate connection with the Tijāniyya. The *muqaddim* of Fez, according to Duveyrier, welcomed him as a brother or son, and as a man.

Moreover, Duveyrier responded within the bounds of propriety. "I will not talk to you however of their [i.e., the women's] physique, because I had decided to maintain during this entire visit the role of a a well-instructed, proper man, according to the notions of the milieu in which I found myself, and I hailed them by voice without looking at them."[44] Not for Duveyrier the titillating voyeurism of so many ethnographers. The presence of women weaves a narrative about Duveyrier's masculinity. He used the Tijāniyya women as a sign pointing to his status as both male and honorary Tijānī. In depicting this scene of Moroccan mores, he presented a gendered honor and the personal obligation that masculinity entailed. Even Henri himself conceded its significance. "Perhaps," he wrote, "you will find that I have extended myself too long on this episode of [my] voyage? My excuse would be that I consider it as the most interesting experience that I have had" – no mean admission from Henri Duveyrier.[45]

Nevertheless, none of Duveyrier's works represent the unmediated musings of the young explorer. Text and emotion ultimately remain separate, and reading does not reconstitute the ethnographic moment. Moreover, the texts of Duveyrier offer another challenge. They bear the traces not only of their author's silences, but also of the heavy hand of subsequent editing.

Toward the end of his voyage to the Sahara, Duveyrier fell deathly ill with typhoid fever. It left him mentally enfeebled. The loss of his memory

[43] Duveyrier, *Chemin des Ambassades*, 361, but cf. chapter 3.
[44] Duveyrier, *Chemin des Ambassades*, 361. [45] Duveyrier, *Chemin des Ambassades*, 361.

devastated Duveyrier.[46] At nineteen, he had the experience of a lifetime, and at twenty-one he forgot it. The material traces remained, but his own recollection vanished. In 1862, he received the Cross of the Legion of Honor, but upon his death, the eulogies mentioned an honor he never remembered receiving.[47]

His illness reoriented Henri Duveyrier's life; at twenty-three, he lost both the memory of his most significant accomplishment and the ability to replicate it. Never again could he undertake the kind of sustained ethnographic voyage he made at nineteen. Although his intellectual life did not end, it reached its pinnacle. In the words of Emile Masqueray, his perspicacious and poignant eulogist, "buried slowy in an irrevocable past," Duveyrier "must have said to himself it would have been better for him to die at twenty-three in the splendor of his youthful glory, when no disappointment had yet struck him." He both did, and did not, die in the desert. "[S]ince then he had done nothing but witness the ruin of his work like the decline of his glory." Masqueray continued, "[t]he fever was too indulgent when it let go of his useless body."[48] The explorer merely preoccupied himself with "his maps," central, decades later, to events in the Sahara.[49] Dying at twenty-five, he would not die for decades. It was not that he would not achieve again such heights as those of his youth. He simply could not. His greatest achievement always lay behind him.

Into this void stepped Henri Duveyrier's mentor, Auguste Warnier. Yet another Saint-Simonian, Warnier greatly influenced *Les Touareg du Nord*.[50] To describe their relationship as tortured, exploitative, or obscurely Œdipal renders a grave injustice to the depths of both Henri's despair and Warnier's oft-imperious devotion.[51] It was, at the end of the day, a friendship, and, as with many friendships, the scrutiny of analysis tends to dissolve it, unjustly, into a complicated congeries of needs

46 Duveyrier, *Touareg du Nord*, viii–ix.; AGGA, 6X/20, E[mile] M[asqueray], "Henri Duveyrier"; AN, 47AP/3, Henri Duveyrier to Charles Duveyrier, and attached note by Auguste Warnier, Saint-Eugène, February 18, 1862. According to the archivist, Françoise Aujogue, 47AP/3 contains the personal papers of both Duveyrier and Maunoir.

47 Pottier, "Centenaire," 43; Pottier, "Hommage," 141.

48 AGGA, 6X/20, [E]mile M[asqueray], "Henri Duveyrier."

49 AN, 47AP/3. Henri Duveyrier [to his father Charles or to Warnier?], Paris, April 4, 1863.

50 Jean-Louis Triaud attempts the impossible task of ascribing individual authorship to sections of an essentially collaborative work; Triaud, *Légende noire*, vol. I, 109–10.

51 Pottier, "Hommage," 141–2, focused on Duveyrier's anger at Warnier's interference with his text; Pottier, *Un Prince saharien méconnu*, 86–92; letters such as AGGA, 4H/5, Henri Duveyrier to Auguste Warnier, Rhat [sic: Ghaṭ], March 25, 1861, attest to their erstwhile relationship.

and affections. Those intimate ties altered the unfolding of ethnographic scholarship on the Tuareg. In an account of the 1859 voyage, Duveyrier acknowledged "thanks to a revered friend, Dr. Warnier, who put to my service his experiences of things African as well as his talent as a writer, after having saved my life."[52] Even this statement, however, remains open to conjecture; possibly Warnier inserted the self-congratulatory prose himself, as Jean-Louis Triaud contends he did with the treacly dedication to *Les Touareg du Nord*.[53] To conclude that he did so out of malice ignores the possibility that Warnier may have aimed to preserve Duveyrier's dignity. We cannot assume, as René Pottier did, that the damaged Duveyrier's assessment of Warnier's motives was accurate.[54] "Henri Duveyrier," writes Triaud, "was but a little boy in the hands of his ebullient protector," evincing a consistent sense over his project and its results, and anguish over his impuissance.[55] Such a portrayal of Warnier owes as much to the peevishness, depression, misery, and derangement of the ill Duveyrier as to the overweening doctor.

Ultimately, the texts' authorship mattered less than their style. Duveyrier's works relied upon the authority of intimate experience. Of the voyage, the illness, the conflict, remained the texts, the adumbrative letters – the ethnography. First-person ethnographic voices echoed through the written word.

Nevertheless, to romanticize Duveyrier as counter-hegemonic discounts his embedding in colonial politics. Anomalous though he was, he remained inextricably implicated in the colonial project. Gianni Albergoni accuses Henri Duveyrier of having shown himself "too interested or not lucid enough" in his descriptions, "exaggerat[ing]," he writes, "each element of description."[56] Ethnographic narration, whether intimate writings or more "lucid," served as a handmaiden of empire. Despite the fractious nature of colonial discourse, the imperial project contained a multitude of voices. Personal trajectories across colonial Algeria could not escape the context of their articulation. Even Henri Duveyrier, who

52 Henri Duveyrier, "Le Nord du Sahara central," trans. Capt. H. Simon, *Bulletin de la Société de Geographie d'Alger et de l'Afrique du Nord* [*BSGA*] 8 (1903:1): 33.

53 Triaud, *Légende noire*, 108–9; Duveyrier, *Touareg du Nord*, title page, viii.

54 Pottier, "Hommage," 141–2.

55 Triaud, *Légende noire*, 108, and the citations of AN, 47AP/3, Henri Duveyrier to Charles Duveyrier, April 29, 1865, therein. See also AN, 47AP/3, Henri Duveyrier to Charles Duveyrier, with addendum by Auguste Warnier, Saint-Eugène, February 18, 1862; Henri Duveyrier to Charles Duveyrier, Saint-Eugène, March 24, 1862.

56 Gianni Albergoni, "Variations italiennes sur un theme français: La Sanusiya," in *Connaissances du Maghreb: sciences sociales et colonization*, Recherches sur les sociétés méditerranéennes (Paris: Éditions du Centre national de la recherche scientifique, 1984), 113.

had developed a network of friendships and intimate ties, conceived of himself as "a young man isolated among the savages."[57]

The origin of the administrator-ethnographer

In contrast, Louis Rinn rarely used first-person narration. Nevertheless, his personal story offers valuable insight into the intellectual world of Algeria in the late nineteenth century. Arguably the most famous colonial administrator of his time, complete with society-page wife and daughter and a minor scandal involving his prodigal son, Rinn obsessively chronicled media attention, society pages, business cards received, and even programs from diversions in his three-volume scrapbook. Dog-eared and stiffened by paste, these volumes illustrated the intimate connections of a man temperamentally less given to reflection than Henri Duveyrier.

Through the scrapbooks unfolds the family life of a top administrator and prolific author. Louis Rinn viewed the volumes as an exercise in self-commemoration, if not in self-presentation. He grandiosely entitled the first folio "Articles from Journals and Revues on My Acts and Writings: Collected for My Children, in Algiers, since 1880," and stamped it with his seal, reading, in Arabic, "*al-mutawakkid ʿalā al-maʿīn ʿabdahu al-kamāndā rīn*," in English, "the verified seal of his servant Commander Rinn."[58] Out of a supreme belief in his significance, Rinn collected the minutiae of the quotidian for his son and daughter. The flotsam and jetsam of the waves of success and (admittedly less frequent) failure record the daily life of an administrator-ethnographer.

The scrapbooks reveal the exaggerated courtesies and near-courtly intricacies of colonial high society. In a small world, precision of form can take utmost precedence. Prior to the publication of *Histoire de l'insurrection de 1871 en Algérie* (1891), a political tract veiled as an historical account, Louis Rinn sent an advance copy to Corneille Trumelet. Colonel Trumelet had published a two-volume account of an earlier insurrection, *Histoire de l'insurrection dans le sud de la province d'Alger en 1864* (1879) and *Histoire de l'insurrection dans le sud de la province d'Alger de 1864 à 1880, deuxième partie* (1884). The gift represented just another of the affinitive ties that bound the denizens of the intellectual world of colonial scholarship to each other.

Nevertheless, the book demonstrated the ambivalence of those relations, the undercurrent of mutual suspicion, the subtle interplay of state patronage and individual expertise. Though relatively erudite and well

57 AN, 47AP/2, "Carnet No. 3. 20 juin 1859 à 10 juillet 1859," 73–4.
58 AGGA, 3X/1 (Personal Papers of Louis Rinn), frontispiece.

respected, Trumelet wrote as a mere officer in the ministry of public education and a corresponding member of the Société historique algérienne.[59] Trumelet resided in the Drôme, far from the centers of Algerian scholarship. Rinn, however, benefited from the privilege of government association: conseiller d'état, vice president of the Société historique, former head of the Native Affairs Service, resident in Algiers, Louis Rinn drew upon the authority of personal prestige and professional position to bolster his account.[60] Written on the back of a visiting card, Trumelet's prolix and effusive expressions of gratitude gave lie to another layer of meaning behind Rinn's prompt dispatch of an advance copy of *Histoire de l'insurrection de 1871*. Trumelet viewed the "gift" as a warning shot fired off his own intellectual bow. Trumelet

> thank[ed] most cordially his excellent comrade Commander Rinn for . . . his great book – a monument of the highest merit, – work [illeg.] that will give him the greatest honor in the present and in the future; it was a work of great difficulty of execution, which he achieved with all the hommages that it merits, and his good talent of popularization of Algeria. In expectation [i.e., of Rinn's honors], I no longer dare to occupy myself with a work of the same genre.[61]

Rinn, bureaucrat before scholar, convinced Trumelet to abandon his work. In contrast, the administration purchased one hundred copies of *Histoire de l'insurrection de 1871*.[62] Outside of institutional structures of Algerian academia and its dependence on patronage, Trumelet could have damaged the prestige of colonial governance. Though Trumelet's second volume covered the period through 1880, its focus on Saharan insurrections differed in scope from Rinn's work. Calling upon the authority of both his expertise and his employment, Rinn effectively suppressed a rival text by an author not beholden to colonial patronage.

Despite such thinly veiled flexing of professional muscle, Louis Rinn excelled at the niceties of colonial society. Visible, savvy, influential, Rinn and his wife Émilie regularly appeared in the more frivolous items of the Algerian press. He lunched with Cardinal Lavigerie.[63] Rinn and his wife

[59] Colonel C. Trumelet, *Histoire de l'insurrection dans le sud de la province d'Alger en 1864*, vol. I (Algiers: Adolphe Jourdan, 1879), frontispiece. Rinn participated in the 1864 campaign; R. Peyronnet, *Livre d'or des officiers des affaires indigènes 1830–1930*, vol. II: *Notices et bibliographies* (Algiers: Imprimerie algérienne, 1930), 359.

[60] Louis Rinn, *Histoire de l'insurrection de 1871 en Algérie* (Algiers: Adolphe Jourdan, 1891), frontispiece; AGGA, 3X/1, clipping from *Revue africaine* (1894:2): 234.

[61] AGGA, 3X/1, visiting card labeled "Colonel C. Trumelet, Valence (Drôme), le 28 9bre 1890."

[62] AGGA, 3X/1, Secretary-General of the Gouvernement général of Algeria to Louis Rinn, Algiers, March 6, 1891.

[63] AGGA, 3X/1, A. de J., "Chez le Cardinal Lavigerie," *La Dépêche algérienne*, November 14, 1890.

accompanied Jules Ferry and his wife on their visit.[64] Indeed, he demonstrated a certain flair for such spectacle as life in the colonies had to offer: the visit of Czar Nicolas II and Empress Alexandra, an exposition of gymnasts, the circus.[65] The stuff of legend, Louis and Émilie Rinn's ball of 1896 opened the season with such fanfare that the year's subsequent parties would have a hard time living up to it. The breathless *Dépêche algérienne* described the December 7 "Réception mondaine on ne peut plus brillante, . . . chez Mme et M. Rinn, conseiller de Gouvernement" as the event of the season. "The numerous invitations reunited [at the Rinns'] all of high military and civil society." With petty bureaucrats, lawyers, school directors, military officers, members of the chamber of commerce, doctors, city councilors dined the vice-consul of Spain, and a Swedish lieutenant, detached from the cold north to the First Regiment of Zouaves.[66] By the standards of colonial Algiers, the Rinns cut a cosmopolitan and debonair swath through the dismal, rainy winter.

Rinn's daughter Marthe, too, attracted the attention of the colonial press. The scrapbook abounded with clippings from her social appearances. Even her success at the elementary and higher-level diplomas could not escape notice.[67] At society weddings, the mere presence of Marthe and her mother attracted popular attention.[68] Someone lovingly preserved the invitation for Marthe's wedding to Fernand Anduze-Acher (an administrator), inserting it at the very beginning of the first volume of the scrapbook.

Its placement indicated, perhaps, the intended recipient of Louis's clippings. In contrast to Rinn's evident pride in his daughter, his son appeared infrequently. Unlike Marthe, whose intellectual and social achievements demonstrated no little similarity to her father, Edme Rinn lacked his father's ambition. An engineer by training, Edme seemed indifferent to his own success. At a contest for wine-making technologies, Edme failed to present the refrigeration unit submitted, relying only on a series of schematics. Had he shown a bit more initiative, Edme might have won;

[64] AGGA, 3X/1, "Bougie (Algérie)," *La Kabylie*, May 29, 1892. On Rinn's marriage: "Villers-Cotterêts," *Progrès de l'Aisne*, January 3–4, 1896.

[65] AGGA, 3X/3 (Personal Papers of Louis Rinn), *Supplément de la Dépêche algérienne* on the visit of Czar Nicolas II and Empress Alexandra to Algeria, October 6, 1896; AGGA, 3X/3, "Ville d'Alger. Union des sociétés de gymnastique de France. XXIIe Fêe Fédérale. Programme Officiel. Vendredi 3 Avril 1896. Réception des gymnastes au débarquement"; AGGA, 3X/3, "Théâtre-Circus. Esplanade Bab-el-Oued. Aujourd'hui mardi 20 octobre 1896."

[66] AGGA, 3X/1, *La Dépêche algérienne*, December 8, 1896.

[67] AGGA, 3X/1, "Résultat définitif des examens du brevet élementaire, session de juin 1892," *La Vigie algérienne*, June 19, 1892; AGGA, 3/X1, "Brevet supérieure," *La Dépêche algérienne*, June 24, 1894.

[68] AGGA, 3X/1, "Mariages," *Revue algérienne illustrée*, n.d., p. 804.

his father's service as a jury member for the prize no doubt would have helped him, had he put forth much effort. Louis Rinn, however, was not one to reward sloppy or incomplete work, even or perhaps especially among his children.[69]

Edme's sole other appearance in the scrapbooks manifested a rather more serious lapse in diligence. A slapdash engineer at best (his workers suspected his competence), Edme Rinn used shoddy materials and failed to supervise the construction of the Banque de l'Algérie building, resulting in the death of one Frenchman and the injury of a worker. The article pasted into the scrapbook, of course, failed to mention any Algerian casualties.[70] His father presented Edme as slipshod, disappointing, lazy, even of dubious morality. Marthe Rinn came across through her academic achievements and social connections, Edme through his failures. Of his career after the bank collapse the scrapbook kept silent. Between the marbleized covers of the scrapbook, Louis Rinn left his son an ambiguous gift.

In contrast, Louis Rinn demonstrated a near-obsessive diligence in his own professional life. Serving first as head of a battalion, then head of the Service central des affaires indigènes (Native Affairs Service) until its abolition, and finally as conseiller d'état, Rinn pursued with assiduity the policies of the empire.[71] His responsibilities as conseiller d'état included everything from forestry practices to the investigation of the unjust *amende collective*.[72] Personnel and school records revealed an aptitude for both government work and certain kinds of scholarship. He received good marks in Arabic, geography, history, and demonstrated a strong familiarity for the study of "mœurs" – indeed, he was "appreciated and respected by the natives," noted one evaluation. A capable military officer, he fulfilled his duties zealously and enjoyed martial life. Governor General Tirman's adjectives painted a picture of a competent, industrious, colonial soldier: "quiet, calm, firm"; "simple, modest, learned, hardworking." He remarked that, "knowing in depth the natives, their mores, their customs, thus of an uncommonly wide instruction, Commandant Rinn has, to the highest degree, the qualities that required his

69 AGGA, 3X/1, A. Morastel, "Vinification algérienne," *Moniteur de l'Algérie*, September 10 (?), 1893.

70 AGGA, 3X/1, Jean de la Plèbe, "Les Victimes de la Banque de l'Algérie," *Le Reveil Bônois* (Bône / ʿAnnāba, Algeria), March 16, 1895.

71 AGGA, 3X/1, unattributed, untitled clipping from *Le Mobacher*, March 11, 1885; Peyronnet, *Livre d'or*, vol. II, 359–64; Triaud, *Légende noire*, 349.

72 Peyronnet, *Livre d'or*, vol. II, 360–1; Triaud, *Légende noire*, 349; Louis Rinn, *Régime pénal de l'indigénat en Algérie: les commissions disciplinaires* (Algiers: Adolphe Jourdan, 1885); Louis Rinn, *Régime pénal de l'indigénat en Algérie: le séquestre et la responsabilité collective* (Algiers: Adolphe Jourdan, 1890).

delicate functions."[73] He became, in the words of Julia Clancy-Smith, "a self-made soldier-philosopher."[74] Louis Rinn's talents predisposed him to administrative tasks and cultural studies. He not only fitted into the intellectual, military, and above all, colonial world of nineteenth-century Algeria perfectly, he also fashioned it; Rinn became the model for the administrator-ethnographer.

For Louis Rinn, his career proved the perfect opportunity for conducting fieldwork. Indeed, Rinn's writings drew upon his experiences as an administrator and offered recommendations for policy. He understood ethnography as a useful adjunct to his employment.[75] Moreover, the combination of his reputation as an expert and his association with the government enabled him to create a network of personal ties in the intellectual community of Algeria. One informant and friend, Belkassem ben Sedira [Belqāsim bin Ṣadira], used a review of *Marabouts et khouan* to express his gratitude toward Rinn, demonstrating the intimate links forming the locus of colonial intellectual life for French speakers.

> Commander Rinn is one of these *hommes de cœur* – as it is necessary that France have many of in the interest of the Natives – [whom] I have had the good fortune of meeting . . . I owe [him] for having been launched on the path that I follow today. I am happy for the opportunity that is offered me to express personally and publicly to Commander Rinn my . . . hearty gratitude.[76]

Such connections afforded the opportunity to write authoritatively about Algeria. As a government official, Rinn possessed a coercive power and official gravitas that he utilized in his research. The Louis Rinn who enjoyed putting on the ball of the season evinced the same personal traits as the able public servant and the ethnographer. All three combined a

[73] AGGA, 3X/1, dossier labeled "*Notes militaries en Algérie: 1864–1884*," Inspector-General Loysel, "Personnel des Affaires indigènes: Inspection générale de 1884. M. Rinn," with note by Governor General Tirman, Algiers, June 21, 1884; AGGA, 3X/1, "Ecole speciale militaire– 1855–1857 Promotion du Prince. Imperial. Louis RINN. 7979," April 1856, and, for Vincennes, AGGA, 3X/1, "*Notes militaires en Algérie: 1864–1884*," Lt.-Col. Molet, "Notes venues de 83° R^{t} en ligne," July 15, 1863; AGGA, 1K/247, General commanding the Province of Constantine [illeg.], "Personnel des Affaires Indigènes, Inspection Générale de 1873, Rinn Louis Marie, Capitaine au 3e Régt^{t} de Tirailleurs algériens, Chef du Bureau arabe subdivisionnaire," Constantine, September 15, 1873, and similar.

[74] Julia Clancy-Smith, "In the Eye of the Beholder: Sufi and Saint in North Africa and the Colonial Production of Knowledge, 1830–1900," *Africana Journal* 15 (1990): 239.

[75] AGGA, 4H/23, Louis Rinn, "Analyse d'un projet d'expédition saharienne," Algiers, 1886; Louis Rinn, "Les Grands Tournants de l'Histoire de l'Algérie," *BSGA* 8 (1903): 1, 20, 24; AGGA, 16H/2, Rinn's marginalia on *Marabouts et Khouan*.

[76] AGGA, 3X/1, Belkassem ben Sedira, untitled, unattributed press clipping. Rinn collected both positive and negative assessments; see AGGA, 3X/1, *passim*.

supreme confidence in his own august authority with an interest and facility in encouraging the cooperation, respect, or devotion of others.

Nevertheless, not all of Rinn's ethnographic work demonstrated the diligence of *Marabouts et khouan*. Despite his own proficiency in Arabic and Berber languages, Rinn's linguistic work, at best erratic and at worst misleading, manifested an inelegant attempt to force a correspondence between the plasticity of language and Rinn's rigid theories on the "racial" affinities of the Berbers with widely scattered Indo-Europeans – Slavs, Celts, Germans.[77] Henri Duveyrier, René Basset, and Jacques Berque criticized Rinn's more florid etymologies; Doutté, in particular, singled out Rinn's dubious understandings of names.[78] As a philologist, Rinn was an excellent colonial military officer: he saw in his reified Arab and Berber populations differences useful for imperial control. Indeed, one former government interpreter singled out Rinn and his language skills as the kind of scholar-soldier of which the colonial government had greatest need.[79] Rinn's translations are always suspect; reading his ethnographies critically requires a suspicious mind and a good command of Arabic. To cite but one example, he mistook the emphatic consonant *ḍād*, unique to Arabic, in *Ibāḍī*, the name of the branch of Islam practiced in the M'zab, for a *dāl*, an error so basic as to be alarming. Reading Rinn requires literacy in Arabic to prevent the reinscription of his errors – of his belief in racial pseudo-science and fanciful etymologies. Confident to the point of arrogance, Rinn evinced no doubt about the certainty of his imaginative translations and etymologies.

Diligence and scholarly reputation could not save Rinn from forced retirement. Though he immersed himself in the Société de Géographie

77 Louis Rinn, *Les Origines berbères: études linguistiques et ethnologiques* (Algiers: Adolphe Jourdan, 1889), *passim*; Rinn, *Les Premiers Royaumes berbères et la Guerre de Jugurtha*, Géographie ancienne de l'Algérie (Algiers: Adolphe Jourdan, 1885); Louis Rinn, "Lettres de Touareg," *Revue africaine* 31, no. 185 (1887): 321–41, and Rinn, *Premiers Royaumes berbères*; Peyronnet, *Livre d'or*, vol. II, 362. On the Kabyle myth; see Lorcin, *Imperial Identities*.

78 René Basset, *Rapport sur les études berbères, éthiopiennes et arabes, 1887–1891* (Woking, UK: Oriental University Institute, 1892), 1; Edmond Doutté, "Livres nouveaux sur l'Islam: L'Islam, par le Comte Henry de Castries," *Bulletin de la Société de Géographie et d'Archéologie d'Oran* [*BSGAO*] 17 (1897): 108–9; Jacques Berque, "Cent vingt-cinq ans de sociologie maghrébine," in Jacques Berque, *Opera Minora*, vol. II: *Histoire et anthropologie du Maghreb*, ed. Gianni Albergoni (Paris: Éditions Bouchène, 2001), 193. See also AGGA, 3X/1, Ernest Mercier, "La Question du Mulucha," *Revue de l'Afrique française* 4, no. 17 (1886): 178–81, which singled out *Premiers Royaumes berbères*. Louis Rinn, *Marabouts et khouan: étude sur l'Islam en Algérie* (Algiers: Adolphe Jourdan, 1884), 64 n.2 correctly noted Ṣūfī scholars' confusion of *wird* and *ward*.

79 AGGA, 3X/1, F. Gourgeot, "Les Interprètes militaires (1). Suite," *Le Radical algérien*, September 6, 1897, and AGGA, 3X/3, F. Gourgeot, "Les Interprètes militaires. Suite et Fin," *Le Radical algérien*, September 13, 1897.

d'Alger et de l'Afrique du Nord, he felt the ignominy of his departure keenly. He used his scrapbook to correct the government's official account of the end of his term as conseiller d'état. Even after his departure, Rinn offered to Governor General Jonnart the benefit of his counsel and wisdom. As gracious as Rinn was presumptuous, Jonnart invited the former bureaucrat, clearly ill-adjusted to his status as a civilian, to his home in the smart suburb of Mustapha.[80] The governor general, perhaps hoping to replace the longtime administrator with a similar-minded but perhaps more malleable individual, appointed an undistinguished legal scholar.[81] In his scrapbook, at the end of an account of the replacement, Louis Rinn placed a clipping from an unidentified newspaper announcing the "replacement for M. Rinn, admitted, upon his request, to take advantage of his right to retirement," citing the relevant passages of law. Rinn, however, underlined the words "on his demand" and wrote in the right margin, in the same heavy, red ink: "*Mensonge officielle*," official lies, underlined twice, and in the left, "and in formal violation of" the exact same passages mentioned in the clipping.[82] He had faithfully carried out his duties for more than forty years, and Rinn had no intention of retiring; his superiors forced him out, and he made sure his children knew. These marginalia in blood-colored ink offered up this scrapbook as an alternative personal history, a way of controlling the official record. Hence Rinn collected reviews, both positive and negative, of his works; appreciations, good and bad, of his government service; estimations, glowing or disapproving, of his children and their future. His life, how he led it, what happened in it, others' judgment thereon, remained important.

He died in 1905, just short of his sixty-seventh birthday. Eulogies commemorated Rinn's intellect and career.[83] He had "an elite nature," wrote his friend A. Stanislas, "an *homme de cœur* and a learned historian . . . He is one of our most devoted servants, one of its adopted children that Algeria has lost. Our mourning will be equally felt in France, where the name of Rinn had acquired a just reputation."[84]

80 AGGA, 3X/1, Governor General Jonnart to Louis Rinn, Algiers, December 8, 1900.

81 AGGA, 3X/1, "Extrait des Procès-Verbaux du Conseil de Gouvernement. Séance du 8 décembre 1899, Résidence de M. le secrétaire général du Gouvernement"; AGGA, 3X/1, Auguste Hugues, "Le Fonctionnarisme en algérie," *l'Express algérien* (Algiers), November 7, 1899.

82 AGGA, 3X/1, Émile Loubet, "Partie officielle," November 5, 1899.

83 Louis Rinn, "La Femme berbère dans l'ethnologie et l'histoire de L'Algérie," *BSGA* (1905: 2), 461; N. Lacroix, "[Nécrologie] Le Lieutenant-Colonel Rinn," *Revue africaine*, 49 année, no. 256 (1905): 130–2; A. Stanislas, "Nécrologie: Le Lieutenant-Colonel Rinn," *BSGA* 10 (1905:3): 183–193.

84 Stanislas, "Nécrologie Rinn," 193; "Séances," *BSGA* 10 (1905:3): lxxi.

For the history of French colonial ethnography, Rinn's biography proved exemplary. He wrote, he lived, in a particular world of colonial privilege. To ignore, as Triaud does,[85] the intellectual and social formation of a man simultaneously a learned expert and a political leader omits the manifest links between these different aspects of his career and personality, between the two realms of intellectual production and statecraft. A military officer, a competent speaker of many languages (if maverick linguist), a trusted authority, a diligent bureaucrat, Rinn, his life, his scrapbook-memoirs, demonstrated the social and intellectual structures that gave rise to colonial ethnography. The trajectories across this ethnographic, colonial, authoritarian world matter because they make real the opportunities, foreclosures, and choices available to individuals.

Different kinds of institutions: female ethnographers in colonial Algeria

Nevertheless, opportunities and foreclosures accrued unequally. Ethnographically inclined women never benefited from the authority, training, and institutional support that Louis Rinn received. His daughter Marthe, smart and vivacious though she was, could not even aspire to the failed career of her brother. She disappeared from her father's scrapbook after her marriage, just as women too often disappear from intellectual histories piecing together texts clipped from various institutionally ensconced authors. The patriarchal structures of intellectual life barred women from administration and faculty positions. Nevertheless, colonial women found alternative forms of ethnographic expression. Women criticized empire and articulated gendered conceptions of Algerian identity in ways that differed from those of male administrators.[86] With so many avenues closed, some responded by turning toward applied ethnographic projects: workshops, teaching, exploration, travel. To limit the history of ethnography to academic, institutionalized anthropology reinscribes a profoundly gendered ordering of Third Republic intellectual life; focusing on disciplinary development excludes anew most women thinkers. In Algeria, French women resisted their exclusion and tested the limitations placed on the exercise of the mind. Although academic circles

85 Triaud, *Légende noire*, 347.

86 Julia Clancy-Smith, "Islam, Gender, and Identities in the Making of French Algeria, 1830–1962," in Julia Clancy-Smith and Frances Gouda, eds., *Domesticating the Empire: Race, Gender, and Family Life in French and Dutch Colonialism* (Charlottesville, Va.: University Press of Virginia, 1998), 162–72; Jeanne M. Bowlan, "Civilizing Gender Relations in Algeria: The Paradoxical Case of Marie Bugéja, 1919–1939," in Clancy-Smith and Gouda, *Domesticating the Empire*, 175–210.

remained closed to women, men by no means monopolized ethnographic discourse.

In particular, labor attracted the interest of women ethnographers. In 1910, G. Laloë published *Enquête sur le travail des femmes indigènes à Alger*, an ethnography of women's work in colonial Algiers. For Laloë, assigned to the inquest by the governor general himself, her ethnography of working conditions indicted the conditions of Algerian women's lives.[87] At the same time, however, she combated the underlying assumptions about women's work prevalent in ethnography. She emphasized that "the number of native women who work outside their homes is much larger than what is generally thought."[88] Laloë interpreted her task as trifold: communicating basic information about Algerian women's labor, describing its cultural relevance, and establishing a moral context for colonial social welfare.

Laloë's depiction of the lives of female workers deftly wedded ethnographic description to imperial paternalism and salvage ethnography.[89] Echoing metropolitan urban sociology, Mademoiselle Laloë visited four female "gatherers of grasses" in their homes. She found them simple, but clean:

> They live in . . . holes dug out of the thickness of walls and where one could not even extend oneself . . . , where it is impossible to stand upright . . . A curtain in rags delimits the domain of each one – the bed is represented by a heap of rags, dishes by a remnant of some kind of procelain, – but it is rare that this misery is not scrupulously clean.
>
> May one not lose sight [of the fact] that these women often have children to raise and one wonders how they arrived at that state.[90]

Their propriety and poverty marked these women as both virtuous and victimized. According to Laloë, family situation provided the impetus behind child and female labor.[91] On her visits to "native" houses, Laloë uncovered ill-treated, underpaid women working in less than ideal conditions.[92] The conditions of women's labor represented an ill that empire alone, she argued, could rectify.

That rectification, Laloë contended, lay in regulation of Algerian women's work. "[T]his work could be done by a careful, attentive intervention, . . . full of tact, . . . by a tutelage that, tenderly maternal, . . . not [by] being blunt," "would lead . . . the child that is the

[87] G. Laloë, *Enquête sur le travail des femmes indigènes à Alger* (Algiers: Adolphe Jourdan, 1910), 1.

[88] Laloë, *Enquête*, 1.

[89] See also p. 148 on salvage ethnography.

[90] Laloë, *Enquête*, 4.

[91] Laloë, *Enquête*, 13.

[92] Laloë, *Enquête*, 25.

Muslim woman, . . . valiant and truly brave, to become . . . a worthy worker whose labor would give help to her family, without the family hearth being deprived of the indispensable and sweet presence of the wife and mother."[93] Laloë's ethnography revolved around feminized paternalism, the civilizing administrator rescuing the benighted colonial child. Her status as a government employee and as a woman allowed her to carve a space in which to write ethnographies.

Similarly, Marguerite Bel published, with the aid of the colonial government, *Les Arts indigènes féminins en Algérie* (1938). Marguerite Bel, married to ethnographer Alfred Bel, focused on the cultural expressions to which her job exposed her.[94] She "held the post of inspector of artistic and professional instruction for the native girls' school," designed to perpetuate "traditional" handicrafts among Algerian women.[95] Julia Clancy-Smith identifies in Marguerite Bel's writings both salvage ethnography and a record of socioeconomic change.[96] However, her text also represented a milestone in the development of French colonial ethnography. Both Laloë and Bel undertook ethnographic research not as the handmaidens to men, but in realms in which their identity as women proved most useful. They created separate structures to further their interests and research, selecting subjects readily accessible to women. Although they lacked the institutional and personal connections of Louis Rinn, G. Laloë and Marguerite Bel succeeded in writing ethnographies.

Much like Rinn, Laloë utilized her government employment for fieldwork. Rinn had far more such occasions to conduct research, and published voluminously. Of Laloë, only the *Enquête* survived. Nevertheless, she took advantage of her position in order to advance her interests in Algerian culture; Laloë and Rinn alike contributed to colonial ethnography. Despite the circumscriptions placed on their education and employment, French women in Algeria used similar means to shape colonial ethnographic discourse.

Moreover, workshops functioned as the intersection of the civilizing mission and the ethnographic impulse, allowing women a space to write and to undertake what they conceived of as social welfare policies. Yet,

93 Laloë, *Enquête*, 94.

94 Marguerite A. Bel, *Les Arts indigènes féminins en Algérie* (Algiers: P. Fontana, c. 1938); see also Georges Marçais, "Nécrologie: Alfred Bel (1873–1945)," *Revue africaine* 89 (1945:1–2): 106

95 Julia Clancy-Smith, "A Woman Without her Distaff: Gender, Work, and Handicraft Production in Colonial North Africa," in Margaret L. Meriwether and Judith E. Tucker, eds., *A Social History of Women and Gender in the Modern Middle East* (Boulder, Colo.: Westview Press, 1999), 131.

96 Clancy-Smith, "A Woman Without Her Distaff," 31–3.

"by 1900," writes Clancy-Smith, "the social laboratory that was Algeria had come to be viewed as a failure . . . a case study in what not to do."[97] Clancy-Smith correctly notes that colonial understandings of gender "were forged, debated, and ultimately realized in concrete educational institutions," such as colonial workshops.[98] Hence, they functioned as part of the apparatus of both ethnographic scholarship and applied anthropology. In the early 1900s, Simone Bernard d'Attanoux established workshops to train and provide workspace for Algerian women to sew and weave. Colonial administrators provided circumspect support. Various married and unmarried French women – schoolteachers, midwives, the wives of administrators – and the occasional Algerian man provided the organizational impetus behind the workshops.[99] Bernard d'Attanoux herself conducted almost all of the fundraising, drawing up an official-looking form letter requesting stipends from administrators.[100] Women's handicrafts played a central role in the economy of rural North Africa;[101] Bernard d'Attanoux saw them as sites of intervention for the state. In twenty workshops, women made traditional Algerian garments with supplies furnished by Bernard d'Attanoux herself. The women kept the pieces made, and once a month received lessons in hygiene.[102] By November of 1902, more than 115 students attended workshops in four cities.[103] Conscientiously both exploiting the government's

97 Julia Clancy-Smith, "Envisioning Knowledge: Educating the Muslim Woman in Colonial North Africa, *c.* 1850–1918," in Rudi Matthee and Beth Baron, eds., *Islam and Beyond: Essays in Middle Eastern History in Honor of Nikki R. Keddie* (Costa Mesa, Calif.: Mazda Publishers, 2000), 99.

98 Clancy-Smith, "Envisioning Knowledge," 100, 102–6.

99 AGGA, 14H/32, "Rapport: Confidentiel," n.d., 1902, Administrator [illeg.]; Administrator Bollero of the Commune mixte of Fort-National [Kabylia] to the Prefect of Algiers, "Au sujet de Madame Bernard d'Attanoux," Fort-National, October 13, 1902; "Rapport," Commissioner of Police [illeg.], 2nd Arrondissement, No. 3858, Algiers, October 16, 1902; Prefect of the Departement of Constantine to the Governor General of Algeria, "MISSIONS. Madame BERNARD D'ATTANOUX," Constantine, November 6, 1902; Prefect of Algiers to the Governor General of Algeria, Algiers, November 8, 1902; Prefect of the Department of Constantine to the Govenor General, November 6, 1902.

100 AGGA, 14H/32, Simone B[ernard] d'Attanoux, Exploratrice, Officier d'Académie, to administrator, Algiers, May 8, 1902.

101 Clancy-Smith, "A Woman without her Distaff," 27–8, 33–7.

102 AGGA, 14H/32, Bollero to the Prefect of Algiers, October 13, 1902; AGGA, 14H/32, "Rapport," No. 3858, October 16, 1902; AGGA, 14H/32, Commissioner of Police [illeg.], 3rd Arrondissement, No. 4469; "Rapport," Algiers, October 16, 1902; AGGA, 14H/32, Special Commissioner Venges, "Rapport. Objet: Ouvroirs indigènes. Impression sur les indigènes," Algiers, October 30, 1902; AGGA, 14H/32, Prefect of Algiers to the Governor General of Algeria, "Au Sujet des ouvroirs indigènes créés par Madame Bernard d'Attanoux," Algiers, November 8, 1902.

103 AGGA, 14H/32, Madame Bernard d'Attanoux to M. Luciani, Director of Native Affairs, Algiers, November 6, 1902.

financial resources and sagaciously appealing to administrative paternalism, Simone Bernard d'Attanoux created a network of workshops for Algerian women.

Moreover, she advertised her workshops. The poster for Algiers illustrated her understanding of the workshops' role and institutional structure. "The Native Workrooms of Madame d'Attanoux (Courses in Sewing, Cutting, Ironing)," the flyer baldly announced the belief that French women must instruct Algerians in the arts of ironing, not to mention the fabrication of *Algerian* clothing.[104] That most Algerian women knew how to make, or at least iron, a *gandoura* did not occur to the organizers. Nevertheless, in her selection of the locations of the workshops, Bernard d'Attanoux demonstrated an understanding of the social dynamics of gender relations; each of the four Algiers-Mustapha workshops assembled in the homes of Algerians.[105] She faced a problem, however: with one exception, only men hosted the workers' assemblies. Thus, she added a discrete note at the bottom: "One knows that men do not have access to Muslim interiors; on the other hand women who would like to visit the workrooms will always be welcome there," thus forestalling criticism that her workshops violated appropriately gendered space.[106] Overtly addressing relations beween men and women, she inserted herself in the colonial reordering of Algerian family life.

That discrete, italicized note was disingenuous, for Bernard d'Attanoux created her workshops to modify Algerian cultural life. They became an exercise in applied anthropology, yet another front in the French empire's longstanding war against expressions of Algerian culture. "The history of female education," contends Clancy-Smith, "belongs in part to the sociology and anthropology of the state," or rather, state*s*, both colonial and North African.[107] Although she claimed the workshops' respect for social boundaries, Bernard d'Attanoux initiated them to provide the civilizing mission with access to women. "It is through the woman that the native spirit is penetrated," claimed Simone.[108] She interpreted women as the first step in "reconciling" men and children to empire. In her form letter, she advertised her workshops as part of "the

[104] AGGA, 14H/32, flyer labeled "Ouvroirs indigènes de Madame d'Attanoux."

[105] AGGA, 14H/32, flyer labeled "Ouvroirs indigènes de Madame d'Attanoux."

[106] AGGA, 14H/32, "Ouvroirs indigènes de Madame d'Attanoux." AGGA, 14H/32, "Rapport," No. 3858; AGGA, 14H/32, "Rapport," No. 4469.

[107] Clancy-Smith, "Envisioning Knowledge," 101.

[108] AGGA, 14/H32, Simone Bernard d'Attanoux to unnamed administrator, Algiers, May 8, 1902. Cf. Bowlan, "Civilizing Gender Relations in Algeria," 177. See also Julia Clancy-Smith, "L'École rue du Pacha, Tunis: l'enseignement de la femme arabe et 'la plus grande France,' *c.* 1900–1914," Special issue of *Clio: histoire, femmes et sociétés* 12 (2000): 43, on girls' schooling in Tunisia.

mission of French propaganda."[109] The workshops "establish between the natives and us, ties of sympathy perforce rendering truly efficacious the collaboration of our Muslim subjects."[110] The lessons in ironing, in clothes-making, in hygiene masked the true educational project of the workshops: the creation of a class of women who would turn their husbands and children into collaborators. As Clancy-Smith has noted for colonial schooling in Tunisia, "education is never an innocent enterprise, in the imperial case in which the colonial state always sought to form and co-opt . . . 'evolved' *indigènes*."[111]

Moreover, Simone Bernard d'Attanoux depicted her foyers as ethnographic field sites and as places for the inculcation of morality. "Having visited numerous interiors, having at length chatted with women and having made myself trusted enough by them to be able to study them up close, I remain more and more convinced that these women are accessible to our action, and that their influence in the conjugal home is of the most real."[112] Or, in the words of one prefect, "Madame d'Attanoux was not inspired . . . except by humanitarian considerations . . . and by the patriotic concern to exercise on Arab and Kabyle women an influence favorable to French interests."[113] More than almost any other project, the workshops demonstrated the close relationship between scholarship and imperial domination: Bernard d'Attanoux studied Algerian culture to change it. Discourses of salvation and emancipation scarcely masked empire's impulse toward cultural annihilation. However Bernard d'Attanoux marketed them, the workshops conflated the civilizing mission's paternalist social impulse and ethnography.

Many administrators, however, denigrated the workshops' efficacy. Although he acknowledged the vital importance of "the amelioration of the fate of the native women," one administrator contended Kabyles saw the workhouses for what they were: ill-concealed attempts at fostering cultural assimilation.[114] Others explained that what little popularity the foyers had resulted from the combination of their teaching of

[109] AGGA, 14/H32, Simone Bernard d'Attanoux to unnamed administrator, Algiers, May 8, 1902.
[110] AGGA, 14/H32, Simone Bernard d'Attanoux to unnamed administrator, Algiers, May 8, 1902.
[111] Clancy-Smith, "L'École rue du pacha, Tunis," 35.
[112] AGGA, 14/H32, Simone Bernard d'Attanoux to unnamed administrator, Algiers, May 8, 1902.
[113] Fonds ministériels, F80/1727, Prefect of Algiers to the Governor General of Algeria, No. 6028, "Demande d'Attanoux," Algiers, June 17, 1903. See also AGGA, 14/H32, "Rapport," No. 4469, Algier, October 16, 1902.
[114] AGGA, 14H/32, "Rapport. Confidentiel," n.d., *c.* 1902. See also AGGA, 14H/32, Venges, "Rapport," Algiers, October 30, 1902.

useful skills and their complete inability to effect any kind of moral or social change.[115] No administrator ever admitted that perhaps the entire assimilationist philosophy underpinning both the workshops and the civilizing mission doomed her project to failure; to do so would have admitted a kind of defeat that did not yet seem obvious to most administrators in 1902, apparent though it was to most Algerians.

Faced with lukewarm support among Algerians and administrative inertia, Simone Bernard d'Attanoux turned to other means of perpetuating empire. In 1912, she requested government aid for a voyage to Morocco, "to get into contact with the native woman . . . to make penetrate into the Muslim home the notion of ideas of justice, tolerance and bounty that characterize French action, and to dissipate . . . instinctive prejudices." This plan, she explained, proceded logically from her years of dedicated service through her Algerian workshops.[116] Over ten years, she moved from applied anthropology to ethnographic voyages to propagate French expansion. She inhabited a utilitarian ethnographic world in which any cultural knowledge or contact served empire.

Like Henri Duveyrier, Simone Bernard d'Attanoux traveled throughout North Africa, accompanied by her husband. Much like G. Laloë, both Bernards d'Attanoux interpreted the relationship between men and women as vital to the civilizing mission. Like Laloë, Bernard d'Attanoux concluded with the practical implications of gender relations.[117] Although he gave frequent speeches about their travels together, he emphasized the centrality of her interests and participation in their research. Why, exactly, Simone Bernard d'Attanoux remained silent at the meetings of geographic societies to which she also belonged remained unclear.[118] However, her husband underlined the primary importance of his wife's trip. "Over the course of the voyage of study and propaganda that Madame Bernard d'Attanoux has just undertaken . . . we were led to make authentication of . . . the situation of the Arab woman in native society and on the role that this woman plays in relation to the masculine

115 AGGA, 14H/32, Administrator Bollero of the Commune mixte of Fort-National to Prefect of the Department of Algiers, October 13, 1902; AGGA, 14H/32, Venges, "Rapport," Algiers, November 7, 1902; AGGA, 14H/32, Prefect of the Department of Algiers to the Governor General of Algeria, Algiers, November 8, 1902.

116 AGGA, 4H/34, Simone Bernard d'Attanoux née de Montigny, to the Ministers of Foreign Affairs, of Public Education, and of Work, February 17, 1912; AGGA, 14H/32, "Rapport. Confidentiel"; [Monsieur] Bernard d'Attanoux, "Conférence sur le Maroc," *BSGA* 7 (1902:1): 72–85.

117 M. Bernard d'Attanoux, "Du rôle de la femme arabe dans la société indigène," in *Congrès national des Sociétés françaises de géographie: compte rendu des travaux du Congrès. XXIIIme session. Oran. 1er–5 avril 1902* (Oran: Paul Perrier, 1903), 148.

118 "Membres," *BSGA* 7 (1902:1), lvi.

element of the country."[119] He depicted himself as her scribe, writing up the conclusions to questions that her voyages led her to ask and answer. Like Duveyrier, Simone Bernard d'Attanoux undertook "voyages of study and propaganda." Though the official opportunities to do so were scarcer, women participated in the creation of colonial ethnography. She never occupied a chair at the École d'Alger, or the *madrasa* at Tilimsān, or even an appointment as an adjunct administrator in some backwater. She could not. She did, however, follow a particular trajectory as a woman, as an ethnographer, and as a servant of empire.

Neither muse nor *enfant terrible*

European women traveled extensively in colonial Algeria. Indeed, the colonial government in Algeria supported the publication of accounts of the voyages of Abel Brives and his wife to Morocco (1901–7). Like Simone Bernard d'Attanoux, Brives's wife did not narrate her own account of the story. Nevertheless, she represented more than just an intrepid traveling companion.[120] Although she spoke little Arabic, Brives portrayed his wife as an entry into otherwise closed realms.[121] Though such comments reflected masculinist fantasies of unattainability, female ethnographers participated in the production of texts written by their husbands. When "Madame Brives went to visit the women[,] she returned disheartened and thus recounted her visit," which Brives quoted.[122] Madame Brives played a pivotal role in the fieldwork behind the narrative. Reading Brives's ethnography for personal revelation illuminates the centrality of women ethnographers, not in academic centers around, but in the field.

Not all women delegated writing to men. Magali-Boisnard achieved renown for voyages and presentations at the Société de Géographie d'Alger. In her publications, Magali-Boisnard declined to use her first name or a title, referring to herself as "Magali-Boisnard." Her experiences as a participant-observer revealed both the challenges and the recompense of traveling as a lone woman. In the Aurès, a shaykh's wife attempted to convince Magali-Boisnard, a *mademoiselle* though not particularly young, to marry his son. Magali-Boisnard instead seized the

[119] Bernard d'Attanoux, "Du rôle de la femme arabe," 144. See also AN, 47AP/10 (Fonds Henri Duveyrier), "Affaires coloniales, la mission d'Attanoux," Touggourt, March 28, [*c.* 1894] and AN, 47AP/10, "Mission Bernard d'Attanoux: l'audience en congé. – Le retour," Touggourt, April 4, [*c.* 1894].

[120] A[bel] Brives, *Voyages au Maroc 1901–1907* (Algiers: Adolphe Jourdan, 1909), 377, 443–4.

[121] Brives, *Voyages au Maroc*, viii, 332, 372.

[122] Brives, *Voyages au Maroc*, 365.

opportunity to investigate the differential status of the shaykh's various wives.[123] Magali-Boisnard confronted a gendered problem of colonial travel: as an unmarried woman traveling alone, she threatened to undermine strictly gendered patterns of behavior. At the same time, however, she benefited from intimacy that no male had experienced: she sat with the shaykh's wife and her friends, joining in their weaving of a *ḥā'ik*.

Although vital to her fieldwork, gender remained an ambivalent element in the unfolding of the ethnographies themselves. Magali-Boisnard shared her unique experiences, yet also never explicitly called upon the authority of her gender in establishing authorship. Only one reviewer emphasized her gender, repeatedly referring to her as "mademoiselle." Her work he lauded as "truly poetic," "with an elegance of style and a delicacy of expression"; he managed to stop himself before damning her as dainty, but only just.[124] Magali-Boisnard wrote robustly, stridently, in a not especially poetic manner. The unnamed commentator's descriptions exemplified the difficulties women ethnographers faced in ethnographic institutions; her gender, which facilitated participant observation, also facilitated the dismisssal of Magali-Boisnard's scholarship. In summarizing another presentation of Magali-Boisnard, he claimed that "the listener felt charmed by the marvelous talent of the 'African Muse,' who merits more than ever the flattering title."[125] Magali-Boisnard offered a rigorous ethnography, grounded in participant observation, that transformed her gender into a methodological tool. She nevertheless ended 1908 belittled in print, condescended to by her peers as a classical muse calling men to greatness.

Juliette Salmon clearly enjoyed playing with the gendered preconceptions of the Société. Indeed, she addressed her "Une Visite au M'zab" (1908) to "Mesdames, Messieurs," and roguishly explained that "the austere lady that is the Société de Géographie resembles those cute grandparents with white hair, who smile at the whims of *enfants terribles* and love them all the more the more insufferable they are."[126] She seemed determined to demonstrate her enumeration among the *enfants terribles*. In the *Bulletin*, Salmon chided explorers for their devotion to the soft pleasures of littoral Algeria, which she compared to the spa towns of Vichy or Aix-les-Bains. She hectored them to leave the "pretty women"

123 Magali-Boisnard, "L'Aurès barbare," *BSGA* 13 (1908:1): 50–1. See also Magali-Boisnard, "Nos Sœurs musulmanes," *BSGA* 13 (1908:4).

124 "Séances: Rapport des Conférences," *BSGA* 13 (1908:4): lxxxx.

125 "Séances: rapport des conférences," lxxxxiii.

126 Juliette Salmon, "Une Visite au M'zab," *BSGA* 13 (1908:3): 325. See also Juliette Salmon, "Visite à Beni-Ounif et à Figuig," *BSGA* 10 (1905): 3.

1. "Ghardaïa," from Juliette Salmon, "Une Visite au M'zab," *Bulletin de la Société de Géographie d'Alger et de l'Afrique du Nord* 13, no. 3 (1908).

of Algiers, and to travel, as she had, to the distant Mzab.[127] With no "chères madames" with whom to compete, women, too, could leave the trappings of the *toilette* behind.[128] Excluded though they were from the inner echelons of ethnographic institutions, women like Juliette Salmon forced their way in. Contemptuous of the boundaries drawn to keep her out, Salmon asserted her place in ethnography. The jealously guarded institutions of privilege excluded them, but the decentralized nature of ethnographic writing encouraged women to travel, research, and write. Women like Salmon participated in the epistemic violence of empire: "let us sing hosanna!" wrote Salmon, "to the colonizing genius of France."[129] They contributed to the complicated politics of the production of cultural knowledge about Algerians. Perhaps less indebted to the structures of empire, Salmon nevertheless could only sing the praises of the imperial project.

Magali-Boisnard's reviewer ignored entirely Salmon's challenge to gender roles in the Société. Abandoning the condescension he used with

[127] Salmon, "Une Visite au M'zab," 325–6.
[128] Salmon, "Une Visite au M'zab," 326.
[129] Salmon, "Une Visite au M'zab," 334.

2. "Cour de la mosquée de Ghardaïa," from Salmon, "Une Visite au M'zab."

"mademoiselle Magali-Boisnard," he underlined that "*Madame* Salmon terminated her picturesque recital by declaring that the annexation of [the Mzab] has been for it a great good."[130] He subsumed the *enfant terrible*'s critiques into their shared espousal of the political philosophy of empire. Salmon's commitment to empire allowed others to dismiss the more radical elements of her address to "the austere lady." A promulgator of imperial doctrine, Salmon vitiated the radical potential of her own critique of the Société and, by connection, of the gendering of colonial intellectual life.

Neither Salmon, nor Magali-Boisnard, nor Simone Bernard d'Attanoux challenged the fundamental political assumptions underlying the imperial project. They undertook significant research in spite and because of their gender: they rejected many limitations and used others as analytical whetstones. Nevertheless, the imbrication of imperial power and ethnography respected no gender boundaries. Their ethnographies, like those of Henri Duveyrier or Louis Rinn, perpetuated the inequalities

130 "Séance: rapport des conférences," lxxxxi. Emphasis added.

of empire. In this, if not in the halls of the Société de Géographie, they achieved equality.

Aptitudes and inclinations

Edmond Doutté followed a perhaps more typical route into the world of colonial ethnographic scholarship. A teacher, Doutté began his career at the *madrasa* in Tilimsān, an Arabic-language school and a center of ethnographic scholarship in Algeria.[131] In the west of Algeria, Tilimsān had long drawn those interested in Morocco, orienting the young professor's interests toward Algeria's western neighbor.[132] Despite his isolation from embryonic centers of sociology, Doutté found a vibrant, ethnographic community.[133] He conducted the fieldwork for *Les Aïssâoua à Tlemcen* entirely in the eponymous city, the historical capital. Tilimsān in the 1880s offered the most congenial locale for fieldwork-based ethnographic research in the colonial world. The *madrasa* united a group of scholars with a common aptitude for participant observation. A city famed for its beauty, the French who lived there came to love it. Among Doutté's closest friends he counted Alfred Bel, husband of Marguerite and a respected ethnographer.

By 1898, Doutté had moved to Algiers to "furnish . . . missionaries of science" at the École Supérieur des Lettres.[134] There he drew closer to the colonial administration. Nevertheless, his intellectual roots in Tilimsān predominated. In 1908, Alfred Bel dedicated his *La Population musulmane de Tlemcen* to "Edmond Doutté, in testimony of my cordial affection and my admiration for his precious works on the Muslims of Algeria and of

131 The ethnographer Auguste Mouliéras was his mentor; see Edmond Doutté, *Notes sur l'Islâm maghribin: les Marabouts* (Paris: Ernest Laroux, 1900), dedication; Edmond Doutté, "Les Djebala du Maroc, d'après les travaux de M. A. Mouliéras," *BSGAO* 14 (1899): 313–54.

132 Paul Ruff, "Chronique géographique," *BSGAO* 20 (1898): 295; "Membres," *BSGAO* 23 (1903): 5.

133 Lucette Valensi, "Le Maghreb vu du centre: sa place dans l'école sociologique française," in *Connaissances du Maghreb*, 241–3; Marcel Fournier, *Marcel Mauss* (Paris: Fayard, 1994), 360–1; 492 n.1, 581; Sibeud, *Une Science impériale pour l'Afrique?* 188; AGGA, 44S/1.

134 Doutté, "Les Djebala du Maroc," 354. See also Berque, "Cent vingt-cinq ans de sociologie maghrébine," 195; Fanny Colonna, "Présentation," in Émile Masqueray, *Formation des cités chez les populations sédentaires de l'Algérie (Kabyles du Djurdjura, Chaouïa de l'Aourâs, Beni Mezâb)*, repr. with intro. by Fanny Colonna (Aix-en-Provence: Édisud, 1983), xii; Daniel Rivet, "Exotisme et 'pénétration scientifique': l'effort de découverte du Maroc par les Français au début du XXe siècle," in *Connaissances du Maghreb*, 98, 103.

Morocco."[135] Those same works allowed Doutté to enter into the world of government-sponsored ethnography.

Though Bel and Auguste Mouliéras had influenced Doutté's methodological development, his association with the administration determined the use of his intellectual talents. Doutté codified the political utility of ethnography. Only his near-abandonment of ethnography, however, spurred administrators to make official use of him. In 1901, poor, suffering from respiratory ailments, unable to provide for his family, Doutté could no longer afford the cost of fieldwork and publishing. He had, noted one administrator, provided relevant, detailed, information about Morocco and Algeria with only the smallest recompense. Out of fear that poverty would end his contributions, the administrator recommended Doutté's appointment as a part of the Native Affairs Service (Service des affaires indigènes), marking in legal fact the ethnographer's longstanding collaboration with the imperial project.[136] In the reports from his 1901–2 mission to Morocco, the first undertaken as part of his government employment, Doutté attempted to ascertain the boundaries of identity among Moroccan Arabs and Berbers, expressing doubts about the utility of "race" as an analytical category.[137] He detailed the social and political role of Ṣūfī orders in Morocco, offering to the governor general insights on their potential as a locus for anti-European resistance, and purchased important books for the Bibliothèque nationale in Algiers.[138]

[135] Alfred Bel, *La Population musulmane de Tlemcen* (Paris: Paul Geuthner, 1908), dedication.

[136] AGGA, 4H/32, "Rapport à Monsieur le Gouverneur Général. Au sujet de M. Doutté," Algiers, June 3, 1901; AGGA, 4H/32, Governor General, "Note pour le Secrétaire-Général du Gouvernement," n.d. See "Note pour Monsieur le Sécrétaire Général du Gouvernement, by Monsieur le Chef de Bataillon," Algiers, Feburary 26, 1901; Edmond Doutté, *L'Islam algérien en l'an 1900*, Exposition Universelle de 1900, Algérie (Algiers-Mustapha: Giralt, 1900).

[137] AGGA, 4H/32, Edmond Doutté, "Troisième Voyage d'études au Maroc. Rapport sommaire d'ensemble," Tangier, November 6, 1902; Edmond Doutté, "Figuig: notes et Impressions," *BSGP* 8th ser., 9 (1903): 177–202; AGGA, 4H/32, Secretary-General Charles Maunoir, Société de géographie de Paris, to M. Revail, Governor General of Algeria, Paris, Octobre 29, 1902, and Novembre 28, 1902.

[138] AGGA, 4H/32, Edmond Doutté to Governor General, Rabat, June 17, 1901; AGGA, 4H/32, Edmond Doutté to Governor General, Tangier, July 16, 1901. Cf. AGGA, 4H/32, "Programme des études qui seront poursuivies par M. Doutté dans sa mission au Maroc," n.d.; AGGA, 4H/32, Edmond Doutté to Governor General, Marrakesh, April 26, 1902; AGGA, 4H/32, Edmond Doutté to Governor General, Mogador, May 18, 1901; AGGA, 1K/288, Governor General to the General commanding the Division of Constantine, Algiers, March 12, 1902; AGGA, 1K/288, Colonel Rougon, Commander of the 3rd Regiment of Spahis, to General commanding the Division of Constantine, Batna, March 28, 1901; Edmond Doutté, "À Rabat, chez Abdelazîz: notes prises en 1907," *BSGAO* 33 (1910:1): 21–68; Brives, *Voyages au Maroc*, 358–60; Ch. René-Leclerc, "Bibliographie: le Maroc connu," *BSGAO* 23 (1903): 359–66.

Doutté marshaled for his new employer all of the catholicity and virtuosity typical of incipient ethnography. Nevertheless, his ethnographies subordinated methodological and analytical concerns to the overarching political interest of empire. Doutté's reports evinced no real interest in Moroccan culture for its own sake, an interest he demonstrated elsewhere, focusing instead on its political import. Doutté knew well his employer's interests and aimed to gratify them. Indeed, he even offered political recommendations of his own regarding "the indefinite extension of civilization" from Algeria to Morocco.[139] As shrewd a politician as he was perspicacious an ethnographer, Doutté's reports from Morocco coincided perfectly with the governor general's assessment of the reason for hiring Doutté in the first place. Wrote the governor, "[a]fter making himself noticed for his numerous writings on Islamic questions on North Africa, [Doutté] has recently rendered again brilliant services to the Gouvernement Général de l'Algérie, in exploring Morocco, where he reported useful intelligence and knowing studies on the most varied subjects."[140] Doutté's wide-ranging interests marked him as eminently useful. "He is," the governor concluded, "one of the most precious agents" in Algeria.[141]

The interests and aims of ethnography coincided with the grandiose and violent projects of empire. Few ethnographers had to make a conscious decision to bend the results or goals of his or her project to the will of empire. Doutté not only exemplified the concordance of ethnography and politics, he and E. F. Gautier collaborated to produce ethnographic texts for the Algerian colonial government. In 1904, the two undertook a major research project on the Algerian Saharan oases.[142] The nameless administrator who received Gautier's report endorsed his

139 AGGA, 4H/32, Edmond Doutté, "Les Deux Politiques," n.d.

140 AGGA, 4H/32, Governor General of Algeria, "Note pour le Secrétaire-Général du Gouvernement," n.d.

141 AGGA, 4H/32, "Note pour le Secrétaire-Général." See also AGGA, 10H/74, Chief of the Service of Native Affairs to Edmond Doutté, "Renseignements sur le mode d'habitation de l'Annexe du Gourara," October 18, 1911; AGGA, 10H/74, anonymous, "Rapport," August 21, 1913; AGGA, 10H/74, Edmond Doutté to Commander Chartenet, Paris, October 17, 1913; AGGA, 10H/74, Commander Chartenet to Edmond Doutté, "Enquêtes ethnographiques," Colombes (Seine), December 8, 1913; AGGA, 10H/54, Edmond Doutté, "L'Imamat," November 25, 1914; Edmond Doutté and E. F. Gautier, *Enquête sur la dispersion de la langue berbère en Algérie, faire par ordre de M. Le Gouverneur Général* (Algiers: Adolphe Jourdan, 1913); *Bulletin du Comité de l'Afrique française* 15 (1905:4): 172; Paul Pascon, "Le rapport 'secret' d'Edmond Doutté: situation politique du Hoûz 1er janvier 1907," *Hérodote,* no. 11 (July–Sept. 1978): 132–59.

142 AGGA, 4H/33, E.-F. Gautier to unnamed commander, "Rapport sommaire sur un inventaire scientifique des Oasis Sahariennees et du Sahara." Mustapha (Algiers), January 28, 1904.

selection of Doutté. "The attached note from M. Doutté shows under which form a slightly divergent ethnographic questionnaire seems to have been conceived. We rally completely to the ideas expressed by M. Doutté," he wrote.[143] Doutté envisioned a politically interested, administratively directed ethnography. His "Note sur l'établissement d'un questionnaire ethnographique" (1904) advocated the codification of participant observation and ethnography as bureaucratic duties. Particularly in the Sahara, Doutté contended, administrators possessed both the time and the will to conduct ethnographic research. They lacked, however, the sustained methodological rigor that "ethnographic and sociological studies demand."[144] Lest his superiors criticize him for academic frivolity, Doutté scrupulously defended the utility of his proposal. "If one considers that these studies are the very data of our Saharan politics, better yet its sole fundaments . . . one could not too much encourage our Officers to apply themselves" to ethnographic research, "and a guide that would permit them to orient themselves a bit in this vast department of science would render real services."[145] Drawing upon the positivist logic underpinning the nascent social sciences, Doutté argued that ethnographic research created a corps of scientifically rigorous administrators. Thus, elite scientists expert in the sociology of desert culture would replace haphazard and dangerously inept governance.

A questionnaire offered a logical means of organizing data and orchestrating analysis. Doutté, however, methodically demolished the utility of questionnaires, forms, and the other impedimenta of colonial bureaucracy. The fragmentary results made systematization into "an anthropological, ethnographic, and sociological monograph" impossible.[146] He objected primarily to questionnaires' superficiality, to the lack of expertise required. Because of such homogenizing rigidity, "the documents thus collected . . . will not have any scientific character, because but one of the paragraphs of [such a] program would demand a long preparation and special aptitudes that are found together but rarely. Moreover, this inquiry not only will not be scientific, but will even harm the progress of science because, well edited, written neatly, well presented, it will have a deceptive aspect of the 'complete' and the 'definitive' that will" discourage additions; "real science," claimed Doutté, "never is and never will be finished. Finally, the time that is allotted to conduct [the research] is

143 AGGA, 4H/33, anonymous, "Observations sur la note de M. Gautier," n.d. (1904).
144 AGGA, 4H/33, Edmond Doutté, "Note sur l'établissement d'un questionnaire ethnographique," n.d. (1903–4).
145 AGGA, 4H/33, Doutté, "Note sur ethnographique."
146 AGGA, 4H/33, Doutté, "Note . . . ethnographique."

most short."[147] A devoted practitioner of participant observation himself, Doutté remained convinced of the need for detailed, long-term study.

Never hesitant to express his convictions, Edmond Doutté gave administrators an example of methodological failure. Its provenance perhaps indicates something about the state of ethnography in the colonies; that Algeria led, Doutté did not doubt. The text in question, "L'Inventaire méthodique des territoires de la Sénégambie-Niger," came from the interim governor general of French West Africa (AOF).[148] Doutté vehementally rejected the worth of "L'Inventaire méthodique," distributed to functionaries in AOF, because of its superficiality, demanding information on everything from history to ichthyology to cartography.[149] For Doutté, the ethnographic monograph represented nothing less than the culmination of a scientific methodology; no mean recitation of responses to questions could equal the achievement of a narrative ethnography. Anything less representated a dereliction of scientific and administrative duty.

Instead, Doutté outlined the different kinds of scholarship useful for the colonial enterprise. The scientifically inclined, he felt, ought to pursue botanical and biological studies, while the naturally sociable and linguistically gifted should take up ethnography. Outdoorsmen would take naturally to the study of agriculture and sport; the dry study of history, alas, he reserved for the pedantic loner.[150] Expertise comprised the fortuitous alignment of interests and abilities (for the ungifted enthusiast, Doutté offered nothing). "It is in taking into account these varied dispositions," he contended, "that it is necessary to try to utilize good will" among administrators.[151] Although his texts lacked the revelations of Henri Duveyrier, Doutté revealed more of himself than, perhaps, he intended in his proposal. Quite simply, his ethnographic manual represented the apotheosis of his methodology; through it Doutté triumphed over metropolitan academics, who often ignored him. Doutté found in colonial administrative monographs an ethnographic impulse, but one that demanded management, a pruning into a shape commensurate with notions of ability and expertise he himself embodied. Thus, the fundamental impulse to detailed cultural study by which Doutté lived lay at the heart of ethnographic practice and administrative need. He merely pointed out that the first answered to the requirements of the second.

147 AGGA, 4H/33, Doutté, "Note . . . ethnographique."
148 AGGA, 4H/33, "L'Inventaire méthodique des territoires de la Sénégambie-Niger," *La Dépêche coloniale*, October 21, 1903.
149 AGGA, 4H/33, "L'Inventaire méthodique des territoires de la Sénégambie-Niger."
150 AGGA, 4H/33, Doutté, "Note . . . ethnographique."
151 AGGA, 4H/33, Doutté, "Note . . . ethnographique."

Whether the colonial administration implemented Doutté's project remains irrelevant: since the advent of French colonialism, administrators constructed narrative ethnographies to facilitate control. Although Doutté could propose manuals or vituperatively castigate questionnaires, he could change little, for administrators had already reached the same conclusions he had.[152] Narrative ethnography arose out of the necessities of political control. Though he never recognized it, Doutté offered less of a research proposal than a state of the field. In Algeria, ethnographic scholarship provided the keystone upon which scholar-administrators erected the edifice of empire. The future of empire depended on its bureaucrats' understanding of colonial cultures. Doutté little realized that its future depended, too, on their misunderstandings.

In a dimly-lit café in Tilimsān

On February 2, 1903, the director of the *madrasa* in Tilimsān meticuously recorded propitiations aimed at conjuring rain. Alfred Bel was conducting research for an ethnography of drought rituals. The vast preoponderance of Bel's ethnographies unfolded in the city of Tilimsān, a city Bel knew and loved. At the time one of the most beautiful cities in Algeria, "Tlemcen," as Bel noted, "[was] the only city in Algeria where one encountered so many still imposing vestiges, so many ancient monuments, eloquent witnesses to Arab civilization, at the time of its disappearance in the Maghrib and Spain."[153] Hence, it served as the ideal site, not only for ethnographers such as Doutté and Bel, but for scholarly visitors. "Since Tlemcen became French, scholars, tourists, the admirers of this old Muslim city have written the results of their research and their observations in a large number of works, in brochures and articles in Reviews and Journals."[154] Although located in a provincial city, Bel, like Doutté, fashioned in Tilimsān a center of scholarship. He worked alongside ethnographers, both Algerian and European.[155] No

152 FM GEN 236 (1688), Conseiller d'état, Minister of the Colonies, Service of Geography and Archives, "Rapport au ministre," Paris, March 14, 1896. See also AGGA, 12H/4, "Note sur les Administrateurs de C[om]m[une] M[ix]te," Dossier: Projet de loi Albin Rozet 1909–1910, n.d. Cf. AGGA, Oasis//46, Chef d'Escadron Payn, Military Commander of the Territory of the Oases, to the Captain, Head of the Annex, In-Salah, May 7, 1912.

153 Alfred Bel, "Bibliographie: *Les monuments arabes de Tlemcen*, par Mm. William et Georges Marçais," *BSGAO* 23 (1903): 256.

154 Bel, *Population musulmane*, 1. See also Marçais, "Nécrologie Bel," 104–5.

155 Marçais, "Nécrologie Bel," 104, on Bel's ties with Basset, Douttté, and Destaing, like Bel, from the Franche-Comté; see also 105, 107–8. See also Sibeud, *Une Science impériale pour l'Afrique?*, 187–8; Bel, *Population musulmane*, dedication; Aboubekr

more vibrant ethnographic community existed in the French empire. Bel contended that his generalizations "on the religious habits of the people of Tilimsān apply equally well to all the Muslims of North Africa."[156] Never mind the faulty transposition underpinning Bel's claim; he had made it so. Ethnographies of Tilimsān used its inhabitants to substitute for North Africans as a whole. Bel's authority allowed Tilimsān to serve as a universal field site, a methodological shorthand to generalize about North African Muslims.

Thus, Bel seized that dry February day to observe Algerians throughout the Oranais. He relied on the web of personal contacts made in Tilimsān. Bel's "Quelques rites pour obtenir la pluie en temps de sécheresse chez les musulmans maghribins" (1905) demonstrated his relationship to Tilimsān and his unique place in ethnography. Drawing on his colleagues, students, and neighbors, Bel interrogated them about drought rituals, observed their practices, recorded them, compared them. Bereft of close ties to the state, he made do with an unusual degree of familiarity with Algerians, conferred by virtue of his position at the *madrasa*. "The examples given" of rituals "were observed directly by me in the department of Oran, or else were furnished me by Muslims who recounted to me the detail of these festivals for rain in their region," and he could have included even more.[157] Moreover, he "personally attended the rogations of the blacks [*nègres*] at Tlemcen, the second of February 1903."[158] Bel lived in greater proximity to Algerians and the events of importance in their lives. Though other ethnographers wrote on ritual,

Abdesselam ben Choaïb, "Les Marabouts guériesseurs," *Revue africaine* 51 (1907): 250–5; ben Choaïb, "Les Croyances populaires chez les indigènes de algériens," *BSGAO* 27, no. 29 (1906:2): 169–74.

156 Bel, *Population musulmane*, 8. See also pages xi–xiii, xviii–xxvi, 31, 35–6, 39–40, 42–3, 52–7; Alfred Bel, "Quelques rites pour obtenir la pluie en temps de sécheresse chez les musulmans maghribins," *Recueil de mémoires et de textes publiés en l'honneur du XIVe Congrès des Orientalistes par les professeurs de l'École supérieure des lettres et des médersas* (Algiers: Imprimerie orientale Pierre Fontana, 1905); and Alfred Bel, "La Fête des sacrifices en Berbérie," *Cinquantenaire de la Faculté des lettres d'Alger (1881–1931)* (Algiers: Société historique algérienne, 1932), 87–125.

157 Bel, "Quelques rites," 49. On *madrasas*: Bel, "Sidi Bou Medyan et son maître Ed-Daqqâq à Fès (notes hagiographiques et ethnographiques)." *Mélanges René Bassel: études nord-africaines et orientales* 1 (1923): 31; Charles-Robert Ageron, *Les Algériens musulmans et la France (1871–1919)*, vol. II (Paris: Presses universitaires de France, 1968), 923–62; Allan Christelow, *Muslim Law Courts and the French Colonial State in Algeria* (Princeton, NJ: Princeton University Press, 1985), 23, 249.

158 Bel, "Quelques rites," 72–3. On "Quelques rites," see also I. Goldziher, Review of *Recueil de mémoires et textes publié en l'honneur du XIVe Congrès des Orientalistes par les professeurs de l'École supérieure des lettres et des Médersas*, *Revue de l'histoire des religions* 50 (1905): 1–18.

none did so with Bel's casual familiarity. No other ethnographer could boast of the surfeit of research materials that he could.

Bel's geographic trajectory in the ethnographic world of colonial Algeria remained largely limited to Tilimsān. Intellectually, however, it knew no bounds. He communicated with Algerians in Tilimsān and with metropolitan academics, with tourists and teachers across the Francophone world. It extended, too, to that dismal café in Tilimsān whose image begins this chapter. As so many of us have, Arnold Van Gennep found himself at a dreary spot in an unfamiliar town because of the recommendation of a local friend. That friend directed the *madrasa*, and had become the foremost scholar of Islam of his time. "There were exceptions," noted Van Gennep, to the settlers' injunction against mixing, their denigration of that démodé little café, and Bel was one of them. "[T]he director of the Medersa [sic], a good old friend of mine, . . . indicated this café to me, where there came at times to keep me company a professor at the Medersa and the justice of the peace. But, most often, I was there alone. And I passed hours watching the coming and going of the men in burnouses."[159]

Bel called Van Gennep's attention to the warp and weave of the daily fabric of communal life in Tilimsān. By temperament interested in cultural life, and passionately devoted to Tilimsān, Bel uniquely positioned himself to conduct fieldwork. His ability to quote lengthy, untranslated Arabic passages and to refer to personal connections with Algerians created an authoritative voice. In the *madrasa*, in the dimly lit café, Bel formulated research questions, selected informants, asked probing questions – conducted fieldwork. This dingy space where Algerians met the audacious French visitor – Bel, Van Gennep, the adventurous justice of the peace – marked precisely the kinds of rare experiences that contributed to the formation of fieldwork methodology. Out of these "disreputable" visits emerged notions of ethnographic expertise. Bel and Van Gennep were two in a long and mostly anonymous line of colonial ethnographers; separated by the institutional strictures of colonial politics, metropolitan academe, and jealously guarded disciplinary privilege, Bel and Van Gennep met on the muddy cobbles of the café and exchanged ideas about the structure, practice, and writing of ethnography.

Upon his visit to Tilimsān, Van Gennep enacted Doutté's conception of ethnographic expertise. Although he spoke no Arabic, Van Gennep seized the opportunity of the intimate contact of the café to

[159] Van Gennep, *En Algérie*, 20–1. See also Bel, review of "A. van GENNEP: la formation des légendes," *BSGAO*, 31 (1911:1): 81–3. Van Gennep also counted William Marçais among his friends; see *En Algérie*, 132.

conduct ethnography in miniature. "[I]n Tlemcen only," wrote Van Gennep, "the Algerian nature has so much gentleness, and so much likable richness."[160] Abandoning armchair theorizing, Van Gennep interrogated the café patrons about their cultural lives. He met the Beni Ournid (Banī 'Urnīd), mountain-dwellers who visited the café on market days and stayed in nearby *fanādiq*. "At the beginning," Van Gennep explained, "I took care not to bump into these cumbersome brigands; but after several days, I was known by them."[161] Moreover, later, "several free cups of coffee showed me in these terrible savages good, unpolished, young children, with guileless smiles."[162] The mere process of making the Banī 'Urnīd's acquaintance manifestly did not remove Van Gennep from the predominant tropes of colonial ethnography.

Nevertheless, Van Gennep's first interactions with Algerians altered his relationship to methodology: he changed his opinion on the Banī 'Urnīd after actually meeting them. In addition, after dismissing his early notion, replacing it with an equally imperialist view of them as benighted children, Van Gennep saw the café differently. It becomes, in the text, "mon café" – Van Gennep took ownership over the liminal, filthy spot in which he began his investigations. Ethnography became a compulsion. After his visit to Tilimsān, "[T]o do research in ethnography and folklore, it's already no longer a work, or an occupation, or a distraction; it's an organic necessity," he contended, "to make people speak and to extract from them legends and stories."[163] He asked the Beni Snous (Banī Sanūs), weavers at market, about production and decoration.[164] Indeed, one member of the ethnic group would bring interesting examples for Van Gennep to examine at "his café." Having rejected the injunctions of French settlers to shun contact with Algerians, Van Gennep instead threw himself into the cultural life of his little café, and observed their habits. His *Ethnographie algérienne* (1911) drew on his conversations about textiles and handicrafts with the Banī Sanūs. He acknowledged his methodological debt in *Ethnographie algérienne* to the teachers at the *madrasa*.[165] Moreover, his "friend Bel led [Van Gennep] to an old man who was weaving," an informant for *Ethnographie*.[166] Arnold Van Gennep learned his participant-observation methodology at the same school where Bel instructed Algerians in Arabic.

160 Van Gennep, *En Algérie*, 11, 13–17.
161 Van Gennep, *En Algérie*, 21.
162 Van Gennep, *En Algérie*, 22, 129.
163 Van Gennep, *En Algérie*, 125–6.
164 Van Gennep, *En Algérie*, 23–4; see also Clancy-Smith, "A Woman Without Her Distaff," 38–43.
165 Arnold Van Gennep, *Études d'ethnographie algérienne: les soufflets algériens, les poteries kabyles, le tissage aux cartons, l'art décoratif* (Paris: Ernest Leroux, 1911), 1–5.
166 Van Gennep, *Ethnographie algérienne*, 68.

This café in Tilimsān witnessed no fundamental moment in the formation of ethnographic expertise. Van Gennep did not sit reverently at the feet of Bel, absorbing wordy discourses on methodology. I am not tracing a *silsila*, the transmission of divine inspiration back through history from one great to another. What happened was far simpler: Bel had advised his friend to sit, watch, listen, ignore the hectoring voices that deemed scandalous his association with Algerians. Nearly ten years earlier, Bel and Doutté imbued ethnography with a particular set of skills and methods – linguistic fluency, participant observation, daily interaction with Algerians. Dedicating *En Algérie* to Bel, Van Gennep remained more ambivalent; his hesitant interactions in the Tilimsān café indicated his reluctance. He was no expert on Algeria, but rather a fumbling novice. His time in Algeria proved a rite of passage, opening his mind to new forms of experiential, authoritative writing. In *En Algérie*, Van Gennep explained that "when one researches ethnographic problems, one chats. Good practice requires that one speak of many things before formulating technical questions."[167] Although Bel, Doutté, and Van Gennep differed greatly in academic training, their work coalesced around new conceptions of methodology and writing. The history of ethnography arose as much out of affinities, out of haphazard interactions, out of chance meetings in dimly lit cafés as it did out of concerted, disciplinary developments.

Ethnographies yield only tantalizing glimpses of the intimacies of ethnographers and informants, and of ethnographies. Pretensions to scientific authority often excised personal voices from ethnography. The ethnographic moment remained evanescent, and no historian could hope to reconstitute the complexity of personal ties. Neither new nor inherently liberatory, the turn towards reflexivity in ethnography draws upon pre-existing, if concealed, intimacy. Colonial ethnographers marshaled the authority of the personal as yet another weapon in the intellectual battles of empire. Hence, the greatest legacy of attention to the construction of narrative authority lies in critical reading of ethnographies as texts concealing and revealing the intimate connections of participant observation. Eschewing a deterministic view of fieldwork, such techniques allow for the psychological, political, social, and cultural construction of ethnographic texts.

Some texts, however, remain opaque. The difficulty in recapturing the ethnographic moment eerily recaptures the difficulty of ethnographic research itself. Even Henri Duveyrier at times revealed only ambiguity. In the Sahara in the autumn of 1861, Duveyrier witnessed "a frightful thing," a horrific public execution. "The son" of the murder victim "cut

[167] Van Gennep, *En Algérie*, 8. On p. 73, he even used the term "informant" (*informatrice*).

3. "Le Lieutenant Roussel donne aux Touareg une audition de gramophone," from Captain Florent-Alexis Métois, *La Soumission des Touareg du Nord*, preface by F. Foureau (Paris: Augustin Challamel, 1906).

off the head of the murderer . . . in a barbarous manner. The well-dressed wives of the deceased . . . drank the blood of the annihilated one. A frightful thing."[168] The terrifying, revolting passage strains credulity, threatens to dissolve the credibility of other passages of Duveyrier's other writings. What did he exaggerate, fabricate, not comprehend? No reading unearths anything further. The questions hang in the air.

Other words hang, other texts remain, impenetrable. Captain Florent-Alexis Métois's *La Soumission des Touareg du Nord* included an inscrutable photograph. Lieutenant Roussel bends rigidly toward a phonograph, giving an audience of waiting Tuareg . . . what? What concert, what musical piece, what spoken word did he bring to the desert? The photograph bears a mute witness only to the watchful attentiveness of the Tuareg audience, the spotted dog, to the stage managing of Roussel – and the photographer. Voiceless, not faceless but effaced, the Tuareg listen to a vanished message whose content will never again echo in the desert. Its message is obliterated, but we can only assume the voice from the phonograph spoke in French.

[168] AN, 47AP/2, Henri Duveyrier, Carnet of Sept. 29–October 1861, 66.

3 "Au coin des rues Diderot et Moïse": the ethnography of the esoteric and the politics of religious sociability

In February of 1896, in the Algerian littoral town of Berrouaghia, a French colonial administrator took a photograph. In it a dark-skinned, bearded man in his late thirties sits next to a white-washed, thatch-roofed stone house. On his knees a large, elaborate, gilt-edged book lies open, neatly framed by the white of his robes and the dark color of his sash. Next to him stands a small boy, perhaps seven or eight years old. Both stare solemnly at the camera. The photograph, sepia-toned and faded, adorns a report on Islamic religious orders, one of many similar reports that provided the research for the seminal studies on North African Islam.[1] Possibly this nameless administrator saw this photograph as a way of emphasizing the veracity of his report, or perhaps even of making his work seem thorough enough to merit promotion out of his position as a low-level bureaucrat in Berrouaghia.

For Berrouaghia was something of a backwater in the 1890s. Despite its location on a major road running from the coast to the south, it had yet to attract the attention of many French tourists, or, in fact, of almost anyone. In the words of one visitor, in 1887, "Berrouaghia is a beautiful village, well built, animated . . . The hot, sulfurous baths of Berrouaghia, much appreciated by the inhabitants, will be for this interesting little place a source of wealth, when the magnificent bathing pavilion that is being built is completed."[2] It was a place of potential. The French governed the town, with its surrounding area, as a *commune mixte*, meaning that it had a considerable amount of rural territory attached to it, a sizable

The author would like to thank Duke University Press for permission to reuse in this chapter portions of material that originally appeared in George R. Trumbull IV, " 'Au coin des rues Diderot et Moïse': Religious Politics and the Ethnography of Sufism in Colonial Algeria, 1871–1906," *French Historical Studies* 30, no. 3 (2007): 451–83.

[1] Archives du Gouvernement général de l'Algérie (AGGA), 16H/8, [illeg.], "Études sur les confréries religieuses musulmanes de la commune mixte de Berrouaghia. 1895," Berrouaghia, February 17, 1896.

[2] Zeys, *Voyage d'Alger au M'zab (1887)* (Aix-en-Provence: Centre des archives d'Outre-Mer, 1971). Microfiche.

indigenous population (in 1890, about 250 in the village from which the *commune mixte* took its name), and few Europeans; it had vineyards, Roman ruins, a single hotel.[3] The more than thirty thousand residents of the commune were, thus, a mix of Algerian Muslims and scattered Europeans – French, Spanish, Italian, Anglo-Maltese, and others. One rare traveler referred to it as "neither European country nor Arab country, that area, it's Algerian country."[4] Infamous in the 1990s for terrorist violence and a massacre at its prison, Berrouaghia in the 1890s was famous for nothing.

Hence, Berrouaghia might seem an odd place to look for the encounters that determine ethnographic texts, for colonial relations of participant observation, and for a seminal moment in the history of French Orientalism. However, the colonial state in Berrouaghia, and in Algeria in general, adopted ethnographic methodology in the hopes of understanding and controlling the political role of Islam. Just as Third Republic leftists expressed profound anxieties over Catholicism as a danger to secular governance, and just as vitriolic, anti-Semitic elements of the extreme right attempted to portray Judaism as a political threat, French administrators in Algeria perceived any organized form of Islamic piety as a menace to colonial control. Apprehensions about religion's role in politics extended to the colonies, even to remote Berrouaghia; as a result, French administrators took a lively interest in Islamic mysticism and ritual from the beginning of the occupation of Algeria. Ambivalence regarding the political role of religion dominated republican discourse through the Third Republic.[5] The threat, real or imagined, of religious communities engaging in political activity destabilized both metropolitan France and its colonies.

Most obviously, resurgent Catholicism seemed to pose the greatest threat to French republicans. The association of Catholicism with monarchism cemented, in the minds of many during the 1870s and 1880s,

[3] On the distinction between *communes mixtes* and *communes de plein exercice*, see Charles-Robert Ageron, *Les Algériens musulmans et la France (1871–1919)*, vol. II (Paris: Presses universitaires de France, 1968), 612–22; Charles-Robert Ageron, *Histoire de l'Algérie contemporaine*, vol. II: *De l'insurrection de 1871 au déclenchement de la guerre de libération (1954)* (Paris: Presses universitaires de France, 1979), 19–38; Alain Mahé, *Histoire de la Grande Kabylie, XIXe–XXe siècles: anthropologie historique du lien social dans les communautés villageoises* (Paris: Éditions Bouchène, 2001), 239–40; on the population and attractions of Berrouaghia, see V. Almand, *D'Alger à Ouargla* (Algiers: Adolphe Jourdan, 1890), 18.

[4] Dr. Marius Bernard, *L'Algérie qui s'en va* (Paris: Plon, Nourrit, 1887), 119.

[5] On "les deux France": Maurice Larkin, *Religion, Politics and Preferment in France since 1890: La Belle Epoque and its Legacy* (Cambridge: Cambridge University Press, 1995), 3; see also John Ruedy, *Modern Algeria: The Origins and Development of a Nation* (Bloomington, Ind.: Indiana University Press, 1992), 100.

Catholicism's ties with the forces of ultramontane reaction.[6] In his definitive *Social History of French Catholicism*, Ralph Gibson notes that "the hostility that most republicans felt toward the *congrégation* [Catholic religious organization] sprang from the deepest roots of republican ideology. The Jacobin tradition in France was nationalist, individualist, and statist . . . The congrégations appeared to be foreign, repressive of the individual, and a threat to the authority of the State."[7] This tension between the politicized elements of Catholicism and republicanism resulted in both dynamic contestation between church and state and in increasing anxieties over the threat of politicized religion in general.[8] Until the 1892 *Ralliement* of the Catholic Church to French republicanism, "the anticlerical tail," in the memorable phrase of John McManners, "had been wagging the Republican dog."[9] The *Ralliement* only began the long process of reintegrating mainstream French Catholicism with republicanism and the forces of political moderation in *fin de siècle* France. Obviously, not all Catholics "rallied" to the Third Republic, and, perhaps more importantly, activist Catholicism loomed as a menace discursively, if no longer politically, long after the *Ralliement*.[10]

The tragedy of the Dreyfus Affair illustrates that the political tensions of republican France involved not only Catholicism, but also Judaism. Dreyfus was, of course, entirely innocent of the calumnies against him; nevertheless, his identity as a Jew condemned him, in the eyes of too many, as a traitor. Viewing Jews as incapable of loyalty to France, the anti-Dreyfusards engaged in a politicization of religious identity that resembled the left's fears about reactionary Catholic politics, despite the fact that French Jews never showed any signs of disloyalty to the principles

[6] John McManners, *Church and State in France, 1870–1914* (London: Church Historical Society, 1972), 36; René Rémond, *L'Anticléricalisme en France de 1815 à nos jours*, new edn (Paris: Fayard, 1999), 175.

[7] Ralph Gibson, *A Social History of French Catholicism* (New York: Routledge, 1989), 131.

[8] Christian Sorrel, *La République contre les congrégations: histoire d'une passion française (1899–1914)* (Paris: Éditions du Cerf, 2003), especially 78–89. "Secularism," notes Frederick Cooper, "was more often beleaguered than triumphant." Frederick Cooper, *Colonialism in Question: Theory, Knowledge, History* (Berkeley, Calif.: University of California Press, 2005), 20; J. P. Daughton, *An Empire Divided: Religion, Republicanism, and the Making of French Colonialism, 1880–1914* (Oxford: Oxford University Press, 2006), 116.

[9] McManners, *Church and State*, 64; Daughton, *An Empire Divided*, 117.

[10] The year 1892 also witnessed Jules Ferry's reforms of the Algerian colonial government; see Charles-Robert Ageron, *"L'Algérie algérienne" de Napoléon III à de Gaulle*, La Bibliothèque arabe, ed. Pierre Bernard (Paris: Éditions Sindbad, 1980), 72–93. The 1905 Separation attests to the continued tensions between Catholicism and republicanism in France; McManners, *Church and State*, 64–75; Bruno Dumons, *Catholiques en politique: un siècle de Ralliement* (Paris: Desclée de Brouwer, 1993), 14–30; Daughton, *An Empire Divided*, 87.

of the republic. Although their views had roots in opposite ends of the political spectrum, the anti-Semitic anti-Dreyfusards and the radicals who feared a resurgent ultramontanism evinced profound anxieties about the role of religion in politics. Neither the right nor the left held a monopoly on the politicization of religion during the Third Republic.

If leftist fears of extremist Catholic politics and the extreme right's anti-Semitism both reflected larger anxieties about the relationship between faith and the state, then the Third Republic's relationship to Islam should illustrate other forms of the politicization of religion, not as an expression of a purely metropolitan trope,[11] but as a constituent and defining element of a politicization of religion created both colonially and in the metropole. "By the late 1880s," notes J. P. Daughton, "Catholicism was not the only proselytizing religion in France: the other was republicanism."[12] A history of ethnographies of Islam demonstrates the relationship between Islam and attempts at defining republicanism. The politicization of religion in France took place as much outside of Europe as it did in metropolitan France, and ethnographers took such an interest in Islam precisely because of the challenges republican secularism faced, both at home and abroad. Thus, ethnographies intervened in a political environment in which officially sanctioned narratives about Islam interpreted it as politically dangerous.

Nevertheless, the acquisition of knowledge of Islam demanded systematized ways of familiarizing scholars and bureaucrats with other peoples.[13] While nearly every French person possessed at least rudimentary knowledge about Catholicism, experiences with other religions largely remained confined to stereotypes. Long-entrenched views of Jews and Judaism merged with new scientific discourses to produce a particularly virulent form of anti-Semitism, while scholars of Islam marshaled the very same racial science in their quest to understand Islam.[14] Faced with

[11] Ann Laura Stoler and Frederick Cooper, "Between Metropole and Colony: Rethinking a Research Agenda," in Cooper and Stoler, eds., *Tensions of Empire: Colonial Cultures in a Bourgeois World* (Berkeley, Calif.: University of California Press, 1997), 16. Julia Clancy-Smith, "L'École rue du pacha, Tunis: l'enseignement de la femme arabe et 'la plus grande France,' *c.* 1900–1914." Trans. Anne-Marie Engels-Brooks, special issue of *Clio: histoire, femmes et sociétés* 12 (2000): 55; Alice L. Conklin, *A Mission to Civilize: The Republican Idea of Empire in France and West Africa, 1895–1930* (Stanford, Calif.: Stanford University Press, 1997), 8–13; Daughton, *An Empire Divided,* 7–9, 261; Christopher Harrison, *France and Islam in West Africa, 1860–1960* (Cambridge: Cambridge University Press, 1988), 4, 29–56.

[12] Daughton, *An Empire Divided,* 55.

[13] Edward Said, *Orientalism* (New York: Vintage Books, 1978); Ageron, *Les Algériens musulmans et la France (1871–1919)*, vol. II, 891–922, and Ageron, *Histoire de l'Algérie contemporaine,* vol. II, 168–82, for a broader view of what Ageron calls "la politique religieuse" – albeit a view rather uncritical of colonial sources on Islam.

[14] Michael Burns, *Rural Society and French Politics: Boulangism and the Dreyfus Affair, 1886–1900* (Princeton, NJ: Princeton Univesity Press, 1984), 123. Patricia M. E. Lorcin,

unfamiliar and hostile Algerians, bureaucrats, scholars, tourists, settlers, and others combined racist interpretations of the nascent human sciences with the distinctive narrative and methodological conventions of ethnography to interpret Islam politically. Knowledge of Algerian Islam came about almost exclusively through the production of ethnographic texts.

Because Third Republic administrators understood the Algerians they ruled primarily through the lens of participant observation, ethnographies of Islam in French Algeria demonstrate an obsessive focus on sociability and performance. Because of its inherent illegitimacy, colonial governance restricted political participation and hence equated public display of dissidence with resistance. French domination of political expression also implied a need to regulate public discourse; any irruption of Islam threatened to subvert colonial authority. Hence, ethnographic texts (whether state-authorized or other) juxtaposed acts of worship and devotion with the potential for resistance.[15] Thus, French ethnographers interpreted the various Ṣūfī orders as organized, politically subversive cultural elements threatening colonial social organization. Communally organized, sophisticated in the ways of local politics, intimately linked with the larger Islamic world, and collectively influential, these Ṣūfī orders seemed, to the ethnographically inclined observer fixated on religion, the ideal foyer for political contestation. And, indeed, they often did serve as precisely such a foyer: throughout Algeria, minor conflagrations, often inspired by religious leaders, flared throughout the period.[16] More broadly, chiliastic movements and religiously organized anticolonial dissent flourished throughout the Sahara and Sahel, from Algeria to Khartoum.

In general, Ṣūfī orders (*ṭuruq*, paths, ways; sing., *ṭarīqa*) consist of men and women committed to attaining spiritual enlightenment and closeness to God by following (whence the use of *ṭarīqa*, with its association with the idea of a path) the mystical practices set out by the divinely inspired founder, whence the order's name. A *shaykh*[17] (pl., *shuyūkh*) presides over each order, claiming intellectual and spiritual authority by virtue of the *silsila* (chain, series), or genealogy demonstrating the succession of leaders and transmission of beliefs of the order and of the founder's *baraka*,

Imperial Identities: Stereotyping, Prejudice and Race in Colonial Algeria (London: I.B. Tauris, 1995). On the political uses of science in anthropology and religious studies, see Jacqueline Lalouette, *La République anticléricale: XIXe-XXe siècles* (Paris: Éditions du Seuil, 2002), 246–55.

15 Sossie Andezian, *Expériences du divin dans l'Algérie contemporaine: adeptes des saints dans la région de Tlemcen* (Paris: CNRS Éditions, 2001), 24–5.

16 Julia Clancy-Smith, *Rebel and Saint: Muslim Notables, Populist Protest, Colonial Encounters (Algeria and Tunisia, 1800–1904)*, Comparative Studies on Muslim Societies, ed. Barbara D. Metcalf (Berkeley, Calif.: University of California Press, 1997).

17 Also a generic term of respect.

4. Frances E. Nesbitt, "Un Marabout mendicant," from Brieux, *Les Beaux Voyages: Algérie*, Les Arts graphiques (Paris, 1912).

divine blessing.[18] The shaykh has a series of deputies, *muqaddimīn* (sing., *muqaddim*) who lead smaller, localized groups of *ikhwān* and *akhawāt*, members (lit., brothers and sisters), in acts of devotion and common prayer (*ḥaḍra*), carried out at a *zāwiya* (pl., *zawāyā*), a meeting-house that doubled as a hotel, home for vagrants, and distributor of food and aid in times of strife.[19] Frequently, the *zāwiya* also held land in common as *waqf*, or a religious endowment.[20] Holy men and women administered justice and mediated local disputes.[21] At a minimum each order has a special series of prayers and recitations, a *dhikr*, unique to its members, who learn of its details upon initiation, though many orders have other distinctive practices as well.[22] In North Africa in particular, individuals could, with a few exceptions, affiliate with numerous different orders, though most chose to join ones to which they had a family or social tie. Even as late as 1884, the interpreter Colas could note with some vexation that "there is no real agreement on what must be learned or done to be a Sufi."[23]

Ṣūfī *ṭuruq* respected no colonial boundary. Nearly every *ṭarīqa* present in Algeria counted adepts in other parts of the Muslim world, from India to Nigeria. It was precisely this transnational scope that drew the attention of the colonial state in Algeria. Ṣūfism's refusal to countenance state boundaries undermined the fragile lattice of imperial power. Ṣūfīs and scholars spread far and wide through the *dar al-islām*. In large part, Algerian ethnography records a state's attempt to control religious phenomena throughout North Africa.

Despite the international scope of Ṣūfism, ethnographic studies of Islamic mysticism often appeared as state-centered, government-directed publications; bureaucratic reports, tourist literature, and, of course, scholarly studies contributed to the acquisition of knowledge about

18 Abdellah Hammoudi, *Master and Disciple: The Cultural Foundations of Moroccan Authoritarianism* (Chicago: University of Chicago Press, 1997), 138–9.

19 On religious space: Muṣṭafā ʿAbd as-Salām al-Mahmāh, *Al-mrāʾa al-maghribiyya w-al-taṣawwuf fi-l-qarn al-ḥādī ʿashr al-hijri* (Casablanca: Dar al-Kitāb, 1398 h. / 1978 AD), 43.

20 David S. Powers, "Orientalism, Colonialism, and Legal History: The Attack on Muslim Family Endowments in Algeria and India," *Comparative Studies in Society and History* 31, no. 3 (1989): 535–71.

21 Allan Christelow, *Muslim Law Courts and the French Colonial State in Algeria* (Princeton, NJ: Princeton University Press, 1985), 18–21, 37.

22 On Ṣūfism: Alexander Knysh, *Islamic Mysticism: A Short History*, Themes in Islamic Studies, vol. I (Leiden: Brill, 2000). See especially 175–6, 301–25; Jacques Berque, *L'Intérieur du Maghreb: XVe–XIXe siècle*, Bibliothèque des Histoires (Paris: Éditions Gallimard, 1978), 423–9.

23 AGGA, Division of Oran, Subdivision of Tlemcen, 16H/7. Colas, *Notices sur les ordres religieux*. 1884.

5. "Family Tree" of Ṣūfī Ṭuruq, including major leaders, from Octave Depont and Xavier Coppolani, *Les Confréries religieuses musulmanes* (Algiers: Adolphe Jourdan, 1897).

mystical Islam. Juxtaposing such state-centered publications and archival documents with scholarly studies and popular tourist literature emphasizes commonalities in the use of ethnography as a means of politicizing Islamic religious sociability. Although scholars have long recognized Ṣūfism's impact in Africa, none have examined its relationship to ethnographic narrative and the perpetuation of colonial authority in Algeria.[24] Focusing on ethnographic studies of these Islamic religious orders as a negotiated space between piety and politics integrates the colonial history of domination with metropolitan conceptions of political religion.

Nevertheless, French ethnographic texts form no coherent school of thought on Ṣūfism. Though various authors shared a common orientation toward problems of religion and politics, their resultant texts on Islamic mysticism form not a uniform "école algérienne,"[25] but rather a dynamic, manifold discourse. Instead of a simple set of assumptions reinscribed through repetition, ethnographic texts on Ṣūfism became a constantly evolving renegotiation of empire, republican politics, and religious faith. Historians would do well to remember that not all French men and women in the Third Republic were, in fact, republicans, but at the same time must recognize that even the most virulently anti-Islamic passages may simultaneously reflect an author's hostility to religion *in general*; moreover, ethnographers had institutional reasons to provide information congruent to various government policies and institutions, despite personal political allegiances. Conversely, ethnographic texts *intervened* in contested debates about the nature of religion and politics. As Abdellah Hammoudi notes, "one has to keep in mind that the homogenous and homogenizing colonial discourse does not always keep its word. Instead of a single discourse, we find several discourses, which contradict each other."[26] Colonial ethnography consisted more of a series of methods, intentions, and styles, a process of imagining colonized cultures into reality, than a unified school of thought.

Ethnographers perceived the structure of Ṣūfī orders as a threat to secular control of Algeria. The seemingly impenetrable hierarchical organizational structure of the *ṭarīqa* lent itself to the subversion of French domination.[27] Answering only to God, the *shuyūkh* pursued their own goals in spite of, or without reference to, French claims of temporal

[24] Jean-Louis Triaud, *La Légende noire de la Sanûsiyya: une confrérie musulmane saharienne sous le regard français (1840–1930)*, vols. I & II, (Paris: Éditions de la Maison des sciences de l'homme, 1995); and David A. Robinson, *Paths of Accommodation: Muslim Societies and French Colonial Authorities in Senegal and Mauritania, 1880–1920*, Western African Studies (Athens, OH: Ohio University Press, 2000), 3–4, 37–54.

[25] Triaud, *Légende noire*, 347–74. [26] Hammoudi, *Master and Disciple*, 112.

[27] Abdelbaki Hermassi, "The Political and Religious in the Modern History of the Maghrib," in John Ruedy, ed., *Islamism and Secularism in North Africa*, Center for Contemporary Arab Studies (New York: St. Martin's Press, 1994), 88. Archives du

6. Origins of the Four Madhāhib (Legal Schools) within Islam, from Depont and Coppolani, *Confréries religieuses*.

authority.[28] The Baron Estournelles de Constant even claimed that "the shaykh makes disappear, like so many moral stains, the reasoning, the initiative, the thought of he who delivers himself to [the shaykh]; a being who becomes between his hands not a cadaver, but a blind instrument that fanaticism can lead to the excess of good or evil."[29] Indeed, the fear of the members of Ṣūfī orders as fanaticized automatons permeated ethnographies. The mere idea of the ease of marshaling thousands of "blind instruments" obsessed administrators. In both cultural discourses and official political documents, Ṣūfīs appeared as a religious fifth column threatening to undermine French governance in Algeria. Ethnographies transformed religious sociability into ethnographic objects embodying the political fears of the dominating power.

Indeed, the idea of organized forms of religious sociability as profoundly destabilizing political structures extended beyond Algeria. As Julia Clancy-Smith notes, "[t]he colonial model held that certain Sufi orders... were inherently political, thus resolutely opposed to Algeria's French masters throughout the past century..."[30] Moreover, the ethnography of Islamic sociability drew upon French conceptions of *Catholic* religious orders; the antagonism to Islamic sociability that Clancy-Smith points out echoed similar concerns about Catholicism.[31] Since at least 1789, French republicans had posited Catholic orders as a fundamental threat to secular governance, and it required only the easiest of transpositions to extend the image to Ṣūfī orders, as well.

Until World War I, ethnographers focused on Ṣūfī orders as threats similar to the threat once posed by Catholic religious orders. Indeed, no lesser expert than Louis Rinn proposed nationalizing religious figures, including Ṣūfīs, as government bureaucrats in Algeria, just as republican

Département d'Alger (ADA), 2U/20, anonymous, Rapport sur les confréries religieuses, Division of Algiers, Subdivision of Laghouat, Annex of Ouargla, 1903.

28 Louis Rinn, *Marabouts et khouan: étude sur l'Islam en Algérie* (Algiers: Adolphe Jourdan, 1884), 59; AGGA, 3X/1, Ernest Masqueray, review of Louis Rinn's *Marabouts et khouan*, *Bulletin de Correspondance africaine* 4 (1885): 178–83; AGGA, 3X/1 (Personal Papers), Maurice Wahl, "Les Congrégations dans l'Islam," *Revue de l'Afrique française* 6, no. 29 (Septembre 1887): 286–8.

29 Le Baron d'Estournelles de Constant, *Les Congrégations religieuses chez les Arabes et la conquête de l'Afrique du Nord*, Bibliothèque ethnographique, ed. Léon de Rosny (Paris: Maisonneuve et Leclerc, 1887), 18. AGGA, 16H/9, anonymous, "Notices détaillées sur les Zaouias, Chioukh et Mokaddem, établies en conformité des instructions contenues dans la dépêche préfectorale du 13 mars 1895 No. 989 (cabinet)." Commune mixte of Hillil, July 4, 1895.

30 Clancy-Smith, *Rebel and Saint*, 5. Clancy-Smith also cites Marcel Simian, *Les Confréries islamiques en Algérie (Rahmanya-Tidjanya)* (Algiers: Adolphe Jourdan, 1910), 44.

31 See Charles-Robert Ageron, *Modern Algeria: A History from 1830 to the Present*, trans. and ed. Michael Brett (London: Hurst, 1991), 71; Gibson, *Social History*, 132.

7. Etienne Dinet, "Le Muezzine appelant les fidèles à la prière" (1914).

governments had once done in France.[32] Not surprisingly the proposal generated much opposition. One prominent newspaper in Constantine contended that

[32] Rinn, *Marabouts et khouan*, 110–1. Octave Depont and Xavier Coppolani, *Les Confréries religieuses musulmanes: publié sous le patronage de M. Jules Cambon, Gouveneur général de l'Algérie* (Algiers: Adolphe Jourdan, 1897), 283–4.

what happened in France will happen in Algeria. For, during the Revolution, the juring clergy, held aloof by the faithful, could but increase disorder, and it is a gross illusion to believe [in the ability to] bypass a religious movement by giving its priests salaries.

And in effect, since 1870, have the members of the Catholic clergy ceased to oppose with all their force the consolidation of the Republic that accords them a salary?[33]

Because, as Gibson notes, "the hostility that most republicans felt towards the [Catholic] *congrégation* sprang from the deepest roots of republican ideology,"[34] many ethnographers felt a similar hostility to the Islamic equivalent of the Catholic *congrégation*.[35] Debates over religious sociability in large part determined ethnographic interpretations of Ṣūfism.

Ethnographers focused on Ṣūfī practices as sites of potential resistance. In the context of French anxieties over Islam in general, ethnographers depicted mystical retreats, tribute, and pilgrimages,[36] though primarily *religious*, as *politically* subversive. Louis Rinn called "the love of the contemplative life . . . an unproductive idleness that distances [the *ikhwān*] from all progress and all relations with Europeans."[37] For Rinn, both the organizational structure and the mystical beliefs of Algerian Ṣūfism impeded the establishment of French control by hindering contact. By 1897, Octave Depont and Xavier Coppolani had further exaggerated the threat, portraying Ṣūfism as a Pan-Islamic reservoir of resistance. "Whether they come from Morocco, from the edges of the Bosphorus, from Egypt, from the extreme south or the Far East, . . . armed with their rites, their miraculous legends and their faith, [Ṣūfīs] penetrate the huts of the poor and the mansion of the rich, with the same dominating power that troubles their souls and makes of these pilgrims demi-gods."[38] Casting proselytism as subversion, Depont and Coppolani created an ethnographic portrait that focused, in its essence, on only the political implications of a religious act.

Naturally, ethnographers and administrators did not merely address the problem of religious sociability in the abstract but rather discriminated among the various Ṣūfī *ṭuruq*. Colonial ethnography reified their identities, condensing multitudinous, locally determined practices, beliefs, and political orientations into more manageable representations.

[33] AGGA, 3X/1 (Personal Papers of Louis Rinn), anonymous, untitled. *L'Indépendant* of Constantine, August 23, 1884.
[34] Gibson, *Social History*, 130; Triaud, *Légende noire*, vol. I, 10–14.
[35] Harrison, *France and Islam*, 42, 61.
[36] On *ziyāra*, see Clancy-Smith, *Rebel and Saint*, 29, 36–8.
[37] Rinn, *Marabouts et khouan*, 77.
[38] Depont and Coppolani, *Confréries religieuses*, 192.

Historicizing the ethnography of religion in relation to each individual order reveals the perpetuation of French Orientalist understandings of Islam.

Moreover, the binary distinction between resistance and collaboration itself adopts the positionality of colonial domination and ignores cultural dimensions of resistance.[39] What France deemed "collaboration" and "resistance" cannot be reduced to simple binary choices because of the complexity of the internal dynamics of Algerian society.[40] Religious orders often obeyed a series of principles without regard to the expectations of republican authorities. Nevertheless, the colonial state's political agenda pervaded ethnography through the near-obsessive quest to unearth resistance. In Algeria at least, colonized peoples did not always acquiesce *or* revolt; often, Algerians manipulated European misunderstandings to their own advantage. Analyzing the discrepancies in ethnographic analyses of the individual Ṣūfī orders reveals a polyphonous and at times disharmonious set of colonial discourses considerably more complex than reductions into collaboration and resistance.

Ethnographic images: the ethnographer and the mystic

The road to Berrouaghia leads one way; archival evidence allows us to reconstruct only the observations of the nameless administrator who took the photograph described at the beginning of this chapter, and not the perceptions of those he observed. His signature present but illegible, he seems to embody, eerily, the phantom positionality, the ghostly personality, of the ethnographic observer, present but self-effacing, attendant but vaporous, illegible. His presence marks an absence: all knowledge of the Islamic order about which he wrote, the Shādhiliyya,[41] passed through the distorting prism of the anonymity of ethnographic authority. In vanishing ink he marked the text as his own, leaving smudged traces of the interpretive choices he made; in his report, the Shādhiliyya existed, in no

39 See Homi Bhabha, "Signs Taken for Wonders," in Homi Bhabha, *The Location of Culture* (London: Routledge, 1994), 112–13, 120, on hybridity as "the articulation of the ambivalent space where the rite of power is enacted," and a means of "deformation and displacement."

40 Clancy-Smith, *Rebel and Saint*, 263–4. For an analysis of the *problématique* of "collaboration" in French West Africa, see Robinson, *Paths of Accommodation*.

41 Even the identification of the order remains problematic; often confused with the Darqāwiyya or other offshoots, French references to the Shādhiliyya appear to have addressed most frequently the ramifications known as the Shādhiliyya Jazūliyya and the Shādhiliyya Zarrūqiyya. See Knysh, *Islamic Mysticism*, 216; Depont and Coppolani, *Confréries religieuses*, 455, 466.

small part, as the object of his creation. When we see the Ṣūfī order, we see through the eye[42] of power.

We see a photograph, we read a name. The man in the photograph was named Ṭayyib bin al-Ḥājj Bāshir, and he was a holy man by both inheritance, through his maraboutic family, and choice, as a shaykh of the Shādhiliyya. A former colonial soldier, Shaykh Ṭayyib bin al-Ḥājj Bāshir eventually left the army, devoted himself to mystical study, and became shaykh at the age of twenty-eight, settling on fifty hectares of land near Berrouaghia.[43]

The photograph emphasized the personal characteristics of Ṭayyib that made him a reliable, ideal informant. In his discussion of the photograph, the administrator indicated a close familiarity, demonstrated his reliance on Ṭayyib and the information he could provide. "His appearance," noted the administrator,

> is mild and his physiognomy sympathetic; benevolent to all those who approach him, he has always known how to maintain good relations with all the representatives of authority and in many circumstances he has given proof of tact and open-mindedness in lending without too much difficulty information on the Muslim religion and on his sect in particular. Si Taïeb [*sic*] having expressed to us the desire to be photographed with his young son Yahia, the only male child of his descent who is, moreoever, called to succeed him in his religious title, we thought it a necessity to give him this small satisfaction.[44]

Despite the incredulity of Depont, who queried in the margins, "Is this actually true?", the administrator's explication of the photo juxtaposed his personal connections with Ṭayyib and the professional role the latter played in serving as an informant for such ethnographic texts. Each ethnographic text consisted of just such innumerable personal interactions. The exchange of favors, the affiliative ties made through personal connections, the sympathy of one administrator for a father's affection for and pride in his son; such cultural interactions determined the conditions of the production of ethnographic knowledge.

Knowledgeable in the ways of both French administrators and Algerian mystics, Ṭayyib served as the primary informant for the administrator's study of the Ṣūfī *ṭuruq* in Berrouaghia. Acknowledging his reliance on Ṭayyib bin al-Ḥājj Bāshir for most of his information, the administrator

[42] See chapter 1 for a further deconstruction of this eye; on "resisting the 'I' of the ethnographer as a privileged eye, a voyeuristic eye, an all-powerful eye," see Ruth Behar, *The Vulnerable Observer: Anthropology that Breaks your Heart* (Boston: Beacon Press, 1996), 21.

[43] AGGA, 16H/8, "Étude sur les confréries . . . de Berrouaghia," 1895, 23–4; A. Joly, "Étude sur les Chadouliyas," *Revue africaine* 51, no. 264–5 (1907): 243

[44] AGGA, 16H/8, "Étude sur les confréries . . . de Berrouaghia," 1895, 21–3.

nevertheless defended him as providing a less interested kind of information:

> It is true that commentators are numerous in Muslim lands . . . the representatives of each order are pleased to introduce certain unique variations to enhance themselves in the eyes of [fellow Muslims] . . .
>
> [W]e thought it interesting to expose them in our study, inasmuch as the cheikh Si Taïeb [*sic*] who is very intelligent is deeply literate in the matter of the Muslim religion above all.[45]

Deeming information from most Muslims politically motivated, the administrator depicted Ṭayyib as less biased: his education and study qualified him as a commentator on mysticism, and his time as a French soldier made him less suspect.

In the Berrouaghia texts, Ṭayyib emphasized aspects of the order's practices least disruptive to French control. Consciously downplaying the order as a political threat, the Berrouaghia text established a precedent that deemed Shādhiliyya piety not threatening, but instead anodyne, even munificent. In general, the order benefited from its founder's reputation for knowledge and piety, as well as orthodoxy.[46] Traditionally, new initiates to the *ṭarīqa* undertook two months of itinerant begging, demonstrating the the order's emphasis on poverty.[47] The practice, however, fell out of favor during the colonial period, due in part to French discouragement of potentially disruptive peripatetic mystics.[48] Similarly, the Berrouaghia report recorded changes in the order's behavior over time. Remarking that Ṭayyib bin al-Ḥājj Bāshir's information (on the *dhikr*, for example) differed from that of *Marabouts et khouan*, and indicating that Ṭayyib demurred from Rinn's conclusions, the administrator also contended that Ṭayyib had eschewed proselytism in favor of charity and hospitality.[49] In these reports, a clear distinction emerges between dangerous mendicant practices and an emphasis on perpetuation, and a lapse into a pious, charitable quiescence deemed innocuous.

The challenges that Ṭayyib bin al-Ḥājj Bāshir faced came not only from the French, but from other Muslims as well. Incipient Wahhābism in North Africa targeted the Shādhiliyya as a syncretistic, deviant, and fundamentally un-Islamic religious form because of its emphasis on retreat

45 AGGA, 16H/8, "Étude sur les confréries . . . de Berrouaghia," 1895, 13.

46 AGGA, 16H/8, "Étude sur les confréries . . . de Berrouaghia," 1895. On Shādhiliyya practices in Tunis, see Richard J. A. McGregor, "A Sufi Legacy in Tunis: Prayer and the Shadhiliyya," *International Journal of Middle East Studies* 29, no. 2 (May 1997): 255–77.

47 Knysh, *Islamic Mysticism*, 217,

48 AGGA, 16H/8, High Commander of the Circle of Djelfa [illeg.], "Rapport au sujet des confréries religieuses," Djelfa, June 4, 1895.

49 AGGA, 16H/8, "Étude sur les confréries . . . de Berrouaghia," 1895, 13, 16–7, 19, 27.

8. "Illustration of the Ṭuruq," from Depont and Coppolani, *Confréries religieuses*.

and contemplation.[50] In Ottoman Syria and Ottoman and Muhammad Ali's Egypt, where the Shādhiliyya had spread with much success, the rise of new governing elites in the nineteenth century bound Shādhilī leaders in allegiance to Muslim states, while simultaneously diminishing the political rule of the Ṣūfīs.[51] The intellectual and urban nature of the Egyptian Shādhiliyya allowed only for Wahhābī critiques of religious ideology, and not politics.[52] In North Africa, however, the Shādhiliyya suffered from a reputation as troublemakers who prevented Islamic unity. The Salafī apologist Ṣāliḥ bin ʿAbdallah bin ʿAbd al-Raḥmān al-ʿUbūd contends that North Africa "was already unfree because of the discord between Arabs and Berbers and the prevalent, deviant Sufis – especially the order of the Shādhiliyya and its illicit innovation in religion."[53] In other words, according to the Wahhābīs, the Shādhiliyya's religious excesses had sown discord (though al-ʿUbūd shies away from the loaded term *fitna*) and prevented Muslim unity. Ṭayyib would have faced much criticism from Wahhābist-influenced groups.

Other ethnographers, moreover, suspected the veracity, or at least the intent, of Ṭayyib bin al-Ḥājj Bāshir's contentions. Like the Berrouaghia report, A. Joly's "Étude sur les Chadouliyas" (1907) relied overwhelmingly on one particular informant. However, Joly availed himself of one of Ṭayyib's rivals, one Muḥammad al-Misūm, whom Louis Rinn also thanked in his preface to *Marabouts et khouan*.[54] Interestingly, al-Misūm, like Ṭayyib, dismissed French fears of Shādhiliyya hostility.[55] Furthermore, Joly's ethnography brought to the surface tensions within the Shādhiliyya. By 1907, Ṭayyib bin al-Ḥājj Bāshir may, in fact, have no longer *been* a shaykh of the Shādhiliyya. Tensions with al-Misūm and other Shādhiliyya leaders had drawn the adepts of Berrouaghia closer and closer to the Madaniyya, a much smaller, related order.[56] Joly also remarked, however, that al-Misūm, and his followers in general, suffered from a reputation for laxity. In the words of one shaykh,

[50] ʿabd al-Fatāḥ Fūʾād, *Al-Filāsifa al-islāmiyyūn wal-ṣūfiyya wa mawqif ahl al-sunna minhum* (Cairo: Dār al-Daʿwa lil-Ṭabʿa al-Nashar wa al-Tawzīʿ, 1997), 116.

[51] Rachida Chih, *Le Soufism au quotidien: confréries d'Éypte au XXe siècle*, La Bibliothèque arabe (Arles: Éditions Sindbad, 2000), 29, 33, 36–8, 44–7.

[52] Éric Geoffroy, *Le Soufisme en Égypte et en Syrie sous les derniers Mamelouks et les premiers Ottomans: orientations spirituelles et enjeux culturels* (Damascus: l'Institut français d'Études arabes de Damas, 1995), 172–5, 208, 262, 263. Minăl ʿabd al-Munʿim Jād-Allah, *al-Taṣawwuf fī Miṣr wa al-Maghrib* (Alexandria: Munshāʾa al-Muʿārif bil-Iskandriyya jalāl ḥazī wa sharkaḥ, 1997), 208 notes the imbrication of religion, ideology, and politics.

[53] Ṣāliḥ bin ʿAbdallah bin ʿAbd al-Raḥmān al-ʿUbūd, *ʿAqīdat al-shaykh Muḥammad bin ʿabd al-Wahhāb al-Salafiyya wa Athr-ha fī al-ʿĀlim al-Islāmī*, vol. I (al-Manūra: Maktba al-Ghurbāʾ al-Athriyya, 1996), 47.

[54] Rinn, *Marabouts et khouan*, viii. [55] Joly, "Étude sur les Chadouliyas," 24, 240.

[56] Joly, "Étude sur les Chadouliyas," 232–3, 243.

"the zaouiya of Cheikh Elmiçoume, it's an orange tree planted in a dunghill."[57] Al-Misūm, despite his protestations of his own innocousness, portrayed the rival Ṭayyib as an instigator who, noted Joly, "probably entertain[ed] secret relations with the Orient."[58] Nevertheless, in 1907 many Berrouaghia still revered the late Ṭayyib bin al-Ḥājj Bāshir, a reverence extended to his son who succeeded him.[59] These contradictory interpretations of the role and beliefs of Ṭayyib bin al-Ḥājj Bāshir indicate the paramount importance of personal contact in the creation of a colonial ethnography of Islam; al-Misūm's information on Ṭayyib differed greatly from that provided by Ṭayyib himself or his son, and what we know of Ṭayyib and al-Misūm comes only from how each presented himself or his rival. Reliant on the fieldwork of administrators utlizing the most compliant or familiar Algerians within their circumscription, ethnographies reflected the concerns of both informant and ethnographer.[60] Algerians, such as Ṭayyib, living in contact with French ethnographers mediated all information presented in ethnographic texts. Colonial archives reflect the unspoken self-representations, determined by local politics and individual interests, of Ṭayyib and others. As a direct result, the ethnographic texts of colonial Algeria must be read reflexively, for the constitutive moments of personal encounter that determined their content, but with an acknowledgment that few marks of intent remain engraved on the text.

These concerns with the Berrouaghia report (and, implicitly, with other such reports) surfaced only after the publication of the Depont and Coppolani text. Thus, not only did Ṭayyib bin al-Ḥājj Bāshir provide nearly all of the information on the Shādhiliyya in the Berrouaghia report, he also determined the analysis of Octave Depont and Xavier Coppolani's *Les Confréries religieuses musulmanes*; Depont and Coppolani drew most of their conclusions from fieldwork conducted by hundreds of administrators, across Algeria, including the Berrouaghia report. As a result, Depont and Coppolani did not accord the Shādhiliyya the same status as a menace that they ascribed to other Ṣūfī *turuq*, articulating few

[57] Joly, "Étude sur les Chadouliyas," 237. [58] Joly, "Étude sur les Chadouliyas," 244.

[59] ADA, 2U/21, Administrator of the Commune mixte of Berrouaghia, [illeg.], "Confréries religieuses musulmanes. 1e Semestre 1907. Rapport," Department of Algiers, Arrondissement of Médéa, Commune mixte of Berrouaghia, June 30, 1907"; "Renseignements individuels pour servir au Recrutement du Personnel Administratif Indigène" Chadouli Yahīa ben Tayeb [*sic*], Berrouaghia, 1910.

[60] Mary Louise Pratt refers to this phenomenon in the New World as as "autoethnography . . . instances in which colonized subjects undertake to represent themselves in ways that *engage with* the colonizer's own terms" (italics in the original). Mary Louis Pratt, *Imperial Eyes: Travel Writing and Transculturation* (London: Routledge, 1992), 7; see also Robinson, *Paths of Accommodation*, 3–4.

connections between their analyses of practices and beliefs of the *ṭarīqa* and the politics of colonial authority.

One knows the doctrines of the Chadelian mystical school: a purified spirituality, the abandon of the self to the profit of God, prayer at all times . . . in order to live in constant union with the Divine. It is eternal ecstasy, but ecstasy without mystic raptures, the ecstasy provoked by this ardent love of the Divine, which distances the world and procures inexpressible sensations.

Among the Chadelïa, no retreat, no monastery; no noisy charlatanism; – the errant and contemplative life with, for the profession of faith, unity of God (the *Touahid* [*sic*: *tawḥīd*]), and, for education, the *Tessououf* [*sic*: *taṣṣawuf*, the Ṣūfī way], or a science of spirituality that must lead the neophyte to live in the divine essence.[61]

In other ethnographies, such practices appeared as subversive and frankly hostile; among the Shādhiliyya, they serve to mark the *ṭarīqa* as both pious and innocuous. Surveillance documentation on individual adepts of the order manifests a corresponding inattention to the order's political import. One such document noted one adept as particularly learned and, "forty years ago, led by a most imperious mystic vocation," to join the order – yet still did not categorize him as a menace.[62] The experiences of various administrators followed a pattern established by Ṭayyib and, most importantly, determined the predominant analytical trends in synthetic ethnographies.

Colonial ethnographic discourses, however, did not view religious elements of Algerian culture through the obfuscating lens of the collaboration/subversion binary. Instead, the Shādhiliyya moved in a polyvalent narrative world in which they seemed both non-threatening *and* subversive, depending on the authority consulted. Even Depont and Coppolani, among the greatest propagandists for the vision of a quiescent Shādhiliyya, expressed concerns about the potential for Pan-Islamist doctrines arising out of the *ṭarīqa*.[63] Perversely, the two authors portrayed the order as non-threatening in its *practices*, but potentially

61 Depont and Coppolani, *Confréries religieuses*, 443.

62 AGGA, 16H/30 (Enquête de 1910), anonymous, "Renseignements individuels pour servir au Recrutement du Personnel Administratif Indigène à la surveillance politique et administrative des populations musulmanes. 1re catégorie: Confréries religieuses musulmanes (chiouks, mokaddems, marabouts locaux [*sic*])," Kaddour ben Salah [*sic*], Department of Algiers, Commune mixte of Ouarsénis, 1910. For similar treatments of other individuals, see anonymous, "Renseignements . . . ," Tahar ben Boubeker [*sic*], Ouarsénis, 1910; anonymous, "Renseignements . . . ," El Hadj Kaddour [*sic*], Ouarsénis, 1910; anonymous, "Renseignements . . . ," Chadouli Yaḥīā ben Tayeb [*sic*], Berrouaghia, 1910; AGGA, 1I/151, Governor General Jules Cambon to the General commanding the Division of Algiers, April 20, 1893, paid particular attention to the Shādhiliyya as collaborators – albeit in tension with the Tijāniyya.

63 Depont and Coppolani, *Confréries religieuses*, 261.

generative of dissent in its *beliefs*; the dynamics of politicization of religion did not vacillate between the two (artificial) poles of collaboration and resistance, but rather fluctuated in a kind of indeterminate, politically charged valence-space. No less an authority than Jules Cambon (who later acknowledged the order's cooperation[64]) ascribed to the order a defining role in the genesis of the Sanūsiyya and the perpetuation of Pan-Islamism.[65] Ethnographies reached seemingly contradictory conclusions about the Shādhiliyya. In fact, however, they reveal less of a contradiction than a discursive splitting, a double-speak in which organized religious networks would come to signify, even to enact, an entire range of politics in the vast spaces between hostility and collaboration.

The suspicion of the ethnographic state

In contrast to the Shādhiliyya, the Qādiriyya[66] are not Algerian in origin; nor are they of recent formation. Founded in Baghdad in the twelfth century by 'Abd al-Qādir al-Jīlānī, the Qādiriyya represents the oldest and most widespread Ṣūfī *ṭarīqa*, ranging from Senegal to Chechnya, and from Morocco to India. This wide geographic range inhibited the development of strong central authority in the order, which remains a diverse group of affiliated *zawāyā*.[67] From 1832 to 1847, the Amīr 'Abd al-Qādir led his famous rebellion that associated the Qādiriyya with armed resistance to the French.[68] The rebellion's temporal distance from the Third Republic, however, allowed for a more nuanced ethnographic view of the Qādiriyya than one that merely focused on armed conflict. Thus, ethnographic texts focusing on the Qādiriyya exhibit a different relationship to the politics of resistance, and more attention to other aspects of the *ṭarīqa*.

The Qādiriyya emphasis on charity attracted particular attention from French ethnographers. For Ṣūfī orders, charity represented as much a social as a mystical practice, allowing the redistribution of tribute

64 AGGA 1I/151, Cambon to the General commanding the Division of Algiers, April 20, 1893.

65 AGGA, 16H/44 Jules Cambon, Resident of the French government at Tunis, to M. de Freycinet, President of the Counsel and Minister of Foreign Affairs in Paris, Tunis, May 20, 1882; Duveyrier, "La Confrérie musulmane de Sîdi Mohammed ben 'Ali Es-Senoûsî," 162; see also AGGA, 1I/151, General de Savigne to the General commanding the Division of Algiers, March 1, 1891.

66 French ethnographers occasionally mistook the *qāf* of "Qādiriyya" for the *khā'* of "Khādiriyya," a *ṭarīqa* absent from Algeria.

67 Knysh, *Islamic Mysticism*, 187.

68 On 'Abd al-Qādir's resistance, see Aḥmad Kamāl al-Jazzār, *Mafākhir fī ma'ārif al-Amīr 'Abd al-Qādir wa al-sāda al-awliyā' al-akābir*, intro. by Muḥammad Zakī Ibrāhīm (Cairo: Maṭba'a al-'Umrāniyya l-l-Awfasat, 1997), 31–2; Clancy-Smith, *Rebel and Saint*, 71–2.

(*ziyāra*) and a means of attaining a closer relationship with God. The military ethnographer Lieutenant-Colonel de Lartigue maintained the Qādiriyya concentrated on "philanthropic principles developed to the highest degree without distinction of race nor religion; an ardent charity; a rigourous piety; humility in all instances." Though he overstated the "hysterical practices" in the *zawāyā*, unusual among Algerian Qādiriyya, Lartigue emphasized the philanthropic aspects of the *ṭarīqa*.[69] Ethnographic generalizations about Qādiriyya practices highlight the most beneficent and politically anodyne of their behaviors, portraying the Qādiriyya as altruistic and generous to all, regardless of creed or national identity.

The association of the Qādiriyya, like the Shādhiliyya, with charity testified to the Qādiriyya as a politically quiescent *ṭarīqa*. In one administrator's report, the unnamed author, a functionary in a small city south of Ghardaïa, depicted the trajectory of one female initiate in the order. He described

> the negress Messaouda bent Salem [*sic*], a true sister of charity admirable for her devotion and courage, who goes to families to collect the alms that she consecrates wholly for good works.
>
> This woman told us that she was led to consecrate herself to the duties that she has filled for fifteen years following a dream, in which Sidi Abdelkader el Djilani [*sic*] appeared to her, saying "Messaouda, go serve in my zaouia [*sic*] and you will be healed of your infirmities." She obeyed and the violent pains in her head and heart from which she suffered disappeared almost entirely.[70]

Masʿūda bint Sālim devoted her life to charity, good works, and the service of God; at first glance, she appears to have played little political role in the eyes of the administrator, and in her conversation with the ethnographer-administrator appears to have emphasized the pious aspects of her work.

A closer reading, however, reveals a subtly politicized and unambiguously gendered interpretation of mystically inspired piety. The administrator contended that "[t]he women affiliated to the order of the Kadrya [*sic*] are numerous: it is the preferred order of the fair sex which, being

69 Lt.-Col. de Lartigue, *Monographie de l'Aurès* (Constantine: Marle-Audrino, 1904), 380; Rinn, *Marabouts et khouan*, 75,183; Simian (plagiarizing Rinn?), *Confréries*, 15; AGGA, Oasis//40, anonymous, "Rapport Annuel," 1908. Territories of the South, Territory of the Oases, Annex de Tidikelt.

70 AGGA, 16H/8, anonymous, "Renseignements politiques. État des confréries religieuses musulmanes au 15 juin 1895," Division of Algiers, Subdivision of Laghouat, Circle of Ghardaïa, Annex of El-Goléa, 1895, 33.

also weaker, above all has an interest in protection."[71] In a neat piece of ethnographic synecdoche, Mas'ūda, as part of the Qādiriyya, comes to stand in for both her entire gender and her religious co-adepts. For this administrator, sickly, weak Mas'ūda and her devotion to a life of charity stood in for her order's philanthropic orientation and appeal to women.

The administrator drew a political conclusion from the object-lesson of Mas'ūda bint Sālim. Without further transition, he followed his discussion of the Qādiriyya as the order of choice for the weak and the feminine by excusing the Qādiriyya from the suspicion of any resistance. "[T]he order of the Kadrya [*sic*] is like a true charitable organization and gives no opposition to our government; consequently, it does not deserve to be disturbed and, while surveying it intently to assure that it does not deviate from its maxims, it must be left to freely pursue its religious and humanitarian work."[72] The nameless administrator began with a discussion of one particular woman's spiritual fulfillment and ended with the political implications of an entire cultural trope, creating a chain of causality equating Mas'ūda with charity and the feminine role, and ultimately with the order's political reliability.

Nevertheless, French ethnographers very clearly defined a *spectrum* of behaviors abetting colonial domination. Like many other ethnographers, Louis Rinn observed that the Qādiriyya proved deferential to those in power.[73] The Qādiriyya's participation in armed rebellion seemed distant enough for forgetting, and intervening years of calm succeeded in banishing from French memory thoughts of the Qādiriyya as a foyer of effective resistance.

However, the French did identify one potential threat from their theoretical allies. Presciently comprehending just how disruptive ties to colonial powers proved, many colonial functionaries feared that the order's association with French power diminished its prestige in the eyes of indigenous Algerians, and hence its efficacy as a tool. To cooperate with a non-Muslim occupier undermined the Qādiriyya's popularity, and, in at least one case, a specific act of collaboration precipitated a decline in

71 AGGA, 16H/8, anonymous, "Renseignements politiques," El-Goléa, 1895, 33. Unlike some orders, the Qādiriyya admitted nearly all as members.

72 AGGA, 16H/8, anonymous, "Renseignements politiques," El-Goléa, 1895, 33. See also p. 31; Calderaro, "Beni-Goumi," *Bulletin de la Société de Géographie d'Alger et de l'Afrique du Nord* 9 (1904), 329, and AGGA, 16H/9, "Renseignements politiques. État des confréries religieuses musulmanes au 15 juin 1895," Palikau, June 4, 1895.

73 Rinn, *Marabouts et khouan*, 186. See also AGGA, 10H/22, Governor General to General commanding the Division of Constantine. Service of Native Affairs and of Military Personnel, no 82, "Envoi d'un travail d'hiver"; AGGA, 16H/49, Octave Depont, "Les Tidjânia [*sic*] et leur rôle politique," April 15, 1899.

the *ṭarīqa*'s importance.[74] While the colonial state discriminated against individuals and networks of religious sociability on the basis of their amenability to European bureaucratic practices, many Algerians castigated those who undermined indigenous social, political, and cultural systems through support for the French.

Any form of religious sociability, even innocuous ones, threatened instability. Despite their cooperation, the Qādiriyya nevertheless still required active surveillance, argued one bureaucrat, "as . . . it would suffice [for] one respected moqadem [*sic*] departing from the true doctrine . . . to lead all of the Kadria . . . into an order with idea[s] opposed to our domination."[75] While no longer suspicious of the Qādiriyya for their role in ʿAbd al-Qādir's rebellion, French administrators nevertheless supervised the *ṭarīqa* for signs of imminent collapse – or explosion. Similarly, the avoidance of conflict only deflected the panoptic eye of colonial power; strategies aimed at defusing discord could not wholly erase the stigma attached to religious orders as a whole; as with the Shādhiliyya, the Qādiriyya loomed in ethnography as both aid and enemy. From the perspective of colonial power, the Qādiriyya represented the best elements of a cultural order nevertheless fundamentally unstable, threatening, and dissident.

"The Tijāniyya do not dance"

The Tijāniyya negotiated their association with the French in response to internal political dynamics. Hostile from their inception to the Ottoman Empire,[76] the adepts of the Tijāniyya saw the French as a potential ally in their struggle against both Ottomans and other *ṭuruq*.[77] Through the order's shaykh, Aḥmad al-Tijānī, and in particular through the auspices

74 Rinn, *Marabouts et khouan*, 516–7. AGGA, 16H/8, General commanding the Division of Algiers, "Rapport résumant les faits intéressant les Ordres religieux, les Mosquées ou les Zaouia [*sic*] pendant la périod du 1er juillet au 31 décembre 1898," Algiers, February 9, 1899.

75 AGGA, 16H/8, anonymous, "Renseignements politiques. État des confréries religieuses musulmanes au 15 juin 1895," Laghouat, 1895. Rinn, *Marabouts et khouan*, 200; Camille Sabatier, *La Question du Sud-Ouest*, (Algiers: Adolphe Jourdan, 1881), 72.

76 See Estournelles de Constant, *Congrégations*, 36; Paul Soleillet, *L'Afrique occidentale: Algerie, Mzab, Tidikelt* (Avignon: F. Seguin Aîné, 1877), 52–5; Berque, *L'Intérieur du Maghreb*, 240–82.

77 Louis Petit, *Les Confréries musulmanes*, 2nd edn (Paris: B. Bloud, 1902), 23. On the Tijāniyya and other orders: ADA, 2U/20, Chief of Battalion, Vandenbavière, High Commander of the Circle of Djelfa, to General commanding the Division of Algiers, September 25, 1903; AGGA, 16H/8, Lieutenant [illeg.], "Rapport sur les confréries religieuses musulmanes au 15 juin 1895," Ouargla, May 27, 1895; AGGA, 16H/49, Octave Depont, "Les Tidjania et leur rôle politique," April 15, 1899; Rinn, *Marabouts et khouan*, 420.

9. Aḥmad al-Tijānī and Aurélie Picard, from Elise Crosnier, *Aurélie Picard 1849–1933: première Française au Sahara* (Algiers: Éditions Baconnier, n.d.).

of his French wife Aurélie Picard, the Tijāniyya entered into a close relationship with the French, cemented by decades of cooperation and mutual aid. French ethnographies nevertheless evinced a distinct ambivalence about the Tijāniyya's role in colonial politics. The *ṭarīqa*'s internal tensions, subversive behavior in other colonies, and preponderance in the restive and discontinuously controlled Sahara generated considerable anxiety. Any dissent within organized forms of religious sociability, especially those most closely linked with French rule, threatened the underpinnings of colonial hegemony.

Tijāniyya practices differ significantly from those of most other Ṣūfī orders. Founded in Algeria in 1815, the order aimed at reforming Ṣūfī Islam. Eschewing the ties of fictive kinship implied in the terms *ikhwān* (brothers, siblings) and *akhawāt* (sisters), members of the order, emphasizing the voluntary aspects of Tijānī sociability, referred to each other as *aḥbāb*, friends.[78] The founder elucidated no *silsila*, instead claiming

[78] But cf. p. 61: Duveyrier's experience differed. ADA, 2U/20, [illeg.], "Rapport sur les confréries religieuses," Bou-Saâda, February 11, 1903. More broadly, see Jamil Abun-Nasr, *The Tijaniyya: A Sufi Order in the Modern World* (London: Oxford University Press, 1965), 45, 53.

10. Etienne Dinet, "Terrasses à Bou-Saâda" (n.d.).

direct revelation from God, alienating other orders.[79] Nevertheless, the Tijāniyya enjoyed a reputation as open-minded, just, and tolerant, particularly toward Europeans.[80] Perhaps because of the Tijāniyya's enmity with the Ottomans, the order justified French domination as divinely ordained, a sort of spiritual test of the rejuvenation of Islam in Algeria.[81] One administrator notes that "[t]o receive the dikr [*sic*], the adept must place himself in front of the mokhadem [*sic*] and testify to respect the goods of others, never to lie in any circumstance, and to keep all engagements that he would contract" with others.[82] This portrayal of the initiation inverted precisely the behaviors colonial administrators feared most in their subjects: theft, dishonesty, duplicity. As a result of such inversion, the Tijāniyya came to embody the idea of the "good native."

Hence, French ethnographers and administrators claimed profound knowledge of the Tijāniyya. Government archives recorded the Tijānī

[79] Abun-Nasr, *Tijaniyya*, ch. 2, esp. 29, 34, 37–9; Rinn, *Marabouts et khouan*, 419; Depont and Coppolani, *Confréries religieuses*, 420–1.

[80] Rinn, *Marabouts et khouan*, 75–6. [81] AGGA, 16H/49, Depont, "Les Tidjania."

[82] AGGA 1I/95, anonymous, "Situation des Ordres religieux musylmans dans le Cercle de Boghar,"1883.

dhikr in Arabic.[83] The military officer V. Parisot identified in depth the practices that Tijānī *aḥbāb* used in reciting their rosaries, made up of "600 beads; [the members] can walk, talk, and do whatever they wish while saying their rosary."[84] Like the string of words in the *dhikr*, the string of beads is deceptively simple; it marked various rogations but also identified members by sight, visually conferring the protection of the influential order and safe passage in the Sahara. Henri Duveyrier even received the rosary of the Tijāniyya and status as a (most likely honorary) member for his travels in the Sahara.[85] The *misbaḥa* (rosary) and the *dhikr* represented a passport into the order. Detailed French knowledge may indicate close ties with the order, though it is probably safe to assume that that knowledge, however detailed, was incomplete.

Nevertheless, ethnographers did not hesitate to make authoritative claims about their familiarity with Tijānī practices. Indeed, that presumption of familiarity stifled dissenting information about the Tijāniyya. In a report made as part of the Algeria-wide inquiry into religious orders that served as the fieldwork and notes for the Depont and Coppolani masterwork, *Les Confréries religieuses*, one administrator observed that, among the Tijāniyya, "mystical practices . . . varied little; a general custom practiced in the zaouïas [*sic*] that represent this order . . . is to mingle long days of prayers and devotions with dances and religious singing."[86] Dancing, singing, and even more astonishingly violent acts were integral to the practices of many Ṣūfī *ṭuruq*. Nevertheless, an uncharacteristically stern margin note in the hand of Octave Depont silenced the administrator and explains the passage's absence from *Confréries religieuses*. "The Tidjaniya," Depont noted, "*do not dance*."[87]

But they did. Jamil Abun-Nasr accentuates a long and acrimonious debate of the role of *raqṣ* (dance) and music in the *ḥaḍra*.[88] Because it contradicted French knowledge about the Tijāniyya, Depont censored the text supplied by this particular observer; as Homi Bhabha notes, "the field of the 'true' emerges as a visible sign of authority only after

[83] The Tijānī *dhikr* resembles that of the Ṭayyibiyya; both begin with "Forgive me, God" and end with "There is no god but God"; the Tijānī *dhikr* has only three elements, with the middle one significantly longer than any part of the Ṭayyibiyya *dhikr*, and showing some affinities with that of the Madaniyya. AGGA, 1I/151, anonymous, "Renseignements politiques sur les confréries religieuses musulmanes," Laghouat, June 1895.

[84] Parisot, "Ordres," 567.

[85] Henri Duveyrier, *Les Touareg du Nord: Exploration du Sahara* (Paris: Challamel Aîné, 1864), 309.

[86] AGGA, 16H/9, anonymous, untitled report on religious orders in the Commune mixte of Sedrata, Sedrata, 1895, 11.

[87] AGGA, 16H/9, anonymous, untitled report on religious orders in the Commune mixte of Sedrata, Sedrata, 1895, 11. Emphasis in the original.

[88] Abun-Nasr, *Tijaniyya*, 54–5.

the regulatory and displacing division of the true and the false . . . The acknowledgement of authority depends upon the immediate – umediated – visibility of its rules of recogntion as the umistakable referent of historical necessity."[89] Colonial discourse both does not, as Hammoudi notes, keep its word *and* must simultaneously maintain the semblance of its internal coherence, constantly reaffirming the visibility of the signs it uses as cultural reference. As a direct result, nowhere in *Confréries religieuses* do the Tijāniyya dance. Ethnographers of religion believed the image they had created, made that representation "real" by freezing it in time and perpetuating it in text. This self-reproducing, triumphant supremacy of discourse distinguishes Orientalist writings from other kinds of text.[90] Colonial ethnographers trusted their assumptions more than their evidence. If Salman Rushdie is correct that "[e]verything must be made real, step by step . . . [that] [t]his is a mirage, a ghost world, which becomes real only beneath our magic touch,"[91] – and he is, at least in the world of (post)colonial representation – then Depont proves the greatest conjurer of all, creating and making real out of the ethnographic ether the "Tijāniyya" as the object of a totalizing French knowledge. Colonial ethnography existed to make concrete generalizations about Algerian culture. And so "the Tijāniyya do not dance."

Ethnographers and administrators collected alike their information about the Tijāniyya from two main sources, the shaykh Aḥmad al-Tijānī and his French wife, Aurélie Picard. Though the Tijāniyya proved useful to the French in numerous ways (in particular in serving as a counterbalance to the Sanūsiyya) in the Sahara,[92] it was primarily through the auspices of these two individuals that the French and the Tijāniyya

[89] Bhabha, "Signs Taken for Wonders," 110. [90] Said, *Orientalism*.

[91] Salman Rushdie, *The Ground Beneath Her Feet* (London: Vintage, 2000), 268.

[92] On the construction of the Sanūsiyya as an object of fear and political enmity by the French, see Jean-Louis Triaud's recent *La Légende noire de la Sanûsiyya*. The Gouvernement général in Algiers had an interesting text published (in Arabic) in an attempt to combat "fanaticism" (al-taʿṣṣub): Fonds ministériels, Généralités 305 (1998), Shaykh Sīdī Muḥammad bin Muṣṭafā bin al-Khūja al-Jazāʾirī, *Iqāmat al-Brāhin al-ʿiẓām ʿalā nafī al-taʿʿṣub al-dīnī fī al-Islām* [Great Liturgical Proof of the Rejection of Religious Fanatacism in Islam] (Algiers: Pierre Fontana, 1902); Knysh, *Islamic Mysticism*, 249; Robinson, *Paths of Accommodation*, 145; Triaud, *Légende noire*, 111–12; Depont and Coppolani, *Confréries religieuses*, 441; David A. Robinson, "Conclusion: A Research Agenda," in Jean-Louis Triaud and David A. Robinson, eds., *La Tijâniyya: une confrérie musulmane à la conquête de l'Afrique* (Paris: Karthala, 2000), 502; Abū ʿAbdallah Muḥammad bin Muḥammad bin Yūsuf Sanūsī, *Matn al-Sanūsiyya fī al-tawḥīd: petit traité de théologie musulmane, texte arabe publié par ordre de M. Jules Cambon, Gouverneur Général de l'Algérie, avec une traduction française et des notes par J.-D. Luciani* (Algiers: Imprimerie orientale [note typographic error in the Arabic: for *sharkāya* read *sharqîyya*] Pierre Fontana, 1896). See al-Jazzār, *Mafākhir*, 26–31, a most interesting account with useful references to other Arabic language source material.

interacted. Al-Tijānī manipulated both administrators and rivals. Indeed, reluctant to leave the comforts of home, he proved far more effective at providing information than he did at commanding obedience.[93] Louis Rinn listed Tijānī as one of the religious figures with whom he had "personal relations . . . [that] permitted us to verify and complete information" for *Marabouts et khouan*.[94] Aḥmad al-Tijānī even authored lengthy reports that then circulated among bureaucrats. One such report, "A Descriptive Memoir of the Services Rendered to France by Sidi Ahmed Tijani and of the Manifest Proofs of His Inalterable Loyalty," focused entirely on trumpeting his own loyalty and service to the French, castigating those who opposed his marriage and the Shaykhiyya. He carefully explained the inconsistencies in his colonial service; the administration in 1869–70 had, after all, exiled Aḥmad al-Tijānī to France for his attempts to subvert colonial control.[95]

The eventful summer of 1870 forced Aḥmad al-Tijānī's evacuation to Bordeaux.[96] This exile proved a fateful move for Aḥmad al-Tijānī, for in Bordeaux he met Aurélie Picard. Aurélie Picard had traveled to Bordeaux as a domestic for a wealthy family when she met Aḥmad al-Tijānī. Her father's ill health had prevented him from realizing his dream of raising his family in Algeria, but Aurélie would make the dream of a life there her own, holding fast to it as a refuge from bourgeois tedium. In equal parts ambitious and adventurous, Aurélie Picard saw in al-Tijānī the opportunity for a new life. The actual marriage, however, proved difficult; Governor General Gueydon refused an exemption from the law prohibiting marriages between Muslim men and French women. Refusing to elope, Picard fashioned with Tijānī an ingenious solution:

[93] AGGA, 16H/49, Swiney, General commanding the Division of Algiers, to the Governor General of Algeria, Algiers, January 12, 1882. See also AGGA, 1J/174, Louis Rinn's copy of de la Tour d'Auvergne, "Renseignements fournis par Si Ahmed Tedjini [*sic*] sur le nommé Si Hamou ben Attar, Oukil de la Zaouïa de Tlemcen, ainsi que sur les Mokkadem de son Ordre dans l'Ouest," Médé, June 12, 1880. After the shaykh's death, Octave Depont voiced some suspicions over the depth of Aḥmad al-Tijānī's commitment, openly questioning whether he cleverly manipulated the French while conducting secret arrangements on the side. See AGGA, 16H/49, Depont, "Tidjania," April 15, 1899; cf. AGGA, 16H/49, General Collet Meygret, commanding the Division of Algiers, "Extrait. Division d'Alger. Rapport annuel de 1895, "Algiers, April 14, 1896. On the stipend, see AGGA, 16H/46, anonymous, "Au sujet de Si Ahmed Tedjini," Algiers, October 8, 1881.

[94] Rinn, *Marabouts et khouan*, viii; see also V. Largeau, *Le Sahara algérien: les déserts de l'Erg*, 2nd edn (Paris: Hachette, 1881), 95–6.

[95] AGGA, 16H/49, Aḥmad al-Tijānī, "Mémoire présenté à Monsieur le Gouverneur Général. Mémoire descriptif des services rendus à la France par Sidi Ahmed Tidjani et des preuves manifestes de sa fidélité inaltérable," April 19, 1893. The title reflects what in Arabic al-Tijānī would have considered elegant style.

[96] Rinn, *Marabouts et khouan*, 433; AGGA, 16H/49, Depont, "Tidjania."

no less than Cardinal Lavigerie himself and the grand mufti of Algiers performed two separate ceremonies, spiritually binding the two without either spouse renouncing their respective faiths.[97] From the perspective of colonial authorities, Aurélie Picard and Aḥmad al-Tijānī remained unmarried, a fact waspishly noted in government reports. Some viewed her as uppity, as an unnatural woman whose avarice, love of expensive jewelry, and arrogance did not endear her to colonial officials, despite her commitment to relieving the grinding poverty of indigenous Algerians in the pre-Sahara.[98]

Despite their distaste, administrators had to reckon with her influence. Like Isabelle Eberhardt, she occupied a peculiarly imprecise cultural space: French, but identifying by choice with Algerian Muslims, both Eberhardt and Picard Tijānī threatened the cultural politics of colonialism. Administrators' suspicions grew as Picard Tijānī took over the more mundane operations of the *zāwiya* of ʿAyn Māḍī, while her less organizationally capable husband concerned himself with the Tijāniyya's spiritual direction.[99] Picard Tijānī managed Tijāniyya finances, establishing a farm at Kourdane,[100] site of her 1933 burial in a Muslim cemetery after Catholic last rites.[101] She leveraged her status as a French citizen to procure for the Tijāniyya unique privileges by providing valuable information;[102] arguing that the redistribution of tribute provided a social service, that she and her husband served as agents of propaganda, and that she could deliver the support of the *ṭarīqa*, she convinced

97 Élise Crosnier, *Aurélie Picard 1849–1933: première Française au Sahara* (Algiers: Éditions Baconnier, [1947]), 17, 20, 23, 25–6, 43–4, 51–2, 54; Marthe Bassenne, *Aurélie Tidjani, "Princesse des Sables"* (Paris: Plon, Nourrit, 1925); Jean Déjeux, *Femmes d'Algérie: légendes, traditions, histoire, littérature* (Paris: La Boîte à documents, 1987); AGGA 8X/56, anonymous, "Jurisprudence de la Cour d'Appel en Matière Musulmane. Les Kadis n'ont pas qualité pour procéder au mariage d'un musulmane [*sic*] avec une française," *Le Mobacher*, August 10, 1875. AGGA, 1I/96, General commanding the Subdivision of Médéa to the General commanding the Division of Algiers, "Au sujet de Si Ahmed Tedjini [*sic*]," Médéa, May 19, 1873.

98 Crosnier, *Aurélie Picard*, 111, 117–18, 121.

99 AGGA, 16H/8, "Renseignements politiques, Laghouaṭ, 1895; Oasis//85, "Rapport Annuel. Année 1909," Military Territory of Ghardaïa, Annex of Laghouat, 1910; AGGA, 16H/49, copy of Lt.-Col. De Ganay, "Rapport sur la conduite tenue par le marabout Si Ahmed Tedjani [*sic*] depuis la dernière période insurrectionnelle," Laghouaṭ, April 16, 1887; see Jean Tharaud and Jérôme Tharaud, "Préface," in Crosnier, *Aurélie Picard*, 5–6, and Crosnier, *Aurélie Picard*, 34, 105, on Picard's natural affinity for leadership – and her husband's lack thereof.

100 Abun-Nasr, *Tijaniyya*, 75; Madame Jean Pommerol, *Islam africain: chez ceux qui guettent* (Paris: Fontemoing, 1910), 330; and Soleillet, *Afrique occidentale*, 62, in Abun-Nasr, *Tijaniyya*, 75.

101 Crosnier, *Aurélie Picard*, 146–51.

102 See, for example, AGGA, 16H/46, anonymous, "Au sujet d'un indigène d'Aïn Madhi qui se ferait passer pour le marabout Si Ahmed Tedjini," Oran, February 9, 1881.

French administrators to permit al-Tijānī's travel for the collection of *ziyāra*, a privilege nearly unheard of in colonial Algeria, but one of many similar privileges accorded to Aḥmad al-Tijānī.[103] Aurélie herself even received the *palmes académiques* for her work at Kourdane and for the French.[104]

Not surprisingly, the preponderant role of a French Catholic woman in the Tijāniyya threatened to fracture the order.[105] Aurélie Picard adroitly hustled Aḥmad al-Tijānī's previous wives into seclusion, though not without a spirited fight from her rivals, and had introduced her husband to champagne – though he claimed the miraculous ability to transform it into water before drinking it.[106] In the 1880s and 1890s, a *muqaddim* in Tammasīn chafed under her charismatic economic and political domination, and attempted to claim the title of shaykh.[107] After Aḥmad al-Tijānī's death in 1897, the French colonial administration found a simple way to mitigate these tensions: coercing the remarriage of the economic and spiritual realms through the literal marriage of Aurélie Picard Tijānī and the new spiritual head. The influence of the French woman in the *ṭarīqa* solved numerous problems for administrators: she furnished invaluable information and influenced the politics of the order, but also resolved the potentially dangerous schism (to which she contributed) that developed in an important French ally.

The Tijāniyya appeared compliant in colonial ethnographies because of the influence of al-Tijānī and Picard. In light of their cooperation, Rinn and other ethnographers denigrated the idea of the Tijāniyya as a threat. Other administrators, however, harbored no illusions about the

103 Abun-Nasr, *Tijaniyya*, 76; Crosnier, *Aurélie Picard*, 95–6.

104 AGGA, 16H/52, copy of Secretary-General of the Government M. Vaince for the Governor General to the Minister of Public Education at Paris, "A[u].S[ujet]. d'une proposition pour les palmes académiques faite en faveur de Madame Aurélie Picard," Algiers, March 29, 1906.

105 AGGA, 16H/49, Aḥmad al-Tijānī, "Mémoire présenté à Monsieur le Gouverneur Général. Mémoire descriptif des services rendus à la France par Sidi Ahmed Tidjani et des preuves manifestes de sa fidélité inaltérable," April 19, 1893; see also AGGA, 1I/96, copy, High Commander Paul Flatters to the General commanding the Subdivision of Médéa, "A.S. de la position des frères Tedjini [*sic*]," Laghouat, July 10, 1878.

106 Crosnier, *Aurélie Picard*, 75, 77; AGGA, 16H/8, anonymous, "Renseignements politiques. Etat des confréries religieuses musulmanes au 15 juin 1895," Laghouaṭ, 1895.

107 The French occasionally referred to this rival subsection of the Tijāniyya as the Tijājna. Abun-Nasr, *Tijaniyya*, 78; Robinson, "Conclusion," 500; AGGA, 16H/7, Colas, "Notice sur les ordres religieux"; AGGA, 16H/45, Lt.-Col. P. Paret to the General commanding the Division of Constantine. Batna, May 25, 1895; Depont, "Les Tidjania"; Crosnier, *Aurélie Picard*, 129–45; Depont and Coppolani, *Confréries religieuses*, 426; AGGA, 16H/44, [illeg.] to the Governor General of Algeria, Constantine, March 17, 1883; AGGA, 16H/46, Chief of Battalion Bélin to the General commanding the Subdivision of Médéa, Laghouat, March 26, 1881; anonymous, "Rapport annuel. Année 1911,"Laghouat, 1912, AGGA, Oasis//85.

insurrectionary capacity of the order should the shaykh's allegiances change.[108] Viewing the Tijāniyya's quiescence not as loyalty to the French, but rather as loyalty to Tijānī himself, they implicitly acknowledged that the shaykh's close ties could camouflage alienation and the menace of revolt by blinding administrators to the fundamental nature of the order. Depont and Coppolani remained convinced that, at best, "the temporal and the spiritual occupy the same rank" with the Tijāniyya.[109] Lieutenant Pierre Castel went further, referring to the Tijāniyya as "the most dangerous and the order the most hostile to our domination" in his region.[110] French administrators rooted the primary dangers of the Tijāniyya in internal tensions or imports from elsewhere in Africa.[111] Near Morocco, the Tilimsān Tijāniyya remained particularly closed to the intrusion of colonial administrators, forming the locus of suspicions of rifts in the Tijāniyya as a public peril.[112] Similarly, the governor

108 AGGA, 16H/46, General La Tour d'Auvergne, "Renseignements demandés par lettre confidentielle de Monsieur le Général Commandant la Division d'Alger en date du 2 avril 1880, No. 13, sur les indigènes de la Subdivision de Médéa, affiliés à l'ordre religieux des Tedjadjna et sur les principaux personnages de cet ordre," Médéa, April 11, 1881, undated *copie conforme*; AGGA, 16H/46, General Loysel, commanding the Division of Algiers, to the General commanding the 19th Army Corps in Algeria, Algiers, 17 October 1881. Note also that the shaykh's occasional flirtations with the Awlād Sīdi al-Shaykh (Shaykhiyya) caused considerable concern. Abun-Nasr, *Tijaniyya*, 74; anonymous, "Rapport résumant les résultat des enquietes auxquelles il a été procédé au sujet du projet insurrectionnel organisé par le Nommé Mouley Yacoub ben Mouley el Arbi, pour le compte de l'ordre religieux des Tedjadjna[*sic*], au sujet des agissements du chef et des membres de cet ordre, et enfin au sujet de l'entente qui existe entr'eux et Si Kaddour ben Hamza, chef des Oulad Sidi Cheikh [*sic*] dissidents," Tilimsān, August 26, 1889; AGGA, 16H/9, anonymous, untitled report on religious orders in the Commune mixte of Sedrata, Sedrata, 1895; AGGA, 3X/1 (Personal Papers of Louis Rinn); Maurice Wahl, "Les Congrégations dans l'Islam," *Revue de l'Afrique française*, sixieme année, no. 29 (September 1887) (Paris: Librairie africaine et coloniale, 1887), 289.

109 Depont and Coppolani, *Confréries religieuses*, 421. Doutté echoed their emphasis on the political aspects of the Tijāniyya. Edmond Doutté, *L'Islam algérien en l'an 1900*, Exposition universelle de 1900, Algérie (algiers-Mustapha: Giralt, 1900), 77–8.

110 Pierre Castel, *Tébessa: histoire et description d'un territoire algérien*, vol. I (Paris: Henry Paulin, 1905), 156.

111 On the Tijāniyya in sub-Saharan Africa, see AGGA, 16H/10, [illeg.], "Rapport semestriel sur les confréries religieuses. 1e Semestre 1899," Division of Constantine, Subdivision of Batna, Circle of Touggourt, June 19, 1899; AGGA,16H/45, Governor General of Algeria to the General commanding the Division of Constantine, "Nouvelles en circulations dans le Ksar d'Aïn-Madhi," Algiers, June 19, 1884; AGGA, 16H/51, General Pédoya, commanding the Division of Algiers, to the Governor General of Algeria, September 27, 1899; Robinson, "Conclusion," 499–500; Knysh, *Islamic Mysticism*, 254–5, 263; Robinson, *Paths of Accomodation*, 86. See also the notes written in Louis Rinn's hand in his own copy of *Marabouts et khouan*: AGGA, 16H/2, Rinn, *Marabouts et khouan*, 451.

112 AGGA, 16H/7, Colas, "Notice sur les ordres religieux"; Robinson, "Conclusion," 500; unattributed translation of a letter from Aḥmad al-Tijānī to the Governor General of

general feared the Tunisian Tijāniyya's ties to Pan-Islamism and the Moroccan Tijāniyya's anti-Christian rhetoric.[113] Despite the cooperation of al-Tijānī and Aurélie Picard Tijānī, administrative discourses on the Tijāniyya remained embedded in the larger political context of religious sociability. Even close collaboration and a French director could not mitigate the discursive effects of a dominant political climate that portrayed cultural elements of religion as issues of colonial security.

The menace of reticence

In the far reaches of the Algerian Sahara, a military ethnographer stumbled on an Algerian dressed in a patched, ragged burnous. The thick camel-hair cloak served many uses in the climatic and ecological extremes of the desert, from warmth to improvised bedding, and its condition could speak for the social status of its owner. This tattered burnous, however, misled the Frenchman in the Sahara, for underneath its brown bulk lay an opulent and expensive caftan, insulating the Algerian from the scratchy, coarse camel hair of the outer cloak. This incongruity caught the attention of the ethnographer-colonel, as it enabled him to place the Algerian in a very specific cultural and religious context.[114]

The man wearing the raggedy burnous and elegant caftan belonged to the Darqāwa[115] *ṭarīqa*. Perhaps more than any other order, the Darqāwa embodied the failures of French ethnography as a technology of colonial control. Founded in Fez in 1823 as a ramification of the Shādhiliyya, the Darqāwa aimed to regenerate its parent order, purify it of its perceived decadence, and return Islam to its roots. The founder's reputation for austerity, doctrinal severity, and devotion won him many followers, particularly among the poor.[116] The order rapidly developed practices that

Algeria, September 17, 1881; anonymous, "Rapport résumant les résultats... Oulad Sidi Cheikh dissidents," August 26, 1889; Depont and Coppolani, *Confréries religieuses*, 430–5.

113 On Tunisia and Pan-Islamism: AGGA, 16H/44, Cambon to Freycinet, May 20, 1882; E. Duclerc to Governor General of Algeria, Paris, August 19, 1882 (copy); AGGA, 16H/45, Governor General of Algeria to General Vilmette, Algiers, September 2, 1882; on Morocco: AGGA, 1I/151, Governor General of Algeria to the General commanding the Division of Algiers, Algiers, November 30, 1896.

114 See Colonel Trumelet, *Les Français dans le désert: journal historique, militaire et descriptif d'une expédition aux limites du Sahara algérien* (Paris: Challamel Aîné, 1885), 177.

115 In fuṣḥa, Darqāwiyya; the colloquial, "Dergāwa or Darqāwa." On the Darqāwa in the eighteenth and early nineteenth centuries, see Berque, *L'Intérieur du Maghreb*, 272–82.

116 Knysh, *Islamic Mysticism*, 216, 248; Depont and Coppolani, *Confréries religieuses*, 503; Archives privées, personal papers of Henri Duveyrier, 47AP/5, Archives nationales de France, "Depouillement des manuscrits de M. le colonel Forgemol"; AGGA, 16H/7, Colas, "Notice sur les ordres religieux," 50.

marked it in ethnographic texts as hostile to French domination and generative of dissent. Darqāwī practices embodied, for French ethnographers, not culturally specific, socially embedded expressions of personal and collective piety, but rather politically subversive acts of contestation and conflict.

As a set of behaviors and character attributes, the order's practices readily distinguished its adepts from those of other orders. In addition to the distinctive *dhikr*,[117] the Darqāwa especially emphasized visual markers of affiliation. While every order possessed its unique *misbaḥa*, the Darqāwa developed a far more elaborate system of visual cues, which even extended into written texts. Colas, a near-fluent Arabic speaker and government interpreter, noted that the Darqāwa wrote the name of the prophet Muḥammad in a characteristic way so as to represent the human form. The first *mīm* formed the head, the *ḥā'* the arms, the second *mīm* the torso, and the *dāl* the legs.[118] While this distinctive textual form – the bisection of the *ḥā'* by the axis of writing is highly unusual – may not have been the exclusive preserve of the Darqāwa, Colas and others associated it with the order.

Visual markers extended to Darqāwa adepts' clothing. One military ethnographer, Colonel Trumelet, noted that they "affect the greatest scorn for the things of this world" and singled out their manner of dress as particularly indicative of the order's fundamental anti-materialism. "One recognizes these sectarians by their burnouses in tatters or impossibly patched together, their rosaries with coarse beads, the long staff that they hold in their hands, and a certain affectation in the pronunciation of the guttural letters." Indeed, these outward cues effectively set the Darqāwa apart from other orders. Trumelet went on to note, however, the danger of reliance on appearances as the indication of the rejection of the corporeal world; "very often," he remarked, "the Darqāwī is so only on the surface; we met one in the south who, under his mended burnous, wore a luxurious caftan."[119] For Trumelet, the outward markings of the rejection of materialism embodied not doctrinal adherence or spiritual

[117] See AGGA, 16H/7, Colas, "Notice sur les ordres religieux," 51, 54–5; Rinn, *Marabouts et khouan*, 251–2, 254–5.

[118] AGGA, 16H/7, Colas, "Notice sur les ordres religieux," 49; see also P. Kiva (Lt.-Col. Paul Waché), *En Algérie (Souvenirs)* (Paris: Henri-Charles-Lavauzelle, 1894), 92.

[119] Trumelet, *Français dans le Désert*, 177. Note also that his remark on the pronunciation of the guttural letters may not, in fact, have indicated Darqāwī affiliation, but rather regional or class differences. On the order's distinctive dress: Colonel Corneille Trumelet, *Histoire de l'insurrection dans le sud de la province d'Alger en 1864*, vol. I, 129; G. Salmon, "La kherqa des Derqaoua [*sic*] et la kherq Soûfya," Archives marocaines: publication de la mission scientifique du Maroc 2, no. 1 (1904): 127–43. On class and labor: AGGA, 16H/7, Colas, "Notice sur les ordres religieux," 50.

piety, but rather dissimulation, deceit, and an implied spiritual poverty. Ethnographic discussions of a Ṣūfī order as a cultural object focused on its potential to serve as a pretense for political subversion.

One administrator's ethnographic observations of the order underlined the literal and figurative visibility of the Darqāwa in Algeria. Montière, the administrator of the commune mixte of Renault, in the west of Algeria, paid particular attention to the practices of the numerous Darqāwa in his commune. Enumerating the practices unique to the Darqāwa, he highlighted common prayer at the *zāwiya*, dancing spectacles in public, "demonstration by . . . sustained labor that the affiliate feels no fatigue from the dances or the prayers," and unique manners of dress, greeting, and prayer.[120]

In short, the emphasis on external representations of interior, spiritual states made the Darqāwa easily identifiable to ethnographer-administrators. Because of the order's self-conceptualization as a reform movement rejecting previous, more decadent Ṣūfī *ṭuruq*, Darqāwa adepts, at least in theory, attempted to bring into congruence their spiritual and worldly lives. To take the *wird* of the Darqāwa in colonial Algeria implied both a religious commitment and a commitment to a particular manner of living one's life.

Paradoxically, the Darqāwa remained poorly understood by French ethnographers and administrators. Although most colonial bureaucrats readily identified Darqāwī members, most expressed profound ambivalence about the order's aims. Evinced in dress and practice, the *ṭarīqa*'s cohesiveness proved an effective barrier to French penetration of the Darqāwa's political motives. Such secrecy did not accidentally result from Darqāwī practices; rather, the order demanded very specific relations to temporal authority from its adepts. As a corollary to the *ṭarīqa*'s emphasis on reform, the Darqāwa rejected all forms of temporal political authority. Just as the Darqāwa had fiercely opposed Ottoman hegemony,[121] so Darqāwa adepts refused to participate in colonial governance. As Louis Rinn noted, "[O]ne must never ask the Derqaoua [*sic*] to be the devoted auxiliaries of our political agents . . . we will not succeed in making them actively cooperate in the work of progress and civilization . . . They

120 AGGA, 16H/9, Montière, "Commune-mixte de Renault. Renseignements politiques. État des confréries musulmans au 15 Juin 1895," Renault, June 10, 1895; Alliot to the Prefect of the Department of Oran, "Ordres religieux. Derkaoua," Saïda, January 15, 1895, Archives departementales d'Oran (ADO), 2U/7 (also AGGA, 16H/9).

121 N. Lacroix, *Les Derkaoua d'hier et d'aujourd'hui: essai historique*, Documents pour le Nord-ouest africain (Algiers: Imprimerie administrative Victor Heintz, 1902), 6–7; Rinn, *Marabouts et khouan*, 242–3.

refuse moreover all employment in the administration."[122] Whereas some orders actively resisted or aided French domination, the Darqāwa openly disputed the very foundations of secular governance; the Ottoman and French empires proved anathema to devout Darqāwa.

The Darqāwa's refusal to cooperate deprived French administrator-ethnographers of their main source of information about Ṣūfī politics. Unlike other *ṭuruq*, the Darqāwa furnished the administration with few functionaries. The *ṭarīqa* remained more or less politically indifferent, unlike, for example, the Tijāniyya, Ṭayyibiyya, or Shaykhiyya. Individual members did resist or provide information to the French, but the order as a whole undertook no insurrection. Although the Darqāwa adepts remained readily identifiable, and their more overt practices became common ethnographic knowledge, their distance from colonial politics proved a constant source of concern. The *ṭarīqa*'s impenetrability particularly vexed one administrator, in Saïda.

> What exactly is the goal pursued by the Derkaoua [*sic*]? None of the affiliates with whom I conversed was in a position to inform me... [I]t is revealed only to the initiates of a higher grade. Despite the declarations of the Mokeddems [*sic*] who affirm that their order busies itself but with the prescriptions of religious law, it is beyond doubt that, just as with most of the Muslim orders, they are hostile to our dominion. The doctrine of the Derkaoua teaches, be assured, disobedience to all government whatever it be... [Nevertheless] [t]he attitude of members of this sect certainly gives rise to no unfavorable remark and would not motivate any special measure. They feel themselves strictly monitored and do not gather together as they assuredly used to do in the past.[123]

[122] Rinn, *Marabouts et khouan*, 262; see also Estournelles de Constant, *Congrégation*, 25.

[123] ADO, 24/7, Alliot to Prefect of the Department of Oran, "Ordres religieux. Derkaoua," Saïda, January 15, 1895, pp. 9–11; for other administrators' and ethnographers' similar comments, see also AGGA, 16H/33, "Renseignements individuels pour servir au Recrutement du Personnel Administratif Indigène à la surveillance politique et administrative des populations musulmanes," "Ben Tabet" (Si Abdelouahab Ben Abdelkader) [*sic*], Department of Oran, Mascara, March 10, 1911; AGGA, 16H/9 anonymous, "Renseignements politiques. État des confréries religieuses musulmanes au 15 juin 1895," Commune mixte of Cacherou, June 4, 1895, (on the Habriyya, a closely associated order or subset of the Darqāwa), 31, 33; AGGA, 16H/9; illeg., "Notices détaillées sur les Zaouias... 13 mars 1895 No. 989 (cabinet)," Commune mixte of Hillil, July 4, 1895. AGGA, 16H/33; illeg., "Renseignements individuels pour servir au Recrutement du Personnel Administratif Indigène à la surveillance politique et administrative des populations musulmanes," Confrérie des Derkaouas Hebria [*sic*], Nabi (Hadj Abdelkader ould Elhadj Mostefa [*sic*]), Department of Oran, Commune mixte of Cassaigne, February 10, 1911. illeg., "Renseignements individuels pour servir au Recrutement du Personnel Administratif Indigène à la surveillance politique et administrative des populations musulmanes," Confrérie des Derkaouas, Kherradji (Mohammed) Bouallala Ben Mohammed ben Abdelkader El Kherradji [*sic*], Department of Oran, commune of Tlemcen, June 20, 1900; E. de Neveu, *Les Khouan: ordres religieux*, 3rd edn (Algiers: Adolphe Jourdan, 1913), 121.

The Darqāwa of Saïda responded to the surveillance of the administrator with neither deference, nor cooperation, nor visible defiance. They openly conversed with the administrator, yet prevaricated when asked for details. Although they shared basic facts, they declined to engage in political discussion. With some aggravation he observed that, while the order opposed temporal French authority, their *behavior* offered no particular cause for increased surveillance. Louis Rinn contended that "remoteness from agents of authority is, in effect, the distinctive sign of the derqaoui [*sic*], but, in practice, this remoteness is not at all absolute and in no way has a malevolent character,"[124] noting Darqāwī judges and religious officials, in Saïda and elsewhere. Nevertheless, this distance effectively and *by design* isolated the Darqāwa from French interference. In the case of the Darqāwa, surveillance proved of limited use. From the ethnographic perspective of the colonial state, the Darqāwa remained, paradoxically, known but impenetrable.

This opacity translated into anxieties about the order's political role. In the absence of adequate knowledge, ethnographers interpreted their ignorance as indicative of the *ṭarīqa*'s potential for disruption. One administrator in Cacherou counted the Darqāwa as "not among the less hostile to the French cause. Be that as it may, I could not, despite numerous investigations, obtain the smallest fact . . . that could have a certain importance from a political point of view."[125] As the administrator himself readily admitted, despite his detailed knowledge of their mystical practices and *dhikr*, not one shred of evidence from his informants underpinned his conclusions about the political repercussions of Darqāwa theology. Because of the resulting lack of French familiarity, most ethnographies interpreted the Darqāwa's indifference to worldly power not as a theological imperative, but instead as a pretext cloaking resistance.

No work more contributed to this discursive creation of a threatening Darqāwa than Depont and Coppolani's *Confréries religieuses*. Since they drew upon administrative ethnographers' texts, including those from Saïda, Cacherou, and Hillil, the two depicted Darqāwa reticence as dissemblance, a strategic masking of antipathy to colonial order. Despite the lack of concrete evidence, this reticence may have functioned as resistance but also enacted the Darqāwa's commitment to the necessity of evading worldly corruption. Depont and Coppolani, however, denuded this

124 Rinn, *Marabouts et khouan*, 246.

125 AGGA, 16H/9, anonymous, "Renseignements politiques. État des confréries religieuses musulmanes au 15 juin 1895," Commune mixte of Cacherou, June 4, 1895.

reticence of its spiritual connotations and provided in their place a political agenda.

Thus is, rapidly sketched, the order of these dervishes in rags . . . often presented, with reason, as messengers of instructions tending to cast perturbation in the countries they traverse, or as apostles affecting to preach a complete abstention from the affairs of temporal power. These are the Muslim socialists of North Africa . . . They admit no yoke and are in permanent insurrection against all those who hold power . . .

However, if . . . one yet finds derqaoua [*sic*] disdaining with ostentation honors and riches, we have met them elsewhere as greedy as the other Muslims; under the *khirqa* [robe; lit., rags] of the philosopher, they always hide diplomatic ends aiming only at the overthrow of rulers to substitute themselves for [the rulers] or seeking to reawaken [the rulers'] fanaticism to maintain them [in power] and to direct them toward the will of [the Darqāwa's] ambitions.[126]

Perhaps the Darqāwa did, their anti-materialist doctrines notwithstanding, engage in such politicking; either way, colonial administrators had only suspicions, and little proof. Moreover, the order's disdain for the temporal world makes a sustained effort at political domination unlikely, and Depont and Coppolani cite no evidence for their outlandish claims that the Darqāwa "pursue their work of intellectual obstruction, multiply the number of their affiliates and ceaselessly stir up enemies against us," claims repeated until World War I.[127] What the Darqāwa saw as a

[126] Depont and Coppolani, *Confréries religieuses*, 512–13; see also Depont and Coppolani, *Confréries religieuses*, 261, and AGGA, 16H/8 "Minute de la lettre écrite par M le Gouverneur Général à MM Résident Général [à] Tunis, Consul général de France [à] Tripoli; Ambassadeur [à] Constantinople; Vice Consul [à] Benghazi; Consul [à l'] Egypte; Consul [à] Djeddah; Consul [à] Smyrne." Note James Scott, *Domination and the Arts of Resistance: Hidden Transcripts* (New Haven, Conn.: Yale University Press, 1990), 203: "Any public refusal, in the teeth of power, to produce the words, gestures, and other signs of normative compliance is typically construed – and typically intended – as an act of defiance."

[127] Depont and Coppolani, *Confréries religieuses*, 277; see also AGGA 16H/9, Administrator of Commune mixte of Sebdou [illeg.], "Confréries religieuses: situation au mois de juin 1895," Sebdou, June 28, 1895; AGGA 16H/7, Colas, "Étude," 53; Doutté, *Islam algérien*, 82–4; Lacroix, *Derkaoua*; AGGA, 16H/33, [illeg.], "Renseignements individuels pour servir au Recrutement du Personnel Administratif Indigène à la surveillance politique et administrative des populations musulmanes. 1re catégorie: Confréries religieuses musulmanes (chiouks, mokaddems, marabouts locaux [*sic*])," Confréries des Derkaouas [*sic*], Benzian (Abdelbaki Ben Ahmed), Department of Oran, Douar-Commune of Zemmora, May 5, 1911; AGGA, 16H/9, Prefect of Oran to the Governor General of Algeria, No. 4941, "Confréries religieuses," December 6, 1895; AGGA, 16H/9 anonymous, "Notices détaillées sur les Zaouias, Chioukh et Mokaddem, établies en conformité des instructions contenues dans la dépêche préfectorale du 13 mars 1895 n° 989 (cabinet)," Commune mixte of Hillil, July 4, 1895; AGGA, 16H/9, Alliot, "Renseignements politiques. État des confréries religieuses musulmanes au 15 Juin 1895."

divinely mandated avoidance of worldly corruption marked, in French ethnographies and for the administrators who wrote them, dissimulation.

Hence, the Darqāwa, professedly *indifferent* to politics, served as a locus for French anxieties in politicized ethnography. In such texts, the Darqāwa appeared as dangerous fanatics secretly attempting to overthrow the French. Thus, one of the very few *ṭuruq* to decline political participation became the object of a pervasive, discursive politicization through the medium of the ethnographic text; French ethnographers could not comprehend that the Darqāwa chose *not* to be political, despite their professions to that effect.

Furthermore, Darqāwa adepts' obedience to their *shuyūkh* facilitated comparisons with the Jesuits, projecting the Third Republic's anxieties about Catholicism onto Islam.[128] For one ethnographer-administrator, this obedience implied an especial threat. "The doctrine professed by the Derqaoua [*sic*] is far from being favorable to French domination," though "they would act the same in relation to any other government."[129] Increasing in number, readily identifiable, unified, impenetrable, the Darqāwa not only emerged as a danger but obsessed French ethnographers like no other order, with the possible exception of the Sanūsiyya. An administrator in Hillil described "the members as imbued . . . with egalitarian, antisocial and retrograde ideas liable to pose serious obstacles to the development of modern society."[130] His words, his juxtaposition of adjectives, accentuates the surreal nature of colonial ethnography: through the distorting pen of the ethnographer, the egalitarian, apolitical Darqāwa threaten, antisocially, atavistically, French domination, and indeed the self-deception that was the civilizing mission. Ethnographic inversions made the egalitarian deviant and the apolitical subversive.

"Au coin des rues Diderot et Moïse"

Other ceremonies revolved around the implements of death, whether immediate or lingering. Vipers and iron, fire and poison, knives and hatchets brought with them first a sense of menace, and later spectacle,

128 G. Bonet-Maury, *L'Islamisme et le christianisme en Afrique* (Paris: Hachette, 1906), 241; AGGA, 16H/45, Jules Cambon, to the President of the Council, Minister of Foreign Affairs, Tunis, August 5, 1882 (also 1I/96); Doutté, *Islam algérien*, 82–4.

129 AGGA, 16H/9, Montière, "Commune-mixte de Renault," 1895.

130 AGGA, 16H/9, illeg., "Notices détaillées sur les Zaouias . . . 13 mars 1895 No. 989 (cabinet)," Commune mixte of Hillil, July 4, 1895, AGGA.

and finally menace of a different kind. While the scent of burnt tissue and of warm blood marked for the adepts of the ʿĪssāwa[131] the mortification of the flesh and the pursuit of communion with the divine, it exerted an entirely different pull on the ethnographers, metropolitan tourists, and administrators who watched. Although the order's ecstatic spiritual practices alienated them from other orders,[132] they fascinated the French. In the early 1870s, the ʿĪssāwa practices seemed the embodiment, all the more so because of the violence, of Algerian liminality. The consolidation of French rule transformed not the content of the ceremonies, but rather their context; the danger commodified, the exoticism packaged as ethnographic experience, the ʿĪssāwa developed into an object of tourist fetishization.

By the early 1900s, however, the sense of menace returned, cloaked in the more mundane form of politics. The ʿĪssāwa directed their acts of extreme violence only at their physical selves, yet, at the dawn of the twentieth century, ethnographers deemed them sufficiently threatening to ban their mystical exercises. Thus, the least politically engaged of the Algerian Ṣūfī orders, scorned by other Ṣūfīs, became the only order to have its public practices banned. The history of the ʿĪssāwa follows the transformation of bodily mortification into political subversion, through the means of tourist commodification.

The order originated in Meknes in 1524 from the teachings of Muḥammad bin ʿĪssā, who claimed the divine gift of healing. Evicted from Meknes, the saint and his followers nearly perished of hunger in the desert, until bin ʿĪssā commanded them to eat the snakes, scorpions, and stones before them, which they did, with impunity. He once took forty adherents individually into a house, while the others heard the screams and saw rivulets of blood. In actuality, he had sacrificed sheep and was merely testing his followers' devotion. After the fortieth "sacrifice," he distributed the mutton to the poor. Generating the *ṭarīqa*'s commemorative acts of ritualized violence, these events introduce the charity and poverty for which the order was known in North Africa.[133]

131 Fuṣḥa: ʿĪssāwiyya, French "Aïssaoua." On similar ecstatic practice: Vincent Crapanzano, *The Hamadsha: A Study in Moroccan Ethnopsychiatry* (Berkeley, Calif.: University of California Press, 1973); Depont and Coppolani, *Confréries religieuses*, 367–8; Rinn, *Marabouts et khouan*, 39–40, 120.

132 Rinn, *Marabouts et khouan*, 308–9.

133 Alfred Bel, *L'Islam mystique, suivie de Es-Soût', les dires du prophète* (Mayenne: Imprimerie de la Manutention, 1988 [1928]), 32; Xavier Coppolani, *Confrérie religieuse musulmane de Sidi-Ammar-Bou-Senna ou l'Ammaria en 1893 de notre ère – 1311 de l'hégire* (Algiers: Adolphe Jourdan, 1894), 7; Depont and Coppolani, *Confréries religieuses*, 326, 349–50; G. Delphin, "Les Aïssaoua," in *Oran et l'Algérie: notices historiques, scientifiques et économiques*, vol. I (Oran: Paul Perrier, 1888), 331–6; Edmond Doutté, *Les*

These commemorative and spiritual rituals displayed an unerring sense of the dramatic; they were, above all, sensory exepriences. Music played a crucial part in setting the tone of ʿĪssāwa gatherings. Unfamiliar to French ears, their syncopated percussion and pentatonic scale highlighted the exotic for observers. Ethnographers emphasized music-induced mystical trances in the adherents, connecting their own exoticized experience of the ceremonies with the spiritual contents for the participants.

[I]nvocations are made out loud, on top of a rapid rhythm that supports the musique of the tambourines, and which continues, accelerating, until the excitement and dizziness lead to . . . physical insensibility and cerebral drunkenness favorable to hallucinations, to religious ecstacies and delirium.[134]

Orchestrating their ceremonial brushes with mortality with the otherworldly sounds created an hallucinatory environment for adepts and observers.

Scent also facilitated mystical ecstasy. The perfume of incense, the sharp, metallic smell of glowing iron, the acrid smoke, the stench of charred flesh, the dry dustiness of the reptiles could only have enhanced the disquieting strangeness of the displays.[135] To this sensory background the ʿĪssāwa set their ferocious displays. Amidst this raucous and fragrant tumult, the ʿĪssāwa strove for union with God with a single-minded doggedness. They

play with the serpents that they place on their chest, in their mouth [*sic*], or with which they make a turban; others pierce the hand with a well-sharpened sword, or seize with their teeth a red-hot iron over which they pass the tongue; several vociferate their savage melodies . . . they all begin to dance, turning around each other like dervishes, grimacing, contorting themselves . . . to the sound of the music that began to crescendo, to the point of falling into epilepsy and rolling on the ground, foaming at the mouth, and [with] all limbs writhing in a horrifying manner.[136]

For French ethnographers steeped in both antipathy to superstition and colonial anxieties about Islam, ʿĪssāwa ceremonies appeared threateningly atavistic. Snake-handling particularly impressed French observers,

Aïssâoua, à Tlemcen (Châlons-sur-Marne: Martin frères, 1900), 21, 23; Petit, *Confréries musulmanes*,19–20; Rinn, *Marabouts et khouan*, 40, 304–7; Louis Régis, *Constantine: voyage et séjours* (Paris: Calmann Lévy, 1880), 15–16.

134 Rinn, *Marabouts et khouan*, 329.

135 A. Certeux and E. Henry Carnoy, *L'Algérie traditionnelle: légendes, contes, chansons, musique, mœurs, coutumes, fêtes, croyances, superstitions, etc.*, vol. I: *Contributions au folklore des Arabes* (Paris: Maisonneuve et Leclerc, 1884), 142; Régis, *Constantine*, 14; Henri Dumont, *Alger: Ville d'hiver, notes de voyage* (Paris: Berger-Levrault, 1878), 105.

136 Arthur-Alexandre Behaghel, *L'Algérie: conquête et colonisation, religion et mœurs, armée* (Paris: E. Dentu, 1870), 315.

especially when the vipers and asps appeared to perform tricks on cue, or lunged at the audience.[137] ʿĪssāwa brothers and sisters[138] ate scorpions and nails and glass, walked on sharpened sword blades, performed gravity-defying gyrations, slashed their throats or stomachs. They chewed protruberant, spiny cactus leaves, ripped the flesh from live animals' bodies and ate it, bloody and raw.[139]

The charismatic rituals of the ʿĪssāwa drew the attention of colonial ethnographers. Edmond Doutté's 1900 ethnography, *Les Aïssâoua à Tlemcen*, reflected his preoccupation with ritual and superstition in the history of religions. For Doutté, ʿĪssāwa ceremonies offered an ideal opportunity to put into analytical practice his theoretical approaches to the understanding of religious praxis, analyzing religious rituals as culturally embedded expressions of piety. Thus, while Doutté did not ignore the *ṭarīqa*'s riotous practices, his ethnography accentuated smaller details. A fluent Arabic speaker, he comprehended the sense where others heard only raucous cries, resolving them into *ya Allah* (O God) *Muḥammad ḥabīb Allah* (Muḥammad is the friend / beloved of God).[140] Out of the static, the clamor that other ethnographers heard, Doutté understood meaning.

Through *Aïssâoua*, Doutté related his observations to larger strands within the anthropology of religion. Despite his inextricable relationship with colonial institutions, he understood ethnographic texts as scholarship. More importantly, he explicitly situated his work and analyses within the context of early theories. Singling out of the ʿĪssāwa procession performers dressed as or interpreting animals, such as camels, he reflected early ethnographers' nascent interest in totemism.[141] For Doutté, the *ṭarīqa* represented the ideal opportunity to explore, in a practical environment and through the means of his fieldwork, his own theoretical interests.

Doutté attempted to relate the ʿĪssāwa to other Ṣūfī *ṭuruq*. Uniquely among colonial ethnographies, his *Aïssâoua* paid especial attention to other orders' views on the ʿĪssāwa. During his fieldwork with the *ṭarīqa*,

> We were overtaken by the two processions of the members of the order of the Qâdriyya [*sic*] and the T'ayyibiyya [*sic*]; the Aïssâoua members draw aside to let

[137] J. Canal. *Oudjda: la frontière marocaine. 1885* (Oran: Paul Perrier, 1886), 46.

[138] On female adherents: Depont and Coppolani, *Confréries religieuses*, 353, in Doutté, *Aïssâoua*, 16 n.4.

[139] Parisot, "Ordres," 569; Certeux and Carnoy, *L'Algérie traditionnelle*, 143; Doutté, *Aïssâoua*, 7–8; Petit, *Confréries musulmanes*, 19–20. On colonial ethnography's overemphasis of the hysterical among the ʿĪssāwa: Andezian, *Expériences du divin dans l'Algérie contemporaine*, 112.

[140] Doutté, *Aïssâoua*, 8.

[141] Doutté, *Aïssâoua*, 7–9.

them pass; the moqaddem [*sic*] of each order embrace each other. Is it an illusion? . . . we see in the eyes of several members of these two other orders a somewhat disdainful look for their Aïssâoua brethren . . . probably too the Qâdriyya and the T'ayyibiyya, generally the most learned, scorn somewhat the Aïssâoua because of the rude practices and the gymnastic tricks.[142]

Doutté addressed the ʿĪssāwa's strained ties with other orders, introducing questions of authority and subversion: it is no accident that he mentioned the "most learned" Qādiriyya and Ṭayyibyya, among the most cooperative Algerian *ṭuruq*. Most importantly, the passage indicates Doutté's interest in the comparative analysis of religious behavior and its larger implications on colonial life. His equation of ʿĪssāwa practices with those of *ṭuruq* elsewhere re-situates these spectacles within the context of larger studies of Islamic mysticism.[143] Adopting the perspective of a comparative history of Islam, Doutté's ethnography reincorporated the seemingly aberrant ʿĪssāwa into discourses on the Qādiriyya, Ṭayyibiyya, and other Ṣūfī orders.

Ethnographic interest in the ʿĪssāwa generated tourist interest. As a result, ʿĪssāwa ceremonies became, throughout the 1890s, more spectacles than demonstrations of religious faith. After attending the *ṭarīqa*'s spectacles, tourists tended to portray the ʿĪssāwa as *emblematic* not only of Islamic mysticism, but of Algeria. Indeed, attendance at an ʿĪssāwa spectacle reduced Algerian exoticism into a single, commodified event. Dr. Amédée Maurin, one of the seemingly endless parade of winter tourists, exemplified the ʿĪssāwa's enactment of the colonial exotic, remarking that "these soirées are indescribable, and if we have tarried sometimes in these bizarre scenes, it was so as not to remain estranged from the intimate details of the oriental life."[144] He described the ʿĪssāwa ceremonies as "a symbol incomprehensible for the Europeans,"[145] yet made sense of this symbol by reducing it to an Orientalist cliché.

Few travelers failed to observe the ʿĪssāwa's unusual ceremonies. With exasperation, Doutté contended that "there is no tourist who, having visited Algeria or Tunisia, did not attend their strange exercises," and that tourists had bastardized their content, with the exception of those he observed in Tilimsān.[146] The ʿĪssāwa defined the Algerian experience

[142] Doutté, *Aïssâoua*, 9; Edmond Doutté's *Missions au Maroc: En Tribu* (Paris: Paul Geuthner, 1914), 426.
[143] Doutté, *Aïssâoua*, 24–5.
[144] Dr. Amédée Maurin, *La Saison d'hiver* (Paris: G. Masson, 1874), 179.
[145] Maurin, *Saison*, 179.
[146] Doutté, *Aïssâoua*, 5. Travel writers' descriptions do not differ substantively from those of ethnographers: Viscount Félix Augustin de Pulligny, *Six Semaines en Algérie*, new edn (Paris: Canson, 1884), 25–8; Charles Barbet, *La Perle du Maghreb (Tlemcen): visions et*

for French tourists, a synecdoche in which the ecstatic, violent, mystic practices of the order embodied the exoticism and difference of the colony.

At the center of this process of synecdoche lies a transformation: the increasing vogue for colonial travel during the early Third Republic converted the ethnographer's participation in and observation of the ʿĪssāwa into the commodified spectacle of the tourist. As travelers sought out in the ʿĪssāwa an ostensibly "authentic" experience, they simultaneously created an ethnographically oriented theater of tourism. Chimerical though this search for authenticity was, the Orient required physical representation to the traveler. Tourists and travel writers came to Algeria in search of the exotic, and found it among the ʿĪssāwa.

The ʿĪssāwa ceremony as theater is not metaphorical. Rather, ʿĪssāwa adepts and tourists participated together in ethnographic performance, transforming religious rituals into rituals of earthly power and representation. The ʿĪssāwa embraced the institutions of the *fin de siècle* spectacle, of the modern theater, welcoming European observers as a means of making money. Henri Dumont attended his first spectacle after the approach of an adept advertising the event in the local patois.[147] Through advertisement and word of mouth, the ʿĪssāwa encouraged European tourists and their donations. They even participated in the Colonial Exposition of 1889, where they left such an indelible mark that, in 1895, one journalist appealed to memory of their performance to explain Ṣūfism.[148]

As another travel writer, J. Rosier, witnessed, advertising marked only one element more often associated with professional entertainment than with Islamic mysticism. In contrast to the raucous, eerie procession in Doutté's *Aïssâoua*, the ceremony Rosier attended seemed orderly. The ʿĪssāwa rituals had become ritualized again, not as spiritual ceremonies, but as commercial ones: Rosier, guided by an administrator friend named Cherbonneau, arrived at a rented hall, took his appointed chair in the audience, and awaited the performers. At the appointed time, the ecstatic practices began. Cherbonneau counseled Rosier to "[be] patient; the actors that you look for, are behind you and perhaps [will] touch you; only, instead of waiting for the signal of *trois coups* as in our theaters, they wait for the inspiration or rather the presence in their bodies, of the

croquis d'Algérie (Algiers: Imprimerie algérienne, n.d. [1907]), 65–9, 121–4; Bernard, *L'Algérie qui s'en va*, 338–49; Canal, *Oudjda*, 42–6; Mme. A. Gaël, *En Algérie* (Paris: Librairie centrale des publications populaires, 1881), 60–6; Albert Laporte, *Souvenirs d'Algérie* (Paris: Théodore Lefèvre, 1882), 59–65.

147 Dumont, *Alger: ville d'hiver*, 100–1.

148 AGGA, 16H/8, F. Polvère, "Les Khouans [*sic*] d'Algérie," *Petit Marseillais*, February 12, 1895.

Spirit who must make them move."[149] Cherbonneau and Rosier expressly equated the ʿĪssāwa spectacle with the theatrical experience, with the caveat that the ʿĪssāwa "actors" took stage direction from divine inspiration. The otherworldly ʿĪssāwa procession of Tilimsān has vanished. In its place came ethnographic theater in the round, rituals conducted by appointment with God and advertised by street hawkers.

Advertisement and rented space do not guarantee an attentive audience, however, and Rosier and another companion quickly tired of the gyrations and dancing. They made a move to leave, but Cherboneau restrained them. "[Y]ou asked me to see the Aïssaouas, you will see them through and through . . . one cannot leave now, we would be poorly judged. These worthy people would figure that it is fright and not disgust that drives us away."[150] Even the theater of the ethnographic had its own peculiar etiquette, one that revolved around not evincing any kind of weakness in the face of the performers. Tourist-ethnographers did not focus on the spiritual professions of the ʿĪssāwa. Rather, they interpreted them as a kind of performative challenge, a stylized defiance that played out on stage. Travel literature reduced the ʿĪssāwa to an exoticized commodity, denigrating religious beliefs of the *ṭarīqa* by transforming them into a litmus test for French stoicism and power.

The French colonial government in Algiers not only knew about ʿĪssāwa spectacles but promoted them as tourist attractions. With administrators or their spouses, visiting dignitaries participated in ʿĪssāwa rites as a packaged Orientalist miniature. In Algeria for a conference, the Viscount Félix de Pulligny attended an ʿĪssāwa meeting put on especially for the attendees at the request of the mayor of Algiers; usually, according to the viscount, such ceremonies took place only once a week, and those wishing to attend made preparations in advance.[151]

Perhaps the most interesting of such spectacles occurred in the presence of no less than Madame Jules Cambon, wife of the famous governor general. Paul Eudel, a prolific travel writer, was yet another winter tourist, profiting from the Mediterranean climate of the littoral. Madame Cambon arranged for Eudel's attendance and accompanied him; the projected line-up was so lavish that Eudel "doubt[ed] that all the numbers of the program would be" performed. The evening proved his fears unfounded; when one ʿĪssāwī ate a scorpion numerous women in the audience fled.[152] The colonial government perceived the ʿĪssāwa spectacles as

149 J. Rosier, *Souvenirs d'Algérie* (Paris: Delhomme et Briguet, 1892), 259–61; see also Gaël, *En Algérie*, 63.

150 Rosier, *Souvenirs*, 262.

151 de Pulligny, *Six Semaines*, 114.

152 Paul Eudel, *Hivernage en Algérie* (Paris: Hérissey et Fils, 1909), 50–5; see also Laporte, *Souvenirs d'Algérie*, 59.

representative enough to organize them as a special event for an important scholarly conference, or to use them to honor a particularly distinguished visitor. Despite other *ṭuruq*'s antipathy toward colonial society, the ʿĪssāwa cared little for privacy.

The cultural analysis of the ʿĪssāwa undertaken by Doutté and the commodified ethnographic theater sought out by tourists embodied only two of the myriad anthropological approaches to ecstatic mystical practices. Lucien Rabourdin, professor of political economy and member of various anthropological and geographical societies, perceived in the ʿĪssāwa rituals a challenge to the positivism of the nascent human sciences. While Doutté considered the ʿĪssāwa from the perspective of the cultural history of religions, and tourists saw the *ṭarīqa* as the epitome of Algerian exoticism, Rabourdin's perspective was decidedly neurological. In essence, his ethnography of Algeria attempted to link the cultural expressions of the ʿĪssāwa with physical attributes of the body and structural elements of the mind.[153] In the process, Rabourdin contributed to the politicization of ʿĪssāwī practices: his reduction of their rituals into pathology facilitated their concomitant transformation into demonstration of the potential for subversion. Rabourdin divided the rituals into discrete events, "composed with veritable science," aimed at achieving specific medical states of delirium and alienation from consciousness.

> They lead themselves little by little to nervous crisis by a swaying . . . of the body and of the head; . . . the faces bunch up and contract, the eyes are slightly convulsed, the singing of the psalms is now but a series of cries, of hoarse, hurried barks, and hysterical vertigo begins to make all these naked chests pant. But, under these conditions, exhaustion would come before the crisis. Also movement slows, in a manner so as to rest, while maintaining the effect already produced, and this easily managed succession of violent enthusiasm and relative repose, during which the nervous state acquired is preserved, perforce acts on all temperaments.[154]

While some adepts flinched during self-mortification, "behind these standard-bearers . . . the mass of the faithful . . . truly fall into [a state of] anesthesia and often also into hysterico-epileptic convulsions." For Rabourdin, the ʿĪssāwa benefited from a self-induced trance state that accorded them insensitivity to physical suffering.[155] His medical

[153] On neurology: Doutté, *Aïssâoua*, 26; Delphin, "Les Aïssaoua," 330, 338; Commandant de Pimodan, *Oran. Tlemcen. Sud-Oranais (1899–1900)* (Paris: Honoré Champion, 1902), 140–2.

[154] Lucien Rabourdin, *Algérie & Sahara* (Paris: Challamell Aîné/ Guillaumin, 1882), 85. Interestingly, other ethnographers remarked upon the ʿĪssāwa's reputation as both spiritual and medical healers. See Rinn, *Marabouts et khouan*, 331.

[155] Rabourdin, *Algérie & Sahara*, 87–92.

diagnosis – a medical diagnosis from a professor of political economy – reduced ʿĪssāwa rites to bodily mechanisms; marshaling the resources of nineteenth-century positivist human science, Rabourdin successfully transformed the exotic rites of the ʿĪssāwa and relegated mystics to the status of bodily curiosities, neurological freaks.

Lucien Rabourdin did so for a very specific purpose. For him, the ʿĪssāwa "was perhaps of all the Muslim sects the most fanatical as well as the most dangerous for Christians."[156] Just as his positivist explanation denied the spiritual elements of ʿĪssāwa practice, his interpretation of the ʿĪssāwa as a political entity arose out of anxieties about religion. "Bound together by secret signs . . . , bent under the yoke of a passive obedience to . . . their priests [*prêtres*; note word choice], they are all the more frightening as the exercises to which they deliver themselves up . . . lead them to disregard pain, as they think they can brave with impunity fire, iron and poison."[157] Rabourdin's language of the sciences of mind and body addressed the cultural and political challenges posed by the ʿĪssāwa. Through the medium of ethnography, explanations of the corporeal offered a means of combating the seemingly anti-republican and anticolonial threat of Islamic mysticism.

Throughout the 1880s and 1890s, ethnographers, tourists, and administrators began to see the ʿĪssāwa less in terms of religion than artifice, dismissing ʿĪssāwa practices as mere *jongleries*,[158] as ethnographic parlor tricks. While Rabourdin used quasi-scientific theories of the body–mind interaction, others contented themselves with dismissing the ʿĪssāwa as fakes without explanation.

For many ethnographers, the artifice of the superstitious mysticism of the ʿĪssāwa was self-evident in the context of the Third Republic secularism. The tourist Henri Drouët perceived the ʿĪssāwa as fakes, as entertainers rather than mystics: "performers of rather vulgar tricks . . . jugglers and magicians, nothing more."[159] While Drouët gave no cause for their decadence, Rosier did. "Unfortunately for them," he noted, "this tradition and its veracity have been weakened by the frequency of their testing . . . They are adroit jugglers and nothing else."[160] The incessant repetition of the spiritual tests – in tourist ceremonies – stripped the rites of their mystical meaning, of authenticity. For Drouët and Rosier, performance for a European audience transformed the ʿĪssāwa from exemplars of the exotic into charlatans, living testaments to colonial bastardization.

156 Rabourdin, *Algérie & Sahara*, 88 n.1. 157 Rabourdin, *Algérie & Sahara*, 88 n.1.
158 Literally, juggling; chicanerie, charlatanism.
159 Henri Drouët, *Alger et le Sahel* (Paris: Hachette, 1887), 130.
160 Rosier, *Souvenirs*, 265.

The colonial search for ethnographic authenticity culminated with the relegation of the ʿĪssāwa to the realm of the no-longer-authentic. The ʿĪssāwa no longer embodied the exotic Orient, and had become mere performers, impostors. The ethnographies that portrayed an ʿĪssāwa decline into artifice bears the unmistakable taint of salvage ethnography, expressing French anxieties about the consequences of colonization without actually desiring to halt its march. "This order loses . . . every day its true character to transform itself into a school for jugglers or fetishists," lamented one administrator.[161] This ethnographic nostalgia for a vanishing and nonexistent authenticity betrays colonial equivocation. In reality, Drouët or Rosier or the unnamed administrator regretted what they perceived as the loss of the picturesque, not the philosophy of destruction and replacement underpinning empire.

Ethnographers did not solely depict ʿĪssāwa rites as anthropological curiosity, clinical object, or mark of authenticity. For some, the ʿĪssāwa represented another Ṣūfī danger to French governance. Although they did not participate in colonial politics and joined no uprisings, the ʿĪssāwa nevertheless threatened, at least in ethnography, the underpinnings of colonial society. The extremity of the rituals exacerbated French fears; ʿĪssāwa adepts in the middle of their spiritual communion "are no longer human beings, but veritable demons possessed of a furious madness."[162] Others saw the *ṭarīqa*'s transience and marginality as potentially disruptive. Madame Gaël identified in the peripatetic ʿĪssāwa whose performances she attended the dissemination of nefarious plots.

> According to the most credible opinion, this sect hides, under a religious exterior, a political goal to which only the principal leaders hold the secret . . . By the intermediary of the Aïssaouas, the Muslim priests or marabouts can easily entertain relations from one end of the coast to the other . . . to call the fanaticized populations . . . to a holy war against the *Roumis* [the Christians].[163]

Others shared Gaël's rather incredible claim; in 1882, Governor General Tirman received warnings from the French representative in the Arabian Peninsula (where there were few ʿĪssāwī outside of the ḥajj) of ostensible ties between the ʿĪssāwa, Qaïrouan, and a mysterious secret

[161] AGGA, 16H/9, Administrator [illeg.], "Renseignements politiques. État statistiques et notices détaillées sur les confréries religieuses musulmanes au 15 juin 1895. (Exécution de la riculaire Préfectorale du 13 Mars 1895. N° 989. Cabinet)," Department of Oran, Arrondissement of Tlemcen, Commune mixte of Aïn-Fezza, June 8, 1895, 11. cf. Rinn, *Marabouts et khouan*, 303–4, 328–9; Paul Bert, *Lettres de Kabylie: la politique algérienne* (Paris: Alphonse Lemerre, 1885), 25.

[162] Certeux and Carnoy, *L'Algérie traditionnelle*, 142.

[163] Gaël, *En Algérie*, 52–3. Emphasis in the original.

society.[164] Depont and Coppolani depicted the order's cohesion and ties to Morocco as distinctly troubling.[165] Difficult though it may seem to imagine in fire-eating the transmission of messages (the content unknown even to the performers), administrators and ethnographers created a reality in which religious display, and particularly rites as foreign as those of the ʿĪssāwa, coded for political dissent.

Hence, as early as 1881, the colonial administration had banned *foreign* Muslims from charming snakes or performing musically in public. The edict prosecuted mostly Moroccans and probably aimed at limiting contact between Algerian ʿĪssāwa and the *ṭarīqa*'s headquarters in the kingdom.[166] By 1906, the tourist spectacles proliferated to such a degree that the Prefect of Oran, the department closest to the Moroccan border, demanded a total prohibition of ʿĪssāwa practices. The governor general, however, demurred, declining to ban the ceremonies entirely in favor of the cessation of the *public* displays of "grotesque and repugnant spectacles."[167] Thus, the French administration, "considering that the external practices of the Muslim sect of the Aïssaoua [*sic*] constitute, by reason of their repugnant character, manifestations of a nature to trouble public tranquility," officially extended the prohibition to Algerian, as well as foreign, ʿĪssāwa. They prohibited public displays and required governmental approval for private ceremonies, which, to facilitate French surveillance, took place at prearranged times and places.[168] In the eyes of administrators, the shocking displays of the ʿĪssāwa menaced public order and hence demanded a political response.

The response they crafted achieved the goals the colonial administration had set out for it. Eliminating the public elements of ʿĪssāwa performances prevented the adepts from testifying to the greatness of Sīdī ʿĪssā. As a result, the number of those following the ʿĪssāwa *ṭarīqa* seems to have fallen in the years after the 1906 prohibition. In 1907, the Oranais witnessed a few naturalized ʿĪssāwa attempting to assert their rights as

[164] AGGA, 1H/84, Suret, Vice-Consul of France in Jeddah, to M. de Freycinet, President of the Council, Minister of Foreign Affairs in Paris, May 19, 1882; Archives privées, personal papers of Henri Duveyrier, 47AP/5, Archives nationales de France, "Depouillement des manuscrits de M. le colonel Forgemol."

[165] Depont and Coppolani, *Confréries religieuses*, 351–2.

[166] AGGA, 9H/9, Governor General Tirman, "Circulaire No. 13. Mesures à prendre contre les Musulmans d'Algerie ou étrangers exerçant les professions de musicien, bateleur, chanteur[,] charmeur de serpents, vendeur d'amulettes," Algiers, July 22, 1882; AGGA, 9H/4, "Instructions du Gouverneur Général, 25 Janvier 1895."

[167] ADO, 2U/6, Governor General of Algeria to the Prefect of the Department of Oran, Algiers, February 1, 1906.

[168] ADO, 2U/6, Copy: Prefect of the Department of Oran, "Arrêté," May 30, 1907. ADO, 2U/6, Secretary-General of the Government, for the Governor General, to the Prefect of Oran, Algiers, April 29, 1907.

French citizens by continuing their public rites. The decree, after all, only forbade *Algerian* ʿĪssāwa, not French citizens, from engaging in the ceremonies. The prefect and governor rapidly disabused these hardy souls of their notion that French law applied equally to all citizens; the intent of the law aimed at punishing a cultural group (the ʿĪssāwa), and not delineating rights for a legal identity.[169] Elsewhere, however, the decree immediately diminished the *ṭarīqa*'s vitality. Even in Tilimsān, where Doutté reveled in what he interpreted as the most vital ʿĪssāwa rites, participation declined in the eleven months after the decree's issue, albeit with a renaissance in 1913.[170] Lest the French adminstration acquire a reputation for laxity, in 1912 they thoroughly policed the decree in the Oranais, shuttering a "Moorish café" for three months for having permitted an ʿĪssāwī French soldier to dance on the premises.[171]

Through the 1906 decree, the colonial administration in Algeria managed only to diminish the importance of perhaps the most politically anodyne Ṣūfī *ṭarīqa*. Louis Rinn numbered the ʿĪssāwa among most compliant *ṭuruq*.[172] Openly hostile *ṭuruq* remained untouched, primarily because of the inefficacy of colonial cultural politics, while the French antagonized[173] the previously more-or-less quiescent and marginalized ʿĪssāwa. Little given to political demonstration, the ʿĪssāwa nevertheless suffered the greatest from French rule.

169 ADO, 2U/6, Governor General to the Prefect of Oran, "Fêtes indigènes. Aïssaoua [*sic*]," Algiers, May 25, 1907.

170 AGGA, 16H/5, Administrator [anon.], "Rapport sur les confréries religieuses musulmanes dans les Communes de plein exercice de l'Arr de Tlemcen. Exécution des prescriptions de la Circulaire de M. le Gouverneur Général en date du 7 Août 1906," Tilimsan, January 15, 1907; AGGA, 16H/5, Administrator attached to the Sub-Prefecture of the Department of Oran [anon.], "Rapport sur les confréries religieuses musulmanes des Communes de plein exercice de l'arrondissement de Tlemcen. 2e semestre 1913," Tilimsân, February 19, 1914. Doutté himself noted the passing of the decree in Edmond Doutté, *Magie et religion dans l'Afrique du Nord* (Algiers: Adolphe Jourdan, 1909), 483. On tourism's effects on the ʿĪssāwa: AGGA, 16H/5, Assistant Administrator [anon.], "2e semestre 1913. Rapport sur les faits intéressant les zaouias et les confréries religieuses," Clinchant, Commune mixte of la Mina, December 31, 1913.

171 AGGA, 16H/5, administrator seconded to the Sub-Prefecture of Mascara [anon], "Rapport sur les confréries religieuses musulmanes des Communes de plein exercice de l'Arrondissement de Mascara. 2e semestre 1912," Department of Oran, Mascara, December 31, 1912; ADA 2U/21, Administrator of the Commune mixte of Beni-Mansour [illeg.], "Rapport sur les Confréries religieuses. 2e sémestre 1914," Department of Algiers, Commune mixte of Beni-Mansour, Maillot, January 7, 1915.

172 Rinn, *Marabouts et khouan*, 109, 332–3; AGGA, 16H/7, Division of Oran, Subdivision of Tlemcen, Colas, *Notice sur les ordres religieux* (1884), 95.

173 Pierre Castel warned that intervention would incite resistance. See Castel, *Tébessa*, vol. I, 159–60.

The true magicians of colonial Algeria were not the adroit performers of the ʿĪssāwa ceremonies, but the ethnographers who described them. In writing, they conjured up a cultural system that justified the political order in which they had insinuated themselves; an ʿĪssāwa made real as a political threat through ethnographic codification buttressed authoritarian colonial politics by providing the pretext for intervention. That intervention came in the form of the colonial government's prohibition of public enactment of ʿĪssāwa ceremonies. The ʿĪssāwa's political apathy allowed the partial prohibition: a more politically connected *ṭarīqa*, such as the Tijāniyya, or openly hostile one, such as the Sanūsiyya, could have brought to bear more effective pressure. The expressly apolitical ʿĪssāwa, impoverished and frequently shunned by other Algerians, formed an easy target for the French.

From the perspective of colonial authority, the ʿĪssāwa, whose performances first embodied the exotic, dangerous, and liminal Orient for so many tourists and ethnographers, came to represent a more sinister, politicized Orient. After 1907, the *ṭarīqa* came to exemplify for the French yet another Orient, a performative, colonized Orient stage-managed into closing the show. Driven underground (or, rather, inside), their numbers (ostensibly) diminished, their (imaginary) menace dissipated, the ʿĪssāwa faded from the minds of most ethnographers. After first making the ʿĪssāwa real for Europeans as tourist spectacle and Orientalist stereotype, ethnographies imagined the ʿĪssāwa out of European reality, banishing them to the realm of threats restrained. The ʿĪssāwa continued in their beliefs and rites, honoring the memory of their founder and testifying to the greatness and compassion of God. In private, their rituals persist, most notably in Tilimsān and, ironically, Aix-en-Provence, the home of the colonial archives.[174] During the colonial period, the ethnography of the ʿĪssāwa revolved less around the order itself and more around constantly varying the discursive reconfigurations through which the French administration made sense of the *ṭarīqa*'s behavior.

The ethnography of the ʿĪssāwa illustrates both the fundamental methodological unity and contradictory conclusions of French texts on Ṣūfism. Underpinning ethnographies of religion lay a belief that the nascent social sciences could abet the colonial project; simultaneously, however, the resulting studies often led to conflicting conclusions and internal contradictions. Nowhere are such contradictions as evident as in ethnographies of the ʿĪssāwa. At the most basic level, these ethnographies

174 Andezian, *Expériences*, 33, 114, 177; cf. Émile Dermenghem, "J'ai vu les Aissaouas [*sic*] d'Afrique du Nord jouer mystiquement avec le fer et avec le feu," *Sciences et voyages*, February 1949, 37–41.

struggled to reconcile lavish, ecstatic religious practices with an intellectual and political climate that often dismissed religion as pretext for dissent, as both camouflage and catalyst for rebellion.

Ethnographies of the ʿĪssāwa perforce situated themselves at the crossroad of republican debates and rapidly changing conceptions of the role of religion. In the town of Médéa, midway on the road from Algiers to Berrouaghia, the ʿĪssāwa's "savage demonstrations attract[ed] them much sympathy and their festivals [were] much frequented." Fittingly, "their 'hadras' [took] place in a Moorish house sitting at the corner of Diderot and Moses Streets."[175] No other *zāwiya* possessed such an apt address.

Itself situated at the intersection of the Third Republic's anxieties about secularism and the political role of religion, French ethnography depicted Islamic sociability as a roadblock, an obstacle to French domination. Thus, ethnographic representations of Ṣūfī orders reflect the interests of contested republicanism and disputed religion. Politicized through its authors' associations with colonial bureaucracy, ethnographers perceived Ṣūfī *ṭuruq* in two different, yet inextricably linked, political contexts: that of Third Republic France – which at times posited religion as the impetus behind political instability – and that of colonial Algeria – which continuously and dialogically reevaluated conceptions of "resistance" and "collaboration." Concealed within these texts lie the daily interactions of participant observation, the connections and conversations among administrators and *shuyūkh*, among *ikhwān* and tourists, among bureaucrats and writers.

Multiplicity and representation

The Berrouaghia file contained another photograph. Not surprisingly, Ṭayyib bin al-Ḥājj Bāshir figured prominently in this photo, as well. Indeed, the image consciously echoes the themes of the portrait of Ṭayyib and Yaḥīā. In the center, in front of a white-washed, thatch-roofed, stone house, sit not one, but fifteen adepts of the Shādhiliyya, all dressed in white, many with sashes like Ṭayyib bin al-Ḥājj Bāshir's, each holding open an unidentified book on his lap, all looking at the camera. It is an image of multiplicity, of the reproduction of Ṭayyib in the other members of the *ṭarīqa*. "The group represented in the included photograph,"

[175] AGGA, 16H/4, Administrator attached to the Commune de plein exercice of Médéa [anon.], "Offrandes et Ziaras perçues dans les Taams, Zerdas et Ouadas des Communes de plein exercice de l'arrondissement de Médéa," Department of Algiers, Arrondissement of Médéa, February 15, 1902.

explained the administrator, "is composed of students, of mokkadems and of several khouan."[176] Whoever staged this photograph conscientiously highlighted the internal coherence of the order; the signs that marked Ṭayyib bin al-Ḥājj Bāshir as a cooperative informant, appear multiplied into fifteen.

The history of French Orientalism demands a critical reengagement with its source material and the methods of its production through evanesecent moments of encounter only rarely captured on film. Perhaps the Berrouaghia photographs illustrate this need best: the administrator remarked on his acquiescence to Shaykh Sī Ṭayyib bin al-Ḥājj Bāshir's demands to include his son in the photograph, but we know little else. The report does not indicate whether the administrator chose the pose or whether Sī Ṭayyib did, whose house looms in the background, the color of the dark sash Sī Ṭayyib and the others wear, the exact day or time or reason for the photograph. Even the title of the books open on the laps of Sī Ṭayyib bin al-Ḥājj Bāshir and the other Shādhiliyya remains obscure. This book is not a sign taken for a wonder; it reverses the signification Homi Bhabha attributed to the book in India.[177] It is not Bhabha's biblical signifier of the colonizer, reappropriated as a weapon of cultural resistance. Its anonymity, the colonial archive's ignorance of its title or author or import, marks it as a fundamentally different kind of text. As a symbol, the Shādhiliyya book remained outside the scope of systematized cultural knowledge, marking, in a fading sepia photograph, the silences of ethnographers and their texts. Photographs are always silent, with what Rushdie calls "the silence of great horror . . . the eternal silence of faces and bodies and animals and even nature itself, caught . . . in the grip of the fear of the unforeseeable."[178] If pictures keep silent, texts do not; Rushdie reminds us, "the inside of a book is there whether you read it or not. Even if nobody ever reads it, it's there, doing its work."[179] Sī Ṭayyib bin al-Ḥājj Bāshir's book did its work.

French ethnographers realized Ṣūfī orders as political threats; through the reification of religious sociability in cultural description, administrators, tourists, travel writers, and scholars created the *ṭuruq* as objects of European anthropological knowledge. This chapter has traced how ethnography made Islam "real" for those exercising colonial power. Out of a ghost-world, ethnographic texts crystallized these representations as objects of power, subject to the discriminating effects of the colonizing

176 AGGA, 16H/8, "Étude sur les confréries . . . de Berrouaghia," 1895, 27.
177 Bhabha, *The Location of Culture*. For a photo of a *different* (Moroccan) Si Tayeb (1950s), with yet another meaning, see Hammoudi, *Master and Disciple*, 125–6.
178 Rushdie, *Ground Beneath Her Feet*, 13.
179 Rushdie, *Ground Beneath Her Feet*, 448.

state. Historians and anthropologists of religion who too often blithely cite representations from colonial ethnographies of Ṣūfism without regard to the coercive political context of their creation would do well to heed Camille Brunel's words. While he intended them as an admonition to French administrators to pay attention to millenarian prophecies, they read as an eerily apt indictment of the very representations to which he contributed: "it is of little import to us, in effect, that they be authentic or not; the important for us is that they be considered as such."[180]

[180] Camille Brunel, *La Question indigène en Algérie: l'Affaire de Margueritte devant la cour d'assises de l'Hérault* (Paris: Augustin Challamel, 1906), 19.

4 "Les mauvais génies dans tous les contes de fées": the ethnography of popular religion and the fashioning of Algerian primitivism

"Nous sommes," wrote Jules Liorel, "les mauvais génies dans tous les contes de fées." We are the evil genies in all of the fairy tales. The French, Liorel contended, represented creatures of inexplicable wrath and caprice. Why did Algerians manifest "this defiance . . . this hate . . . this incomprehensible savagery" in the face of the French? "Because," Liorel answered, "the absurd legends, the improbable legends, represent us in the eyes of the young, of the weak, of the disarmed, as dangerous, harmful beings, without faith, without virtue, without honor."[1] Or, in the words of Henri Duveyrier, Algerians "confuse the genies and the French in a single race of mischievous and cannibalistic beings."[2]

Such assertions exposed the fundamental concern underpinning the ethnography of popular religion in Algeria: colonial administrators worried that legend and local rites concealed metaphorical statements about colonial politics. Through narratives about popular religion, ethnographers opposed Islam to the values of republican France. Rituals appeared in ethnographies as the intrusion of religion into politics, contesting secularism and marking the backwardness of Algeria, and hence justifying the civilizing mission.

Third Republic France provided a ready set of characteristics that colonizers marshaled in the ideological construction of the civilizing mission.[3] The civilizing mission, however, had to *create* cultural objects on which to act.[4] Consequently, the ethnography of ritual in colonial Algeria reflected two overlapping and mutually reinforcing conceptions: the first posited

1 Jules Liorel, "Dans Le M'zab,"*Algérie artistique & pittoresque* 3 (1893:1): 28–9.
2 Henri Duveyrier, *Journal d'un voyage dans la province d'Alger: février, mars, avril 1857*, ed. Charles Maunoir (Paris: Augustin Challamel, 1900), 71.
3 Alice L. Conklin, *A Mission to Civilize: The Republican Idea of Empire in France and West Africa, 1895–1930* (Stanford, Calif.: Stanford University Press, 1997); Herman Lebovics, *True France: The Wars over Cultural Identity, 1900–1945* (Ithaca, NY: Cornell University Press, 1992), 6.
4 Cf. Nicholas B. Dirks, *Castes of Mind: Colonialism and the Making of Modern India* (Princeton, NJ: Princeton University Press, 2001), 194.

11. "Le Mzab," from Jules Liorel, "Dans Le M'zab," *Algérie artistique et pittoresque* 3(1893:1).

the export of morality as the ideological motivation behind colonialism, while the second defined those characteristics as embodied by the republic. Hence, debates over republican secularism and suspicion of "superstitious" piety[5] inflected colonial ethnography projects.

Primitivism and salvage ethnography

Primitivism in Algeria drew heavily on long-established discourses of salvage ethnography.[6] The idea of saving cultural elements deemed authentic from the deliquescence of Algerian culture revolved around the search for cultural relics. Primitivism embedded salvage within emerging European self-conceptions. By ascribing to these "survivals"[7] an ideological content as determinants of intellectual capabilities, primitivism reintroduced notions of evolutionism that ethnography had only recently

[5] Ruth Harris, *Lourdes: Body and Spirit in the Secular Age* (London: Allen Lane, 1999).

[6] On salvage, see James Clifford, "On Ethnographic Allegory," in James Clifford and George E. Marcus, eds., *Writing Culture: The Poetics and Politics of Ethnography* (Berkeley, Calif.: University of California Press, 1986), 112–13, 115.

[7] On survivals, see Abdellah Hammoudi, *The Victim and its Masks: An Essay on Sacrifice and Masquerade in the Maghreb*, trans. Paula Wissing (Chicago: University of Chicago Press, 1993), 19, 49.

discarded.[8] For many French ethnographers during the Third Republic, the secular positivism of republicanism had replaced Christianity as their evolutionary endpoint.[9] Hence, the "primitive" of colonial ethnographies in Algeria referred to a normative Europe and its self-conceived progress. The civilizing mission required an evolutionary understanding of identity, in which the politically dominant served as model for colonial development.[10] Thus, many ethnographers interpreted ritual as evidence of Islam's failure to follow a normative teleology, proof that Algerians remained "primitive" objects ripe for French civilizing – and civilization. Primitivism refers to the overlap between salvage ethnography and a renascent, if latent, evolutionism; simply put, primitivism combined the imperial belief in the normative nature of colonizing cultures *and* the concomitant denigration of the colonized as incomplete and atavistic. As an ideological system, primitivism exposes the evolutionary ideology of the civilizing mission. In Europe, contestations over reconfigurations of relations among individuals, religion and the state rarely agreed on their consequences.[11] Despite the use of common trends and tropes, colonial ethnographers created differing and often contradictory forms of primitivism for the civilizing mission.

From ethnographies of popular piety emerge three primary themes. First, the majority of ethnographers of ritual in Algeria utilized primitivism as an object for the civilizing mission. Second, narratives focused on popular beliefs as "primitive" philosophy or history, reserving high intellectual production for Europeans. Lastly, ethnographic texts portrayed ritual as an ineffectual intellectual system constructed in the absence of science as inadequate explanations of natural events. Popular

8 George W. Stocking, Jr., *Delimiting Anthropology: Occasional Essays and Reflections* (Madison, Wisc.: University of Wisconsin Press, 2001), 273.

9 On Christianity as the endpoint, see Hammoudi, *Victim and its Masks*, 26. See also Hammoudi, *Victim and its Masks*, 9, 19, 24–8. On Doutté and the ethnography of sacrifice; Edmond Doutté, *Magie et religion dans l'Afrique du Nord: la société musulmane du Maghrib* (Algiers: Adolphe Jourdan, 1909), 495. Driss Mansouri neglects the connections between colonial power and the trope of sacrifice; Driss Mansouri, "Manifestations festives et expressions du sacré au Maghreb," *Prologues* 1 (April/June 1993): 5–11. See also Talal Asad, "The Concept of Cultural Translation in British Social Anthropology," in Clifford and Marcus, eds., *Writing Culture*, 161.

10 Abdellah Hammoudi, *Master and Disciple: The Cultural Foundations of Moroccan Authoritarianism* (Chicago: University of Chicago Press, 1997), 111; and Lebovics on the political context of folklore studies: Lebovics, *True France*, 6–8, 29, 32–9, 49–50, 139–40, 146, 163, 189–203.

11 James C. Scott, *Seeing Like a State: How Certain Schemes to Improve the Human Condition Have Failed* (New Haven, Conn: Yale University Press, 1998), 331, and James Ferguson, *The Anti-Politics Machine: "Development," Depoliticization, and Bureaucratic Power in Lesotho* (Cambridge: Cambridge University Press, 1990), in Scott, *Seeing Like a State*, 331; Lebovics, *True France*, 94–7.

religious beliefs served as the antithesis of rational science.[12] The ethnography of popular religion in colonial Algeria created a primitivist object from which it exiled philosophy and science. These three themes delineated entire realms of thought as the exclusive purview of the colonizer.

Rituals[13] to end drought and legends about genies reveal the pervasiveness of these three forms of primitivism in colonial ethnography. An analysis of these two tropes uncovers the discontinuities within French colonial ethnography; though many ethnographers used these three themes as analytical reference points, their resulting ethnographies of drought rituals or of genie beliefs often proved dissimilar. The ethnography of religion played an essential role in conceiving of various primitive Algerian cultures in need of regeneration through French colonization. As even Jacques Berque conceded, the trope of the mystical, magical Maghreb was an overused theme even as early as 1954.[14] Primitivism functioned primarily not as a statement about the colonized culture, but rather as statements, embedded in European politics, about the values of the ethnographer. Primitivist ethnographies reveal ethnographers' conception of France's imperial project.

Survivals, secularism, and the new evolutionary ethnography

Ethnographies of Algerian popular piety manifested the impulse toward salvation by positing relics from a primitive past. The preponderance of French ethnographers conceived of the ostensible paucity of such traits in European culture as evidence of their own progress; scientific, secular, bourgeois culture had effaced the traces of the process of cultural development. Like flotsam left in the wake of a retreating wave, in colonial ethnography survivals attested to the obfuscated presence of a vanished past, while their comparative absence from *French* culture marked the latter's evolution. They testified not to chronology, but to teleology, progression with hierarchy.

[12] Cf. Dirks, *Castes of Mind*, 172.

[13] I have adopted here Hammoudi's definition of ritual as "enactment-discourse." Hammoudi, *Victim and its Masks*, vii–viii, 5, 31, 106. See also Lawrence Rosen, *The Anthropology of Justice: Law as Culture in Islamic Society* (Cambridge: Cambridge University Press, 1989), 36.

[14] Jacques Berque, "Une exploration de la sainteté au Maghreb," in *Opera Minora*, vol. II, *Histoire et Anthropologie du Maghreb*, ed. Gianni Albergoni (Paris: Éditions Bouchène, 2001), 171; cf. Stefania Pandolfo, *Impasse of the Angels: Scenes from a Moroccan Space of Memory* (Chicago: University of Chicago Press, 1997), 41–2.

Edmond Doutté devoted much of *Magie et religion dans l'Afrique du Nord* (1908) to a search for relics. A synthetic work, *Magie et religion* represented less an ethnography than an encyclopedia, summarizing not only Doutté's own fieldwork experiences, but also those of other scholars. Fundamental to Doutté's synthesis lay the theory that survivals revealed traces of collective development. "But," Abdellah Hammoudi notes, "what interests [Doutté] is less a theory of sacrifice . . . than finding the debris of ancient Berber religion in . . . Muslim practices."[15] If Doutté did not utilize these survivals to create a theory of sacrifice, to what narrative work, then, does Doutté put this "debris"?

Doutté exploited the concept of survivals to represent Islamic popular culture as primitive. For some ethnographers, the question of primitivism and religious cultural development remained primarily one of academic interest. In *Les Fontaines des génies* (1903), J. B. Andrews represented rites and rituals as "a survival of a very primitive cult, that is connected to the problems of evolution of religion . . . which they will aid in resolving."[16] Andrews found "the origin of this evolution in primitive ideas" that were "destined to disappear soon from Algeria."[17] Although *Magie et religion* appears, at first, less overtly political, Doutté himself embodied the kind of ethnographer-administrator colonial France hoped to create; early on in *Magie et religion* Doutté announced that "applications of contemporary sociology will be able to show us what use the studies are from a practical point of view."[18] Hence, while *Magie et religion* may have served as yet another salvo in the debates over sacrifice and totemism in early anthropology, more importantly, it articulated the narrative relationship between the ethnography of salvage and the civilizing mission.

For Doutté, popular piety marked North Africans as insufficiently evolved. He posits one "civilization musulmane" for the entire region because of what he interpreted as the totalizing penetration of religion.[19] Simultaneously, however, he attempted to ascertain "in studying Muslim institutions, which is the part . . . [of] anterior civilizations and which is that of Islam," reserving the possibility of local difference.[20] Doutté

15 Hammoudi, *Victim and its Masks*, 26.

16 J. B. Andrews, *Les Fontaines des génies (Seba Aioun): croyances soudanaises à Alger* (Algiers: Adolphe Jourdan, 1903), 9.

17 Andrews, *Fontaines des génies*, 32, 36.

18 Doutté, *Magie et religion*, 25. 19 Doutté, *Magie et religion*, 13.

20 Doutté, *Magie et religion*, 18. See also Alfred Bel, "Bibliographie: [review of] Edmond Doutté, *Magie et religion dans l'Afrique du Nord*," *Bulletin de la Société de Geographie et d'Archéologie de la Province d'Oran* [*BSGAO*] 13 (1909): 118.

created an "Islamic culture" at once totalizing and monolithic, but also imperfect, beset with the inherited legacy of the past.

The role of the scholar revolved around making legible that legacy through a minute sifting of details to lay bare the remains. When discussing folkloric festivals, Doutté clarified his methodology and his aims:

> [T]he puritans have often prohibited them [folkloric festivals]. They are extremely precious for us: they are the fossils of sociology. They represent in effect ancient magical practices, having had a religious force and which are disarticulated, in some fashion, from religion. Moreover the representations linked to these practices, the myths that they put into action, the beliefs that they manifest have generally disappeared and we must reconstitute them with the debris of rites which survive: this is what Tylor called survivals.[21]

Doutté interpreted ethnography as reconstruction. The European ethnographer arrives, pen in hand, to dust off festivals and rites and to capture their meaning before their inevitable extirpation at the hands of "puritans," at the hands of a totalizing yet incomplete Islamic orthodoxy. This text reminds us of what too many current critics of anthropological narratives have forgotten: salvage ethnography not only implies the condescension of rescue; it also implies a rescue from a particular enemy.

The reification of Islamic orthodoxy as the enemy of salvaging ethnographers resulted from evolutionism latent in the ethnography of religion. From the perspective of Third Republic France, "Islamic civilization" and Europe had diverged; Islam had decayed; the conquering hordes transformed themselves into the colonized subject. According to Doutté, "the cult of relics does not appear to have *attained* in Islam the *development* that it underwent in Catholicism."[22] The ostensible lack of a popular tradition of relic use in Islam deviated from the patterns of evolution established by European Christianity. Doutté's Islam halted early in its cultural evolution. "Primitive magic disappeared in the face of Islam, but we have sought to reconstitute it with the debris that survive: some are popular practices, tolerated by the orthodoxy, others have been admitted by [orthodoxy]; but there remains a forbidden magic . . . that is in opposition to the ends of religion."[23]

Between the sorcerer and the ethnographer, Doutté placed the Muslims who formed the object of his study: intolerant of the past's historical legacy yet unable to transcend it, they became a new primitive object for ethnographers like Doutté. This was not the primitivism of Montaigne,

[21] Doutté, *Magie et religion*, 347.
[22] Doutté, *Magie et religion*, 443, citing Carl Albrecht Bernoulli, *Die Heiligen der Merowinger* (Tübingen: J. C. B. Mohr, 1900), 237ff, 261ff. Emphasis added.
[23] Doutté, *Magie et religion*, 599.

12. Etienne Dinet, "La Lecture du Coran" (n.d.).

or Diderot, or Montesquieu; instead, latent evolutionism condemned to primitivism those deemed incompletely intellectually developed. For Doutté, Islam was "excessively poor" in terms of mythology and "grand religious ceremonies," yet rich in subsumed and incorporated rites.[24] It occupied a peculiar hybrid space, intolerant of and locked in constant struggle with "magic," yet ridden with its remains. It was precisely this liminality that embodied the new primitivism.

In contrast, Alfred Bel depicted the relationship between Islamic orthodoxy and surviving rituals not as antagonism, but rather as coexistence, symbiosis. As for "magico-religious customs from early antiquity," Bel

[24] Doutté, *Magie et religion*, 603.

maintained, "one finds them [in Algeria] even in the Festivals of orthodox Islam."[25] His conclusion that Islamic orthodoxy *facilitated*, rather than extirpated, "survivals" rejected Doutté's artificial dichotomy of popular religion and orthodoxy. Nevertheless, the conceptual consequences of this shift remain identical; Bel's Algerian festivals remain riddled with the detritus of antiquity, and his Algerians seemingly carry out their rites under the guise of "orthodoxy," ignorant of their classical heritage.

Frequently, ethnographers made the evolutionary ideology behind the survivals concept explicit; for Auguste Pomel, the senator from Oran, the religious edifice of Algeria invited an exposition of its evolutionary failings. His analysis imbricated primitivism and politics through the reintroduction of evolution. "*Mahométisme* [*sic*] seems most especially to suit societies whose social evolution has stopped at the stage of Barbaric patriarchy. Arab society is the type best characterized by this political constitution, which appears to have reached its embodiment in perpetuity in [this] race."[26] Reducing Islam to a fetishization of the prophet, Pomel represented religion as arrested development, the teratological result of abbreviated evolutionary processes. According to Pomel, race interrupted those processes, leaving Arabs politically, culturally, and socially stunted – leaving them "Barbaric" (Pomel clearly intended a close association between *barbare* and the near-cognate *berbère*), primitive. Pomel distinguished only vaguely among politics, culture, social process, and religion, yoking them to evolutionary racism that demeaned Algerians as byproducts of stunted evolution.

The connection between colonial ethnography's attachment to survivals and its roots in racial theory was not academic; it was political. The representation of Algerian Islam as primitive resulted from the inseparability of colonial ethnographers from authoritarian politics. Alfred Bel summarized it best in two separate passages from his last work (1938):

> The study of the past and the present of the Muslim religion in North Africa does not only interest the science of Religions[;] it must bring also and above all precise notions necessary to all those who, from near or far, have to govern and administer

[25] Alfred Bel and Maurice Eisenbeth, *Les Principales Races de l'Algérie: Les Berbères, les Arabes, les Juifs* (Paris: L'Encyclopédie coloniale et maritime, [1938]), 85; also Bel, "Bibliographie . . . *Magie*," 118–35.

[26] Auguste Pomel, *Races indigènes de l'Algérie, et du rôle que leur réservent leurs aptitudes: Arabes, Kabyles, Maures et Juifs* (Oran: Typographie et lithographie Veuve Dagorn, 1871), 4–5. See also Victor Largeau, *Le Sahara algérien: les deserts de l'Erg* (Paris: Hachette, 1881), 142.

the indigenous North Africans, to all those who are simply in relation with these Muslims.[27]

This ignorance of the religion and mores of *Indigènes*, . . . this misunderstanding of Islam by public powers and by a certain number of those who have to direct communes or administrative services in the lands of Islam[,] is at the very base of many of the errors, understandings, and faults that accentuate or provoke an unfortunate ideology and an obdurate sentimentalism.[28]

In French Algeria, indeed in France, the study of Islam created politically useful, administratively oriented knowledge. The discursive turn that posited "survivals" as a constitutive element of Algerian religious life permitted colonial ethnographers to tack easily back and forth between the past and the present of Algerians. Colonial ethnographers predicated their understanding of religious culture in North Africa upon precisely this purported eruption of the past into the present of colonized peoples.

Primitivist rituals and alternative histories

Such ethnographers posited rituals as an alternative history, as Algerian narratives about their history. Simultaneously, however, colonial ethnographers *demeaned* legend as historical knowledge, comparing it unfavorably with a reified and ill-defined notion of history. The ethnographer-administrator Métois contended that

Certainly, those of these legends that address the past of peoples have but a distant relation with history . . . But these accounts always offer us a precious means to capture the popular mentality, and we have no other [means] than this . . . When, in addition, it is not a question only of people, but of a doubly ignored people, first because they are common, then because their customs are absolutely different from ours, popular stories become yet more useful, because . . . they constitute . . . information on ignored customs. The little details of existence that frequently escape the sociologist . . . appear in these accounts in a form that cannot be doubted, for it is given by those concerned themselves. In the enthusiasm that continues to inspire him of heroes that he transforms so that they always resemble him, the storyteller permits himself to unveil secrets that he would never otherwise have dared express, least of all to a stranger.[29]

While legend offers useful sociological and historical information, it nevertheless appears as bastardized history, tainted by the romanticism of the

[27] Alfred Bel, *La Religion musulmane en Berbérie: esquisse d'histoire et de sociologie religieuse*, vol. I, *Etablissement et développement de l'Islam en Berbérie du VIIe au XXe siècle* (Paris: Libraire orientaliste Paul Geuthner, 1938), 10.

[28] Bel, *Religion musulmane*, 12.

[29] Capitaine Florent-Alexis Métois, "Contes Sahariens," *Bulletin de la Société de Géographie d'Alger et de l'Afrique du Nord* [*BSGA*] 14 (1909): 509.

storyteller. Through legend, a "common" people inadvertently reveals in narrative what it otherwise hesitates to reveal about itself. A Trojan Horse for ethnography, popular stories revealed to Métois details that the storyteller ignored or withheld. Métois remained indifferent as to whether legend offered information on the present or past of his "common people." Their historicity and their present remained undifferentiated, its heroes reduced to facsimiles of its storytellers; the historical and the contemporaneous bleed together into an arrested present. "One will perhaps be astonished," Métois claimed, "to find [among one Saharan ethnic group] . . . but historical legends. The fact is that I have never seen their imagination exercise itself except on subjects of this nature."[30] History, for Métois, became an imaginary exercise for Algerians. In their massive ethnography of "the folklore of the Arabs," A. Certeux and Henry Carnoy maintained that "legend . . . falls somewhat under the heading of history . . . The storyteller *believes* it generally. Its domain is vast and embraces all the supernatural."[31] For Certeux and Carnoy, legend is somewhat-history, the not-quite narration of the past: the authors' italics and emphasis on the supernatural emphasize both the genre's instability and the ethnographers' unwillingness to ascribe historical validity to legend. In the succinct words of Corneille Trumelet, for colonial ethnographers, "legend, in effect, is the history of peoples who have not written any."[32]

The construction of a primitivist philosophy

In essence, some ethnographers represented popular narratives as debased philosophy attesting to intellectual primitivism. The comparisons implicit in the conception of legend as inferior history became explicit in the discussion of popular religion as a system of thought.

The ethnographic analysis of popular Islam invited comparisons with non-clerical Christianity. Moreover, ethnographers' interest in the role of the belief in genies in North African Islam echoed similar debates about popular (or "superstitious") Catholicism.[33] While deliberations about Catholicism often framed the question in terms of class (populist

[30] Capitaine Métois, "Contes Sahariens," 511.

[31] A. Certeux and E. Henry Carnoy, *L'Algérie traditionnelle: Légendes, contes, chansons, musique, mœurs, coutumes, fêtes, croyances, superstitions, etc*, vol. I: *Contributions au folklore: des Arabes* (Paris: Maisonneuve & Leclerc, 1884), 17. Italics in the original.

[32] Col. C. Trumelet, *L'Algérie légendaire: en pèlerinage ça et là aux tombeau des principaux Thaumaturges de l'Islam (Tell et Sahra [sic])*, (Algiers: Adolphe Jourdan, 1892), 1.

[33] A. Behaghel, *L'Algérie: conquête et colonisation, religion et mœurs, Armée* (Paris: E. Dentu, 1870), 269–70. On popular Catholicism, see Harris, *Lourdes*.

ritual and elite clerical orthodoxy), French republican ethnographers cast this dynamic in Islam in terms of civilization: rituals and legends marked Islam as religiously less evolved. With self-congratulatory authority, many Third Republic ethnographers deprecated belief in genies, angels, and the intercession of saints as evidence of primitivism. Alfred Bel compared superstition's role in Islam to its role in Catholicism. "Islam – like Catholicism moreover – while recognizing the reality of sorcery (*sih'r*) [*siḥr*], formally prohibited the practice. The sorcerer, in the view of orthodoxy, attributes to himself powers that belong only to God."[34] For Bel and others, superstitious belief in ritual and legend formed the basis of religion, yet rarely did they depict *French* rituals as primitive, despite a burgeoning and at times primitivist body of folklore studies on rural France.[35] Nevertheless, ethnographers inclined toward the positivism of the human sciences interpreted popular religious belief as an outmoded form of thinking. The prevalence of "superstition" in both Algeria and France could not erase the fundamental distinction between colonizer and colonized. For many, religious ritual within France seemed to represent the remnants of a way of thinking soon to disappear, while they understood ritual and religion in Algeria as the basis of thought.

Thus, colonial ethnographies not only compared popular religion in Algeria with religion in France, but rather also interpreted ritual and legend as lesser, alternative philosophy,[36] the dominant mode of Algerian thought. In his *La Condition sociale des indigènes algériens*, Henry Drapier depicted a reified "Islamic civilization" as intellectually stagnant, decadent.

> The Muslims after having attained a demi-civilization comparable to that of European peoples before the Renaissance took pleasure in a routine that soon distanced them [from the European model]. Once the traditions were ruptured, the intellectual and material resources accumulated by the preceding generations were rapidly annihilated. They were ignorant of [that fact] that a nation, to avoid decadence, must not stop and that it is necessary for them as for their competitors to aim at a continuous perfecting.[37]

34 Bel, "Bibliographie . . . *Magie*," 125, 129.

35 But cf. Octave Depont and Xavier Coppolani, *Les Confréries religieuses musulmanes: publié sous le patronage de M. Jules Cambon, Gouveneur général de l'Algérie* (Algiers: Adolphe Jourdan, 1897), 141. Ethnographers of Islam, although aware of primitivist tendencies within European folklore studies, largely eschewed comparisons between Christian and non-Christian traditions.

36 See Paul Rabinow, "Representations are Social Facts: Modernity and Post-Modernity in Anthropology," in Clifford and Marcus, eds., *Writing Culture*, 234–61.

37 Henry Drapier, *La Condition sociale des indigènes algériens* (Paris: Ar. Rousseau, and Algiers: Adolphe Jourdan, 1899), 74.

Drapier's analysis generated a void at the heart of intellectual life and "social condition" for Muslims.

Into that void, ethnographers like Edmond Doutté placed ritual and superstition. Doutté considered that North Africans resorted to magic as a means of "pursuing . . . utilitarian ends," but also "to acquire intelligence" or for other, more metaphysical goals.[38] He saw magic as a means of enacting individual desires, of rendering emotional states visible and concrete. More importantly, Doutté made this magic, as a system of making emotion into action, the centerpiece of intellectual life. In a chapter entitled "Magic, Science and Religion," he noted

> the preponderant role of affective states in the mentality of the primitive: man and primitive man less than any other do not think except in images. It is a fault in the English school [Edward Tylor and James George Frazer] not to have sufficiently taken into consideration the enormous distance that there is between our mental life with its efflorescence of abstract representations and that of the savage, which is felt rather than thought.[39]

Doutté used the presence of magical beliefs among North Africans to condemn them as automatons incapable of abstract thinking, slaves to the literal. For Doutté and others, popular religious belief offered a primitive alternative to philosophy, an entire system of thought filling the void French ethnographers posited in colonial Algeria. According to Doutté's theory, the primitive mind existed solely to give voice to desire, action to impulse, not to reason abstractly.

Edmond Doutté's hypothesizing about the mind of savages did not remain at the level of the theoretical. He based *Magie et religion* on fieldwork in Algeria and Morocco.[40] Doutté did not create the "primitive mind" of this passage as a theoretical construct; lest it be assumed that he excluded North Africans from the status of "primitives," he cited various North African practices for healing scorpion bites by killing the scorpion or healing jaundice with saffron and carrots as evidence of "the logic of savages."[41] Citing Henri Hubert and Marcel Mauss on the homeopathic principle of using like to cure like, Doutté questioned whether "this relatively complicated reasoning was truly within the grasp of savages."[42] Although embedded in general debates about the "primitive mind,"

[38] Doutté, *Magie et religion*, 304. See H. Marchand, *Masques carnavalesques et carnaval en Kabylie* (Algiers: Société historique algérienne, n.d. [1938?]), 4 on festivals and morality.
[39] Doutté, *Magie et religion*, 309, and A. Binet, "La pensée sans images," *Revue philosophique*, 55 (1903), 138–52, in Doutté, *Magie et religion*, 309.
[40] On Doutté's lectures at the École des lettres d'Alger, see Bel, "Bibliographie . . . *Magie*," 118.
[41] Doutté, *Magie et religion*, 310–11. See also 171, 173, 187–8, 275.
[42] Doutté, *Magie et religion*, 311, citing "Hubert and Mauss, *Magie*, 81."

Doutté's analysis started with examples drawn from North Africa. Alternating between the healing rites of North Africans and the philosophical concept of the primitive mind, Doutté effectively posited magical beliefs as an intellectual system that defined North Africans as primitives.

In 1904, Octave Houdas reached a similar conclusion about the incapacity of Muslims for abstract thought. Like Doutté, Houdas worked as a colonial functionary; his translations and ethnographies formed an integral part of the colonial canon. Houdas, however, posited not the accidents of evolution as the cause for arrested intellectual development, but rather malign will.

> Superstition... permits simple and naïve spirits to represent to themselves, in a concrete guise, abstract principles that they are incapable of understanding... [Superstition] fortifies religious sentiment more that it destroys it. Also, the weakening of superstitious practices constitutes a first step towards skepticism, which certainly kills all religions. The Muslims appear to have recognized this consequence of a too-active struggle against superstitions, and they have never combated them but rather listlessly.[43]

For Houdas, Muslims attempted to halt the inexorable evolution toward skepticism. Colonial ethnographers defined Muslims as primitive because superstitious, and superstitious because primitive. Such reasoning offered no way out of the intellectual abyss established by Drapier; by design it represented Algerians as primitive objects who had failed to achieve the evolutionary development of French culture.

Such ethnographic representations served a political function. Claiming a theory of the functioning of the so-called primitive mind, the ethnography of religion purported to offer knowledge of the minds of Algerians. Its authoritative claims rendered ethnography a useful political tool; Trumelet emphasized

> the interest that the study of religious mores of Muslim groups in the countries of North Africa that we have conquered-[groups of] whose body if not spirit we have charge – could present, and in those countries where the needs of politics, commerce and civilization will yet irresistibly push us . . .
>
> For, to acquire this force of penetration..., we must first study the hidden things, the mysterious practices of the groups to which we are exposed to encounter on our tenebrous, silent, mute route.[44]

For Trumelet, colonialism embodied a near-moral imperative, the fulfilling of a destiny at once collective and national. Ethnography opened up the intellectual space of Algeria for the civilizing mission. Requiring a

[43] Octave Houdas, *L'Islamisme* (Paris: Dujarric, 1904), 259–60.
[44] Trumelet, *L'Algérie légendaire*, 1.

culture in need of civilization, the civilizing mission found, in the ethnographic fables of Doutté, Trumelet, and others, primitive Algerians.

Ethnographic primitivism invited the penetration of the myth of colonialism as intellectual uplift into Algeria. In a polemic on regeneration, Ferdinand de Béhagle underlined superstition as the signifier of the primitive:

> Just as one cannot begin the instruction of a child by the study of abstract sciences, similarly one would not begin the education of a yet savage race by putting into action . . . our civil and religious laws that are the synthesis of thousands of centuries of refined civilization.
>
> The misrecognition of these principles [,] there is the real cause of the successive failures of Christianity in Africa and the success of Islam.
>
> To the poor intellects of savages Islam presents itself in a simple form that they can understand. In the place of the complicated mysteries of our religion, of the refinements of our ethics . . . that our peasants themselves scarcely understand, and the Africans not at all, the Muslim brings a simple dogma, a simple ethics . . . Religion, ethics, hygiene, it is all one, and very simple; the savage understands and accepts.[45]

For Béhagle, Islam provided the "savage" with a network of superstition that undermined social functioning, determined freedom and bondage, offered a code of behavior and a way of life. The very universalism that Béhagle perceived in "Islamic culture" articulated an intellectual void for the evolutionist civilizing mission.

The ethnographic fetish: "science is charged with sorcery by an ignorant society"

Similarly, colonial ethnographers constructed popular religion as anti-science; in the eyes of French writers, ritual and legend served as a systematized way of explaining natural phenomena and interpreting causality. Colonial ethnography depicted popular religion as the superstitious alternative to the reason of science. Denigrating ritual and legend as irrational, ethnographers interpreted popular religion as primitivist cultural logic. While evolutionist ethnographies of religion posited science as a characteristic of European thought, ritual and legend signified a system of intellectual organization that characterized the primitive.

Arnold Van Gennep exemplified the use of scientific rhetoric as a discriminating tool of colonial control. Despite his exclusion from its institutions, Van Gennep utilized the principles of science as the

[45] AGGA, 4H/22, Ferdinand de Béhagle, *Des Moyens de combattre la dépopulation en Afrique*, (Paris: Joseph André, 1895), 20.

exemplar of French intellectual achievement to mark difference in *En Algérie* (dedicated to Bel). "It is," Van Gennep maintained, "to the natural sciences that we owe our [i.e., French] intellectual emancipation; it is to the physico-chemical sciences that we owe our power over nature: the great abyss that separates us from the indigenous populations of North Africa is caused by their scorn for those sciences."[46] Van Gennep ascribed the purported intellectual inferiority of North Africans to "scorn," willful ignorance. For Van Gennep and other ethnographers "Islam, by its uniquely literary aspect and its recourse to the principle of authority, imposes incuriosity in regard to natural phenomena and in general in regard to all biological and social phenomena."[47] Thus, this spurious Muslim resistance to science prevented Algerians from the investigation of nature, biology, or even society.

Van Gennep reinscribed the conclusions of early ethnographers. In an ethnography published as part of the "Bibliothèque instructive" in 1885, Dr. F. Quesnoy remarked,

> The Arab has the love of the marvelous, of extraordinary stories, of sorcerers, of ghosts, of magic . . . [T]he most natural things take on grand proportions when they have been treated by the imagination. The direction of his faculties does not render him suitable for the interpretation of natural phenomena . . . All his works are still what they were in past centuries. These are men of tradition, refractory to all progress.[48]

The ethnographic devaluation of popular religion never engaged with the rich history of science in the Islamic world, revealing instead the predominant place of scientific thought in French evolutionism. It was less a case of Algerian undervaluation of science than of European fetishization of it. Prewar ethnographers reflected the narrative style's debt to and imbrication with evolutionary anthropology. Science, as a discursive tool if not as a practice, became yet another sign pointing to the ostensible intellectual inferiority of Algerians.

Whereas Van Gennep, Quesnoy, and others discussed science primarily as a category of knowledge, some focused on specific legends as revealing a primitive anti-science underpinned by alternative conceptions of causality. In an article on Algerian folklore, Achille Robert highlighted Algerian explanations of the source of the pollution of a particular stream: running through an ancient Roman cemetery, the water

[46] Arnold Van Gennep, *En Algérie* (Paris: Mercure de France, 1914), 158. Dr. Bonnafont, *Pérégrinations en Algérie, 1830 à 1842: histoire, éthnographie, anecdotes* (Paris: Challamel Aîné, 1884), 212.
[47] Van Gennep, *En Algérie*, 180.
[48] Dr. F. Quesnoy, *L'Algérie* (Paris: Librairie Furne, Jouvet, 1885), 266.

collected, according to legend, the fluids and remains of the centuries-old corpses.[49] In including the tale in a section labeled "Nature," Robert expressly juxtaposed the rules of the natural world, whereby scientific explanations accounted for polluted wells, and the rules of the supernatural world, whereby the corpses of long-dead Christians and pagans did. A Lieutenant Brouard equated the arrival of the French railroad in the Sahara with previous tales of monsters associated with the same geographic region; "the legendary well," he noted, now "feeds the reservoirs of the railroad."[50] Ethnographers like Brouard cast natural or technological phenomena as reflecting, for Algerians, pre-existing legends. Where French ethnographers supplied scientific explanations, they represented Algerians as utilizing popular religious themes to clarify the origins of natural phenomena.

In *Magie et religion*, Edmond Doutté reconciled his belief in Algerian primitivism with his interpretation of superstition as a necessary step in an inevitable evolution toward scientific reason. For Doutté, magic embodied a means by which intellectually stunted peoples made sense of the natural environment.

> The savage does not yet have the notion of the invariable relationship between cause and effect; if he had it, science would be founded. His representations are much more confused and his practices still move in the obscure domain of the affective . . . One cannot say . . . magic is a false science,[51] at least in its origins: it is nothing but a practice, ill adapted to its goal and sensed rather than perceived.[52]

Thus, Doutté conceived of magic as science's inverse. Lacking a theoretical conception of causality, bereft of effective perception, and devoid of regularity in its observations, magic embodied precisely the superstitious, irrational, anti-positivist values that ethnographers such as Doutté abhorred. The stakes were, for Doutté, if anything more personal: isolated from established academic sociology by geography, temperament, and research interests, he had to protect the scientific credentials of his

[49] Achille Robert, "Contribution au folk-lore des indigènes de l'Algérie," in *Actes du XIVe Congrès international des Orientalistes: Alger, 1905*, vol. IV: *Troisième partie (suite): langues musulmanes (arabe, persan et Turke)* (Paris: Ernest Leroux, 1908), 565. See also Marchand, *Masques carnavalesques*, 8–9; H. J. Arripe, *Essai sur le folklore de la Commune mixte de l'Aurès*, (Algiers: Adolphe Jourdan, 1912), 17; Louis Voinot, "Le Tidikelt," *BSGAO* 29 (1909): 438.

[50] Brouard, "Méchéria (Légende et Histoire)," *BSGAO* 10 (1890): 218.

[51] Edmond Doutté, citing James George Frazer, *Le Rameau d'or*, trans. R. Stiébel and J. Toutain, vol. I, *Magie et religion: les tabous* (Paris: Schleicher, 1903), 61 seq., and F. B. Jevons, *An Introduction to the History of Religion*, 163.

[52] Doutté, *Magie et religion*, 313, and Salomon Reinach, *Cultes, mythes, et religions*, vol. II, 19–20, in Doutté, *Magie et religion*, 313.

own work. He imbued his definition of magic with his own anxieties about his ability to conjure the appropriate scholarly response.

That Doutté saw magic as somehow inimical to scientific praxis he made clear;[53] nevertheless, he articulated magic as a stage in the evolution toward reason. His descriptions of magic seem intentionally to echo descriptions of scientific methodology. "The processes by which one can capture and enslave magical forces are . . . strictly determined and one must follow them strictly. Otherwise the redoubtable forces that one puts into play could miss their goal and so they would return against the operator."[54] In this passage, Doutté illuminated a fundamental aspect of his theory of magic: magic relied not on relations of cause and effect, but, nevertheless, on a complicated and equally rigid set of rules.[55] "Magical phenomena are . . . caused by an invisible force, transmissible at a distance, acting in relation with the impulses and desires of man and which is nothing other than these impulses and desires conceived of as existence outside of the human mind."[56] Doutté's North African magic had nothing of the haphazard or chaotic about it; rather, it obeyed a specific set of requirements. Indeed, magic conducted outside of these rigid rules became subject to, for want of a better phrase, lab accidents. In deviating from Frazer's conception of magic as "false science," Doutté instead defined magic as inverting science: magic revolved around methodology without causality, redress without observation, solutions without knowledge of origin. *Magie et religion* reappropriated discursive notions of scientific positivism as elements of rational ("civilized") thought and marshaled them, in the inverse, as signifiers of Algerian primitivism.

A necessary precursor to scientific thought, magic represented a developmental period, not a culmination. "The belief in divination . . . gave birth to types of sciences," contended Doutté, and hence it attested to Algerian primitivism;[57] divination without the subsequent development of science failed to meet the evolutionary tests set forth by the scholar-mouthpieces of colonial hegemony. As that evolutionary scale placed theism between magic and science, colonial ethnographers of religion had to clarify the transition between magic and orthodoxy. Doutté conceived of the "the god . . . invented for society" as the individual embodiment of the forces magicians called upon for various "physical" and "moral" needs; instead of invoking forces, theists invoked a god.[58] The efficacy of certain rites despite variations or failures in practice introduced, according

[53] Doutté, *Magie et religion*, 314.
[54] Doutté, *Magie et religion*, 97.
[55] Doutté, *Magie et religion*, 163–4.
[56] Doutté, *Magie et religion*, 419. See also 598.
[57] Doutté, *Magie et religion*, 351.
[58] Doutté, *Magie et religion*, 331.

meet with the disapprobation of representatives of orthodoxy; according to Doutté's model, "science is charged with sorcery by an ignorant society."[60] The progression Doutté envisioned began with magic, proceeded through theism, and culminated in science. Nevertheless, this ostensible ascent was far from assured; science faced the threat of an orthodoxy attempting to purge it as sorcery. Doutté's conception of the relationship between orthodoxy and innovation became nearly dialectical; thus, Doutté "could conceive of a society where the belief in science would be obligatory and where religion would be forbidden and relegated thus along with sorcery; science would become itself a religion."[61] Doutté missed the apparent irony of the remark. As the Third Republic debated state secularism, anticlericalist and anti-religious elements combated organized religion by demeaning it as superstitious. Constructing popular religion as a systematized form of anti-science, colonial ethnography represented Algerians as primitive.

Analyses of folk medicine functioned as case studies in Algerian conceptions of science. Such texts focused on popular treatments as evidence of a primitive understanding of physiology and causality. Achille Robert, in *L'Arabe tel qu'il est* (1900), perceived in folk medicine a philosophical orientation toward fatalism and indifference to logic.

> The Arabs blindly accept all that the doctors mindlessly repeat to them, without astonishment: genies, exorcisms, incantations, pilgrimages, talismans, the strangest remedies . . . if the patient does not get better, which, one can imagine, happens almost always, he does not fear and limits himself to declaring that "God did not want to bestow healing"

upon the patient.[62] Robert's "Arab as he truly is," reified as one individual, ultimately surrendered his life in an act of superstitious belief. Such extreme denigrations of the knowledge and lived experiences of Algerians composed the primitive colonial object necessitated by the civilizing mission. Capitain Bérenger, a military ethnographer, wrote of the Algerians in Beni-Abbès that "their fatalist ideas and their credulity make them admit improbable things," such as genies and sorcerers who caused

[59] Doutté, *Magie et religion*, 332. [60] Doutté, *Magie et religion*, 335.

[61] Doutté, *Magie et religion*, 340.

[62] A. Robert, *L'Arabe tel qu'il est: études algériennes et tunisieunes* (Algiers: Imprimerie Joseph Angelini, 1900), 100–1. On ritual and fatalism: Jules Liorel, *Races berbères: Kabylie du Jurjura* (Paris: Ernest Leroux, [1893]), 508. On alternative healing in contemporary North Africa, see Dr. Mustapha Akhmisse, *Médecine, magie et sorcellerie au Maroc ou l'art traditionnel de guérir,* 4th edn (Casablanca: Dar Kortoba, 2000).

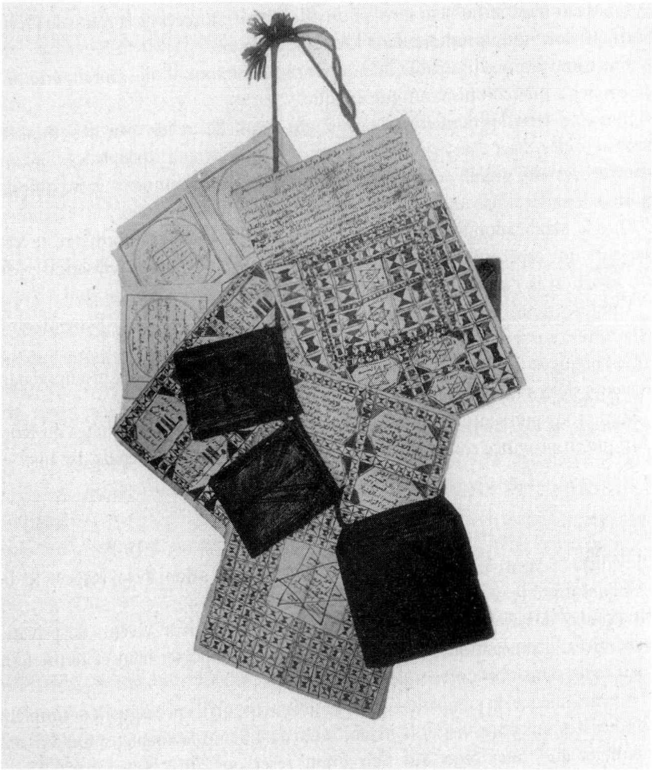

13. "Amulets," "Talismans," Letters of Introduction, and Other Ṣūfī Ephemera, from Liorel, "Dans le M'zab."

illness.[63] Some ethnographers discriminated between French and Algerian by constructing popular beliefs and medical practices as "primitive."

Not surprisingly, colonial administrators latched onto the medical practices of local religious figures as significant for understanding. The regional reputations of healers offered a platform for the variety of public influence administrators feared when exerted by Algerians. In Aïn Ghoraba, one "Khaldi" (ʿAlī wālid Aḥmad)

enjoys a great reputation as a healer. He is a rival of Pasteur and . . . makes in the region great competition for the Institut [Pasteur] of Algiers. He radically cures rabies and this in the blink of an eye and without pain.

His procedure is simple: he takes a raisin[,] writes on the skin several cabalistic words and then makes the patient swallow this new type of pill . . . Cost: 0,F50

[63] Captain Bérenger, "Notice sur la région de Beni-Abbès (avec cartes)," *BSGAO* 27 (December 1906). Oran: L. Fouque, 1906, 452.

Never is this price exceeded. Rich and poor pay the same price.

The product of these truly miraculous cures is religiously turned over by our man to the *marabouts* of Kerzaz.[64]

From all parts of the Oranais, Algerians came for ʿAlī wālid Aḥmad's miraculous rabies cure. "Europeans and . . . Israelites [*sic*] do not hesitate in the least . . . to find this therapy of which the treatment is doubtless less effective than that of the Institut Pasteur [but which] at least has the advantage of being less long[,] less painful and more economical."[65] Invoking that most authoritative figure of French science, Louis Pasteur, the administrator effectively belittled the beliefs of ʿAlî wạlid Aḥmad's patients. That ʿAlī wālid Aḥmad's raisin probably did not cure any rabies cases imports little for the history of ethnography. The persistence in the belief in traditional healing attested to the well-reasoned mistrust that Algerians had for the colonial administration. Flippant in tone, dismissive in its intellectual implications, this administrator's ethnography converted an act indicative of French failures into an indication of the primitive mind. Through the magical narratives of the ethnography of medicine, the mistrust of Western medical practices associated with colonial power became, not a failure, but rather the proof for Europeans of the *necessity* of their colonization.

The creation of Algerians as the primitive object for the civilizing mission rested as much upon more narrative forms of ethnographic writing as upon thematic discussions of inheritance, philosophy, and science. Most ethnographers constructed narratives around specific rites. Though survivals, philosophy, and science provided theoretical reference for the construction of a colonial primitive, most ethnographers drew on *each* theme through the dissection of specific rituals. Discourses about survivals,

64 Archives du Gouvernement général de l'Algérie (AGGA), 16H/4, administrator [illeg.], "Confréries religieuses," Sebdou, February 24, 1904. See also Aboubekr Abdesselam ben Choaïb, "Les Marabouts Guérisseurs," *Revue africaine* 51 (1907): 251.

65 AGGA, 16H/4, "Confréries religieuse," Sebdou, February 24, 1904. On local healers: Jules Maistre, *Mœurs et coutumes kabyles* (Montpellier: Imprimerie de la Manufacture de la charité, 1905), 15–17, 37. Dr. A. Marty, *Islamisme: mœurs médicales et privées: Climatologie de l'Algérie, considérations sur l'Atmosphère* (Monaco: Imprimerie du "Petit Monégasque," 1903), 11–21; see Archives militaires de Vincennes, Service Historique de l'Armée de la Terre, 1M/2260. Maurice Joppé, "Étude de la position militaire de Bizot," Army of Africa, Division of Constantine, 3rd Regiment of Chasseurs d'Afrique, Constantine, December 7, 1875, 30–1; Bel and Eisenbeth, *Principales Races*, 92; Depont and Coppolani, *Confréries religieuses*, 142; Doutté, *Magie et religion*, 109, 178, 194; Liorel, *Races berbères*, 509. See ben Choaïb, "Les Marabouts Guérisseurs," 264–5, 255, and Maistre, *Mœurs et coutumes kabyles*, 73; Dr. Charles Amat, *Le M'zab et les M'zabites* (Paris: Challamel, 1888), 281; Bel, "Bibliographie . . . *Magie*," 119; Doutté, *Magie et religion*, 35, 36, 38, on doctors combating "superstition."

philosophy, and science did not compete, nor did they exist independently of ethnographies of specific rites.

Primitivist ethnography and the rites of supplication

Because rituals to end drought constituted a symbolic whole, colonial writers mined them for the ostensible primitivism of those who enacted them. Undoubtedly the most significant of the ethnographies of rain rituals was Alfred Bel's influential "Quelques rites pour obtenir la pluie en temps de sécheresse chez les musulmans maghribins" (1905). Drawing upon his experience as a teacher at the *madrasa* in Tilimsān,[66] Bel interpreted rites to end drought as evidence for Algerian primitivism. Rain rituals allowed Bel to uncover survivals, primitive philosophy, and indigenous resistance to science. When combined, these three intellectual strands proved a far more effective tool for the construction of a primitive Algeria than each would separately.

The construction of a primitive Algeria arose out of such analysis of specific ceremonies. In Tilimsān, a French schoolteacher watched, fascinated, as the people of the city struggled to end the drought. It was February 2, 1903, and Alfred Bel was taking notes. Perhaps he read Mauss or composed a letter to Arnold Van Gennep. But he watched. Singing, chanting, wailing, the despondent of Tilimsān toured the innumerable *zawāyā* and shrines of the beautiful city, invoking Muḥammad, Fāṭima, Abū Bākir, 'Uthmān, 'Umar, 'Alī, the prophet's family, the brilliant caliphs of the classical era, the holy and the powerful of the vanished beginning of days. Throughout the mosques echoed the sounds of the *suwar* of the Qur'ān, repeated in their entirety from memory by the *ṭalaba*. Each took a *sūra*, and as one finished, all cried out together, "God is compassionate with his servants, he blesses whom he wishes and his is the greatest power." At the saints' tombs, the people of Tilimsān shared a couscous, scattering its remnants on the ground for the birds.[67]

The women and children of 'Ayn Ṣafrā' walked slowly, laden with a contribution of flour. It was late winter, 1903, in the south Oranais, and the rains had failed, the flour all the more precious when the grain to replace it was withering. Congregating at one woman's home, they marked the beginning of the *ṭalab al-naw'*, solicitation of the tempest, of

[66] On rain rituals in the Constantinois, see J. Rosier, *Souvenirs d'Algérie* (Paris: Delhomme et Briguet, 1892), 250.

[67] Alfred Bel, "Quelques rites pour obtenir la pluie en temps de sécheresse chez les musulmans maghribins," in *Recueil de mémoires et de textes publiés en l'honneur du XIVe Congrès des Orientalistes par les professeurs de l'École supérieure des lettres et des médersas* (Algiers: Imprimerie orientale Pierre Fontana, 1905), 68–71.

the winter gales – the *ṭalab al-laṭīf*, the request for divine kindness. In an enormous dish the woman of the house mixed the proffered flour with butter and dates, the staple of the pre-desert economy[68] and emblem of the evanescent bounty of desert life. The *rūina*,[69] the communal dish, would later attest to the generosity and compassion of the suffering village. As they watched her subsume their meager flour contributions into their common offering, other women selected carefully, choosing only *al-mighrafa mtāʿ al-maraqa* for their masquerade.[70] Instantly finding it among the other implements, the women and children knew the spoon, they recognized the *mighrafa*, they had used it to make gravy or broth or bouillon. The older women perhaps remembered stretching a scant supply of meat by turning it to liquid,[71] conjuring a meal from dearth. In commemoration of such everyday miracles, marking acts of creation or of desperation, the women and children dressed the ladle in the clothes of a bride. The ladle disappeared, subsumed (like the paltry tributes of flour) into something larger, something communally made, a fetish-object for the village. Transformed, with a few scraps of gaudy cloth, from an object of mere utility into a powerful embodiment of collective need, the *mighrafa* became the *ghanja*.[72] For Berber speakers, *ghanja* signified a sauce spoon, another word for *mighrafa*. Nonetheless, all present knew its Arabic meaning as well. *Ghanja*, the sham bride, was a flirt, a coquette, a tease.[73] Dressed in ill-suited and incongruous finery, the spoon had become an effigy. Sprinkling the doll with water or with milk in desperate hope of conjuring the vital rain, the women and children processed slowly to the shrines of the marabouts, to the holy men. Stragglers and hangers-on joined them in their invocation: "Ghanja, ghanja, her head dissolves in water / O my Lord, moisten her eager supplicators / the ears of grain are thirsty / drench them O our Lord." At each marabout's shrine, the women burned incense, anointing the buildings at the holy sites with henna. In witness to the piety and generosity of the village, testifying to the injustice of the drought plaguing the virtuous, the women distributed the *rūina* to the poor, offering to the most needy

68 Julia Clancy-Smith, "A Desert Civilization: The Pre-Sahara of Algeria and Tunisia, *c.* 1800–1830," in Clancy-Smith, *Rebel and Saint: Muslim Notables, Populist Protest, Colonial Encounters (Algeria and Tunisia, 1800–1904)*, Comparative Studies on Muslim Societies, ed. Barbara D. Metcalf (Berkeley, Calif.: University of California Press, 1997). 11–33.

69 All translations from Arabic are mine. *Ruwina* [fuṣḥa] appears to come from the triliteral root *r-w-y*, as in the verb *rawiya*, to slake one's thirst, to be irrigated, to bring water, but also to narrate, to tell a story.

70 Bel, "Quelques rites," 65–6, transcribed the Oranais pronunciation as *el-mghorfa nt'at al-merga*.

71 Bel, "Quelques rites," 85–6.

72 Bel, "Quelques rites," 85.

73 *Ghanija* in fuṣḥa, from gh-n-j, to flirt or act coquettishly.

the scant fruits of their own harvest. But a few days later, the dust still clung to the feet of the children of ʿAyn Ṣafrāʾ, and the shoots shriveled and browned and the men choked in the fields. Leading a black bull, they gathered together, proceeding to the shrines of the marabouts as their mothers, wives, sisters, daughters had done earlier. In piety they went barefoot, as a mark of their humility. After the procession, the indigent feasted on the stringy meat of the gaunt bull, and perhaps on couscous offered by each household.[74]

Throughout the Oranais, from Alfred Bel's Tilimsān to the edge of the desert, the pious and the desperate performed similar rituals. In fear of the drought's inexorable progression, the women of the Banī Shūqrān divided into two groups. On a dark night, half of the women led a black cow from tent to tent, kicking up the dust of many days' drought and pleading with the cow, "O black cow, madam cow / Ask our Lord to give us rain." Before she rejoined her herd, the women remaining in the tent anxiously sprinkled the cow and her minders with water, desperately waiting for the cow to urinate. Her urination during or after the ceremony marked the successful completion of her obligations to the Banī Shūqrān, presaging the coming of the winter and spring rains. The cow, however, failed; she returned to the herd dusty and dry, and the women made their pilgrimage with the *ghanja* the next day. Their cries disturbed the silence at the shrines; "Ghanja, ghanja, make claim with our urgent request / O Lord, give us rain," or, more simply, "O ghanja of the tempest, O ghanja of the tempest."[75] No storms came, and the men, in turn, in vain, visited the marabouts. Forlorn, bereft of hope and water, the Banī Shûgrân implored the holiest among them, the *ṭalaba* (students) of the Qur'ān, the living saints, the pious, the learned. This last, somber, most desperate procession relied upon the mercy of God and the virtue of the village. Bare-headed the children came, barefoot the learned, and the pious and saintly came nude. Parading their shame and desperation to the blind eye of the marabouts' whitewashed shrines, the men returned slowly to the tents.[76]

For Alfred Bel, survivals offered a framework to comprehend rites. In "Quelques rites" remnants marked specific Algerian ceremonies and their participants as primitive. "These rites," noted Bel, "often being no more than the survival . . . of some most ancient pagan custom, or else the result of an extremely primitive mental state, I have insisted on each of

[74] Bel, "Quelques rites," 64–6.

[75] Bel, "Quelques rites," 86. "Shitā" (with an *alif maqṣūra*) is an example of the idiomatic spellings in Arabic that Bel used to attempt to register Oranais pronunciation; the *fuṣḥa* spelling is for rain is *shitāʾ* (*alif* and *ḥamza* in place of Bel's *alif maqṣūra*).

[76] Bel, "Quelques rites," 67–8.

these practices to try to extract from them [their] particular character."[77] Whereas survivals provided, on a theoretical level, a comparative discussion of cultural evolution, at the level of micro-ethnography, survivals allowed the ethnographer to ascribe specific meanings to the smallest of symbols. Hence, Bel compared the drought rituals to Bulgarian agricultural festivals,[78] or to Welsh rain ceremonies,[79] or could interpret the *ghanja* itself, "an instrument that serves to pour liquid,"[80] as "the symbol of rain personified" and as a pre-Islamic "rain goddess . . . transformed . . . into a simple higher power who can intercede with God," similar to the rain goddesses among peoples he termed "savages."[81] The survival concept enabled Bel to view the *ghanja* as a rain goddess embedded within ceremonies carried out by avowedly monotheistic Muslims, and therefore to denigrate Algerians and their popular religious practice as primitive. The resulting idea that evolution left traces on contemporary civilization permitted Bel and others to make theoretical comparisons.

Alfred Bel emphasized survivals as indicative of the rivalry between popular religion and orthodoxy. Colonial ethnography differentiated Islamic orthodoxy from popular religion by seeking out "primitive" survivals.

> The ancient rites did not delay in penetrating Islam[,] above all when the inefficacy of the Muslim ritual at provoking rain became apparent. In the generality of pagan rites that one finds through the Maghrib, we would be led to think that they have never ceased to coexist with the orthodox ceremonies. I would even add that the latter [the orthodox ceremonies], in certain rural regions, have not succeeded in taking root and have never been practiced there.

Bel highlighted saints, the *ghanja*, and various invocations as particularly un-Islamic.[82] For him, such atavistic remnants undermined Islam's spiritual mastery. With the local rituals he deemed primitive and universal,[83] Bel juxtaposed the idea of an imposed and imposing Islamic orthodoxy. In colonial ethnographies, rain ceremonies attested to the continuing presence of primitive religion.

Bel interpreted rain rites as evidence of a larger, philosophical and religious system. After Hubert and Mauss, Bel depicted in religious thought

[77] Bel, "Quelques rites," 49. [78] Bel, "Quelques rites," 86.
[79] *Revue historique religieuse*, 38, 335, in Bel, "Quelques rites," 81, and Bel, "Quelques rites," 93–4.
[80] Bel, "Quelques rites," 86. [81] Bel, "Quelques rites," 86–7.
[82] Bel, "Quelques rites," 74. David S. Powers found a similar trend toward the designation of certain practices as "un-Islamic" in colonial legal texts; see David S. Powers, "Orientalism, Colonialism, and Legal History: The Attack on Muslim Family Endowments in Algeria and India," *Comparative Studies in Society and History* 31, no. 3 (1989): 570.
[83] See Bel, "Quelques rites," 77.

the inability to differentiate physical harm from divine chastisement for transgression.[84] Furthermore, Bel perceived in the *ghanja* ceremonies a discrimination among different classes of religious subjects (male / female, old / young, holy / unclean, black / white, educated / student) absent from the orthodox *ṣalāt al-istisqā'*, or prayer for rain.[85] Such organizational uniformity marked popular religion, for Bel, as a totalizing philosophy. At the same time, Bel could only conceive of popular religion as aberrant, as heterodox, as infiltrated with the remnants of previous religious systems. Quite simply, Bel combined the intellectual theme of survivals and that of popular religion as an inferior philosophy.

> It is naturally in the countryside that orthodox Islam has least penetrated; it is there too, consequently, that it is necessary to look for pagan survivals. They are sometimes maintained there in remarkable purity. Even in cities, outside of an infinitesimal minority of [the] literate, instructed in the knowledge of dogma, the people have conserved a good number of beliefs and antique rites more or less distorted by contact with Islam.[86]

Bel depicted the problem of drought as essentially a religious problem and Algerians' solutions as rituals invoking the divine. In his ethnography of rain rituals, Bel understood Algerian conceptions of causality as religious; by placing survivals at the heart of religious rituals, he transposed the valorization of religion as primitive to Algerians themselves.

Bel, like the Algerians about whom he wrote, could provide neither explanation nor remedy for the weather patterns that caused drought. French science offered no alternative means to comprehend climatic variations. This rendered difficult the invocation of scientific discourse to distinguish primitive from civilized, colonized from colonizer. Nevertheless, Bel managed to do so. "For the man who takes God as the primary cause of the here-below, every event outside of the habitual order of phenomena and which cannot be explained by scientific causes . . . is for him a warning that God sends him."[87] Deftly, Bel reintroduced the distinction between the realm of scientific explanation and that of religious belief. Even for those events without adequate scientific explanation, Bel implied, a man who did *not* take God as the primary cause, whose philosophical system remained distinct from the religious, would not interpret a warning.

In "Quelques rites," Bel incorporated the notion of salvage, of religion as primitive philosophy, and of science as a distinguishing characteristic of intellectual capability to render Algerians as inalienably primitive.

84 Bel, "Quelques rites," 52.
85 Bel, "Quelques rites," 62. See Doutté, *Magie et religion*, 591–3, on the *ṣalāt al-istisqā'*.
86 Bel, "Quelques rites," 64. 87 Bel, "Quelques rites," 52.

These three intellectual strands allowed Bel to move between universalizing statements about evolution and the microscopic example he analyzed. This purported primitivism erected a totalizing edifice of social scientific knowledge with French intellectual development as the culmination of cultural evolution. This structure denigrated colonized peoples as insufficiently evolved, as atavistic, stultified, and primitive. Upon this edifice, the French colonial apparatus built the civilizing mission.

"Fleeting hallucinations"

Even muttering the *basmala* [*bismillah al-raḥman al-raḥīm*, in the name of God the merciful and compassionate] as an imprecation against evil and possession, few walked alone during the last rays of afternoon sunlight or in the dark night without fear of the *jinn*. Dry creek beds, places of slaughter, wells, streams, hot springs, places of running blood or water, above all the entire Sahara itself, all sheltered the invisible possessors; to appease the *jinn* well-diggers would sacrifice a sheep, mixing blood and water in commemoration or awe of the near-miraculous appearance of water in the midst of the desert.[88] In the form of nearly any animal, or even human, or, most ominously, invisibly, they watched over humans, viciously avenging any perceived slight; many Muslims took simple precautions – discarding wash-water with care, moving deliberately so as not to strike the invisible and ruthless *jinn*.[89] "It is almost impossible to not

[88] Louis Voinot, "Oudjda et l'Amalat," *BSGAO* 31 (June 1911): 181; Bel and Eisenbeth, *Principales Races*, 92; Andrews, *Fontaines des génies*, 10; Captain Léopold Louis Aymard, *Les Touareg* (Paris: Librairie Hachette et Cie, 1911), 78; Edmond Doutté, *L'Islam algérien en an 1900* (Algiers-Mustapha: Giralt, 1900), 101; Henri Duveyrier, *Les Touareg du Nord: exploration du Sahara* (Paris: Challamel Aîné, 1864), 414–19; Fernand Foureau, *Au Sahara: mes deux missions de 1892 et 1893. Le Gassi Touil et le Grand Erg. L'Oudje sud et le Tinghert. Hassi Messeguem et Hassi Imoulay*, 2nd edn (Paris: Augustin Challamel, 1897), 109; Fernard Foureau, "Une Mission chez les Touareg," *Bulletin de la Société de Géographie de Paris* 7th ser., 14 (1893:4): 506; Bonnafont, *Pérégrinations*, 381; Robert, "Contribution au folk-lore," 564; Edward Westermarck, *The Belief in Spirits in Morocco, Acta Academiae Aboensis, Humaniora* I, 1 (Åbo, Finland: Åbo Akademi, and Helsingfors: The Finnish Literary Society, 1920), 19–48; Pandolfo, *Impasse of the Angels*, 240.

[89] Bel and Eisenbeth, *Principales Races*, 92; Andrews, *Fontaines des génies*, 26; Maurice Benhazera, *Six Mois chez les Touareg du Ahaggar* (Algiers: Adolphe Jourdan, 1908), 60; A. Cour, "Le Culte du serpent dans les traditions populaires du Nord-Ouest Algérien," *BSGAO* 31 (1911): 61–73; Certeux and Carnoy, *L'Algérie traditionnelle*, 177–8; Joseph Desparmet, *Coutumes, institutions, croyances des Musulmans de l'Algérie*, vol. I: l'Enfance, le mariage, et la famille, trans. Henri Pérès and G.-H. Bousquet, 2nd edn (Paris: J. Carbonel, 1948), 71; Achille Robert, *Métiers et types algériens* (Algiers: Ernest Mallebay, 1895), 31–4; Westermarck, *The Belief in Spirits in Morocco*, 13.

harm the genies, sometimes, as they are omnipresent while at the same time invisible."[90] The fearful and the learned knew that whistling or even merely speaking their name invited the unwanted attention, the great cruelty or undeserved rewards, of the mercurial, capricious, and pitiless *jinn*.[91] It was better to refer to them as the Believers, the Muslims, the Masters of the House, to placate them with unsalted food, sacrificed chickens, incense. Fend them off with flame or candles or iron or the *basmala*.[92] Best to pass unnoticed, best not to summon them.

Some accepted the perilously ambiguous gifts of the *jinn*; some Algerians called upon them for their costly aid. Their omnipresence, their constant invisible attendance, made contact simple. Sometimes a woman would make a couscous, reserving a small portion of it for the *jinnī*, burning incense, lavender, or sandalwood, and offering rings or keys or other bits of symbolically imbued metal.[93] Just as words could ward off the *jinn*, so, too, could the proper invocation summon them. A woman stood on an earthen terrace at midnight. Perhaps with a brief hesitation, she cast a flowerpot filled with dirt towards the sea, crying, "Peace be upon you, earth of this pot! / Whether you be dry or wet I know not / Give me news of [the desired one], be he lost in the ocean!" From near and far came voices and images, spectral faces and mocking laughter, offering her their intelligence or their malice. Or she could make an effigy out of charred wood, tracing on its carbonized surface, however imperfectly, a face (the eyes, the nose, the mouth, the seat of the soul), clothing it, inviting life into its charred, dead body. As she lay in bed facing the doll, she stumbled over her question, faltered in interrogating the male or female spirit who now possesses the figure; her hesitation only provoked the wrath of the easily piqued spirit. "Why have you summoned me?" the *jinnī* asked in a rage, and the consequences would be dire. Few humans trafficked lightly with the *jinn*. Perhaps she captured a spider, enclosing it in a small box. The *jinn*, confined and temporarily helpless, offered enigmatic responses to her questions.[94]

90 Andrews, *Fontaines des génies*, 24–5.

91 Robert, *L'Arabe tel qu'il est*, 34; Andrews, *Fontaines des génies*, 18.

92 Bel and Eisenbeth, *Principales Races*, 92; Westermarck, *The Belief in Spirits in Morocco*, 49–75.

93 Certeux and Carnoy, *L'Algérie traditionnelle*, 83; L. Bertholon and E. Chantre, *Recherches anthropologiques dans la Berbérie orientale: Tripolitaine, Tunisie, Algérie*, vol I: *Anthropométrie, craniométrie, ethnographie* (Lyon: A. Rey, 1913), 609.

94 Certeux and Carnoy, *L'Algérie traditionnelle*, 83–4, 169–70; Andrews, *Fontaines des génies*, 23; Doutté, *Magie et religion*, 91; and G. Trenga, "Les Chahaouna: notes sur les Mediouna et les Oulad Zian," *BSGA* 14 (1909): 19; Bertholon and Chantre, *Recherches anthropologiques*, 607–8.

Although the *jinn* (genies; sing. *jinnī*) have entered contemporary popular consciousness through popular representations, Islamic cosmology portrayed genies as beings of a different order from humans.[95] Certeux and Carnoy concisely defined the *jinn*:

The *Djinns* [*sic*] or *Djnoun* [*sic*] are . . . good or evil spirits, but ordinarily . . . the latter.

The people represent them as horrible forms and hideous faces, as they occupy themselves only with doing evil and horrifying mortals. At other times they are a kind of fairy, lascivious, enchantresses, inhabiting a superb palace in unfamiliar places, living there in the midst of all the pleasures, and attracting the travelers that happen [upon them] to their pleasure. Or they are . . . water genies, assuming the gracious form of a gazelle or a dove, wandering the countryside on serene nights.[96]

Ugly or beautiful, deformed or perfect, initiating unwitting travelers into unknown pleasures or luring them to their death (or, frequently, both), the *jinn* embodied amoral caprice, uncontrollable whim, and unpredictable intervention. Malicious, outside of the moral order established by the Qur'ān and the *ḥadīth*, genies alternately thwart and aid humankind whimsically, with indifference to the repercussions of their actions.

Ethnographers of religion weaved vivid descriptions of the dire consequences of contact with the *jinn*. Attesting to the amount of detail informants provided to colonial ethnographers, they rendered Algerians exotic by associating popular beliefs and the realm of the incredible and the fantastic.

Sometimes, the djins [*sic*] are taken with a violent passion for a human being, of a different sex from theirs. They manifest, sure enough, their love to the preferred, profiting from [the beloved's] sleep for this, and procuring for him / her veritable sensual ecstasies. Children can be born from these couplings (the case is quite rare), [but] they do not live! The woman beloved of a djin [*sic*], having tasted his caresses, finds without savor the maladroit and selfish embraces of poor mortals[;] also she never marries! Such a union would be, moreover,

[95] Andrews, *Fontaines des genies*, 6; Doutté, *Islam algérien*, 101. P. Kiva (Lt.-Col. Paul Waché), *En Algérie (Souvenirs)* (Paris: Henri Charles-Lavauzelle, 1894), 70. On the *jinn* in Morocco: Pandolfo, *Impasse of the Angels*, 83, 85, 240–6; see Westermarck, *The Belief in Spirits in Morocco.*

[96] Certeux and Carnoy, *L'Algérie traditionelle*, 81–2. On ghouls, see Desparmet, *Coutumes*, 87; René Basset, *Contes populaires berbères: Recueillis, traduits et annotés par René Basset* (Paris: Ernest Leroux, 1887), 60; Aymard, *Touareg*, 59–61 (on vampires).

a certain condemnation to death for the spouse, who would perish infallibly as soon as he attempt to consummate, in effect, the marriage.[97]

The description of the romantic lives of genies did not merely gratify prurient interests. The author, Capitain Léopold Aymard, included the passage as part of his ethnography *Les Touareg*. The exoticized descriptions of the genies' love and the humorous tone belie the facile assumption that the passage represents mere persiflage, an amusing respite within his ethnography. Quite the opposite; the love life of the *janūn* offered important information about the Tuareg: from the perspective of the colonial military officer, it established their naïveté. Ethnographic discourse on the *jinn* articulated a credulous, fantastic Algeria. Colonial portrayals of Algerians as simultaneously exotic and naïve engendered the colonial family romance of a primitive Algeria and a zealous, civilizing France.

Though ethnographic discussions of genies themselves contributed to primitivist discourses, they also arose from an intellectual climate that *already* cast colonized peoples as incompletely civilized. Most ethnographers rarely followed their stories of the *jinn* with explicit references to Algerian primitivism. They did not have to; the colorful accounts of the genies represented exotic "superstition" in a context that equated popular religion with anti-positivism. In essence, primitivism engendered further primitivism: the denigration of popular religion provided the essential framework for understanding primitivist ethnographies. Hence, ethnographers embedded genies in the opposition between science and popular beliefs.

Many French writers interpreted genie legends as a primitive method of explaining causality. The *jinn*'s behavior mimicked the cruel indifference of the natural environment; not surprisingly, genie legends are far more frequent in the Sahara than in urban parts of the Maghrib or Mashriq.[98] Proselytizers of science, many ethnographers focused on beliefs explaining natural phenomena.[99] Popular belief in genies as causal agents and figures to appease and supplicate reaffirmed French convictions that colonized Algerians had constructed a system of understanding that not only failed to account for science but intrinsically opposed it.

[97] Aymard, *Touareg*, 64–78. Punctuation in the original. See also Doutté, *Islam algérien*, 101; Westermarck, *The Belief in Spirits in Morocco*, 9–11. For another take on French understanding of Algerian notions of marriage and childbirth, see Allan Christelow on the "sleeping baby": Allan Christelow, *Muslim Law Courts and the French Colonial State in Algeria* (Princeton, NJ: Princeton University Press, 1985), 128–30.

[98] Aymord, *Touareg*, 59–78 *passim*. On genies associated with the earth and with the sea, see Bertholon and Chantre, *Recherches anthropologiques*, 607. On the association of specific genies with time, see Doutté, *Magie et religion*, 68.

[99] E.g., Certeux and Carnoy, *L'Algérie traditionnelle*, 77–8.

Many Algerians associated the *jinn* with specific illnesses. Legends about genies, invisible, omnipresent, resembled contemporary French ideas of contagion; one informant perspicaciously noted, " 'the *jenoun* [*sic*] are our microbes.' Every malady," the ethnographers continued, "is caused by the incarnation of a *jinn* in the body of the patient."[100] No other ethnographer connected infectious causality and the *jinn*, instead conceiving of genies as a primitive conception of medicine. In *Islamisme: Mœurs médicales et privées* (1903), Dr. A. Marty contended that "the Djinn . . . is considered by *every* Muslim as the *sole author* of all suffering and of all maladies."[101] With the deftly universalizing narrative of colonial ethnography, Marty effectively preserved Algerians as uncomprehending of causality, as uniformly superstitious. Citing theories of cholera infection, by which one genie inscribed the names of those to die and four others caused symptoms, Marty emphasized genies as evidence of Algerians' credulity.[102] In *Coutumes, institutions, croyances des Musulmans de l'Algérie*, Joseph Desparmet argued that Algerian women attributed infants' deaths to a malign genie-twin: for every human child born, a genie gave birth to a genie-child at exactly the same moment; both genie mother and genie infant could cause illness in the human twin.[103] As an experiential expression of medical discourse, the Algerian conception of invisible causality resembled European medical theories of miasmas, poisonous airs.[104] Nevertheless, ethnographers such as Marty and Desparmet disavowed such similarities, presenting instead the role of *jinn* in illness as picturesque detail. In colonial ethnographies, popular beliefs about the *jinn* in medical causality marked Algerians as inferior in their explanations, as exotic.

Methods to combat *jinn* damage interested French ethnographers. Exoticized accounts of combating genie possession reinforced the differentiation between civilizing colonizer and superstitious colonized. In Tidikelt, Louis Voinot recorded the burning of aromatic gums and the recitation of the *bismillah* to chase genies.[105] L. Bertholon and E. Chantre claimed that the ʿĪssāwa cured the possessed by interrogating the genie (answering through the victim) and sacrificing the animal

[100] Bertholon and Chantre, *Recherches anthropologiques*, 607. On the *jinn* and the body in Morocco; see Westermarck, *The Belief in Spirits in Morocco*, 8.
[101] Marty, *Islamisme*, 49. Emphasis added. [102] Marty, *Islamisme*, 50–1.
[103] Desparmet, *Coutumes*, 45. On genies, insanity, and neurological conditions, see Bertholon and Chantre, *Recherches anthropologiques*, 607, on the *majnūn* (insane), which shares the root j-n-n with *jinnī*; Marty, *Islamisme*, 50; Doutté, *Magie et religion*, 224; and Robert, "Contribution au folk-lore," 569.
[104] On contagion as a sociopolitical problem, see Andrew R. Aisenberg, *Contagion: Disease, Government, and the "Social Question" in Nineteenth-Century France* (Stanford, Calif.: Stanford University Press, 1999).
[105] Voinot, "Le Tidikelt," 437; Arripe, "Essai sur le folkore," 17.

demanded. The healer then smeared the blood on the possessed's tongue. However, the process had its own dangers: a genie who departed by the eyes, nose, ears, or mouth left the patient blind, without a sense of smell, deaf, or mute. The only safe means of egress was the toes.[106]

Joseph Desparmet's older female informants recounted the substitution by the *jinn* of genie-children for human infants. Out of fear of just such a switch, parents remained with a newborn for the first four days of life. If not, incessant crying, extreme thinness, raised eyebrows, deadness of the extremities, and subsequent death revealed the changeling. To reverse the substitution, during Friday prayers, the mother placed the child in the center of the room, sweeping dust from four corners into the basket-cradle with the child. Invoking the genies, "O people of this dung heap, give us the child of our house and take back that of the manure pile," the mother threw the cradle over a pile of manure, where a waiting woman caught the basket. Taking a different path, the receiving woman returned to the mother's house. "If the child recovers, one does not fail to say: 'Those believers [*jinn*] have brought back our child; may God render them always sensitive and good in respect to us.'" Desparmet also mentioned another, more sinister, remedy: burying the child, with a bone broken into ninety-nine pieces, in an imitation tomb dug in a dungheap. If, upon her return, the mother found more than ninety-nine fragments, the child's survival – i.e., the return of the human baby – was assured. Another method involved plunging the child in a basket into a well; tears indicated the survival (return) of the human child. Seven submergings without tears denoted imminent death.[107] For Desparmet, changeling rituals demonstrated the centrality of genie legends as explanations of causality; infant mortality became a function of the incompatibility of humans and their spirit brethren. Desparmet in effect interpreted genie legends as an alternative way of understanding inexplicable events.

Not all methods of combating the *jinn* evinced the ferocity of the changeling rites. More frequently, ethnographers such as Marty described amulets as a more predictable means of expelling or warding off the *jinn*, yet more evidence of Algerian primitivism.

> [T]he amulet . . . has the power to combat this evil influence [of the genie] and to heal all ills. The marabouts, under the pretext that the command of spirits gives them the innate science of healing the body, pitilessly exploit . . . the boundless credulity of a people . . . inclined toward superstitious ideas.[108]

[106] Bertholon and Chantre, *Recherches anthropologiques*, 608. On animal sacrifices, see Andrews, *Fontaines des génies*, 11–12, 15; Doutté, *Magie et religion*, 458.

[107] Desparmet, *Coutumes*, 23–4.

[108] Marty, *Islamisme*, 49, 52; Desparmet, *Coutumes*, 42–3; and Duveyrier, *Touareg du Nord*, 419, also discuss amulets; Westermarck, *The Belief in Spirits in Morocco*, 107–19.

14. “Marabout à Berrian – Mzab,” from Liorel, “Dans le M’zab.”

Portraying the marabout as an adroit manipulator, Marty dismissed Algerians as overly superstitious and naïve, reducing "the science of healing" to superstition. He fastened upon curative rituals as another discriminatory facet upon which the civilizing, scientific mission could operate.

Moreover, Marty interpreted genie cures as a collective obsession. In their beliefs in the *jinn*, Algerian Muslims evinced what Marty presented as savagery. About amulets, he wrote:

> [a]ll these practices are pushed to such a degree that, under the influence of fleeting hallucinations . . . , the Muslims are, all the time, tortured by the constant preoccupation with the djinn [sic]. They consult their dreams, forebodings, unlucky days, to make a decision, and their torment disappears . . . only with the help of the amulet . . . [T]his religious sentiment, pushed to the most baleful exaggeration, . . . influences their ethics, and it is certainly not the errant, savage, monotonous, melancholic, and above all isolated . . . life that could ever be the remedy to their superstitious ideas.[109]

Paralyzed by the supernatural, pursued by phantoms of chastisement, Algerians appeared as prisoners of superstition. An ineluctable part of the "savage" lives of Algerians, the *jinn* emerged, not as picturesque exemplars of the exotic Orient, but instead as a site of intervention for French knowledge.

Alfred Bel interpreted methods of defeating genies as survivals, further evidence of Algerian superstition.

> To dominat[e] the *djinns* . . . a sorcerer is necessary, or some specialized tâleb [*sic*: *ṭālib*, Quranic student; generally, a learned Muslim], who knows the technique, the rites and incantations to employ in the matter; still one must omit nothing . . . , for if the operation fails, one incurs the wrath of the djinn . . .
>
> All this is very ancient; and Islam has only brought to the Sorcerer-tâleb several words . . . from the Coran [*sic*], which, mixed with . . . sorcery, serve in the creation of amulets and formulas of magic incantations.[110]

For Bel, the legends of repelling the *jinn* reinscribed Algerian primitivism. The *jinn* furnished yet more evidence of survivals, cultural evolution, and hence of a primitive Algeria. J. B. Andrews devoted *Les Fontaines des génies* to the search for survivals of what he deemed more primitive, sub-Saharan

[109] Marty, *Islamisme*, 53, 56. Edmond Doutté dedicated his *Notes sur l'Islâm maghribin: les Marabouts* (Paris: Ernest Leroux, 1900) to the study of Islamic saints, whose role in curing genie possession Marty had described. Echoing metropolitan tropes of Catholicism as a faith strongest among women, Doutté noted the presence of female saints, whom he portrayed as scarcely tolerated imitations, "relatives of more celebrated [male] saints." See Doutté, *Notes sur l'Islâm maghribin*, 93, 95, 96, 100, and Auguste Mouliéras, "Hagiologie Mag'ribine," *BSGAO* 19 (1899): 374–6.

[110] Bel and Eisenbeth, *Principales Races*, 92.

religion, revealing his indebtedness to a French cultural evolutionism.[111] Where Marty posited savagery in the absence of science, Andrews and Bel found the primitive because of the presence of remnants; interpretations of the *jinn* did not deviate from the primitivist anthropological script established by Doutté, Bel, and others.

"Nous sommes," wrote Jules Liorel of his compatriots in Algeria, "les mauvais génies dans tous les contes de fées."[112] We are the evil geniuses in all of the fairy tales. The French, ethnographers contended, represented creatures of discriminating logic and absolute authority. The fairy tales, however, of late nineteenth- and early twentieth-century Europe differed dramatically from those of Algeria; they were stories, not of *Alif layla wa-layla*'s Aladdin, but of Shelley's *Frankenstein*. The calculated, calculating experimentation of the scientist replaced the enigmatic curses of the *jinn*. They were, nevertheless, more similar than different; much like the *jinn*, these mad scientists performed their transformations through magical words. Through alchemical ethnography the anthropologist converted popular religious expressions into manifestations of primitivism.

Like the *jinn*, the scientist-ethnographers were less evil geniuses than they were beings subject to a foreign and at times incomprehensible moral code, in the case of ethnographers, a code that valorized the secular legacies of French republicanism above all else. This code combined the intellectual inheritance of cultural evolutionism with the fetishization of science to depict Algerian popular beliefs as atavistic – primitive. The affinity of the ethnographic for the creation of primitivism did not represent mere textual sleight of hand or narrative exoticism, but rather arose out of a particular political climate. Placing cultural difference at the heart of the colonial project, the civilizing mission required an object on which to act. It demanded, in short, a culture to civilize; to create one, out of the cloth of popular religious practices, colonial ethnographers wove a narrative of Algerian primitivism.

[111] See, for example, Andrews, *Fontaines des génies*, 28–31, in particular the references to Westermarck.

[112] Liorel, "Dans Le M'zab," 28–9.

5 "Have you need of a model, he will furnish one on command": the gendering of morality and the production of difference in colonial ethnography

The subaltern cannot speak French.[1] To seek to reconstitute gender relations through the lens of colonial ethnography is a project doomed to failure. We cannot recapture the content of the interactions that catalyzed ethnographic moralizing. Like E. M. Forster's Marabar Caves[2], the archive provides only hauntingly empty echoes of cultural interactions neither recorded nor remembered, but rather compulsively and convulsively reverberated, endlessly repeated as statements about morality. The content of those statements, like the events of the Marabar Caves, remain beyond our narrative and analytical ken. Only the moralizing impulse remains, the damning gaze of a colonial power intent on framing interactions between men and women as a pretext for empire. The archive remains silent about the events of the caves, offers only, to borrow from Salman Rushdie, "a framed letter from Morgan Forster describing oddly echoing caves in the side of a scrubby hill," yields only the descriptive and deceptive voices of ethnographic authority, consecrated within the frame of the archive itself.[3] The colonial archive describes, not the voice, but the echo; an analysis of the ethnography of gender in colonial Algeria must acknowledge that the ethnographic text represents a moralizing political project posing as authority.

In Algeria, the moral arguments underpinning the civilizing mission arose out of the colonial ethnography of gender. The civilizing mission cast gender relations as a moral problem requiring a political solution. "The construction," writes Julia Clancy-Smith, "of French Algeria was as much the forging of a . . . spectrum of gazes fixed upon Muslim women – as it was the assembling of mechanisms for political and economic

[1] Cf. Gayatri Chakravorty Spivak, "Can the Subaltern Speak?" in Cary Nelson and Lawrence Grossberg, eds., *Marxism and the Interpretation of Culture* (Champaign, Ill.: University of Illinois Press, 1988), 271–313.
[2] E. M. Forster, *A Passage to India* (New York: Harcourt, 1924; 1984).
[3] Salman Rushdie, *The Ground Beneath Her Feet* (London: Vintage Books, 2000), 315.

control."[4] In Algeria, many ethnographers reduced cultural difference to a function of gender, refined it into the antithesis of European self-conceptions of morality. Moralizing ethnographies presented civil life as a space for colonial reform.

Most ethnographers conceived of gender in Algeria in ways that demanded colonial intervention. At the same time, women in late nineteenth-century Europe began to reconfigure political, social, and cultural forms. The imperial project allowed both men and women to project anxieties and aspirations onto the colonized body. The question remains, however, of how colonial domination, ethnographic narrative, and the production of gendered morality combined to generate the conceptions of difference that underpinned the civilizing mission. "European men and women," Clancy-Smith contends, combined "ethnography with the imperatives of colonial rule" and did so largely through analyses of gender as a colonial object.[5] However, colonial ethnographies portrayed gender relations as both marker *and* effect of Algerian alterity. Gender interaction marked Algerians as in need of the civilizing mission, yet that very need, according to ethnographers, gendered behavior patterns.

In the context of colonial ethnographies, Algerian women emerge primarily as a series of roles. These object-roles marked yet another site for the intervention of the *mission civilisatrice*.[6] For some, the position of Algerian women in relation to Algerian and European women and men came to define Algerian culture. As Clancy-Smith has noted, the "expository strategy for laying bare the condition of the Muslim woman . . . was fundamental to the emerging colonial ethnographic gaze."[7] At the same time, however, the ethnography of gender relations arose out of moral valuations. Colonel Corneille Trumelet, for example, "found himself in the

[4] Julia Clancy-Smith, "Islam, Gender, and Identities in the Making of French Algeria, 1830–1962," in Julia Clancy-Smith and Frances Gouda, eds., *Domesticating the Empire: Race, Gender, and Family Life in French and Dutch Colonialism* (Charlottesville, Va.: University Press of Virginia, 1998), 155.

[5] Christelle Taraud, *La Prostitution coloniale: Algérie, Tunisie, Maroc (1830–1962)* (Paris: Éditions Payot, 2003), 291; Clancy-Smith, "Islam," 167; cf. Mary A. Renda, *Taking Haiti: Military Occupation and the Culture of U.S. Imperialism, 1915–1940* (Chapel Hill, NC: University of North Carolina Press, 2001), 15–6.

[6] François Leimdorfer, "La Condition des indigènes dans l'Algérie coloniale: essai d'analyse socio-linguistique à partir des titres de theses soutenues pendant la période coloniale," in *Connaissances du Maghreb: sciences sociales et colonization* (Paris: Éditions du Centre national de la recherche scientifique, 1984), 198; Sakina Messaadi, *Les Romancières coloniales et la femme colonisée: contribution à une étude de la littérature coloniale en Algérie dans la première moitié du XXe siècle* (Algiers: Entreprise nationale du livre, 1990), 341.

[7] Clancy-Smith, "Islam," 163. See also 163–7, and Gen. Eugène Daumas, *La Femme arabe* (Algiers: Adolphe Jourdan, 1912), 73, in Clancy-Smith, "Islam."

middle of biblical times, with the patriarchs and beautiful girls of Israel."[8] These "beautiful girls" and patriarchal men firmly preserved gender relations as invariable and marked Algeria as atavistic and other. In his *La Condition sociale des indigènes algériens* (1899), the ethnographer Henry Drapier defined "Arab society" as "a group of men ruled by deplorable institutions: polygamy, the debasement of women," and other factors.[9] Drapier expressly defined the object of his ethnography as *men*, but men whose debased women compromised their stature as moral beings. For Trumelet and Drapier, gender relations indicated colonial difference.

Their ethnographic generalizations exemplified the use of gender relations as a synecdoche for difference. Or, as Jean Le Roy phrased it, "if the level of civilization is evaluated for a people [by] the treatment that it reserves for the woman," then he had "to admit," for example, "that the Kabile [*sic*] people has remained at the lowest level of barbarity."[10] The use of gender as a defining characteristic of difference introduced the language of morality, of "barbarity," into ethnography. Ethnographic theories of difference attached moral evaluation to gender reference. The civilizing mission became a moralizing mission.

Ethnographic tourism provided one means of presenting gender relations as the fundamental basis of Algerian cultural identity. Focusing in particular on commodifications of the body, tourists sought out, in miniature and in mimicry, prepackaged cultural performances deemed "authentic." The prurience of ethnography resulted directly from its fascination with the body.[11] At the same time, colonial pornography recalled moral strictures through transgression; colonies became a place in which colonizers violated normative, European codes of behavior. The ethnography of the body in Algeria served primarily to gender morality.

Ethnographic tourism's objectification of the body did not limit itself to heterosexual desire. Both male and female ethnographic observers eroticized the bodies of both genders, and interpreted homo- and heterosocial behaviors in different ways. In an 1899 review of Auguste Mouliéras's *Le Maroc inconnu*, Edmond Doutté depicted homosexual desire in Morocco as indicative of moral degeneration. For both ethnographers, homoerotic desire transformed the Djebala of Morocco into

[8] Col. C. Trumelet, *Les Français dans le désert: journal historique, militaire et descriptif d'une expédition aux limites du Sahara algérien*, 2nd edn (Paris: Challamel Aîné, 1885), v.

[9] Henry Drapier, *La Condition sociale des indigènes algériens* (Paris: Ar. Rousseau, and Algiers: Adolphe Jourdan, 1899), 160–1.

[10] Jean Le Roy, *Deux Ans de séjour en petite Kabylie: un people de Barbares en territoire français* (Paris: Augustin Challamel, 1911), 261.

[11] Nicholas B. Dirks, *Castes of Mind: Colonialism and the Making of Modern India* (Princeton, NJ: Princeton University Press, 2001), 192–3.

lascivious men and weak, permissive women. "The corruption of morals" among the Djebala "attains an unimaginable degree. . . . The Djebala are rotted by sodomy."[12] Doutté castigated both the wives who tolerated their husbands' homosexual affairs, and the men who "glory in having such a companion and promenade with" one of what Doutté referred to as "these foul creatures."[13] Doutté and Mouliéras related the Djebala to the moralized strictures of French ethnography. Sexuality permitted the entrance of moral discrimination into ethnographic description. Above all, the colonial ethnography of gender in North Africa concerned itself with the articulation of *moral* statements about *gendered* interactions.

In *Les Deux Algérie* (1899), Georges Viollier visited a café in which young boys performed dances traditionally reserved for women. This inversion disturbed Viollier, who carefully reaffirmed the boundaries of desire. Disturbingly, he objected, not to the *age* of the child-dancers, but to their gender.

> In a little room filled with men . . . young Arab boys executed . . . a variety of the belly-dance that it would be rather awkward to want to define . . . [They] affect a most accentuated feminine allure.
>
> They come dancing to brush up against the spectators; their eyes have the teasings of courtesans.
>
> In the country, these dancers of the masculine sex enjoy a reputation of the least honorable. Rapidly informed of their identity[,] we went out again.[14]

Viollier depicted objectification of the male body as immorality. As males in a role deemed feminine, these dancers shared the deviance of "courtesans." In his discussion of these dancers, Viollier utilized the language of refusal to impose morality. When he learned of their less than honorable reputation, he departed, emphasizing his rejection. Viollier not only declined to participate in the spectacle, he recounted it as illustrative of Algerian deviance.

Government-sponsored tourist literature in English developed some of the most astonishing eroticizations of the body in colonial ethnographic texts. The December 22, 1913 issue of the weekly newspaper of the Comité d'Hivernage Algérien, published "A Café at Laghouat."[15] In a

[12] Edmond Doutté, "Les Djebala du Maroc, d'après les travaux de M. A. Mouliéras," *Bulletin de la Société de Géographie et d'Archéologie de la Province d'Oran* 14 (1899): 334–5.

[13] Doutté, "Djebala," 335.

[14] Georges Viollier, *Les Deux Algérie*, new edn (Paris: Paul Dupont, 1899), 115–6. See also Paul Eudel, *Hivernage en Algérie* (Paris: Hérissy et Fils, 1909), 51–2; G. de Lombay, *En Algérie: Alger, Oran, Tlemcen* (Paris: Ernest Leroux, 1893), 301; J. Rosier, *Souvenirs d'Algérie* (Paris: Delhomme et Briguet, 1892), 261.

[15] An asterisk attributes the text to S. Barin, *L'Algérie qui s'en va*, while the end of the text attributes authorship or translation to "A.S.G."

"big native café . . . vaulted like a church," enveloped by an exotic atmosphere of "strange odors," the author, A. S. G., observed the "spectral heads" of "magnificent ferocious figures, bare skulls with the Mahometan tuft at the top and grimacing negro faces" and their "fantastic profiles" in shadow.[16] He visited the café to watch the dancing of women, but his description of male bodies evinced the permeation of the eroticized body into nearly all cultural description.

A big buck nigger, bare headed, whose athletic form is set off to advantage by a majestic burnous, is furiously blowing into a haut bois [*sic*: oboe]; an Arab armed with two drumsticks taps frantically on earthenware cymbals and two others beat madly on their *ben dairs* making a noise like that of banging a wooden box. One big blow followed by two less emphatic, as if the hand thrown against the instrument rebounded and fell again of its own weight, constitutes an accompaniment to the deafening clamour [*sic*] of the hautbois and the cymbals. That is their idea of music.[17]

The author conceived of "their idea of music" as an intensely sexualized, racialized, and gendered cacophony, frenetic and loud. "Madly," "frantically," "furiously," the male musicians perform. After the women dance, "another black musician" played music and collected tips. The patrons "stick coins on his forehead streaming with perspiration and he goes on blowing, and with haggard eyes after his turn he kneels down in front of the cymbal player who picks off the collection."[18] At the end of the evening, "a negro . . . yielding to his native taste for fun, grotesquely imitates the . . . dance and as his grimaces do not excite any applause he laughs all to himself and ends by tumbling down in a corner holding his sides."[19] "A Café at Laghouat" exemplified what Clancy-Smith calls "the underground pornographic press of the English-speaking world."[20] Such texts arose as much out of government-sanctioned, ethnographically inflected texts as out of the seamy underground of the publishing world. A. S. G. rendered the African male exclusively in terms of his body. Whether sexualized as "athletic" or "majestic," or demeaned as repulsive and grotesque, these men existed in tourist ethnography as embodiments of physicality, of the ethnographer's desire. Depicting it as a voyeuristic mimesis of participant observation, the ethnographer proffered the eroticized tourist spectacle as both emblematic of Algerian culture and transgressive of French morality.

[16] Archives du Gouvernement général de l'Algérie (AGGA), 14X/8, A.S.G. (S. Barin?), "A Café at Laghouat," *L'Algérie hivernale* (Algiers: Comité d'Hivernage Algérien / Syndicat d'Initiative de l'Algérie), December 22, 1913, 5. See Taraud, *Prostitution*, 158, 173–8, on cafés.

[17] A.S.G., "Café," 5. Cf. Charles Desprez, *L'Hiver à Alger*, 5th edn (Paris: Augustin Challamel, 1898), 175–6, is similar.

[18] A.S.G., "Café," 5. [19] A.S.G., "Café," 5. [20] Clancy-Smith, "Islam," 158

Women, too, combined ethnographic narrative with homoerotic description. In her voyage to "L'Aurès barbare" (1908), Mademoiselle Magali-Boisnard encountered a young beauty. "I met," Magali-Boisnard narrated, "near a fountain, in the gardens, a perfect beauty." She compared the young woman to the eroticized women of male painters: "Gustave Doré would have wanted this ideal for the faces of his Bible. She was called Fathma [*sic*], resembled a princess of legend become shepherdess, offered to me to be her sister and cried because I left."[21] Magali-Boisnard, however, desired more than Fāṭima's offers of kinship. She remarked aloud, "if I were a man, I would marry Fatma."[22] Leaving no room for doubt as to her intentions, Magali-Boisnard expressly placed the "princess of legend" in the context of a homoerotic moralizing that recast the masculine as repulsive. "The antithesis of her grace is the ugliness of the idiot Tahar." This simpleton aroused no malice in the hearts of the people of the Aurès, "despite his filth."[23] Magali-Boisnard, however, conceived of Ṭahar as an object of disgust, as the loathsome, unclean, and masculine antithesis of the object of female desire. In contrast to the beloved female beauty, she placed an image of male repulsion for which she expressed no compassion.

Moreover, Magali-Boisnard's desire implied a political message. She inserted herself as a political actor in the moral empire. Magali-Boisnard's desire stemmed from her perceived ability to rescue Fāṭima from what the author portrayed as the harsh, ugly iniquities of "native" life. "Her house was a somber hole . . . Maggots swarmed there; her ageless mother and her brothers the youngest of whom still hung to a dried-up breast."[24] Magali-Boisnard reduced Fāṭima's aged mother and her brothers to human insects, decrying the cursed state of her beloved beauty. Magali-Boisnard's traveling companion, "Si Ahmed," commented that his three wives prevented his own marriage to and rescue of Fāṭima. Algerian men and women alike remained imprisoned in the home, men unable to escape the shackles of wives, and women unable to escape the binding embrace of the family. Without rescue by a European woman, "What will become of Fathma?" wondered Magali-Boisnard. The homoerotic desire of Magali-Boisnard could not conceal the political context of her ethnography; in the end, "L'Aurès barbare" reinscribed a cultural politics whereby only the civilized French could rescue the benighted native.

Ethnographies rendered the body as commodified object for voyeuristic consumption. Even a seemingly innocuous trip to the markets, as in

21 Mademoiselle Magali-Boisnard, "L'Aurès barbare," *Bulletin de la Société de Géographie d'Alger et de l'Afrique du Nord* [*BSGA*] 13 (1908:1): 48.

22 Magali-Boisnard, "Aurès," 48.

23 Magali-Boisnard, "Aurès," 48–9.

24 Magali-Boisnard, "Aurès," 48.

Félix Hautfort's *Au pays des palmes: Biskra* (1897) exerted the objectifying ethnographic gaze. In the market, "the moved chroniclers stop to gather precious snaps of exoticism, the photographer points his lens and each wishes to rob [*ravir*] the Arab spirit [*âme*] of one of the secrets that it conceals from us."[25] At first glance, the passage seems yet another example of the ethnographic fascination with the mysteries of other cultures. The text, however, relies upon discourses of penetration. Because of the earlier reference to the feminine noun *âme*, the subject of "conceals" is *elle*. Thus, the passage can also scan as: ". . . each wishes to rob the Arab spirit of one of the secrets *she* conceals from us." The pornographic violence of Hautfort's description equates description with theft, or worse. The predatory tone of the first reading gives way to a menacing, gendered one. While gender relations attested to the state of the cultural, contact between French ethnographers and Algerians simultaneously provided Europeans with the opportunity for violence. The conflation of pornography and ethnography facilitated the conception of Algeria as a place of license.

In no text do the intimations of violence appear as explicitly as in G. Guiauchain's *Winter in Algeria* (1901), a governnment guide selling ethnographic tourism to British and American travelers. According to Guiauchain, "the inhabitants are as interesting as the town,"[26] and represented a primary tourist attraction for the peripatetic English speaker. One Madame René advertised her naked "Andalusian dancers" in English.[27] The packaged experiences of Algerian culture that *Winter in Algeria* offered relied upon an implicit violence predicated upon the commodification of the body. "Above all," Guiauchain noted, "the visitor should find his way into an Arab house and surprise the Arab women in the midst of their home, busy preparing the *cousscouss* [sic], the national dish, or weaving carpets and stuffs."[28] *Winter in Algeria* marketed illicit entry as the consummate ethnographic experience. This uninvited invasion of the home, not once but repeated in the homes of numerous "wom*e*n" (note plural), intimations of penetration and of sexually violent power, represented the "above all," the primary cultural experience of ethnographic tourism. Ethnographic tourism permitted,

25 Félix Hautfort, *Au Pays des palmes: Biskra*, 2nd edn (Paris: Paul Ollendorff, Éditeur, 1897), 9

26 G. Guiauchain, *Winter in Algeria* (Algiers: Imprimerie algérienne, 1901), 12.

27 Eudel, *Hivernage*, 137–8. Clancy-Smith, "Islam," 158, on English discourse.

28 Guiauchain, *Winter*, 12. Italics in the original. The government encouraged Algerians to allow Europeans into the home as guests for "fêtes"; Desprez, *L'Hiver*, 167; cf. Ernest Fallot, *Par delà la Méditerranée: Kabylie, Aurès, Kroumirie* (Paris: Plon, Nourrit, 1887), 49.

even encouraged, the tourist to engage in acts of epistemic or physical violence forbidden in the metropole.

British and French tourists frequented Algeria in large part for prepackaged and highly gendered experiences of Algerian culture, for sexualized tourism.[29] As tourists sought out experiences mimicking participant observation, they hunted spectacles of the commodified erotic. Georges Viollier offered a disturbing spectacle of sex tourism. In Kabylia, he encountered "little Fatma, a delicious little girl of a dozen years, already almost formed, conscious of her beauty, [who] follows us closely casting teasing glances at us . . . This vulgar, brutal word of *sordi! sordi!* escapes like a sort of divinely tempting music from her laughing lips, making her poetic, idealizing her."[30] Just as the young age of the (male) child dancers did not alarm Viollier, neither did the prospect of a (female) child beggar. Rather, he took predatory pleasure in his power. "It is not a banal piece of copper that she demands of you, it's a treasure of beauty, of the world of voluptuaries that she lets you glimpse . . . that she offers you. Her regard is at once a prayer and a conquest. Charity has nothing to do with such alms."[31] Viollier traveled to Algeria expressly because of "the little Fatma with the suggestive smile,"[32] and exploitation and violation formed an explicit part of his tourist ethnography. The ethnography of spectacle as emblematic of Algerian culture arose out of narratives of coded violence.

Charles Desprez's *L'Hiver à Alger* (1898) similarly alluded to a paradise of the illicit. Like Viollier, Desprez overtly sexualized child dancers. Rejecting mature women dancers, he instead focused on "a little ballerina, a miniature of the *almée*."[33] She was "still free of the veil because of her youth," her prepubescence.[34] In the eyes of Desprez, "she delivers herself to all glances, she exposes to all loves her fresh and plump cheeks, her smiling, pink mouth, her long, braided hair, floating on her shoulders and her large eyes[,] so beautiful that kohl, far from adding anything, could only detract from them."[35] While Desprez dismissed the mature dancers, he lavished detail on an eroticized description of a child. The ethnographer-tourist represented Algeria through a sexualized lens that viewed gender relations as both a moral system fundamental to

[29] Louis Bertrand, *Le Jardin de la mort: le cycle africain*, new edn (Paris: Ollendorff, n.d.) 235. Edmond Doutté, *Magie et religion dans l'Afrique du Nord: la société musulmane du Maghrib* (Algiers: Adolphe Jourdan, 1909), 501.

[30] Viollier, *Deux Algérie*, 135. Italics and ellipsis are in the original. On French prevention of child marriage: Allan Christelow, *Muslim Law Courts and the French Colonial State in Algeria* (Princeton, NJ: Princeton University Press, 1985), 124–8.

[31] Viollier, *Deux Algérie*, 135–6. Ellipsis in the original.

[32] Viollier, *Deux Algérie* 136.

[33] Desprez, *L'Hiver*, 175–7.

[34] Desprez, *L'Hiver*, 175–7.

[35] Desprez, *L'Hiver*, 175–6.

understanding the colony, and an opportunity to engage in eroticized violence.

Highlighting the skills of various Algerian guides, Desprez portrayed Algeria as a place of infinite possibilities, where the covetous tourist had but to ask. "[P]erfectly current with the habits, the wants, the least caprices of the travel, [the guide] is in a position to render you an infinity of services . . . Painter, sculptor, have you need of a model, he will furnish one for you on command, muscled how you wish, Negro, Mozabite or Biskri; marvelously gracious, Jewess, Andalucian woman, or Mauresque."[36] The tourist returned to the body, the physicality of "racial" types. In Algeria, the artist in search of the bodily representation of an authentic type had his – or her – needs easily met. Though only obliquely sexual, Desprez's passage attests to the omnipresence of gendered images of the muscular male or the gracious female body in tourists' cultural experiences.

Even colonial administrators succumbed to the thrills of sexualized ethnography. In his monograph *Les Touareg* (1911), Léopold Aymard took evident voyeuristic pleasure in his role as participant-observer. In addition to his photograph of a topless woman,[37] he also described young Tuareg women collecting water. In a lengthy, eroticized passage rife with voyeurism, he echoed Desprez's presentation of the colonized body as inanimate, sexualized, and objectified in art.

> The European, deliciously surprised, contemplates, amazed, the charm of the confused visages, the superb firmness of their young chests, the pure design of the arms and legs, the harmonious broadening of the haunches, the smallness of the feet! Entranced, ecstatic, he thinks himself to be in the midst of a dream of art, among the masterpieces of painting and of sculpture, animated, vivified by the fire of a new Prometheus! But his ecstasy is of short duration. For his presence has, alas! frozen the laughs and hardened the visages. Even after a short hesitation, all these young beauties, such supple woodland nymphs, having jumped on their horses, fled in the copses, light, gracious, abandoning their mules and goatskins to the importunate stranger. The latter, disturbed, spurs his horse and leaves, at a gallop, in the opposite direction, feeling himself hated because he represents the detested conquerors![38]

Once again, ethnography combined ecstacy and art, the cultural and the sexual, to discipline colonized women as objectified bodies. Aymard's gaze dehumanized *and* sexualized; the women fled like frightened animals from the predatory, huntsman-like intruder, who pursued them for

36 Desprez, *L'Hiver*, 168.
37 Léopold Aymard, *Les Touareg* (Paris: Librairie Hachette, 1911), 88–9.
38 Aymard, *Touareg*, 107.

sexualized sport. Their body parts, like horns or antlers, served as a kind of trophy for Aymard. At the same time, however, he could not claim his trophy except through enshrining the women in photographs or in text. His sexualized ethnography of the "woodland nymphs" presented him as impotent, voyeuristic but immobile.

Dancing, prostitution, and moral commodification in ethnography

No ethnographic spectacle put on for tourists attracted as much textual attention as dancing women. The colonial government even organized spectacles of erotic dance for distinguished tourists.[39] In particular, the experience, presented as authentic, appealed to tourists who, in the words of Hubertine Auclert, "dreamed of knowing the beautiful, mysterious and magic country."[40] Mimesis of participant observation, these spectacles functioned as synecdoche to allow tourists to participate in Orientalist Algeria. Embodying both sexual and political power, spectacles reflected simultaneous French fascination and repulsion with dance. In ethnography, dancing marked the Algerian female body as the sexualized embodiment of the colonized culture.[41] The proximity to "native culture" gave rise to a voyeuristic, sexualized ethnographic narrative. "Monotonous in its lascivity,"[42] the dance nevertheless succeeded in sexualizing the mimetic ethnographic spectacle of tourism.

Though travelers attended these spectacles as experiences, in miniature, of Algerian culture, they presented them in sexualized narratives. Intimations of arousal permeated many descriptions. The explorer Paul Soleillet maintained that "a sensation, which courses through you like the shivering of fever, seizes you when you find yourself in contact with this painted, perfumed, totally striking, fantastically luminous creature."[43] The experience of controlled participant observation has turned expressly objectifying; the second person plural inculpates the reader in the author's voyeurism. Soleillet rendered the Algerian woman as an immediate and eroticized presence.

Indeed, some tourists acknowledged dancing spectacles as ethnographic commodification. The thrill of illicit contact with dancers formed

[39] Viscount Felix-Augustin de Pulligny, *Six Semaines en Algérie*, new edn (Paris: Canson, 1884), 121; Eudel, *Hivernage*, 50–5.

[40] Hubertine Auclert, *Les Femmes arabes en Algérie* (Paris: Société d'éditions littéraires, 1900), 188.

[41] Messaadi, *Romancières*, 222, notes a similar pattern in literature.

[42] de Lombay, *En Algérie*, 300.

[43] Paul Soleillet, *L'Afrique occidentale: Algérie, Mzab, Tildikelt* (Avignon: F. Seguin Aînés, 1877), 43.

an essential part of the ethnographic theater of sexual politics. Paul Duval evoked the "caresses" and physical pleasures of witnessing the dancing of one Algerian woman, "Fathma."[44] Wrote Duval, she "was the Arab type in all her beauty."[45] Duval offered the sexualized, ethnographic attraction to her dancing. "Thanks to Fathma, the tourists of the Cook agencies could thus penetrate the pseudo-mysteries of an Arab interior."[46] In a remark of either astonishing perspicacity or astounding obliviousness, Duval deftly wedded the pornographic and the ethnographic. The desire of the ethnographer remained inexplicably linked to observation and penetration.

No one better illuminated the connections between ethnographic tourism and dancing spectacles than Paul Eudel. In his winter in Algeria, Eudel and some American friends had stumbled upon Madame René's dancers. The world traveler, however, rejected them as insufficiently beautiful,[47] insisting on dancers in keeping with his romantic images of the Oriental belly dance. Cut from the same cloth as Charles Desprez's guides, Eudel's guide led the party to a spectacle of women dancing nude. "We wanted," Eudel explained, "to see the belly dance without veils, like in Cairo."[48] For the ethnographer-tourist, the Arabic-speaking world represented a homogeneously gendered, Orientalist expanse; whether Cairo or Qaïrouan imported little for the tourist in search of "authentic" ethnographic experiences. Upon their arrival at the spectacle, the Algerian policeman accompanying the group rapidly left, as "our *almées* did not want to dance in front of the authorities,"[49] or perhaps in front of an Algerian male.

Indeed, the women hesitated to dance *at all.* Only when Eudel's companion "got angry and made the *patronne* come" did the women begin.[50] Even once the music had started, Eudel complained, "no veil fell. We insisted," his traveling companions "got angry and demanded that they execute."[51] Under extreme duress, "timidly, bit by bit," did the women remove their clothes. Eudel commented on the breasts of one, inevitably "Fatma," but found her dancing clumsy.[52] Another dancer, "Zeina undressed slowly, stopping to look at us, hesitant." Repeatedly Eudel emphasized the unwillingness of the tentative dancers, the rage of the European observers. "Seized by modesty," Zeina "draped herself within and retired behind the door, showing only her laughing head. Two of her companions had to intervene, and when, a bit sharply, they snatched from her the last veil, Zeina took the pose of the *Venus of the*

[44] Jean Lorrain [Paul Duval], *Heures d'Afrique: Chroniques du Maghreb (1893–1898)*, ed. Fathi Glamallah (Paris: L'Harmattan, 1994), 137–140.
[45] Lorrain, *Heures*, 140. [46] Lorrain, *Heures*, 138. [47] Eudel, *Hivernage*, 278–80.
[48] Eudel, *Hivernage*, 282. [49] Eudel, *Hivernage*, 283. [50] Eudel, *Hivernage*, 284.
[51] Eudel, *Hivernage*, 284. [52] Eudel, *Hivernage*, 284.

Medicis."[53] Eudel narrated the spectacle as one of astonishing violence. It embodied either a scene of reluctant dancers forcibly undressed for lascivious male eyes, or one of a European narrator most eager to cast the spectacle in terms redolent of sexual violence.

Neither the implications of violence nor the reluctance of the participants disturbed Eudel. Eudel, it seems, found them most unconvincing as representatives of Algerian dancing. "They certainly did not," he complained, "know how to dance. Only Fatma, from time to time, gauchely tried the movements of professional dancers."[54] The ethnographic spectacle had failed to correspond to the Orientalist image, and thus became, for Eudel, inauthentic. "In sum, what we saw was not what we wanted. We addressed lively reproaches to" their guide. "He led us into a simple brothel, probably to gain a commission."[55] The erotics of the dancing spectacle proved inextricably bound up with the voyeurism of ethnography. Searching for exotic experiences of Algerian culture, ethnographic tourists sought out romanticized and sexualized performances because prevalent Orientalist discourses had deemed them authoritative, had represented them as emblematic of Algeria. In seeking out the exotic in dance spectacles, ethnographic tourists sexualized their representations of Algerian culture.

Similarly, H. de Rothschild's *Notes africaines* (1896) familiarized readers with colonial cultures. Imitating previous travelers in their search for dancers, he found, instead, exhausted, freezing, desperate, women who, "if you give them the generous offering of a hundred *sous*, they will dance the dance of the *almées* that you have all seen at the Exposition of 1889. Then, they will wrap themselves up again in their shawls, and one of the them, carrying a smoky lamp, will lead you back to the door, and say to you 'bonsoir' in good French."[56] Rothschild retraces the steps of the ethnographer-tourist, reinscribing it with an image of the female dancer debased by meaningless repetition. In contrast to Soleillet, Rothschild's use of the second person plural becomes nearly accusatory, incriminating his reader in the guilt of the destruction of Algeria. Ethnographic tourism had rendered pathetic the dancing so emblematic of Algeria for the audiences of the 1889 Exposition.

Ethnographers and tourists associated dancing with one Algerian ethnic group in particular. The women of the Awlād-Nāïl (Ouled Naïl) traveled throughout Algeria, earning money for their dowries through their

[53] Eudel, *Hivernage*, 284–5. Italics in the original.
[54] Eudel, *Hivernage*, 285. [55] Eudel, *Hivernage*, 285.
[56] H. de Rothschild, *Notes africaines* (Paris: Calmann Lévy, 1896), 55–6; cf. Denise Brahimi, ed., *Maupassant au Maghreb: au soleil, la vie errante d'Alger à Tunis, Tunis, vers Kairouan* (Paris: Le Sycomore, 1982), 111–19.

artistic dancing. Sakina Messaadi notes that colonial literature incorrectly used the term "Awlād-Nāïl" as a synonym for prostitute, "a commercial label without which all work would lose its documentary and touristic value."[57] For tourists and ethnographers alike, the Awlād-Nāïl came to mark the experience of participant observation of authentic Algeria. Brahim Bahloul, the former director of the dance section of the Théâtre National Algérien, remarks that the women "adopted the dance to make of it an attraction destined for tourists, for soldiers, and for a certain clientele avid for exoticism and eroticism."[58] Or, in the memorable words of one commentator, "the belly dance imposes itself in Biskra as, in Paris, [does] a visit to the Opera."[59] The spectacle represented a cultural imperative for the European tourist. Even the President of the French Republic, noted one general, saw an Awlād-Nāïl dance spectacle in Biskra.[60]

French ethnographers rendered the Awlād-Nāïl a site of intervention for empire's moralizing mission. The ethnography of gender among the Awlād-Nāïl did not merely describe women as prostitutes.[61] Rather, it reinvented a whole category of women as immoral. Edmond Doutté claimed that the discourse of the Nāïliyya as prostitutes was so pervasive that "the natives of this tribe who rub shoulders with our civilization voluntarily renounce this custom."[62] Prostitutes required policing; the representation of the Awlād-Nāïl as prostitutes justified colonial intervention.

Paul Soleillet placed the Awlād-Nāïl within the moral framework of the civilizing mission. According to Soleillet, "among the Berbers, prostitution [was] seen as an indifferent thing," and, "among the Oulad-Naïd [*sic*], . . . an institution."[63] He cast prostitution in terms of societal permissiveness: the nature of Berber culture allowed for the perpetuation of the institution. In Soleillet's ethnography, prostitution characterized the nature of the ethnic group. Soleillet went further, however. For him, "the men of this tribe are also very beautiful, but very effeminate and

57 Messaadi, *Romancières*, 197; Camille Lacoste-Dujardin, "Génèse et evolution d'une representation géopolitique: l'imagerie kabyle à travers la production bibliographique de 1840 à 1891," in *Connaissances du Maghreb*. More broadly: Taraud, *Prostitution*, 77–9, 83–5.

58 Brahim Bahloul, "La Danse en Algérie," in Djamila Henni-Chebra and Christian Poché, eds., *Les Danses dans le monde arabe, ou l'héritage des almées* (Paris: L'Harmattan, 1996), 159; cf. Messaadi, *Romancières*, 224.

59 Pierre Batail, *Le Tourisme en Algérie* (Algiers: Imprimerie algérienne for the Gouvernement général de l'Algérie, 1906), 27.

60 General Donop, *Lettres sur l'Algérie 1907–1908* (Paris: Plon-Nourrit, 1908), 223.

61 Clancy-Smith, "Islam," 158, and 305, nn. 17–18.

62 Doutté, *Magie et religion*, 560.

63 Soleillet, *L'Afrique occidentale*, 118.

15. Awlād-Nāïl Dancers in Ghardaïa, from Liorel, "Dans le M'zab."

of dissolute morals."[64] Dancing debased men and women alike. Soleillet conceived of the Awlād-Nāïl, and by extension all Berbers, as irreducibly immoral, corrupted by the moral stain of sanctioned prostitution. He depicted them strictly through the lens of this imperialist, paternalist morality, as a permissive culture of institutionalized prostitution and effeminate men. Despite its presence in France, colonial ethnographers conceived of prostitution as a moral flaw in Algeria that only empire could rectify.

Other ethnographers interpreted prostitution as an open threat to the values of the French republican empire. In *Au pays des burnous* (1898), Charles Barbet interpreted the urban prostitutes as debased and predatory, the defiant forward guard of an immoral, feminine army. To a cacophony of "savage, discordant music,"[65] the Awlād-Nāïl, "immobile, watching their prey, such shrewd spiders in the center of their web, . . . hail in a rasping voice, in a French crossed with Arabic, the tourist or stranger who passes *en flânant*, and looks at them with a curious,

[64] Soleillet, *Afrique*, 118. On the Awlād-Nāïl and homosexuality, see Raoul Bergot, *L'Algérie telle qu'elle est* (Paris: Albert Savine, 1890), 145–6; Clancy-Smith, "Islam," 159–60.

[65] Charles Barbet, *Au Pays des burnous (impressions et croquis d'Algérie)* (Algiers: Ernest Mallebay, 1898), 27.

interested eye."[66] Siren-like, the rapacious women entice by appealing to the (male) voyeur's desires. "Others," he continued, "promenade themselves in the streets of the neighborhood, . . . jostling, with cynical gestures and obscene glances, the natives that they meet[.]"[67] In the eyes of the ethnographer, these aggressive, obscene women tempt native men into immorality. The tourist, however, could resist: "let us enter with them [the women] and have a cup of *kaoua*[68] in their company; that doesn't commit one to anything . . ."[69] No harm could come to Barbet in the company of such women, however tempted "the natives" might be to succumb. His ellipses, however, left the point open to doubt. Barbet depicted the women of the Awlād-Nāʾil, not as women, but as myrmidons of the unholy. With inhuman adjectives – "feline," "ignoble," "serpentine"[70] – Barbet debased these women as inhuman, as immoral temptresses. His was not a moralizing mission that treated prostitutes with much compassion, but rather as a moral danger to men, predatory spiders whose obscenity men must control.

For the ethnographer-tourist Félix Hautfort, the Awlād-Nāʾil menaced empire's moral foundations. Comparing metropolitan strictures to Arab licentiousness, Hautfort feared for the ethical foundations of French society. "In France where one makes allowance for vice, the reserved neighborhood preserves the modesty of the stranger from heinous promiscuities and if, by any chance a passer ventures there, the obscene brand warns him."[71] Hautfort understood French prostitution as circumscribed, and modesty as in constant need of vigilant protection. Although he acknowledged the existence of prostitution in France, its geographic disavowal allowed Hautfort to dismiss it as a determining characteristic of French morality.

In conrast, in Algeria "vice seems to be unknown by force of unawareness . . . another Eden before sin, where evil and good were ill-defined, where the naïveté of a golden age tarried."[72] Hautfort's Algerian ethnography destabilized the moral valorizations attached to prostitution. The restraining boundaries of metropolitan prostitution having vanished, colonial prostitution rendered Algeria at once prelapsarian and immoral, an infernal paradise. Hautfort intimated that prostitution, policed in France, opened the gates of a carnal, colonial heaven. "Tradition has conserved . . . cities of pleasure . . . antique civilization is returned to us and pious dreamers evoke there the haughty cynicism of some dissolute city of the shores of the Nile."[73] The erotic, exotic

[66] Barbet, *Pays*, 31. [67] Barbet, *Pays*, 31. [68] *Qahwa*, coffee.
[69] Barbet, *Pays*, 31. [70] Barbet, *Pays*, 33. [71] Hautfort, *Palmes*, 26.
[72] Hautfort, *Palmes*, 26. [73] Hautfort, *Palmes*, 26.

prostitute, free of constraint, returns the tourist to a blissful Orient of the past.

Félix Hautfort demolished the very image he created. Rather than being emissaries of Eden, women of the Awlād-Nāʾil, he argued, were slaves. Depicting wives as enslaved by the veil, Hautfort argued that "sexual inferiority made of them street performers and slaves, and servility submits them to masculine caprices with, nevertheless, the revenge of easy gain and of the tax deducted from male furor."[74] For Hautfort, gender relations among Algerians (the Awlād-Nāʾil gave way to a generalized Algerian) enraged men and enslaved women. His ethnography described French attempts to limit prostitution and compared them with Algerian licentiousness. Shrewdly appropriating romantic eroticizations of that license, he returned to the paternalist moralizing of Soleillet and Barbet: native women required protection from native men, and all men required protection from native women. The men were pimps, "obscene, indifferent and blasé."[75] Quoting, in English, a guide, Hautfort concluded that " 'their morality does not stand very high,'" a conclusion he did not come to for the safely isolated European prostitutes of the metropolitan *quartiers du vice*.[76]

Félix Hautfort never criticized prostitution as an institution or the metropole's controlled neighborhoods of vice. Instead, he concentrated on the failure to *regulate* immorality as a fundamental element of Algerian identity. The ostensible cruelty of Algerians' gender relations rendered them inescapably different. For Hautfort, immorality arose, not out of prostitution, but out of the manner of its social and cultural regulation. His moral critiques did not develop out of ethical scruples but instead voiced a paternalist narrative, articulated through the ethnographic, recreating colonial gender relations as an object for imperialist moralizing.

Paul Bourde witnessed an Awlād-Nāʾil performance with the parliamentary mission of autumn 1879. Combining elements of travel writing, journalism, and ethnography, Bourde reviled Nāʾiliyya dancing. "The least refinement of mores would have suppressed . . . the coarse parody of brutal love executed with the impassive visage of the Muslim women . . . It is coldly indecent."[77] The coarseness of Algeria, he argued, permitted the continuation of dancing. In the spectacle he saw a disturbing erotics of violence, "brutal love" with "impassive women." Such intimations of

[74] Hautfort, *Palmes*, 26–7. [75] Hautfort, *Palmes*, 32. [76] Hautfort, *Palmes*, 28.

[77] Paul Bourde, *À travers l'Algérie: souvenirs de l'excursion parlementaire (septembre–octobre 1879)*, 2nd edn (Paris: G. Charpentier, 1880), 146.

16. Etienne Dinet, "Exposition coloniale Marseille 1906."

coercion and violence recall imperialist fantasies of salvage. In Bourde's ethnography, moral evaluations of dancing articulated gender relations as a site of imperial intervention.

In *Les Femmes arabes* (1900), Hubertine Auclert, feminist, activist, and assimilationist, echoed some of Hautfort's concerns about prostitution as indicative of immorality. Like Soleillet, Auclert commented on the beauty of both Nāʾiliyya women and "effeminate men."[78] However, she continued, "these children of the desert allow no regulation of prostitution,"[79] recalling Hautfort's emphasis on control. Auclert remained committed to the civilizing mission and its concomitant proselytizing of "republican secularism and modern science."[80] Echoing the apologetics of salvage, Auclert, like Hautfort, portrayed prostitution as uncontrolled, liminal, libidinal. Moreover, Auclert argued that, far from morality regulating prostitution, *prostitution regulated morality*. Assimilationist to the core and openly hostile to Islam, Auclert inculpated religion in the immoral functioning of prostitution.[81] "The general custom of the Oulad-Naïl [*sic*] of offering for a price of gold their daughters to any comer, is a belief that in acting thusly they honor Allah. They are convinced that the women make a meritorious work in prostituting themselves."[82] Hence, prostitution, "the holocaust of the exquisite Oulad-Naïl,"[83] attested to a fundamental moral inversion in Algerian society. According to Auclert, Islam buttressed prostitution by deeming it *moral*. At the same time, she conceived of her own role as an obligation to point out the moral shortcomings she perceived.

Julia Clancy-Smith highlights the imbrication of Auclert's radical politics in metropolitan France and her commitment to the moralizing mission. Her "positions and causes advocated . . . were introduced into her arguments on the moral duty to uplift the Arab women – to turn harem inmates into voters," in Clancy-Smith's memorable phrase.[84] For Auclert, however, her moral role in the colony, unlike her radical activism in the metropole, hinged not only on political enfranchisement, but also on ethnographic description. In America, Louise Newman claims, "white middle class women's emancipation . . . emphasized (white) women's specific role as . . . the 'civilizers' of racial and class

[78] Auclert, *Femmes arabes*, 112.
[79] Auclert, *Femmes arabes*, 113.
[80] Joan Wallach Scott, *Only Paradoxes to Offer: French Feminists and the Rights of Man* (Cambridge, Mass.: Harvard University Press, 1996), 115.
[81] Auclert, *Femmes arabes*, 22–6.
[82] Auclert, *Femmes arabes*, 114; cf. Doutté, *Magie et religion*, 560–2.
[83] Auclert, *Femmes arabes*, 118.
[84] Clancy-Smith, "Islam," 170.

inferiors."[85] Newman's contention may hold true for the civilizing mission more broadly.

Despite her commitment to reform, Auclert actively contributed to essentialist ethnographic moralizing about gender. At times, Auclert depicted Nāʾiliyya women without any agency whatsoever: men prostituted them, sold them, were convinced of their merit. Auclert saw, in "these cloistered women, walled up like Carmelites" because of the injustice of Muslim men, the means of reconciling Algerians to European society, of assimilation.[86] At the same time, she represented the women of the Awlād-Nāʾil as a menace to morality and order. "The crazed virgins of the Sahara enchant the Europeans. These houris transfix the *habitués* of Moorish cafés who have, in watching them dance, a fore-taste of the Paradise of Mahomet [*sic*]."[87] In other words, the women of the Awlād-Nāʾil offer to *European* men a taste of *Islamic* paradise. Depicting prostitution as naturalized in Algerian society, Auclert represented its immorality as contagious, polluting.[88] Auclert represented women dancers as threatening to reverse assimilation. While Auclert avowedly professed the need for Algerian women to abandon their "cloistered" lives and become European, she also worried that female dancers would seduce European men.

Many conceived of prostitution as an ethnographic marker demeaning the cultural practices of Algerians. Ethnography, imbricated with the civilizing mission and salvage ethnography, posited gender relations as the defining moral element of Algerian culture. According to colonial ethnographies, "prostitution [was]," in the words of Octave Houdas's *Ethnographie de l'Algérie* (1886), "in the morals of the tribe of the Oulad-Naïl."[89] The conception of prostitution as a problem of identity and morality, a

85 Louise M. Newman, *White Women's Rights: The Racial Origins of Feminism in the United States* (Oxford: Oxford University Press, 1999), 23. See also pages 8, 10–11, 12, 15. Cf. Marnia Lazreg, "Gender and Politics in Algeria: Unraveling the Religious Paradigm," *Signs* 15, no. 4 (Summer 1990): 755–80.

86 Auclert, *Femmes arabes*, 22–6.

87 Auclert, *Femmes arabes*, 113. This passage inverts the contention, in Ann Laura Stoler, *Race and the Education of Desire: Foucault's* History of Sexuality *and the Colonial Order of Things* (Durham, NC: Duke University Press, 1992), 115, that "[a] European man could live with or marry an Asian woman without necessarily losing rank"; for Auclert, at least, the transgressive sexual experience of the dance threatened to turn the European man native. Nevertheless, Stoler does highlight the dominant identity boundaries of intermarriage.

88 See also Le Roy, *Deux Ans*, 89, 232, 238.

89 Octave Houdas, *Ethnographie de l'Algérie*, Bibliothèque ethnographique, no. 5, ed. Léon de Rosny (Paris: Maisonneuve et Leclerc, 1886), plagiarized in E. Lacanaud, *L'Algérie au point de vue de l'économie sociale* (Algiers–Mustapha: Giralt, 1900), 15.

collective, moral, and cultural problem, facilitated the attribution to an entire society of ethical failings justifying colonial intervention.

Indeed, Henri Drouët, in *Alger et le Sahel* (1887), alluded to the moral valorizations that colonial Algeria attached to women. Public women, according to Drouët, were invariably women of ill repute. Hence, he had difficulty persuading his innkeeper to let him entertain dancers in his rooms. "We had the desire," Drouët contended, implausibly, "to study the dress and cosmetics of these native women . . . who wanted to lend themselves to our fantasy."[90] Whether his fantasy extended beyond clothes and cosmetics, Drouët remained silent. "On the pretext that modest women never go out, entrance to hotels is forbidden to" women.[91] Drouët continued, "by exception, our innkeeper, perfectly convinced of the purity of our motives," or else coerced by the wealthy tourists, allowed the women to visit Drouët in his chambers.[92] Thus, the ethnographer-tourist's motives remained pure, his virtue intact, his morality wholly unquestioned.

Drouët's text left the Algerian woman, however, with a stark choice: either become the secret, incomprehensible, and moral veiled woman, or become an immoral, immodest, uncovered dancer who consorted with men like Drouët. That Algerian women might have their own reasons for their dress did not cross Drouët's mind. The female body became a blank image for the projection of ethnographic moralizing and for the unfolding of male fantasies of private morality and public availability. In the words of another traveler-ethnographer, "the honest women . . . no one sees them; recluses in their white houses as in a convent, they do not count for the world."[93] Or, at least, they counted for the colonial, ethnographic world only as indications of moral disorder.

This conception of publicly "accessible" Algerian women as inherently immodest arose again and again. Charles Barbet dedicated one of the most disturbing of such texts to none other than "Jean Lorrain." In *Au pays des burnous*, Barbet described his relationship with a young Algerian orphan. His account, probably fictionalized in its more sensational aspects, situated the development of the girl in a context that equated maturation among Algerian women with increasing immorality, framing the story as a "Scene of Kabyle mores." Barbet consistently cast the cultural in terms of the moral.

[90] Henri Drouët, *Alger et le Sahel* (Paris: Hachette, 1887), 146.
[91] Drouët, *Sahel*, 146. [92] Drouët, *Sahel*, 146.
[93] Marius Bernard, *L'Algérie qui s'en va* (Paris: Plon, Nourrit, 1887), 33; Alexandre Papier, *Description de Mena'a et d'un groupe de danseuses des Oulad Abdi (Aurès occidental)* (Paris: Librairie africaine et coloniale, 1895), 12.

Barbet ostensibly met the young girl, Zouïna, as she peddled groceries. Although she passed through the city unveiled (and hence not pubescent), he described her in eroticized terms. "Her *gandoura* of muslin . . . hid, as well as poorly, the nudity of her flesh tanned by the intense heat of the sun and allowed [one] to glimpse the gracious contours, the budding roundness of her supple body."[94] "She evoked in my spirit" he continued, "the troubling image of a slightly civilized 'Rarahu'," the pubescent fetish-object of Paul Gauguin and Pierre Loti, "and this analogy . . . charmed me deliciously by its prestigious exoticism."[95] From their first meeting, Barbet interpreted the child as his sexualized fetish-object, *à la style de Gauguin*. His account brought her from the public streets to his private home; he employed her as a servant living in his house, "to satisfy so promptly, [himself], a profane *roumie* [*sic*: Rūmī: Christian] recently debarked in Algeria, [his] arabophile curiosity, irresistible . . . puerile."[96]

This represented a sexualized, ethnographic, and deeply personal fulfillment of the civilizing mission for Barbet. "In leaving the Metropole, I had in effect conceived the seductive project of attaching to me, beginning with my installation on Algerian soil, a young native, of one or the other sex . . . And here is this charming dream realizing itself suddenly as if by enchantment!"[97] Barbet employed Zouïna as a fetishized experiment in moral development. She embodied for him the cultural capabilities of all Algerians. Moreover, he interpreted these capabilities as part of a sexualized and gendered understanding of Algerian culture.

The sexualized embodiment of the native underwent moral collapse. Zouïna, Barbet complained, spent her money on frivolous ornaments. She even rejected his sage counsel to spend more wisely.[98] "I attempted vainly," he noted ruefully, "to curb . . . this untimely and tasteless coquetry that threatened to degenerate into an obsessive passion, habitual harbinger of an ineluctable moral depravity among the young native domestics belonging to the female sex."[99] His obsession with her perceived decadence revealed both metropolitan anxieties about social uplift and colonial fears of assimilation. Zouïna became "arrogant" and rejected "the yoke of the 'roumi,'" preferring to strike out on her own, while Barbet waited in vain for her "honorable amend."[100] The native specimen Barbet hoped to collect became uncontrollable, the epitome of "degeneration" and "moral depravity," reenacting a congenital, culturally predetermined slide into disgrace. Her innocence

[94] Barbet, *Pays*, 204. [95] Barbet, *Pays*, 204. [96] Barbet, *Pays*, 205.
[97] Barbet, *Pays*, 205. [98] Barbet, *Pays*, 207–8. [99] Barbet, *Pays*, 208.
[100] Barbet, *Pays*, 208.

yielded to decadence, sexuality to immorality, youth to tawdry and garish display.

Intimations of discourses of the moral colonizer and his civilizing mission permeated Barbet's description. The account functioned as an ethnographic morality play, recounting what many saw as the inevitable course of cultural relations between colonizer and colonized. As an exercise in the cultural presentation of colonial power, the script required a very particular ending. In Barbet's rigid narrative, the intransigent, degenerate colonized woman had to meet the ultimate dishonor of her immorality. Later he saw Zouïna, lavishly dressed, "in the Moorish cafés of the city," in the background, "the raucous sound of derboukas and tam-tams."[101] Her appearance with the sound of the drums implied that she had become one of the prostitutes who, according to the ethnographers, frequented such dens of immorality alongside colonial tourists and administrators. The naïve and arrogant native had rejected the sage advice of the superior and judicious European, and returned to the inevitable ruin that marked her cultural inheritance.

Zouïna's downfall was, in a sense, scripted. The gendered dynamics of colonial ethnography demanded that she testify to the great moral need of colonized cultures. Her degeneration, however, into prostitution would seem an ambiguous victory for the colonizing masculine, offering release for the sexualized fantasies of empire, but not the attendant ones of rescue. Hence, Barbet encountered her again, "metamorphosed, dressed in the European manner," her "face withered by precocious debauchery." He learned that "Zouïna . . . whom I had appropriated to myself like a decorative trinket, had long since tossed her *gandoura* in the nettles."[102] Chastened and humbled, Zouïna became a pale, tarnished imitation of a European, humiliated into assimilation by her moral failings. Without the guidance of the colonizing man, she had fallen into inevitable, decadent immorality. In the end, she sought escape in the garb of the European. Assimilation, however, required male guidance: her return to European garb was incomplete. Inherent in the images of Algerians presented in ethnography lay a gendered collective immorality seemingly rooted in culture itself. Barbet intended Zouïna's story as a cautionary tale about empire.

The home as the field

Fantasies of rescue and of immorality also centered on home life, conceived of as private. As a frequently inaccessible sphere of the intimate,

[101] Barbet, *Pays*, 209. [102] Barbet, *Pays*, 209–10. Ellipsis in the original.

familial relations offered the ideal site for the projection of the ethnographic moralizing. As Messaadi notes, novelists "saw the enclosing of women [in the home] as the negative and unhappy result of a retrograde masculine mentality and of a pathological jealousy."[103] Ethnographers often interpreted the gendering of the home as, to use Messaadi's word, "retrograde," that is to say, firmly situated within evolutionary discourses of the civilizing mission. However, colonial ethnographers largely did not couch their discussions of gender and the home in terms of the psychobiological language of pathology – a language perhaps better associated with physical anthropologists and ethnologists. Rather, most discussed Algerian family life as an issue of morality, the manifestation of a culturally specific disordering of normative values.

In his tourist ethnography *Un An à Alger* (1887), M.-J. Baudel presented the home as the key to comprehension of Algerian culture. His entrance into a home in Algiers provided the dominant analytical framework for his moralizing. "A visit of several hours," he contended, "teaches more on the character and customs of the natives than the best descriptions and the most studied accounts."[104] Baudel's assertion of the ethnographic value of tourist observation aside, the passage established the home as the foyer for the production of knowledge, the abode of ethnographic experience, and synecdoche for knowledge of "Algerian culture," equating experience in the home, even for an hour, with totalizing knowledge of Algeria itself.

Moreover, that systematized knowledge itself relied upon the elaboration of a moral theory of colonial relations. "Our homes," Baudel explained, "are our prisons, says an old proverb. It could not be better applied than to the habitations of the Algerians."[105] Using the proverb to reverse the signification of "home," Baudel emptied the word of its domestic and familial attachments in order to associate it with punishment, control, and moral policing – with the prison, in all its Foucauldian array. "With their severe and cloistered aspect, their walls pierced with rare and narrow dormers, one would take them for vast dungeons and not beautiful residences."[106] The observer, both present and absent as the pronoun "*on*," transformed the home into the realm of fantastical and phantasmagorical salvation, into the fairy-tale kingdom of dungeons, towers, and virtuous women in need of rescue. Baudel rendered the home the physical exemplar of a disordered moral state of the Algerian male.

[103] Messaadi, *Romancières*, 114. On the ethnography of the home as a gendered, *physical* space, see Zeynep Çelik, *Urban Forms and Colonial Confrontations: Algiers under French Rule* (Berkeley, Calif.: University of California Press, 1997), 88–112.

[104] M.-J. Baudel, *Un An à Alger: excursions et souvenirs* (Paris: Ch. Delagrave, 1887), 59.

[105] Baudel, *Un An à Alger*, 56. [106] Baudel, *Un An à Alger*, 56.

"The Arab is egotistical, he wants to enjoy alone his possessions, and he insists that his residence be indifferent to the passerby and does not awaken his attention."[107] Thus, Baudel attached the moral valorization of the home to the Algerian male himself; if the Algerian home was a prison, then the Algerian male was its warden. The woman has become a mere possession to guard jealously, and imperial paternalism brooked no rival.

Charles Barbet couched his description of the home in highly sexualized idioms. Even the title of his *La Perle du Maghreb (Tlemcen): vision et croquis d'Algérie* implied the discovery of hidden treasure through opening. In *La Perle du Maghreb*, Barbet left no doubt that the pearl referred to the unattainable Algerian woman. In the language of exoticized transgression and violent possession, he depicted his experiences in the "*quartier maure*" of Tilimsān. Attracted by the "hands burnished with henna," he paused in front of one house. "Behind this door[,] refractory to indiscrete, violating glances, extended a vestibule paved and paneled with squares of multicolored pottery."[108] The violating gaze of the roaming tourist upon the harlequin and exotic interior rapidly gave way to Barbet's entrance into the home of gleaming marble, luxurious tile, and the "mysterious murmurings . . . of a fountain." "Pressed by my amiable guide, I crossed over [*franchis*] the doorstep of this rich Moorish habitation . . . The doors of the apartments that the profane *roumis* do not penetrate, opened on to this circular gallery" where Barbet found himself.[109] The verb *franchir*, with its secondary meaning of "to overcome," reiterates the difficulty of the achievement in entering where other Europeans may not, to use his word, "penetrate."

Barbet described his forbidden interactions with the women of the home he had invaded. "At our presence, pretty Mauresques, modest, frightened, fled . . . ; then, half hidden behind a door, furtively looked at us with their black eye, velvety with enamel, with a carmine smile

[107] Baudel, *Un An à Alger*, 56.

[108] Charles Barbet, *La Perle du Maghreb (Tlemcen): vision et croquis d'Algérie*. (Algiers: Imprimerie algérienne, n.d [1907]), 31. The close reading I trace of Barbet's *La Perle du Maghreb* offers an analytical optic onto similar descriptions of the so-called *maison Mauresque*; see Bernard, *L'Algérie qui s'en va*, 33–7; Daumas, *Femme arabe*, 55; Dumont, *Alger: Ville d'hiver*, 48–9; Fallot, *Par delà la Méditerranée*, 200; Ernest Feydeau, *Alger: Étude*, new edn (Paris: Calmann Lévy, 1884), 161; Gustave Guillaumet, *Tableaux algériens* (Paris: Plon, Nourrit, 1891), 131–45; Charles Jourdan, *Croquis algériens* (Paris: A. Quantin, 1880), 47–58, 60–4, 69, 71; Dr. Bonnafont, *Pérégrinations en Algérie, 1830 à 1842: histoire, ethnographie, anecdotes* (Paris: Challamel Aîné, 1884), 155–61; Trumelet, *Français dans le désert*, 290–1; cf. G. Bonet-Maury, "La Femme musulmane dans l'Afrique septentrionale française," *Revue bleue* 5 (February 3, 1906): 133–6; Viollier, *Deux Algérie*, 70–6.

[109] Barbet, *La Perle du Maghreb*, 31–2.

where were suddenly strung out exquisite white pearls."[110] These furtive women observe the intruder with *one* "black eye," their (singular, collective) smile concealing hidden pearls. In contrast, an old woman at work sewing, "surprised unexpectedly . . . brusquely veiled her face and, immobile, as if stopped dead by the sacrilegious presence of two strangers, cast . . . a worried look at us."[111] The "sacrilegious" fear immediately situated the woman's antipathy as a larger moral concern about gendered religious norms. "We did not think it necessary to penetrate further into this dwelling where native mores forbid cloistered women to offer hospitality to *giaours* [*sic*]."[112] *Jwār* comes from the root j-w-r, indicating both proximity and violation – deviance, outrage, and vicinity. From it come the words *jār*, neighbor, refugee; and *jawr*, tyranny, outrage. Barbet's ethnographic mission had reached completion, culminating in the imposition of his observing will upon the women of this *maison mauresque*. If, as Baudel contended, the Algerian home represented a microcosm of the moral ordering of society, then Barbet had seen enough. His sexualized language of penetration and moralizing language of prohibition and transgression conflated the gendered and the moral.

As a hermeneutic device, an author's entrance into the private home united morality and gender. Ethnographers and tourists interpreted the home as a legitimate field site for cultural research, repeating colonial patterns of coercion and authority. Ethnographers, however, disavowed the ethical implications of such coercion.[113] As Julia Clancy-Smith notes, ethnographic observers "disarmed potential critics" of their voyeuristic eye "by maintaining that the scientific aim of narrative keyhole viewing rendered the Arab family suitable for contemplation."[114] The home as a context for the attachment of moral valorizations to gender relations represented yet another means for the production of ethnographic knowledge out of the cultural politics of empire.

By no means did tourist ethnographers entrench the home as both prison and field site on their own. Rather, institutionalized ethnographers also reinscribed the moral gendering of the home through the legitimating power of the emerging social sciences. Despite his real affection for the people of Tilimsān, Alfred Bel nevertheless interpreted their home lives as indicative of gendered immorality. Although Bel maintained that the women of Tilimsān enjoyed an unusual equality, authority, and respect, he gendered public space to invite intervention. "The public life

[110] Barbet, *La Perle du Maghreb*, 32.
[111] Barbet, *La Perle du Maghreb*, 32. [112] Barbet, *La Perle du Maghreb*, 32.
[113] Some were bureaucrats' homes, or those of men condemned to death. Messaadi, *Romancières*, 40, 293; de Rothschild, *Notes*, 140–7. See also Eudel *Hivernage*, 160–3.
[114] Clancy-Smith, "Islam," 165.

of the woman is reduced in sum to several visits to friends [*amies*, i.e., in the feminine] and relatives, to the occasion of familial festivals, and to meetings with other women, be it at the Moorish baths, or near the sanctuaries of marabouts."[115] In contrast, men led lives of public interaction and, quite frequently, leisure. "The man to the contrary is almost never at home . . . ; he passes his day at work or the Moorish café . . . he chats, plays cards and amuses himself; he frequents the mosque regularly enough and never misses the festivals and meals to which he is invited."[116] The actions of the woman, alone in the house, remain obscure. Whereas Bel did not specify what women *did*, he offered a detailed outline of men's pastimes. In fact, Bel *knew* what women did at home through his wife Marguerite's research. Nevertheless, the preponderance of leisure activities in his litany of the male day introduced frivolity: while women mostly sat home alone, the idle Algerian men passed the day in gossip, card playing, and festivities. This gendered division, not of labor, but of *leisure*, invited the reader to draw moral conclusions about gendered indolence.

Moreover, Bel depicted this gendered organization as a culturally specific natural order. "The divisions that one encounters in the family, between individuals of the two sexes, are found naturally in society. The women are always separated from the men."[117] The dynamic of the home, Bel argued, perpetuated itself through the ordering of society. Even a knowledgeable and rigorous scholar like Alfred Bel could only portray the home as a microcosm for Algerian society.

The ethnographic reconfiguring of gender as a moral problem allowed many French writers to conceive of the *solution* in cultural terms. In his "La Femme musulmane dans l'Afrique septentrionale française" (1906), Gaston Bonet-Maury assigned to French men and women an important role in reordering Algerian society. "It is to the French – and especially to French women – that it behooves to work this noble task, . . . the emancipation of the Muslim woman from her double servitude: that of manners and customs . . . and that of ignorance."[118] For Bonet-Maury, the expansion of French women's rights implied imperial duties. He argued that only the radical alteration of Algerian cultural identity and the concomitant reorganization of gender roles could emancipate Algerian women. This argument of the civilizing mission masks powerfully racist calls for assimilation. According to Ann Laura Stoler, "racism," "was not a colonial reflex, fashioned to deal with the distant Other, but part of the

[115] Alfred Bel, *La Population musulmane de Tlemcen* (Paris: Paul Geuthner, 1908), 55.
[116] Bel, *Population musulmane*, 55. [117] Bel, *Population musulmane*, 55.
[118] Bonet-Maury, "Femme musulmane," 135; on Auclert, see Clancy-Smith, "Islam," 169–70.

very making of Europeans themselves," like Bonet-Maury.[119] Algerian women, a "moral" problem requiring an imperial solution, became one of the primary sites for colonial intervention.

Nevertheless, others decried the apparent failure of French attempts to modify Algerian gender norms. Echoing Auclert, Dr. Bonnafont, in his 1884 *Pérégrinations en Algérie*, lamented that "[t]he familial state of the Arab has stayed identically the same," which he attributed to "the arrest of the development of a race."[120] However, neither relinquished preconceptions of the potential of French empire as a positive force in Algeria. Auclert railed more against male colonizers than against colonization, "employ[ing] the discourse of universal sisterhood" to articulate an important role for French women in the civilizing mission.[121] "[T]he family," she complained, "is inaccessible to men to the point that the French government, having but male inspectors, is presently unable to find out civil offenses in it [i.e., the family]."[122] Or, as Dr. Hélène Abadie-Feyguine claimed, "the native woman wants [to] and can be assisted [and] cared for only by a woman."[123] Only with the active collaboration of French women could the colonial state intrude upon civil life in order to reform the family. Auclert objected to colonial male citizenship when Frenchwomen lacked such rights, portraying the Frenchwoman's civilizing mission as preventing a degradation in metropolitan women's status.[124] Abadie-Feyguine and Auclert saw uplift as a duty, imposed by their rights as European women. For Auclert, empire's failures to rectify moral outrages in Algeria resulted from its masculinist ethos, not from any fundamentally flawed organizing logic.

The ethnography of gender relations in colonial Algeria recreated the family and the body as objects for the moralizing gaze. As ethnographers and travelers watched dances and entered the home, gendered distinctions marked moral ones. Ethnographers as varied as Bel and Barbet or Doutté and Auclert understood relations structured around gender as moral problems requiring resolution and reform. Because colonial ethnographies depicted gender as a microcosm for Algerian culture, the

119 Ann Laura Stoler, *Carnal Knowledge and Imperial Power: Race and the Intimate in Colonial Rule* (Berkeley, Calif.: University of California Press, 2002), 144.

120 Bonnafont, *Pérégrinations*, 231–2.

121 Clancy-Smith, "Islam," 170.

122 Auclert, *Femmes arabes*, 25. Magali-Boisnard, "Nos Sœurs Musulmanes," *BSGA* 13 (1908:4): 506, expressed anxiety that some women might not, in fact, accept freedom.

123 Dr. Hélène Abadie-Feyguine, *De l'Assistance médicale des femmes indigènes en Algérie* (Montpellier: Imprimerie Delord-Boehm et Martial, 1905), 65. See also Hugues Imbert, *Quatre Mois au Sahel: lettres et notes algériennes* (Paris: Librairie Fischbacher, 1888), 175; Mme. A de Bachechacht, *Une Mission à la cour chérifienne* (Paris: Librairie Fischbacher, 1901), 68–75, 80, in Morocco.

124 Scott, *Only Paradoxes*, 116–17.

moral evaluation of gender relations opened up the family and the body for the civilizing mission.

The home, like Forster's cave, reverberates with the moralizing impetus of colonial power. Forster remains silent about the cave, offering readers only the echo, the voice without agency, meaning, or sense, endlessly repeated and reinscribed without will. In French Algeria, ethnographers kept a similar vigilance in writing about men and women, reframing their relations to constantly echo the moral judgment of imperial knowledge. The cacophony of echoes in ethnographic texts parrots the moralizing impulse of empire.

6 Discipline and publish: militant ethnography and crimes against culture

On the evening of April 25, 1892, in a quiet copse in France, his back against the trunk of a tree, his Cross of the Legion of Honor in the dirt beside him, the door to his house open, Henri Duveyrier took up the revolver that had accompanied him on his first voyage to the Sahara and shot himself in the head. Bereft since his illness of the capacity to undertake long explorations, shunned and derided by many of his colleagues in the intellectual circles of African geography, Duveyrier ended his own life at fifty. In an obituary, Emile Masqueray wrote that "nothing in his always-precise letters revealed the least trouble. It would be necessary to go further into the secrets of his life to explain such a disastrous resolution, or else one would end up believing that the men born too young for glory are predestined for a rapid death."[1] The intervening years between Duveyrier's exploration of the Sahara and his lonely suicide had destroyed the cultural work to which he had committed himself. The French imperial project had made implacable enemies of the Tuareg, had established an oppositional politics that negated, in fact and in ideology, the worth and import of Duveyrier's mission.[2]

[1] Archives du Gouvernement général de l'Algérie (AGGA), 6X/20 (31MIOM/37: Papier Duveyrier: 1859–1909), E[mile] M[asqueray], "[obituary for] Henri Duveyrier," *Journal des Débats*, May 14, 1892.

[2] AGGA, 6X/20, Masqueray, "Obituary"; René Pottier, "A propos d'un centenaire . . . Henri Duveyrier," *Notre Sahara* 3, no. 15 (October 25, 1960): 41–44; René Pottier, "Hommage à Henry [*sic*] Duveyrier," *Comptes-Rendus mensuels des séances de l'Académie des sciences d'Outre-Mer* 19 (March 20, 1959): 138–45. See Lionel Galand, ed., *Lettres au Marabout: messages touaregs au Père de Foucauld* (Paris: Belin, 1999), 14, citing René Pottier, *Un Prince saharien méconnu: Henri Duveyrier* (Paris: Plon-Nourrit, 1938); René Pottier, *La Vocation saharienne du Père de Foucauld* (Paris: Plon, 1939); René Pottier, *Laperrine, conquérant pacifique du Sahara* (Paris: Bibliothèque de l'Institut maritime et colonial, 1943); Pottier, *Un Prince saharien méconnu*, 237–9; Jean-Louis Triaud, *La Légende noire de la Sanûsiyya: une confrérie musulmane saharienne sous le regard français (1840–1930)*, 2 vols. (Paris: Éditions de la Maison des sciences de l'homme, 1995), especially vol. I, 310–17, 331–41, and vol. II, 1121; Pottier, "Centenaire," 44; Jean Lartéguy, *Sahara: An I* (Paris: Gallimard, 1958), 77–8.

Duveyrier's suicide marked more than the tragic end to the life of the explorer and ethnographer. It lay at the endpoint of a complicated series of events linking colonial ethnography, the construction of morality, experiences of loss, and violent death. After the bloody ends to several Saharan missions, ends associated with Duveyrier, French colonial ethnographers started to attach moralized interpretations of political behaviors to the cultural identities of various Saharan ethnic groups. In essence, many ethnographers utilized Saharan resistance to brand the Tuareg and the Shaʿamba as culturally and inherently criminal. This moral refashioning of the Sahara allowed for ethnographic rationalizations of military conquest. As writers eulogized, lionized, and commemorated the loss of the scions of imperial folly, they simultaneously produced ethnographic knowledge about Saharan peoples that reduced political contestation to an effect of cultural criminality and collective immorality. The often-dramatic circumstances of explorers' deaths and the anonymous notoriety of the killers conspired to present resistance to empire in the Sahara, not as a political act, but rather as *cultural* crime.

The deaths of the Saharan explorers – some foolish, some meticulous, some naïve, all arrogant – captured the imagination of French ethnographers, playing an important role in the development of ethnographic thought. The mourning for these explorers contributed to a corpus of cultural knowledge demonizing entire ethnic groups as unlawful. An understanding of the processes of that ethnographic creation demands an investigation into the forms of mourning and commemoration that, in part, gave rise to them. In colonial Algeria, cultural identity determined an individual's participation in the apparatus of political authority. Simultaneously, however, certain crimes themselves marked entire ethnic groups as, in a sense, serial offenders – as culturally determined criminals. These crimes became ethnographic crimes. Many ethnographers and writers conceived of the death of Saharan explorers as crimes against culture: the perpetrators had rejected, and violently, the limitations attached to cultural identity in a colonial polity. Colonial politics demanded a culture of quiescence. In colonial India, "crime," Nicholas Dirks contends, "was performed without agency; crime was a function of habit . . . an effect of caste rather than an act of will."[3] Owing in large

[3] Nicholas B. Dirks, *Castes of Mind: Colonialism and the Making of Modern India* (Princeton, NJ: Princeton University Press, 2001), 193; also 181, 188. "Amende collective" formed part of ethnographic criminality and political control; see AGGA, 12H/36, 12H/37, 12H/38, and AGGA, 1T/5, "Au sujet de la proposition d'application du principe de responsabilité collective à l'occasion d'une violation de sépulture près de Nemours," Algiers, March 18, 1874. More broadly, see Charles-Robert Ageron, *Les Algériens musulmans et la France (1871–1919)*, vol. II (Paris: Presses universitaires de France, 1968),

part to the sensationalized publicity surrounding the deaths of explorers, in Algeria, crime became a function, not of agency, but of culture.

The idea of ethnographic crime reenacted fantasies of power and powerlessness, anxieties about the differential experiences of domination. Examples of ethnographic crime abound, even in nineteenth-century France.[4] In Algeria, as in France, sensationalized and highly public crimes facilitated the transference of criminality and guilt from individuals to collective cultural groups. Throughout the 1880s and 1890s, various French explorers, engineers, and soldiers, in the Sahara attempted to extend colonial rule to desert Africa. Travelers to the Sahara operated in a world that equated exploration with a responsibility to produce cultural knowledge on the basis of observation of and participation in the daily lives of the peoples encountered.[5] They engaged in what J. V. Barbier called militant geography, became "martyrs of geography."[6] With these missions traveled soldiers, guards, armed Algerians, an entire cohort of men prepared for violent defense. The knowledge these explorations furnished grew out of the threat of political violence, and their narratives served as militant ethnography.

Dozens of explorers met untimely and gruesome fates in the arid lands between the littoral and the savannah, spurred by the romance of the Sahara[7] and by more prosaic political expediencies. The larger world of colonial Africa loomed large in the ethnographic and political imagination of Algeria. Indeed, some deaths resonating most widely in Algeria occurred outside the colony. Three deaths in particular resonated in Algeria and in France. Although dozens died, the interrelated deaths

644–706; Allan Christelow, *Muslim Law Courts and the French Colonial State in Algeria* (Princeton, NJ: Princeton University Press, 1985).

4 Alain Corbin, *The Village of the Cannibals: Rage and Murder in France, 1870*, trans. Arthur Goldhammer (Cambridge, Mass.: Harvard University Press, 1992); Gay Gullickson, *Unruly Women of the Paris Commune* (Ithaca, NY: Cornell University Press, 1996). Anti-Dreyfusards, too, attempted to ascribe criminality to cultural identity.

5 E.g., Ernest Mercier, *La France dans le Sahara et au Soudan* (Paris: Ernest Leroux, 1889), 17–29. See also AGGA, 22H/79, Governor General of Algeria to the military commanders of the territories of Aïn-Sefra-Laghouat-In-Salah-Biskra, August 29, 1913. On the romance of the Sahara, see Jean-Claude Vatin, "Désert construit et inventé, Sahara perdu ou retrouvé: le jeu des imaginaires," *Revue de l'Occident Musulman et de la Méditerranée* 37 (1984): 108.

6 J. V. Barbier, "Géographie militante: Exploration, les deux missions du Colonel Flatters," *Bulletin de la Société de Géographie de l'Est* [*BSGE*] 3 (1881): 604; Léopold Aymard, *Les Touareg* (Paris: Librairie Hachette, 1911), 133 ("martyrs of geography").

7 On the romanticization of the Tuareg; Henri Duveyrier, *Les Touareg du Nord: Exploration du Sahara* (Paris: Challamel Aîné, 1864); Paul Pandolfi, "Imaginaire colonial et litterature: Jules Verne chez les Touaregs," *Ethnologies comparées*, no. 5 (Autumn 2002); Triaud, *Légende noire*, esp. 99, 109–10, 116–17, 305–9; Paul Pandolfi, "Les Touaregs et nous: une relation triangulaire?," *Ethnologies comparées*, no. 2 (Spring 2001).

of Henri Duveyrier in Paris, Paul Flatters in the Algerian Sahara, and the Marquis de Morès on the border of Tunisia and Libya preoccupied administrators, scholars, journalists, and the public, dominating political debate, public memory, and archival records about exploration. Redolent of fantasies of imperial glory, these violent tales provoked public discussion of empire, and, in some cases, collective attempts to commemorate the deaths. Information leaked slowly out of the Sahara. The great ocean of sand washed the remnants of lives onto the shores of littoral Algeria or to the island oases like the flotsam and jetsam of sandy shipwrecks.[8]

Empire and the poisoned fruit of the desert

"The Sahara," wrote Henri Schirmer, "is the country of mysterious disappearances and unknown dramas."[9] Explorer and eulogist of Henri Duveyrier, Schirmer rendered one such drama known to all. Undoubtedly the most sensationalized of the Saharan missions, the 1881 mission of Lieutenant-Colonel Paul Flatters ended not only in the violent death of its leader and most of its participants, but also the denigration of entire Saharan ethnic groups as culturally predisposed to violent crime. As the governor general succinctly phrased it in 1913, "after the massacre of the Flatters mission, one imagined the Sahara peopled by savage hordes, by veiled men whose ferocity equaled that of the most famous bandits in history."[10] By criminals. Flatters's death embodied the interpenetration of exploration and domination. For many French ethnographers, the "massacre" exemplified the elements of Algerian cultural identity that demanded colonization and the civilizing mission. The logic of the colonial state denied legitimacy to resistance as a form of political contestation.

The selection of Lieutenant-Colonel Paul Flatters to lead two missions to the Sahara to establish a route[11] for a trans-Saharan railroad carried an unmistakable aura of failure. At the very inception, the committee selecting a leader expressed doubts about Flatters. His status as a former military officer lent the mission a military imprimatur, something the committee hoped to avoid. In responses, with an astonishing lack of

[8] AGGA, 22H/30, General Servière, Commander of the Division of Algiers, to Governor General Revoil, Algiers, August 6, 1902.

[9] Henri Schirmer, *Pourquoi Flatters et ses compagnons sont morts* (Paris: Augustin Challamel, 1896), 5.

[10] AGGA, 22H/79, Governor General to the Commanders of the Military Territories, Algiers, August, 29, 1913.

[11] Ministère des Travaux Publics. *Documents relatifs à la Mission dirigée au sud de l'Algérie par le Lieutenant-Colonel Flatters* (Paris: Imprimerie nationale, 1884), 79.

foresight and a characteristic arrogance, Flatters offered to renounce armed escort, an offer to which the committee demurred.[12] Instead, he selected an escort from rival subdivisions of the Sha'amba and Tuareg, and paid them poorly.[13]

Too large to pass unnoticed and too small to afford itself adequate protection, the first mission failed, the Tuareg Ajjer halting it before its completion.[14] Deep in the territory of his guides, who, whatever their internal disagreements, concurred in their hostility to Flatters and the extension of empire, the first mission fell apart; Frédéric Bernard, a member of the first mission, blamed Flatter's organizational ineptitude.[15] As a result of his failure, Flatters "separated himself from certain officers of the first mission, [General Frédéric] Bernard, [Henri] Brosselard, A[lfred] Le Chatelier, who seemed to him not to share sufficiently his sentiments on the conduct to take in regards to the Tuareg whose country was traversed."[16] These cast-offs wrote the epitaphs for the second mission, articulating the ethnographic criminalization of Tuareg and Sha'amba alike.

In 1880, Flatters begin his doomed second mission with no fewer than *ninety-two* attendants. In a letter to his mother, Alfred Le Chatelier offered brief descriptions of those killed alongside Flatters. "His number two, Captain [Pierre-René] Masson" carried out topographic studies, "a charming boy, intelligent good colleague; but he [was] incapable of doing anything[,] understanding nothing of the natives nor of Africa. One justice to render him is that he understood it and effaced himself completely."[17] Le Chatelier found the third in command, Émile-Gustave Béringer, the engineer in charge of astronomical and meteorological research,"very intelligent, very learned, amiable, spiritual, who had voyaged much and describes very well what he has seen. Energetic and very calm, . . . [he] exercised a great influence on the colonel." Béringer worked closely with another engineer, Jules Roche, who carried out studies in geology and mineralogy, a "*bon et gros garçon*," who

12 Schirmer, *Pourquoi*, 13, 14.

13 Henri Brosselard, *Voyage de la mission Flatters au pays des Touareg Azdjers* (Paris: Jouvet, 1883), 67–9.

14 Aymard, *Touareg*, 26; Brosselard, *Voyage*, 130, 164–74.

15 General F. Bernard, "Les Deux Missions transsahariennes du Lieutenant-Colonel Flatters," *Bulletin de la Société de Géographie d'Alger et de l'Afrique du Nord* [*BSGA*] 14 (1909:1): 46–9; V. Derrécagaix, "Exploration du Sahara", *Bulletin de la Société de Géographie* [*BSGP*] 7, no. 3 (1892): 184–9.

16 Commander R. Peyronnet, *Livre d'or des officiers des affaires indigènes 1830–1930*, vol. II, *Notices et biographies* (Algiers: Imprimerie Algérienne, 1930), 394–5. Jean Le Chatelier, "*Alfred Le Chatelier 1855–1929: sa carrière africaine*," unpublished manuscript (Centre des archives d'Outre-Mer, Aix-en-Provence, 1986), 31, notes a personal relationship between Le Chatelier and Flatters's wife.

17 Le Chatelier, "*Alfred Le Chatelier*," 28.

handled the horses, and who "alone among us . . . remained pink and fresh like a young girl." Cabaillot, "a worthy, timid, modest boy, an enthusiastic eager beaver," served as a guide. In particular, Le Chatelier mourned the loss of Dr. Robert-Nicolas-Jules Guiard, "with whom I got along with best . . . well raised, intelligent, learned, very calm and not speaking but after having reflected." Le Chatelier did not mention the members added to the second mission, including Joseph-Gabriel-Henri de Dianous de la Perrotine, an officer in the Native Affairs bureau, and Paul Marjolet, a cook, around whom subsequent events revolved.[18] But then, few remembered Marjolet. Together they represented an ordinary and perhaps not terribly distinguished or well-chosen cross-section of Flatters's world. "Béringer, . . . Roche, . . . and . . . Cabaillot," claimed Le Chatelier, in hindsight, "have, alone, of all the members of the [First] Mission, myself included, done anything intelligent or useful. Three, among them me, who did nothing." He left no doubt as to where the blame for the failure of the first mission – and, by implication, the second – lay. "Three, among them the colonel, who made nothing but errors."[19] Some new members of the second mission acquitted themselves bravely in the events that followed; some yielded to madness; some stood out more for their folly and overconfidence than for particular skill. With the exception of those, like Bernard or the lucky Cabaillot (competent, yet rejected) or Le Chatelier himself, excluded from the second mission, all met a grisly end in the desert.

In winter 1881, various Tuareg and Shaʿamba engaged in an intricate plot to preempt the extension of French control, with Flatters's mission as the object of their ire. On February 16, some Targui guides informed Flatters that they had lost their bearings, and the group stopped at Bir el Gharam to regroup. Separating Flatters and several of his officers from their baggage, the guides led them deep into the desert, to the increasing vexation of Flatters. Characteristically, he expressed his futile rage in terms of colonial racial politics. "I did not bring you to give me orders," he pointedly informed some Shaʿamba guides, "but rather to go where I lead you and to do what I will tell you."[20] This particular harangue appears as likely a point as any to choose as the moment when Flatters's guides decided upon his death. The second Flatters mission "was in reality the adoption of the personal ideas of Lieutenant-Colonel Flatters," wrote Bernard.[21] Moreover, the proposed railroad and Flatters's well-known

[18] Le Chatelier, "*Alfred Le Chatelier*," 28. See also AGGA, 22H/27, "Enquête sur la massacre de la Mission Flatters," 386.

[19] Le Chatelier, "*Alfred Le Chatelier*," 31.

[20] AGGA, 22H/27, "Enquête," 350.

[21] Bernard, "Deux Missions transsahariennes," 50–1; Derrécagaix, "Exploration," 201; AGGA, 22H/27, "Enquête," 383–6 [*c.* 1881].

past as a military administrator menaced the Sahara with the extension of colonial control. A military administrator to the core, Flatters could not conceive of his relationship with the people of the Sahara, whose knowledge vastly exceeded his, through any lens but that of a racialized order of command.

Encamped on a small rise near a well, the several French officers never foresaw their vulnerability. Masson and Flatters attended to the well; Dr. Guiard and Roche pursued their hunt for biological and geological specimens. Béringer "rested in the shade of a clump of tamarind trees."[22] Out of the north came a raucous troop of Tuareg on camels. One Targui decapitated Béringer as he reached for his revolver. Flatters and Masson struggled against the Tuareg contesting their presence. A blow from a saber dislodged Flatters from his horse, and several Tuareg dispatched him on the desolate hillside. Blows to his face and chest killed Masson. De Dianous de la Perrotine fired at the attackers and fell, exhausted, at the top of a small rise. At the end of the battle, Flatters, Capitain Masson, Dr. Guiard, Béringer, Roche, and Dennery met their fate by the small well in the desert. De Dianous led a small band of survivors doomed to even greater suffering. The superior firepower of the Europeans could not counter the superior knowledge of the Tuareg and Shaʿamba. At home in the desert, familiar with its topography, aware of both Flatters's arrogance and his total incapacity to fend for himself, and surrounded by allies, the mission's guides registered their contestation of the extension of French power in the most visceral means possible.[23]

Not all, however, participated. As riven with political rivalries as any other part of the world, the Sahara produced internal tensions. Some

[22] J. V. Barbier, *À travers le Sahara: les missions du Colonel Flatters d'après des documents absolument inédit*, Voyages et découvertes géographiques, ed. Richard Cortambert (Paris: Libraire de la Société bibliographique, 1884), 148.

[23] AGGA, 22H/27, "Enquête," 352–43; AGGA, 1H/85, Chief of the Artillery Squadron [illeg.], "Rapport au sujet des renseignements rapportés par M. l'Interprète militiare Djebarri [*sic*], en ce qui touche la 2e mission Flatters," Oran, February 6, 1895; Bernard, "Deux Missions transsahariennes," 52–4; AGGA, 4H/11, *passim*; Aymard, *Touareg*, 26–9; Barbier, *Flatters*, 604–19; Barbier, *À travers*, 148–9; Fonds privés (FP) 65APC/1 (Papiers Paul Flatters), Captain Spitalier, Chief of the Bureaux arabe at Laghouaṭ, "Procès-Verbal de déclaration du décès," June 15, 188; "Correspondance," *BSGE* 3 (1881): 178–80; Le Chatelier, "*Alfred Le Chatelier*," 25–32; Derrécagaix, "Exploration," 234–7. See also Anne-Marie Briat, Janine de la Hogue, André Appel, and Marc Baroli, *Des chemins et des hommes: La France en Algérie (1830–1962)*, (Hélette: Jean Curutchet, 1995), 97; FP 65APC/1, Madame Flatters to "Monsieur Pilastre," Thursday, July 28, and Madame Flatters to Pilastre, July 29; FP 65APC/1, Capitain Spitalier to Madame Flatters, "Télégramme à Madame Flatters onze rue de Condé Paris," Laghouaṭ, undated, no. 894, and General Cerez to Madame Flatters, "Télégramme à Madame Flatters onze rue de Condé Paris," Oran, no. 9807, undated; "Nécrologie," *BSGE* 3 (1881): 189.

Tuareg and Sha'amba did not attack Flatters and his group but rather attempted to defend him. The difficulty of attributing individuals to particular subgroups, and of assigning their motivations to a political agenda, made French attempts at interpretation complicated. The warnings of betrayal that some Sha'amba gave to Flatters met with an arrogant brush-off; " you and the Chambaâ [*sic*]," he fumed, "you annoy me. Since last year, you've been deceiving me. Leave me alone."[24] His decision, made with his customary arrogance, proved fatal. Though another group of guides attempted to warn a *second* group of Frenchmen separated from Flatters, the latter met the same fate as their compatriots. Though surrounded by guides, the Flatters mission manifested a distinct disinclination to be led. The attackers divided the spoils amongst themselves.[25] On the first day, eighteen Algerians died as well, "killed at the well defending the camels" and the mission. Only five of the attackers lay dead, only a handful injured.[26] Among the Algerians dead alongside Flatters on that desolate hillside remained 'Abd al-Qādir bin Ḥamīd, a *muqaddim* of the Tijāniyya, the very order with which Henri Duveyrier had maintained such close ties.[27]

The survivors of the hilltop battle, including more than fifty Algerians, retreated, hoping to survive the night. The remaining Sha'amba and other Algerians convinced de Dianous, the leader, of the futility of an attack on the vastly superior numbers of Tuareg who followed, from a distance, on their desert march. An Algerian soldier informed the five Frenchmen of the pitiable state of the bodies of those killed at Bir el Gharama, left naked and face down, the corpse of Flatters burned, mutilated. Some Tuareg pursued de Dianous's band, while others attacked the Tuareg Ifoghas, French allies. After several days, starvation set in, and the survivors of the Flatters mission ate their dogs. Before their ordeal ended, they would grow hungrier, and they would eat worse. Surprisingly, they remained in close contact with their pursuers, negotiating safe passage. The two sides even entered an agreement for the return of some of the stolen goods;

24 "Correspondance," *BSGE* 3 (1881): 179.

25 AGGA, 22H/27, "Enquête," 348–7. See also AGGA, 4H/11, "Récit fait par le n^{é} Lechleg ben Arfa, de la tribu des Maamera, chamelier-civil de la mission Flatters rentré de captivité le 12 Juin 1883," Division of Algiers, Subdivision of Médéa, Circle of Ghardaïa, Deposition taken June 15, 1883, at Ghardaïa.

26 AGGA, 22H/27, "Enquête," 344–3.

27 AGGA, 4H/11, Chief of Battalion Belin, High Commander of the Circle of Laghouaṭ, to the General commanding the Subdivision of Médéa, Division of Alger, Subdivision of Médéa, Circle of Laghouat, "Au sujet de n^{é} Abdelkader ben Hamidi Mokaddem de Tedjini, assassiné par les Hoggars [*sic*: Ahaggar]. Mission Flatters," Laghouat, June 2, 1884.

four of the five Algerian emissaries that de Dianous sent to recover them met a rapid death.[28]

Weeks after the initial attack, the French leaders reached a truce with their tenacious pursuers. Starvation had driven them past the limits of cultural boundaries. Upon their return from the desert, the Algerian survivors told stories of cannibalism; colonial administrators quietly encouraged their supervisors to offer large sums, in compensation or in exchange for silence.[29] "During their march, . . . officer Pobéguin and his companions were reduced to living on human flesh; every day, lots would designate a victim whose cadaver served as food for the survivors."[30] Lost in the desert, without hope of rescue, the dwindling French explorers and accompanying Algerians alike violated one of the cultural taboos they shared. They had not only eaten human flesh but had taken lives to do so.

Either out of inability to differentiate hostile from friendly subjects, or out of such sheer desperation, the five surviving Frenchmen accepted a gift of dates from their pursuers. Starving, the survivors ravenously consumed the fruit. Arrogating to themselves by force the rights they thought due them as colonizers, the French members of the expedition ate heartily. "Seized by delirium, in prey of a sudden madness, they wandered through the camp pronouncing incoherent speeches. This period of excitement past, they fell into a state of complete prostration."[31] Vertigo felled others, rendering them incapable of moving from their stupor.[32] While Pobéguin injured himself in his delirious ravings, those of de Dianous proved so severe that "his gun had to be taken from him."[33] The cagey Tuareg and Shaʿamba attackers, knowledgeable of the fruit of the desert, had awaited the desperation of the survivors. The effects of henbane, the deadly nightshade poison that they had mixed with the crushed dates, left none of the party untouched; "the natives themselves felt it, they ran everywhere firing gunshots in the air."[34] De Dianous, disarmed

28 Barbier, *À travers*, 150–5. The Flatters missions resulted in the French occupation of ʿAyn Ṣalāḥ; AGGA, 22H/27, "Observations sur les déclarations," 10–11; F. Bernard, *Quatre Mois dans le Sahara* (Paris: Ch. Delagrave, 1881), 149–50; *Documents relatifs*, 245–68.

29 AGGA, 4H/11, Lt.-Col. Belin, High Commander of Laghouat, to the General commanding the Subdivision of Médéa, Division of Algiers, Subdivision of Médéa, Circle of Laghouaṭ, Laghouaṭ August 18, 1884; AGGA, 6X/20, Masqueray, "Obituary."

30 Brosselard, *Voyage*, 217.

31 Barbier, *À travers*, 155; AGGA, 22H/26, "Enquête," 265.

32 AGGA, 22H/27, "Enquête," 331.

33 AGGA, 22H/27, "Enquête," 331; Aymard, *Touareg*, 28; Brosselard, *Voyage*, 217.

34 Barbier, *À travers*, 155.

by force and descending into madness, slumped on the back of a camel, held upright by others; he died, shot in the chest and thigh. Pobéguin, Marjolet, and Brame, all gravely injured, wandered aimlessly in the desert, ever pursued, but the wounded Santin fell behind and presumably died of the effects of the poison. Brame and Marjolet died, too, the former impaled on a lance. The death of the latter, the newly hired cook, killed while defending Brame and several of his Algerian colleagues, nearly passed unnoticed. De Dianous died shortly thereafter. On March 31, Pobéguin, the last French member of the doomed mission, died. After the deaths of many of their number who had pleaded for clemency, the remnants of the Algerian members of the expedition began to disappear as well, fleeing into the desert or dying alongside the foolhardy French leaders; Targui killed Targui, Sha'ambī killed Sha'ambī.[35] A few survived to tell the sad tale of the rest,[36] the story of the incompetence of the Flatters mission's eponymous leader.

For French colonial administrators and the French public alike, the project of making sense of senseless death became an exercise rooting out ethnographic crime. This process of meaning-making revolved around ascertaining causes and assigning responsibility. In his *Le Sahara-Niger ou Transsaharien*, G.-D. Bédier interpreted Saharan resistance as a cultural politics of refusal. Attempts at the perpetuation of Tuareg "domination of the Sahara . . . made perish the unlucky caravan of colonel Flatters of glorious memory."[37] The Tuareg, according to Bédier, permitted non-Tuareg to enter the desert only so far. "These masters of the desert," the Tuareg, "models of loyalty in any other circumstance, believe themselves permitted anything when it is a question of defending this secret of their State, by force, that is to say, the crossing of the Sahara by anyone who is not Tuareg."[38] Setting aside his total ignorance of non-Tuareg populations, Bédier also attributed to the Tuareg a unified, political state, definitively absent from the Sahara. In an intellectual sleight of hand brought off through generalizing ethnographic narrative, Bédier transferred responsibility for Saharan deaths to the Tuareg collectively; he posited their resistance as equal parts political ideology and

[35] AGGA, 22H/27, "Enquête," 329; Barbier, *À travers*, 156–7; AGGA, 22H/27, "Enquête," 345–3, 334-; Aymard, *Touareg*, 27–8; Barbier, "Géographie militante," 620–1; Bernard, "Deux Missions transsahariennes," 55–7; "Correspondance," *BSGE* 3(1881): 180.

[36] Aymard, *Touareg*, 28; AGGA, 4H/11, Féraud, Consul General at Tripoli in Barbary, to the Minister of Foreign Affairs, Tripoli, April 12, 1881.

[37] G.-D. Bédier, *Le Sahara-Niger ou Transsaharien: conference faite à Paris devant le Comité de l'Afrique du Nord* (Paris: Challamel, 1888), 9; Barbier, *À travers*, 164–74.

[38] Bédier, *Sahara-Niger*, 9; AGGA, 4H/11, Consul General of Tripoli in Barbary to the Minister of Foreign Affairs, Tripoli, May 10, 1881.

expression of an ingrained cultural identity. In *Les Touareg* (1911), Captain Léopold Aymard made the transformation more explicitly. Baldly stated, he claimed that, "currently, [the Tuareg] are better known and judged much less favorably" than in Henri Duveyrier's time. "[T]hey are . . . 'liars, thieves, hypocrites, traitors, and beggars.'"[39] Such ethnographers projected the idea of responsibility for Flatters's death onto the Tuareg as an element of cultural identity. As the behavior of a few individuals became attached to their ethnic group as a whole, crime came to mark the ethnographic identity of all Tuareg.

Even the most blithely homogenizing and casually racist of observers could not fail to assign some blame for the massacre to Paul Flatters himself. His spectacular incompetence verged on a willful neglect of his duty to assure the mission's safety. Before the voyage, Flatters had run afoul of some of the Tuareg or Sha'amba. According to Barbier, after death, his "skin had been burned by a Targui, whose son the colonel had killed, and who thus avenged himself."[40] Far more damaging, however, would prove Flatters's organizational incapacity. Again, J. V. Barbier offered the most damning criticism of the "blind confidence" of Flatters.[41] "[H]e wanted to be the absolute master of men and of things . . . he explained that a leader has uncontested prerogatives . . . which create[d] for him an exclusive responsibility, frightening, in all that it was in his work to anticipate and prevent."[42] Unwilling to delegate authority for the most basic tasks, temperamentally unprepared for the rigors of a Saharan voyage, and intellectually incapable of comprehending the very real resistance and risk of failure, Flatters assumed responsibility for the entire success – or failure – of the mission.

One cause of the mission's failure lay in the continuing tensions within the loose confederation of constantly shifting Saharan alliances. His choice of guides and companions drew Flatters into the conflict between the Tuareg Ajjer and the Tuareg Ahaggar, allied with some Sha'amba.[43]

[39] Aymard, *À travers Touareg*, 81–2. [40] Barbier, *À travers*, 152–3.

[41] Barbier, *À travers*, 156.

[42] Barbier, *À travers*, 132–3. See also Barbier, "Géographie militante," in Ernest Mercier, *L'Algérie et les questions algériennes: étude historique, statistique et économique* (Paris: Challamel Aîné, 1883), 111.

[43] Barbier, "Géographie militante," 610, 622–3; Barbier, *À travers*, 167; AGGA, 4H/11, Chief of Battalion Didier, High Commander of the Circle of Ghardaïa, to General commanding the Subdivision of Médéa, Ghardaïa, June 20, 1883; AGGA, 22H/27, Rogny, "Notice sur Abderrahman ben Mekelaoui et sa famille," n.d. [*c.* 1882?]; AGGA, 22H/27, "Observations sur les Déclarations d'Abd er Rahman Meklaoui," n.d. [*c.* 1882?]; F. Bernard, *Deux Missions françaises chez les Touareg en 1880–1881* (Algiers: Adolphe Jourdan, 1896), 97, 104, 318; Fernand Foureau, "Une Mission chez les Touareg," *BSGP* 14 (1893:4): 526–7; AGGA, 1J/141, Consulat Général of France at Tripoli in Barbary, an unaddressed letter signed Feraud, Tripoli, April 7, 1881; AGGA,

Even the lieutenant-colonel himself, in a letter to Henri Duveyrier, noted the barely concealed hostility to his project.[44] His prudence, however, only went so far; he engaged with the Tuareg he encountered without "see[ing] if the visitors were . . . friends or enemies."[45]

In all fairness to Flatters, he was not the only French official who had difficulty in ascertaining which ramifications of the Tuareg would prove hostile. In their monograph on the trans-Saharan railroad, General Philebert and Georges Rolland similarly accused the Ahaggar but exculpated the Ifoghas from any guilt.[46] It never occurred to many that the various ethnic groups of the Sahara possessed a far more nuanced and variable conception of their relationship to the French. On the rare occasion that administrators could attach a name to a party inculpated in the attacks on the Flatters mission, the name often appeared devoid of any larger attachment.[47] If administrators could assign individuals to particular ethnic groups, their generalizations fell flat. Although suspicion fell upon the mission's Shaʿamba guides, and in particular Muḥammad bin Belghitz, ʿAlī bin Maʿtallah, and ʿAlā bin Shaykh, administrators could not ascertain the guilt of individuals.[48] The ultimate organizational impetus probably lay with some Tuareg Ahaggar and dissident Shaʿamba, with the acquiescence of the Ahaggar leader.[49] Nevertheless, these individuals never acted as representatives of all Tuareg or Shaʿamba, even less as emissaries embodying *all* Saharan peoples. The Tuareg and Shaʿamba that Flatters encountered, those who aided him and those who killed him, acted for purposes and aims that had little to do with mistaken conceptions of the unity of Saharan identity. In assigning responsibility to cultural groups, administrators preserved the fiction of their capacity to punish crimes committed in the Sahara. French inability to differentiate Saharans contributed to the recasting of *all* Saharan peoples as culturally criminal, as culturally predestined for immorality. Paradoxically, French failure to weave a neat narrative out of the Flatters mission painted the Sahara in even broader ethnographic strokes.

4H/11, "Traductions," translation of letters from Cheïkh Younes Aïtaghel ben Biskra to friend El hadj Tahar Basidi and to Ben Aïcha, April 16, 1881.

44 *Documents relatifs*, 428; Derrécagaix, "Exploration," 183.

45 Fernand Foureau, *D'Alger au Congo par le Tchad: mission saharienne Foureau-Lamy* (Paris: Masson, 1902), 112.

46 General Philebert and Georges Rolland, *La France en Afrique et le Transsaharien* (Paris: Augustin Challamel, 1890), 45.

47 AGGA, 4H/11, "Récit fait par le n^{é} Lechleg ben Arfa, de la tribu des Maamera, chamelier-civil de la mission Flatters rentré de captivité le 12 Juin 1883," Division of Algiers, Subdivision of Médéa, Circle of Ghardaïa, June 15, 1883, Ghardaïa.

48 AGGA, 22H/27, "Enquête," 346; AGGA, 22H/27, Rogny, "Notice sur Abderrahman ben Mekelaoui."

49 AGGA, 22H/27, "Notice sur les Déclarations."

The most significant legacy of the Flatters mission for ethnography lay in its commemoration. Lauding some as heroes, popular memory forgot others entirely. The "sad end . . . caused very intense emotion in France and in Algeria," noted Frédéric Bernard.[50] In the shock of the death of the colonel, colonial administrators did not even bother to inform the family of one victim. Paul Marjolet, the young cook who bravely defended his French and Algerian colleagues, died unnoticed.[51] Never an administrator, or a soldier, or a scientist, he lacked the social and political ties of a Flatters or a Masson, the ties that intimately bound individuals to the colonial state and project. On June 13, 1881, months after Marjolet's death, the prefect of Algiers wrote a letter to the governor general. "At the request of M. Pélissier, merchant in Marseille, the Mayor of Algiers asks me if the young Paul Marjolet, enlisted in the Flatters mission as a cook, has been one of the victims of the massacre."[52] His body, like that of numerous Algerian companions, lay dead in the Sahara, and no administrator thought to contact Pélissier or the Algerian guides' families. The death of a simple cook or of an Algerian guide lacked, for both administrators and the colonial press, the visceral political import of the death of Flatters. Not all desert deaths were equal.

Nevertheless, the other deaths attracted much attention. The primary means of commemoration lay in texts, the memoirs of Bernard or the analyses by Barbier, Schirmer, and others.[53] Barbier published to illuminate the causes of the mission's failure, but also to mark the passing of the explorers.[54] Similarly, Bernard's various accounts attested as much to his personal loss of his erstwhile companions as to desires to explain.[55] "In colored and limpid sentences, in a lively and purified style," an anonymous commentator noted, Frédéric Bernard "makes live again, in the spirits of his listeners the various vicissitudes of each of the missions."[56] As early as 1882, Lieutenant-Colonel V. Derrécagaix published a lengthy article offering brief biographical sketches and eulogies of most of those who died with Flatters – or, rather, of the Frenchmen who died with Flatters.[57] Even the government in Paris itself got in on the act, with

50 Bernard, "Deux Missions transsahariennes," 58.
51 AGGA, 22H/27, "Enquête," 327.
52 AGGA, 4H/11, Prefect of Algiers to the Governor General, Algiers, June 13, 1881.
53 Schirmer, *Pourquoi*, 11; Henri Duveyrier, "Revues et analyses: livres et brochures. H. Brosselard. Voyage de la mission Flatters au pays des Touaregs-Azdjers," *Revue d'ethnographie*, 3 (1884): 72.
54 Barbier, "Géographie militante," 604–5.
55 See F. Bernard, *Deux Missions*; "*Deux Missions transsahariennes*"; *Quatre Mois dans le Sahara*.
56 "Séances," *BSGA* 13 (1908): lxxxxii.
57 Derrécagaix, "Exploration," 131–3, 258–69.

its 1884 *Documents relatifs à la mission dirigée au sud de l'Algérie par le Lieutenant-Colonel Flatters*.[58] An entire publishing industry developed around causing audiences to relive the deaths: authors used the events to draw moral conclusions about the identity and role of the Tuareg and the Sha'amba.

Public acts of commemoration cemented Paul Flatters in French collective memory. The violence in the desert had captured public imagination; the rigid, arrogant soldier had become an unwittingly apt emblem for France's imperial project. Neither the man himself, nor the scope of his project, nor yet the magnitude of his failure, marked Paul Flatters's mission as monumental, yet to his memory the French state in Algeria erected a monument to embody empire's audacity. That it could also mark its folly occurred to few, certainly not to the *Bulletin de la Société de Géographie de l'Est* in Nancy. It followed with interest the creation of "the monument destined to perpetuate the memory of the Flatters mission" in Paris, on land given in 1882 by the city.[59] "It is a rather noble pyramid, in gray stone from the Ardennes, with ornaments in bronze."[60] It is difficult to imagine a greater contrast than that between the damp Ardennes and the sands of Bir el Gharam. On one facet read an inscription: "To Colonel Flatters, / leader of the mission charged with the studies / of the Trans-Saharan railroad, / and to his companions: / MM. Masson, capitaine d'état major, / Béringer, Roche, engin., chefs de services, / Santin, assistant engineer / de Dianous, lieutenant / Dennery, Pobéguin, sous-officiers, / to Brame and to the entire escort / Massacred in Africa by the Touaregs [*sic*], / the 16th of April 1881, / After having accomplished their mission."[61] They had, of course, not accomplished their mission, and the Algerians who died beside them went unnamed. "On the right side of the pyramid is the motto of the Legion of Honor: *Honor and Patrie*," and "on the left side: *Science – Civilization*."[62] Glory and nation; science and civilization; empire and selective memory; the glorification of arrogance and folly. The last facet of the monument boasted "a medallion, surrounded by palms, [which] reproduces the likeness of colonel Flatters." The fetishization of Flatters *himself* demonstrated the embedding of the mission in romantic conceptions of colonial conquest. Significantly, in 1941, Marshal Pétain and his Vichy government hoped

[58] *Documents relatifs*.

[59] "Nouvelles Géographiques," *BSGE* 5 (1883): 161–2. The Société de Géographie de Paris also proposed a monument to Flatters; see Dr. Harmand, "Actes de la Société, extrait des procès-verbaux des séances," *BSGP* 7 (1881): 379.

[60] "Nouvelles Géographiques," 161.

[61] "Nouvelles Géographiques," 161.

[62] "Nouvelles Géographiques," 162. Italics in the original.

to revive the Trans-Saharan railroad as an homage to Flatters.[63] On the monument, beneath the image of Flatters, "one reads, *For France, they have confronted perils and death.*"[64] So, too, did Paul Marjolet, whose death merited no commemoration in the Parc de Montsouris in Paris. The death of a young, poor cook, a Marseillais who died defending his colleagues (French and Algerian), fit too poorly with the too-neat narratives of betrayal that public acts of commemoration reified. He fared perhaps better than those Algerians who died alongside him. Instead, Flatters's attackers stood uniformly for all Tuareg; memory effaced Paul Marjolet and the Algerian guides, whose deaths attested to the complexity of the Tuareg. In the Parc de Montsouris, all Tuareg were treacherous murderers, all Frenchmen noble explorers piteously betrayed. The monument, it seems, has only so many facets on which to engrave meaning.

The ethnographer Ernest Mercier grasped the importance of the commemoration with clarity. Foreshadowing the obsessive quest to attach responsibility for the deaths to someone, anyone, Mercier connected the violence of the mission's end with exploration, indeed empire, as a patriotic exercise of the pursuit of scientific knowledge. "All human enterprises have their martyrs and nothing is obtained without sacrifice," wrote Mercier. "Some die without glory at the bottom of a mine shaft; others fall on the battlefield; others perish engulfed in unknown seas; others succumb while searching in the laboratory or in the heights of the sky to snatch some secret from nature." For all these scientists, Mercier declaimed, "let us doff our hats in front of these victims of duty! It is by their devotion that nations become great."[65] Above all, for Mercier, the death of the scientist in the lab, the mariner in the cold sea, or Flatters in the desert represented necessary sacrifices for French glory. "After having paid . . . the tribute of regrets that is their due, let us study the conditions in which the disaster is produced and let us draw profit from the experience made. This must in no way cool our ardor. It is a question of taking our revenge and recommencing in conditions that will assure us success."[66]

That process posed difficult questions and found unsatisfactory answers. The drama of the death of Flatters and his companions prevented a fair evaluation of the leader's role in the mission's demise. As Barbier noted, "when . . . the loss of an expedition is accompanied by

[63] Jean Mélia, *Le Drame de la mission Flatters: les pionniers du Méditerranée-Niger* (Paris: Mercure de France, 1942), 5–7.
[64] "Nouvelles Géographiques," 161. Italics in the original.
[65] Mercier, *L'Algérie*, 112. [66] Mercier, *L'Algérie*, 112.

tragic circumstances, the halo that envelops the hero of the enterprise makes him sacred to us, clothes him in a well-merited prestige, moreover, but which dazzles us and blinds us."[67] Even more difficult, contended Barbier, was the dispassionate study of those killed, like Flatters, for "the cause of science and civilization. Of little import the facts and acts that brought catastrophe; with the enthusiastic spontaneity that characterizes us, we French . . . quickly we raise an altar, at the risk, the next death, of reversing our idols" of yesterday.[68]

Duveyrier and the death of Flatters

In the attempts to comprehend these deaths, a deteriorating man in a dingy suburb of Paris shouldered a disproportionate amount of the blame. Yesterday's idol toppled and fell. The success of Duveyrier's youth greatly influenced subsequent explorers. Nevertheless, his illness and the concomitant slow separation from the Sahara isolated Duveyrier from mainstream debate on the Sahara. Many viewed him as a has-been. His *Touareg du Nord* (1864) remained the seminal text, yet by 1881, Duveyrier retained only vestiges of his previous glory. His participation in the Société de Géographie permitted his continued engagement, and he retained something of a reputation as a Sahara expert. However, many paradoxically dismissed Duveyrier as an expert of the *past*, lacking relevance for contemporary explorers. Out of necessity, explorers relied on the maps and knowledge of Duveyrier, while at the same time denigrating his expertise.

Duveyrier's fascination with exploration verged on the obsessive. Through the Société de Géographie, he evinced a commitment to perpetuating knowledge about the Sahara.[69] Ill, impoverished, and distant from his teenaged exploits, Duveyrier's interest in the expeditions of others provided a literal lifeline, offered to him ties to an increasingly remote glory.

An unhealthy fascination with death ran as an undercurrent in Duveyrier's writings. As early as the 1870s, his texts took a decidedly morbid turn. His "L'Afrique Nécrologique" (1874) raised death

67 Barbier, *À travers*, i. 68 Barbier, *À travers*, ii.

69 Dr. Heinrich Barth, "Sur les expéditions scientifiques en Afrique, par le Docteur Barth," foreword by Henri Duveyrier, *BSGP* 6 (1872): 133–49; *Cinquante-Quatrième anniversaire de la fondation de la Société de Géographie* (Paris: É. Martinet, 1875), 11; "Communications: Expédition de Gérard Rohlfs, lettre à M. H. Duveyrier. Ben-Ghâzi le 30 Octobre 1879" *BSGP* 20 (1880): 172–9; Norbert Dournaux Dupéré, "Voyage au Sahara," ed. Henri Duveyrier, *BSGP* 8 (1874): 113–15; Henri Duveyrier, "Historique des voyages à Timbouktou," *BSGP* 1 (1881): 195–8; Le Chatelier, "Alfred Le Chatelier", 89–90.

to the status of fetish-object. A memorial to those dead in explorations, "L'Afrique Nécrologique" relentlessly cataloged traveling death, offering brief biographical sketches describing the circumstances of the disappearance. In the words of Émile Masqueray's obituary for Duveyrier, "he recorded... the baleful adventures, the self-seeking devotions, the useless deaths, that multiplied... terrors and vengeance on every border of the desert." From those records, "he sadly composed a long martyrology."[70] Illness took up more pages in the article than any section on any individual death.[71] Though he mentioned "climate" (illness and biological failure) and "Muslim fanaticism" as the main causes of death, Henri Duveyrier did not distinguish between deaths from illness or from attack; he commemorated each death equally, something lost in the pursuit of knowledge.[72] For Henri, too, had left something behind in the desert. His malady brought to a close in his early twenties the most successful, productive, and spectacular period of his life. Part of Duveyrier died in the desert from his illness. In mourning others, he mourned himself.

Duveyrier included only "the men of science," and several women as well. He aimed "[t]o show at the price of what sacrifices the geography of Africa became known as it is now, and to collect elements for the study of the[ir] causes."[73] Numerous deaths, not least those of the Flatters mission, marked the years between Duveyrier's voyage and his suicide; Duveyrier intended to provide a systematic way of avoiding future deaths. He arranged "these heroes of science" geographically, situating each death within both a historical and a geopolitical context.[74] Duveyrier's association of death with particular geographic spaces mapped death historically, assigning the disappearance of explorers to specific moment-places in space and time. At the heart of Duveyrier's enthrallment with death lay precisely this mapping of violence onto specific places, and most especially the Sahara he knew so well.

Until the death of Flatters, no explorer's death consumed Duveyrier as did that of David Livingstone.[75] Perhaps something of the famous

70 AGGA, 6X/20, Masqueray, "Obituary."

71 Henri Duveyrier, "L'Afrique nécrologique," *BSGP* 8 (1874): 564–9.

72 Duveyrier, "Nécrologique," 563.

73 Duveyrier, "Nécrologique," 561.

74 Duveyrier, "Nécrologique," 562. Archives nationales. 47AP/10 (Fonds Duveyrier), "Carnet de coupures de presse. *Rif et Maroc N° 1*"; 47AP/10, "Les chefs d'In-Salah et les assassinats de Palat et de Douls," *Journal des Débats*, April 3, 1891; and 47AP/10, "Société de géographie. Séance de la commission centrale," *Le Matin*, May 19, 1892.

75 Duveyrier, "Nécrologique," 635–9, 644; Henri Duveyrier, "Les Explorations de Linvingstone [*sic*] dans la Région des Lacs de l'Afrique orientale," *BSGP* 16 (1872): 337–55; Henri Duveyrier, *Livingstone* (Paris: E. Martinet, 1874); Henri Duveyrier, "Livingstone," *BSGP* 16th ser., 8 (1874): 291–308; Henri Duveyrier, "Traversée de la Zone

tale, the cry of "Doctor Livingstone, I presume," the discovery of the explorer lost on his own voyage of discovery, and his subsequent death, appealed to Duveyrier. He saw Livingstone's exploration of southern Africa as parallel to his own project in the Sahara. Priding himself on his close ties with the people he encountered on the way, Henri identified a similar empathy in Livingstone. "The natives," Duveyrier wrote in Livingstone's obituary, "as if instinctively, sensed in him a defender or a benefactor. He thought of their material well-being, at the same time that he preoccupied himself with developing their intellectual and moral faculties."[76] Concealed beneath this paternalism, dramatically different from the stubborn arrogance of Flatters, personal attachment to these values provided Duveyrier with the impetus to write. In his work, reflected through Livingstone, Duveyrier portrayed a certain nobility. Though permeated with imperialist salvage, Duveyrier's obituary for Livingstone eerily presages what Henri might have hoped for as an epitaph had the violence of empire not dismantled the monument of his reputation. "One of the greatest and most noble actors who have figured on the scene of geographic explorations, one of the most generous representatives of modern civilization, just completed his long and brilliant career."[77]

It was not to be. Duveyrier's career, though brilliant by the standards of its day, remained in perpetuity incomplete, aborted by his malady. Recriminations met Duveyrier's suicide, iniquitous critics would offer the oratories, castigation would be written upon his tombstone.

From their inception, the Flatters missions attracted Duveyrier's scrutiny. The two voyages retraced Duveyrier's steps, relying upon his texts and maps.[78] Indeed, Henri corresponded with the mission during their travels.[79] Following the deaths, he offered his expertise to the Algerian colonial government. In an 1885 letter to Governor General Tirman, Duveyrier reminded the governor general of his experience in the Sahara.[80] He published reviews of books on the mission, juxtaposing his own expertise with that of the cast-aside members of the first mission

Sud de l'Afrique Équatoriale 1873–1875 par le Lieutenant Verney Lovett Cameron de la Marine anglaise," *BSGP* 16 (1876): 113–18.

76 Duveyrier, *Livingstone*, 19.

77 Duveyrier, *Livingstone*, 3.

78 AGGA, 18X/28 (Personal Papers of Henri Duveyrier), Henri Duveyrier to René Maunoir, November 25, 1881; Jean-Louis Triaud, *Légende noire*, vol. I, 310.

79 Henri Duveyrier, "Mission du Colonel Flatters dans le Sahara Central," *BSGP* 7 (1881): 250–7. See also *Documents relatifs*, 429–30; Harmand, "Actes de la Société, extrait des procès-verbaux des séances," 378.

80 AGGA, 4H/11, Henri Duveyrier to Governor General Tirman, Sèvres, September 2, 1882.

in the hopes of providing an explanatory synthesis.[81] Henri Duveyrier presented himself as illuminating the cause of the mission's failures. At the heart of his self-conception, he placed a firm belief in his qualifications to explain. His illness prevented subsequent voyages, but no one, Duveyrier thought, could contest his achievements.

Others demurred. Because of Duveyrier's close association with the mission, some attributed to Duveyrier guilt for Flatters's spectacular failures. Unable to ascertain those responsible, reluctant to blame Flatters himself, commentators turned their attention toward Duveyrier's role in encouraging Saharan exploration.[82] That conditions changed between Duveyrier's explorations and that of Flatters occurred to few. Underpinning the assumption of Duveyrier's responsibility lay a racist conception of Saharan society as static, uniform. Although France had changed dramatically since the 1860s, few thought that the Sahara had. "The organization," noted Frédéric Bernard, one of the lucky members of the first mission excluded from the deadly second, "imposed on Flatters, contrary to his proposals and above all to his experience as an old Africa hand, was based on the idea that an exploration among the Touareg [*sic*] could be carried out in 1880 as the voyage of Duveyrier was accomplished in 1859."[83] Shortly before Duveyrier's suicide, a common interpretation of the 1881 deaths squarely placed the blame with Duveyrier.[84] The death of Flatters and his companions annihilated the idea of colonial stasis, shocking many out of the mistaken belief of Tuareg passivity and absence of politics.[85] This belated acknowledgment blamed Duveyrier and maintained a strategic silence about the organizational and managerial failures of Flatters himself.

The most telling of such condemnations appeared in Captain Léopold Aymard's ethnography, *Les Touareg* (1911). Aymard accused the deceased Duveyrier of an innocence, a puerile naïveté. "The Touareg [*sic*] formerly had, thanks to Duveyrier, a reputation of integrity, of justice, of respect for the word given, that they have never merited, and which, alas!, contributed to the misfortune of Flatters . . . and others." Duveyrier's error, Aymard maintained, arose out of ignorance and luck. Condescending to the youth of the explorer, Aymard remarked that "[t]he brilliant and

81 Duveyrier, "Revues . . . Brosselard," 72–6.

82 *Des chemins et des hommes*, 86; Pottier, "Centenaire," 44; Pottier, "Hommage", 143, Pottier, *Un Prince saharien méconnu*, 160–70.

83 Bernard, "Deux Missions transsahariennes," 44.

84 Philebert et Rolland, *France en Afrique*, 48. See also Pottier (1938), in Triaud, *Légende noire*, 311–12; AGGA, 22H/27, "Observations de la Déclaration d'Abd er Rahman ben Meklaoui," 7; Barbier, *À travers*, 90–1.

85 Triaud, *Légénde noire*, vol, I, 311.

learned author of *Les Touareg du Nord* was scarcely twenty years old, when he completed his most interesting voyage, and had the happiness to manage it without hindrance, whence his gratitude and enthusiasm for the nomads and the portrait he made of them." With the smug benefit of hindsight, Aymard went on: "currently, they are better known and judged much less favorably."[86] Aymard's condemnation perpetuated the conception of *all* Tuareg as inherently, collectively criminal. R. Peyronnet's 1930 *Livre d'or des officiers des affaires indigènes* (1930) repeated Aymard's calumnies.[87] Coupled with the difficulty in finding the perpetrators, the idea that Duveyrier must have erred, that his ethnography was aberrant, allowed commentators both to absolve Flatters and to recreate the Tuareg as a criminal object. Blaming Duveyrier sidestepped the the near-impossibility of punishing the perpetrators and prevented a distasteful critique of Flatters.

Duveyrier attempted, if obliquely, to defend his legacy. In a letter to Frédéric Bernard, he recalled warnings he had offered.[88] In "Le Désastre de la mission Flatters" (1881), Duveyrier elucidated his own explanation for the "disaster."[89] In reality, the poor organizational skills of Flatters and the resistance of the Tuareg and the Shaʿamba to French infiltration bore more responsibility for the ill-fated mission than "these unfounded and cruel accusations" led Duveyrier's contemporaries to believe.[90] The cycles of recrimination failed to interpret the mission's end as a statement about colonial politics, as resistance and political contestation, another episode in empire's long litany of violence.

Thus, his contemporaries refused to absolve Duveyrier from culpability. Moreover, Duveyrier's emotional connection to the events of 1881 made the ten years' recriminations between the massacre and his suicide all the more difficult. His writings, "recounted in touching

86 Aymard, *Touareg*, 81–2.

87 Peyronnet, *Livre d'or*, vol. II, 396–7. See also Triaud, *Légende noire*, vol. I, 311; Michael Heffernan, "The Limits of Utopia: Henri Duveyrier and the Exploration of the Sahara in the Nineteenth Century," *The Geographical Journal* 155, no. 3 (November 1989): 347–8.

88 AN, 47AP/4, Henri Duveyrier to Frédéric Bernard, n.d.; AGGA, 4H/11, General commanding the Division of Constantine to the Governor General of Algeria, Constantine, May 15, 1881.

89 Henri Duveyrier, "Le Désastre de la mission Flatters," *BSGP* 7 (1881): 368–74; Jacques Berque, "Cent vingt-cinq ans de sociologie maghrébine," in Jacques Berque, *Opera Minora*, vol. II: *Histoire et anthropologie du Maghreb*, ed. by Gianni Albergoni (Paris: Éditions Bouchène, 2001), 190–1; Triaud, *Légende noire*, vol. I, 310–17. See also AGGA, 6X/20 (31MIOM37), Masqueray, "Obituary"; Gianni Albergoni, "Variations italiennes sur un theme français: la Sanusiya," in *Connaissances du Maghreb: Sciences sociales et colonization* (Paris: Éditions du Centre national de la recherche scientifique, 1984), 113–14.

90 Dominique Casaius, "Les Kel-Ghela," in Galand, ed., *Lettres au Marabout*, 12–16.

terms,"[91] manifest the toll the allegations took on Henri. "More than anyone," he wrote, "I feel the irreparable loss that we have just had; I could call Colonel Flatters and MM. Béringer and Roche my friends."[92] Both the deaths and popular reaction wounded Duveyrier. "These cruel and unfounded accusations," writes Dominique Casaius, "added to the professional and sentimental disappointments, were perhaps not strangers to his suicide."[93] The complex unfolding of events in the Sahara should, however, caution historians about tracing facile lines of causality; to attribute Duveyrier's suicide to the aftereffects of the Flatters mission grossly oversimplifies the life and actions of someone who, in the final account, was neither a discourse nor a symbol, but a man.

More than just these accusations disturbed Duveyrier. The deaths appeared to Henri to reject his own discoveries, the imperial values to which his voyage had attested. Duveyrier saw in Flatters the continuation of his own mission, and he interpreted its failure as his own, even without others' recriminations. The mission's fatal conclusion punctuated the age of exploration to which Duveyrier belonged, ushering in a different relationship between France and the Sahara. "Flatters above all, the nature of his enterprise as much as his death, touched [Duveyrier] with a perceptible blow. I recall," wrote Emile Masqueray,

> when the march on Hoggar [*sic*: Ahaggar] was decided, he rose to say, "You want to get involved in the Sahara with engineers without your assuring in advance the good disposition of the Touareg [*sic*] who wander it, and you claim that 80 guns will suffice for your defense in case of need. You are ignorant of these immense solitudes in which the most sane spirits are taken with vertigo, where number is nothing, where the best led corps of troops can become the toy in the grip of agile men accustomed to hunger and thirst, always ready to fight and to betray.'[94]

Masqueray had little doubt about whom Duveyrier spoke. The vertiginous wastelands of the Sahara molded the young Duveyrier, and he understood the folly, the sheer arrogant recklessness, of the Flatters mission better than anyone. "When Flatters fell under the blow of a lance, and when the other men of his escort, reduced to eating human flesh, reappeared at Ouargla, like ghosts, a black veil extended over" the Sahara.[95]

A black veil descended over Henri, as well. "The Sahara . . . was stamped forbidden and Duveyrier felt the most beautiful half of his life

[91] Derrécagaix, "Exploration," 255. [92] Duvyerier, "Désastre," 364.

[93] Casaius, "Les Kel-Ghela," 14, citing E. Mambré, *Henry Duveyrier, explorateur du Sahara (1840–1892)* (Université de Provence, Institut d'histoire des Pays d'Outre-Mer, mémoire de maîtrise, 1992); Pottier, *Laperrine*; Pottier, *Un prince saharien méconnu*; Pottier, *La vocation saharienne du Père de Foucauld*; Triaud, *Légende noire*, vols. I and II.

[94] AGGA, 6X/20, Masqueray, "Obituary." [95] AGGA, 6X/20, Masqueray, "Obituary."

become useless, fallen into oblivion."[96] His disenchantment with French policy in the Sahara, his inability to continue his work there, the passing of his moment, his mental incapacity left over from his illness, "[f]rom there," wrote Masqueray, "to taking a revolver in an hour of melancholy to blowing his brains out in the corner of a wood, there is but the distance that separates discouragement from madness, and we touch perhaps now on the veritable cause of his suicide."[97] To the cycle of recriminations in which Duveyrier loomed large and tragic, Emile Masqueray added another layer of responsibility. Duveyrier, he wrote, "did not want to survive: he understood too well that France had long since served notice to him that his role was terminated."[98]

Part of Henri Duveyrier died with Flatters and Masson and Dianous and even the forgotten Paul Marjolet. Duveyrier's eulogist expressed no doubts about the role that public scorn played in Duveyrier's suicide. While Duveyrier traveled with the express goal of meeting, of *connecting*, with the Tuareg, Flatters thought only of connecting the Sahara with the littoral through the railroad. The youth who had befriended Ikhenoukhen, who had lived with the Tuareg, who had joined the Tijāniyya, who envisioned exploration as a project both scientific and personal, bound not by the strictures of politics, but rather by the limits of intellect, imagination, and benevolence, died in the desert. The boy died in the winter of 1881, and the man ten years later. With the death of Flatters and the death of that boy died Napoleon III's dream (paternalist, violent, imperialist though it was) of an Arab kingdom, an imperial France unified with its Arab possessions, destroyed, ten years into the Third Republic, by an imperialism explicit about the aims of conquest that the idea of exploration barely concealed. It was the passing of a generation, and Henri Duveyrier passed with it.

The memory of the Flatters mission, however, refused to die. Because twelve out of the ninety-seven original members of the party survived,[99] information trickled out of the Sahara for years. The survivors faced a lot scarcely less bleak than that of those killed at Bir el Gharama or of those poisoned by henbane. At least one remained a slave of the Tuareg until 1889, when the governor general allocated funds to purchase his freedom.[100] Almost certainly, others died in captivity.

96 AGGA, 6X/20, Masqueray, "Obituary."
97 AGGA, 6X/20, Masqueray, "Obituary."
98 AGGA, 6X/20, Masqueray, "Obituary."
99 Georges-Robert, *À travers l'Algérie: notes et croquis* (Paris: E. Dentu, n.d. [1887]) 358.
100 AGGA, 4H/11, Governor General of Algeria to the General commanding the Division of Algiers, December 6, 1889.

Despite the detailed accounts that emerged, the exact number and identity of the survivors remained surprisingly vague. Through the end of the nineteenth century, various Algerians and French alike claimed mysterious survivors of Flatters mission. The ransoming of the occasional survivor from slavery doubtless fueled these rumors. The most vivid accounts of survivors involved Flatters. In the mid-1890s, Jabārī bin Masʿūd ["Djebari ben Messaoud"], an interpreter and erstwhile explorer, repeatedly claimed to have encountered French survivors living as Tuareg slaves. News of survivors was not new. Debris surfaced periodically, whether because some members had escaped their presumed fate or merely because their belongings had.[101] Moreover, Jabārī's extensive physical descriptions of the purported survivors lent credence to his claims.[102] Governor General Jules Cambon found the descriptions to correspond to Guiard, Béringer, Santin or Brame, and Roche, the latter of whom Jabārī identified from a photograph.[103] Furthermore, Jabārī emphasized the difficulty in acquiring information about the men without endangering the captives' lives; nevertheless, he, alone, Jabārī claimed, could provide the information necessary for rescue.[104] The former interpreter tried to reserve for himself the decisive role in determining how the French would proceed. Decisive, for Jabārī, but rather more precarious for the French administrators, who had to rely entirely on the testimony, motives, and good faith of the baffling Jabārī.

A Tunisian naturalized as a French citizen, Jabārī had married the daughter of a wealthy Tunisian doctor and had served as a French soldier.[105] Prior to his irruption into public consciousness with his Flatters stories, Jabārī gave no cause to attract administrators' notice. However, eighteen months after accompanying an exploration deep into

101 Ernest Mercier, review of F. Patorni, *Les tirailleurs algériens dans le Sahara* (Constantine, 1884), in Mercier, *Mélanges africains et orientaux* (Paris: Jean Maisonneuve et Fils, 1915), 176–9; AGGA, 4H/11, Jules Féraud, Consul at Tripoli, to Minister of Foreign Affairs, Tripoli, April 12, 1881; General Ritter, Commander of the Division of Constantine, to Governor General of Algeria, August 4, 1884; AGGA, 4H/11, Ritter to Governor General, September 9, 1884. AGGA, 1H/85, Chief of the Artillery Squadron [illeg.], "Rapport . . . mission Flatters," Oran, February 6, 1895; FP 65APC/1, "Les Débris de la Mission Flattesr," *Le Dix-Neuvième Siècle*, July 4, 1881.

102 AGGA, 1H/85, Captain [illeg.] to Roche, Paris, November 29, 1894; AGGA, 1H/85, Chief of the Military Squadron [illeg.], "Rapport . . . Mission Flatters," Oran, February 6, 1895.

103 Governor General Jules Cambon to the Minister of the Colonies, Algiers, May 24, 1895. AGGA, 1H/85, "Rapport . . . mission Flatters," Oran, February 6, 1895.

104 AGGA, 1H/85, Roche's copy of Djebari to Captain [unnamed], December 9, 1894; AGGA, 1H/85, "Rapport . . . mission Flatters," Oran, February 6, 1895.

105 AGGA, 1H/85, Special Commissioner Jules Carron, "Rapport: Djebari ben Messaoud, Interprète Militaire," Algiers, February 14, 1895; AGGA, 1H/85, Minister of War to the Governor General of Algeria, Paris, May 14, 1895.

sub-Saharan Africa, Jabārī returned to Tunis with improbable stories of survivors.[106] His willingness to share his views with the press alienated officials in Tunis, precipitating his departure. In Algeria, however, his self-promotion made at least one convert, the editor of the newspaper *L'Hiverneur*, who cooperated with Jabārī on the publication of his work. The editor in question was, moreover, a devotee of the anti-Semitic and nonsensical conspiracy theories of the late Marquis de Morès, like Flatters killed in the Sahara.[107] In publishing his account, Jabārī offered a radical, if implicit, critique of French failure to avenge Flatters and the others. Indignantly the impoverished Jabārī protested his prison sentence for continued contact with the colonial press, noting that French explorers had published with impunity and lived off the income their books produced. Jabārī failed to realize, however, that a colonial subject's publication of an account that contradicted the government's official interpretation amounted to a declaration of discursive war, even if undertaken by a naturalized citizen. That Jabārī attributed this opposition to the machinations of the remarried Madame Flatters no doubt did not endear him to many.[108]

Nor, certainly, did his repeated threats to involve foreign powers. Indeed, they only exacerbated his tensions with colonial regimes in Algeria and Tunisia. Although "he prefer[red] to die of hunger than to become a 'second Dreyfus,'" Jabārī failed to comprehend that the French would only respond to intimidation with hostility and repression; his appeals to settler anti-Semitism with his anti-Dreyfusard sentiments also alienated him from the government.[109] Moreover, it was Jabārī himself who initiated contact with foreign powers; the German Consul in Algeria, demonstrating the surprisingly unassailable solidarity of colonial powers in the face of restive "natives," quietly turned Jabārī's letters over to the French.[110] Even Cambon turned on Jabārī, dismissing him as a deranged liar.[111] Jabārī's willingness to circumvent acceptable interaction between colonizer and colonized, and his attempts to claim the rights of free

106 AGGA, 1H/85, Carron, "Rapport," February 14, 1895; AGGA 1H/85, General Leclerc, Commander of the Division of the Occupation of Tunisia, to the General commanding the 19th Army Corps in Algeria, January 12, 1895.

107 AGGA, 1H/85, Carron, "Rapport," February 14, 1895.

108 AGGA, 1H/85, Special Commissioner Jules Carron, "Rapport: indigènes. Djebari ben Messaoud," February 16, 1895. AGGA, 1H/85, Minister of War to Governor General of Algeria, Paris, May 14, 1895, noted a medical evaluation of Jabārī because of the presumption of mental derangement.

109 AGGA, 1H/85, Carron, "Rapport," February 14, 1895.

110 AGGA, 1H/85, Governor General of Algeria to Minister of Finance, President of the Council, Paris, March 31, 1895.

111 AGGA, 1H/85, Jules Cambon to unnamed deputy, Algiers, December 10, 1895.

expression reserved for Europeans, closed the minds of French administrators to his seemingly far-fetched tale.

To promote the plight of the survivors, Jabārī published his *Les Survivants de la mission Flatters* (1895). A peculiar mix of polemic, plea, and personal justification, *Les Survivants* exposed Jabārī's animosity toward the colonial state. Jabārī captivated the press, relentlessly presenting his argument, marketing both his book and his poverty through Algeria's vociferous independent media. The colonial media latched on to the amazing story of the survivors' enslavement, criticizing the government's failure to exact vengeance.[112] One journalist even called for an expedition, as with Livingstone, though only after dispensing with the pesky middleman of Jabārī.[113] In Paris, Jabārī lectured to an audience of more than *one thousand*, including the Prince de Polignac and Masson's brother.[114] Nevertheless, the colonial government's careful refutation effectively killed Jabārī's career as a public speaker, and the fickle colonial press turned on Jabārī. Shortly after his triumphant Parisian début, *le Journal* offered, in response to an earlier article querying, "ARE THEY ALIVE?", a retraction entitled, "THEY ARE DEAD!"[115]

However, some journalists recognized the deft hand of state manipulation at work in the denigration of Jabārī; Jabārī claimed that his French employers had ill used him following work as an interpreter. Ed. Déchaud of *L'Akhbar* shrewdly remarked on the military's aversion to the scrutiny Jabārī's claims would bring.[116] The popular press's interest in Jabārī's story threatened the Algerian administration with discursive representations that escaped their grasp; the purported existence of French slaves, unrescued and incapable of redemption, fashioned the Sahara as a land of cultural criminals, a place of peoples immune to the chastisements

112 AGGA, 1H/85, "Révélations sensationelles sur la mission Flatters," in *La Dépêche algérienne*, November 22, 1894; AGGA, 1H/85, "Le Colonel Flatters," *La Dépêche algérienne*, November 23, 1894; AGGA, 1H/85, Stanislas Bénet, "M. Djebari," *Moniteur de l'Algérie*, December 18, 1894; AGGA, 1H/85, Ed. Déchaud, "Le Droit du Plus Fort," *L'Akhbar*, March 14–15, 1895; AGGA, 1H/85, "En Tunisie," *La Dépêche algérienne*, March 22, 1895.

113 AGGA, 1H/85, C. Allan, "La Mission Flatters," *La Vigie algérienne*, August 25, 1895, No. 5719; AGGA, 1H/85, "L'Affaire Djebari," *La Dépêche algérienne*, March 18, 1895.

114 AGGA, 1H/85, "Pour la mission Flatters: la réunion du Grand-Hôtel," in *Le Journal*, September 21, 1895.

115 AGGA, 1H/85, "ILS SONT MORTS!," *Le Journal*, after September 10, 1895; AGGA, 1H/85, "SONT-ILS VIVANTS?", September 10, 1895; "En Tunisie: Encore Djebari," *La Dépêche algérienne*, March 30, 1895. AGGA, 1H/85, Napoléon Ney, untitled article, *La Vigie algérienne*, August 25, 1895, claimed Jabārī admitted fabricating the story.

116 AGGA, 1H/85, Ed. Déchaud, "L'Incident Djebari," March 19, 1895; AGGA, 1H/85, Ed. Déchaud, "Pour Finir," *L'Akhbar*, March 22, 1895. See also AGGA, 1H/85, Stanislas Bénet, "Centre africain: le rôle de la France dans le Centre Africain," *Moniteur de l'Algérie*, February 2, 1895.

of the colonial state and abiding by a cultural logic that permitted murder with impunity.

Les Survivants expounded Jabārī's unorthodox theories and improbable encounters with the Tuareg. He pleaded for the lives of "four Frenchmen . . . currently among the savages," offering long descriptions of the men.[117] The naturalized French citizen appealed to the nationalist pride and honor of his countrymen, but also to the basest instincts of Third Republic France. "This little work . . . addresses itself. . . . [n]ot to corrupted France, debased by the presence of Jews or foreigners, but to honest and industrious France."[118] Jabārī aligned himself with the assorted madmen whose conspiracy theories plagued the Sahara like the occasional swarm of locusts, framing his work as a call to action, a revival for a sleeping France that had failed to redeem its noble explorers.[119] Hence, Jabārī constantly reaffirmed his French-ness, creating a narrative "we" including himself. In *Survivants*, his intimate knowledge of the survivors granted him privileges promised him by citizenship, yet denied him by state racism.

Jabārī suffered from the colonial state's racial differentiation of citizenship rights. Allusions to his mistreatment echoed throughout *Les Survivants* and his letters. He decried the obstacles erected in his path by his "powerful persecutors."[120] In particular, he excoriated one Commander Rebillet. Rebillet, he claimed, stalled Jabārī's career and suspended his pension.[121] "The fault" for the continued imprisonment of the survivors of the Flatters mission "falls on one and only one person . . . [:] Commander Rebillet."[122] That Jabārī felt injured, he left no doubt: "To recount the maneuvers of this man to satisfy a base grudge against me, this is neither the time nor the place. Another work will contain them all."[123] Their relationship had started well; Rebillet had hired the military interpreter for a mission to Central Africa (resulting in Jabārī's absence from Tunisia and Algeria from November 1892 to May 1894), promising glory and success, and even attested to his honor to Jabārī's prospective in-laws.[124] What, then, had so incensed Jabārī? Doubtless, Rebillet's reluctance to accord any worth to the interpreter's story rankled Jabārī.

Far more significantly, however, Jabārī took exception to Rebillet's ethnographic classification of Jabārī himself. Rebillet referred to Jabārī in

117 Messaoud Djebari (Mas'ūd Jabārī), *Les Survivants de la mission Flatters* (Tunis: Imprimerie Brigol, 1895), 3; AGGA, 4H/11, Djebari, unnamed article, *Le Journal*, September 10, *c.* 1897.
118 Djebari, *Survivants*, 3. 119 Djebari, *Survivants*, 9. 120 Djebari, *Survivants*, 60.
121 Djebari, *Survivants*, 111. 122 Djebari, *Survivants*, 106.
123 Djebari, *Survivants*, 106. That subsequent volume never appeared.
124 Djebari, *Survivants*, 107–8.

print as a native, an *indigène*.[125] "Useless to say that my title as a Military Intepreter was neglected, by design or not, and that my name was preceded by the qualification 'native.'"[126] To bin Masʿūd, this represented an unmistakable and unforgivable slight against a French citizen – an ethnographic crime of generalization that, he asserted, falsely included him under the rubric of "native." The colonial government never would have denied a pension to a French citizen who had ably served them, yet they did precisely that to the naturalized French citizen, Jabārī. Rebillet's categorization came as one in a long line of insults, both trivial and consequential, that consistently buffeted what little equality naturalized citizens could expect. Jabārī felt a victim of a system of ethnographic criminality that equated all "natives" with guilt. A path pursued by very few, naturalization required the de facto renunciation of cultural identity yet offered little in return. Jabārī effectively relinquished his social position in Tunisia, only to find advancement blocked by basic discourtesies and elemental prejudice.

Jabārī's "we" concealed a stinging rebuke of the inequalities of the French colonial system. That rebuke, however, came at a price. Jabārī's vitriolic rejection of the "native" relied upon his own ingrained prejudices, imbricated with discourses of cultural criminality, about Saharan peoples. Jabārī objected strenuously to the association of "native" with the "*nègres*."[127] Rebillet had published an article on Central Africa, relying on one Ḥājj Aḥmad al-Fallātī for his information.[128] Jabārī claimed that Rebillet ascribed to al-Fallātī details learned from Jabārī himself. Moreover, "the absence of [his] title and the qualification of 'native' . . . reduced me to a simple *nègre*, a caravan conductor."[129] Resenting the implication that readers might consider him black, Jabārī objected bitterly when a young Lyonnais expressed astonishment at his appearance, noting "everyone figures, in Lyon, that you are black, some caravan guide who wanted to make a name for himself by his revelations on Colonel Flatters."[130] Jabārī magnified the white supremacist logic of empire; disavowing his status as a "native," he established rigid, racialized hierarchies of worth, and published to contest his place in those hierarchies. Internalizing the discriminatory logic of colonial citizenship, he received only scorn in return.

Despite its express opposition to the colonial administration, *Les Survivants* repeated dominant ethnographic tropes of criminality. *Les Survivants* conceived of the Tuareg through both Jabārī's own white

[125] Djebari, *Survivants*, 108–10. [126] Djebari, *Survivants*, 108–9.
[127] Djebari, *Survivants*, 108–9. [128] Djebari, *Survivants*, 108–10.
[129] Djebari, *Survivants*, 108–10. [130] Djebari, *Survivants*, 108–10.

supremacy and the lens of ethnographic crime. In short, Jabārī depicted the Tuareg literally as a portrait in black and white. "White" Tuareg were good, "black" Tuareg criminal.

> [T]he blacks are serfs, without honor and without rank... They deliver themselves to acts of brigandage... their morals are loose and their customs consist of stealing or pillaging caravans.
>
> Generally, it is they who are employed as guides or porters. It is thus that they attract prey to the people of their race.
>
> The white Touaregs... push honor to the point of exaggeration.
>
> Their occupation consists of mutually making war... their morals are austere and honest.
>
> The white Targui is punished by death... if he lies, if he betrays or if he steals, whomever might be the victim. The Targui is generous by character and by temperament... He is sober and resistant to fatigue.[131]

Needless to say, Jabārī counseled the French to traffic only with "whites."[132] He created a desert mirage, a phantasm whereby "white" signified the romantic, noble savage and "black" the betraying, murderous native. He fabricated artificial divisions between "white" and "black" Tuareg, assigning them diametrically opposed cultural valences. Mimicking French texts, his depictions conflated cultural identity, criminality, and racial pseudoscience into a reifying epistemology of discrimination. Although Jabārī explicitly introduced racial categories into his discussion of Tuareg morality, he did not contest the moralizing mission of colonial ethnography. He traveled with the Tuareg, spoke extensively with them,[133] and wrote cultural descriptions based on colonial conceptions of criminality. Ethnographic generalizing knew few limits.

Around the Flatters mission crystallized representations of Tuareg criminality. These sensationalized deaths transformed resistance into ethnographic crime, made individual actions into encapsulations of the cultural identities of the Sahara. Paul Flatters's militant ethnography began in the desert but finished in the text. Even his so-called "resurrection" in the 1890s marked less the survival of the members of the mission themselves than the continued perpetuation of the discursive consequences of their deaths. For Marjolet, Flatters, Masson, and the rest did, indeed, die in the desert. I, for one, am convinced. Various Tuareg attested to having seen Flatters's burnt corpse.[134] But I also believe, to some extent, Jabārī's account, fabulist, bigot, and disgruntled careerist though he was. I have no doubts about the presence of the

[131] Djebari, *Survivants*, 46–7, 51 (racialization of criminality).

[132] Djebari, *Survivants*, 47–9. [133] Djebari, *Survivants*, 13–14.

[134] AGGA, 1H/85, "Rapport au sujet des renseignements," p. 1.

17. Etienne Dinet, "La Montée de Bou-Saâda" (1894).

occasional European among the Tuareg, whether by choice or as a captive. The Sahara, vast and mysterious, kept more secrets than it revealed. And it revealed, not the inherent criminality of its inhabitants, a claim as spurious as those that attributed blame to Henri Duveyrier, but rather the inability of Europeans to comprehend the ecological, political, and strategic challenges of conquering the desert. The ethnography of criminality represents an ethnography, too, of ignorance. It left bodies in its wake.

"This problem of moral ethnography"

Wrote Auguste Pavy of the Marquis de Morès (1896), "nothing discourages . . . the valiant. For one that succumbs, twenty rise to replace him."[135] So, too, did innumerable explorers rise to replace Flatters. Each of the dozens of missions that ended violently in the Sahara reinforced

[135] Auguste Pavy, *L'Expédition de Morès*, Librairie africaine et coloniale (Joseph André, 1897), 7.

predominant views of Saharan deviance.[136] Later deaths superseded the Flatters mission in collective memory, providing lurid fodder for conceptions of ethnographic crime.

Even Pavy would have found it difficult to find an explorer to replace the marquis. Among the most prominent of these purported object-lessons stood the bizarre life and peculiar death of the Marquis de Morès, explorer, monarchist, anti-Semite, sometime friend of Theodore Roosevelt. A soldier and conspicuously consuming scion of the crumbling French nobility, the Marquis de Morès was born in 1828 to the Sardinian Duke of Vallombrosa and the Franco-Savoyard Duchess of Cars. After spending part of his youth in the American West with Roosevelt, he married Medorah-Marie Hoffmann, a New York banking heiress.[137] By the 1890s, Morès had become enough of a celebrity in France that his 1896 death caused uproar.

The marquis played no small role in publicizing his ill-fated mission. Although his monarchist politics and nobility in many ways marked him as a man of the Second Empire, he mastered the machinery of Third Republic publicity. In 1896, Morès visited Tunisia to rouse support for his mission's political aim, an "anti-bourgeois," anti-capitalist, anti-Semitic alliance between Saharan Muslims and the French. Morès asked for a vote of support from his audience, duly received and expedited by telegrams announcing a "mandate" for his alliance.[138] Morès combined the anti-bourgeois fervor of an unreconstructed monarchist, the anti-Semitism of the far right, an Anglophobia better suited to Napoleonic France, and a romantic view of a French "Royaume arabe" plagiarized from Napoleon III's script. By the time Morès departed, he added to his conspiracy the Rothschilds, the Prince of Wales, and the Ottoman Empire. So fully did he expect the welcome and support of the Sanūsiyya, the Tuareg, and the Sudanese and Kufra mahdis that he telegrammed declarations of war to Queen Victoria and to the Sublime Porte.[139] Their responses went unrecorded, presumably because of the difficulty of transmitting laughter in a telegram, no matter what the language. To describe his voyage as sheer lunacy reflects neither the true depth of its

[136] Théodore Monod, ed., *Fous du désert: les premiers explorateurs du Sahara, 1849–1887, H. Barth, H. Duveyrier, C. Douls*. Le Tour du Monde, ed. Chantal Edel (Paris: Phébus, 1991); AGGA, 4H/23, 1K/288.

[137] Pavy, *Expédition*, 44–5.

[138] AGGA, 4H/29, M. Millet, Resident-General of France at Tunis, to M. Bourgeois, Minister of Foreign Affairs, Tunis, March 30, 1896; Pavy, *Expédition*, 9.

[139] AGGA, 4H/29, anonymous, "Rapport sur l'expédition du Marquis de Morès," n.d. (*c.* 1897); Pavy, *Expédition*, 10, 14–15; AGGA, 3X/3, anonymous, "L'Algérie en France," *l'Akhbar*, October 1895; AGGA, 16H/6, anonymous, "Une Infamie," *La Libre Parole*, May 22, 1899.

preposterousness, its proponent's fervor, the widespread dissimulation of knowledge about it, nor the seriousness of its consequences and collective memory. Morès may have been a crackpot, but he was an important one, or at least a famous one, which more or less amounted to the same thing.

Unwittingly, Morès stumbled into a political environment very much like that of Flatters. Most of the Sahara remained implacably opposed to the colonial project. Morès had offered bread and oil to some antagonistic Sha'amba, an offering they declined.[140] "They probably estimated," claimed Pavy, "out of some leftover modesty, that they could not rightly be the guests of the man whose death they were already probably plotting."[141] The marquis met his death in El-Ouatia, in the desert near the Libyan-Tunisian border, shot in the back by unidentified Tuareg. Some administrators categorically absolved the Ifogha, French allies, from any responsibility, preferring to inculpate the Sha'amba and not to address the potential defection of ostensible allies. As with Flatters, administrators could not identify Morès's assailants, creating an opportunity for the attribution of collective responsibility.[142] Thus, for Pavy, Morès's death marked the level of civilization for a people who possessed only the remnants of scruples, devoted to betrayal. At least he attributed that remnant to the Sha'amba; "[t]he Tuareg did not even have such scruples."[143] Reified images of a criminalized Sahara relied upon moral evaluations drawn from the deaths of Morès and his like.

As with Flatters, the bulk of the responsibility for the mission's failure lay with its organizer. The Marquis de Morès relied upon a guide who knew nothing of the Tuareg or the Sahara; his mere status as a "native" seemed to suffice as expertise for Morès.[144] Moreover, Morès never really recognized that, while some Algerians befriended him, some would oppose him. Despite myriad warnings, Morès "declared that the dissident Châmbâa [*sic*] had rallied to his cause," and "as for the bad faith

140 Pavy, *Expédition*, 74. 141 Pavy, *Expédition*,75.

142 Pavy, *Expédition*, 52, 95–6; AGGA, 4H/29, Governor General of Algeria to the Governor General "des passages Mecherie," Algiers, June 19, 1895; AGGA, 4H/29, General Fontebride, commanding the Subdivision of Batna, to the General La Rocque, commanding the Division of Constantine, Batna, July 15, 1896; General La Rocque to Governor General, July 17, 1896; AGGA, 4H/29, Chief of the Section of Native Affairs to Governor General of Algeria, Algiers, June 19, 1896; AGGA, Oasis//46, Commander Paÿn, "Rapport du Chef d'Escadrons Paÿn Commandant Militaire du Territoire des Oasis sur les individualités marquantes et les tribus nomades en pays Ajjer," In-Salah, September 25, 1911.

143 Pavy, *Expédition*, 75.

144 AGGA, 4H/29, General Rogny, Division of Constantine, to the Governor General of Algeria, Constantine, June 27, 1895.

18. Etienne Dinet, "Le Ksar d'El-Goléa" (1893).

of the Touareg [*sic*], that was a groundless legend."[145] His entire mission accepted the premise of ethnographic criminality, but in the inverse: he assumed that *all* Saharans thought identically and would rally to his revolution. He proceeded with his plan, incautiously, naïvely. "He thought himself," clarified Pavy, "more enlightened than the counselors whose objections he had just heard."[146] Morès acted with the greatest confidence in the manifest logic and rationality of this manifestly illogical and irrational plan, and with blatant disregard for the unambiguous warnings of the aware.

The colonial administration did not appreciate his attempts to sow rebellion but could do little to stop the wily noble other than to deny him an escort. The lone officer they sent to intercept him waited in vain; Morès took another, far more dangerous route. Furthermore, for administrators, "whatever the itinerary . . . , his voyage could but occasion grave inconvenience for France."[147] Indeed, his relationships with the

[145] Pavy, *Expédition*, 22–3; AGGA, 4H/29, "Rapport sur l'expédition du Marquis de Morès."
[146] Pavy, *Expédition*, 20. [147] Pavy, *Expédition*, 24–6.

Sha'amba proved fraught, not surprisingly, as he passed through a region known to Tuareg, Algerians, and Tunisians alike as "the land of fear."[148] Although the Sha'amba made clear their opposition, he continued to hope to "direct [the Tuareg] in a line useful for France."[149] Morès could not imagine that the Tuareg had no desire for his leadership, and that the Sha'amba's rejection of his bread presaged a far more sinister and deeply rooted hostility. Pavy, the most dedicated chronicler of Morès's mission and proselytizer of Saharan criminality, cogently explained the marquis's failure:

> This surprise . . . reserved for him Morès would have easily divined, if less blinded by his unlimited confidence in the Tuareg, he had taken care to inform himself on the people . . . between whose hands he delivered himself . . .
>
> He would have learned . . . that almost all were assassins . . . He would have learned above all, poor Morès, . . . that he had been very strictly observed by the Azdjer [*sic*] . . . For Morès had, most imprudently, moreover, made such a noise surrounding his name, his projects, and his departure that the entire desert knew of his imminent arrival.[150]

Pavy reproached Morès for his refusal to acknowledge the inherent cultural criminality of Tuareg and Sha'amba alike, dooming himself as a case study in ethnographic crime by virtue of not believing in it. Morès's romance of the Sahara never contested the possibility of creating a portrait of the collective characteristics of an entire people. Morès did not resist moralizing ethnographic generalizations; he merely reversed the sign. For this crime, Pavy maintained, Morès had sentenced himself to death. Government representatives recovered his body, forestalling any rumors of his survival.[151]

Fundamentally, the French colonial government in Algeria feared that Morès would do exactly what he ended up doing: antagonize the people of the Sahara, meet an untimely end, rouse public sympathy and outraged collective mourning, and retard French plans for domination of the Sahara. In short, they dreaded a repeat of the Flatters debacle, whence their intensive interest in a death that, after all, did not occur on Algerian soil. In its gestation of wild exaggerations and improbable rumors, Morès's death equaled the Flatters mission. The Marquise de Morès even claimed colonial administrators employed a Qādirī *muqaddim* to lead Morès into ambush.[152] For administrators themselves, the debate

[148] Pavy, *Expédition*, 51–2. [149] Pavy, *Expédition*,79.
[150] Pavy, *Expédition*, 81–2. [151] Pavy, *Expédition*, 142–7.
[152] AGGA, 16H/3, High Commander Pujat, "Rapport du Commandant supérieur de Touggourt sur Si El hachemi ben Brahim, mokaddem Kadria à Hamich (annexe d'El-Oued) [sic]," Touggourt, August 7, 1902.

revolved around the implication of the Tuareg Ifogha. Allied to the French, the Ifogha represented the wedge to prise open the Sahara. Although apparently only two men related to the Ifogha by marriage participated, without the knowledge of the group as a whole, the ethnographic logic of colonial criminality equated kinship with *collective* guilt; the ostensible failure of the Ifogha to punish their kin presaged, for some administrators, a fundamental change in Ifogha politics.[153] Hence, explanations of the death of Morès reinscribed Tuareg criminality; despite increased French involvement in the Sahara, depictions of the Tuareg and Shaʿamba as inherently criminal had not vanished. If anything, the death of Morès reinforced interpretive trends that dominated ethnography generalizations since the death of Flatters.

The Marquise de Morès, however, refused to settle for vague attributions of collective responsibility. A wealthy widow, the American woman attempted to bring to justice those responsible for her husband's death. Whereas administrators worried over questions of ethnographic criminality such as the trustworthiness of the Ifogha, the marquise evinced an alternative interpretation of criminality in which the state could bring to light and justice individuals responsible for crime. For the grieving widow, collective responsibility and ethnographic crime complemented, but could not replace, the punishment of the individuals who had shot her husband in the back. Discourses of Saharan criminality were in no way uniform: both Algerians and French combated the cultural determination of collective guilt as an efficacious theory of justice.

As part of this contestation, the marquise joined forces with Muḥammad Ṭayyib bin Brahīm, a *nāʾib* [deputy to a shaykh] of the Qādiriyya residing near Ouargla. His marriage to a French schoolteacher precipitated no small amount of anxiety among administrators.[154] Thus, bin Brahīm could navigate, to some extent, the bureaucratic maze of

153 AGGA, 4H/29, General Rogny, Division of Constantine, to the Governor General of Algeria, Constantine, September 14, 1896; AGGA, 4H/29, General Fontebridge, commanding the Subdivision of Batna, to Rogny, November 27, 1896; AGGA, 4H/29, Captain Prandière, Chief of the Annex d'El Oued, to High Commander of the Circle of Touggourt, December 15, 1896; Prandière to the High Commander (Touggourt), December 17, 1896. See also AGGA, 4H/30, General Collet Meygret, commanding the Division of Algiers, to the Governor General, Algiers, November 6, 1897, and AGGA, 4H/30, dossier labeled "Touareg et Chaamba supposés être les assassins de M. de Morès. Sghir b. Si Ame. – Mis en liberté. – 28 Août 97. 1896–1897."

154 AGGA, 16H/6 Prefect of Algiers to the Governor General, August 7, 1899; AGGA, 4H/30, Special Commissioner for Security [anon.], "Rapport. No. 4484. Au sujet de la famille Guillier," Algiers, 4 August 1899. See also AGGA, 16H/6, Lt.-Col. Cauvet, "Renseignements individuels pour servir à la surveillance politique et administrative des indigènes non naturalisés. 2e Catégorie. Personnages religieux, Division d'Alger, Subdivision de Ghardaïa, Cercle de Ghardaïa, Tribu des Beni Chour et Rouissat."

colonial identity politics, willing to contest colonial categories and exploit inconsistencies. He in fact apprehended those who killed Morès, delivering them to administrators for punishment.

If bin Brahīm expected their gratitude, he erred. His actions not only subverted the convenience of collective responsibility, but his delivery of the guilty parties demanded that bureaucrats punish the killers, threatening to alienate vital allies in the Sahara. The colonial state punished his contestation. According to the governor general, "the arrest of the assassins of Morès is not the result of any government mission given or even encouraged by the Governor General[;] it is due to the sole initiative of the Naïb [*sic*], desirous to give himself worth in our eyes and to render a service superior to those rendered by" his rivals "who were just installed [as low-level functionaries] in Ouargla [*sic*]."[155] The governor general interpreted bin Brahīm's mission as subversion, impudence, insolence. Because *not* arresting the individuals responsible for the death of Morès may well have been far more convenient for the state than punishing them, bin Brahīm's actions disrupted the functional fiction of collective, culturally assigned guilt.

Bin Brahīm's actions earned him the enmity of many Algerians. The colonial bureaucracy refused the protection he sought from those he alienated.[156] In response to bin Brahīm's request not to return to Ouargla (where he felt threatened), the governor general demonstrated the administration's hostility, exiling him to distant Nafta.[157] He had rendered a service to the French and received nothing but disrespect in return. "Monsieur le Président [of the Republic]," he wrote, in caustic mockery of the bureaucratic lingo of the Third Republic, "I have the honor to bring to your acquaintance [the fact] that you have completely forgotten me; I cannot believe that he who has served France and rendered to her such great service could be thus abandoned by her." He had lost his standing among Algerians in capturing the killers of Morès, and the administration hesitated even to offer him a job.[158] One

155 AGGA, 16H/6, Governor General, "Note," n.d.

156 AGGA, 16H/6, Captain Th. Pein, Chief of Post at Warqala [Ouargla], to the General commanding the Subdivision of Laghouat, November 11, 1899.

157 AGGA, 16H/6, Governor General, "Note," n.d. See also AGGA, 16H/6, Governor General, "Note," Algier, May 28, 1899. AGGA, 16H/6, Reibell, Chef de Battaillon, "Note pour Monsieur le Gouverneur Général," Algiers, May 20, 1899. He and his family received government subsidies; AGGA, 16H/6, "Dossier: Voyage de Si Mohammed Taïeb ben Brahim – Naïb des Kadria de Rouissat, Division d'Alger. Arrestation des assassins de M de Morès. – 1898. Correspondances 1898 – 1899 – 1900."

158 AGGA, 16H/6, Muḥammad Ṭayyib bin Brahīm to President of the Republic, Algiers, October 27, 1899; AGGA, 16H/6, General Servière, commanding the Division of Algiers to the Governor General of Algeria, March 28, 1902.

administrative court forced him to return the reward the marquise had paid for the capture. In a stern letter, she threatened to expose the government's perfidy, bin Brahīm's dire financial straits, and the obstruction of her recompense.[159] For administrators, he represented a threat in need of neutralization: an Algerian who exposed the fiction upon which colonial justice was based and who contested the categories of cultural criminality. If nothing else, Muḥammad Ṭayyib bin Brahīm's capture of the marquis's killers demonstrated what administrators had denied for years since Flatters: they could, at times, determine individual responsibility with ease, if with aid. The corollary, that perhaps not *all* Saharans acted complicitly in the desert deaths, that perhaps cultural identity condemned or even predisposed *no one* to criminality, threatened to destabilize the edifice of colonial "justice."

Even in death, bin Brahīm faced difficulties in his struggle against ethnographic generalizations and their political limitations.[160] Although he had requested an escort of Spahis at his burial, General Grisot demurred in a letter to the governor general. "I estimate like you," he wrote, "that it is just, as much as good politics, to render to the Naïb . . . honors due to a devoted servant, cavalier of the Order of the Legion of Honor, and who has given his life for France, but," continued the general, "it would be inopportune to escort with so much pomp the remains of a native chief, while those of our officers are transported in the most simple and the most modest fashion."[161] By virtue of his identity as French, any one of the soldiers who had failed, for example, to apprehend the killers of Morès merited a more ostentatious funeral than bin Brahīm, whose service eventually cost him his life. Just as they did to Jabārī, culturally determined circumscriptions on the political role of "natives" thwarted bin Brahīm, even in death.

However, for some, the capture of Morès's killers provided neither satisfactory conclusion nor explanation for the events of El-Ouatia. Given the inflammatory rhetoric of Morès and his paranoiac associates, his death gave rise to conspiracy theories attributing blame to improbable sources. The Comité du Souvenir de Morès perceived "a second Dreyfus Affair, in which the Government, the [Masonic] lodges, the Protestants, and the Jews are going to conspire to assure the impunity of the

159 AGGA, 16H/6, Madame la Marquise de Morès to the Governor General of Algeria, Paris, November 1898.

160 Bin Brahīm was assassinated in a small town called El-Ḥamira. AGGA 16H/6, "Au sujet du nommé El Hadj Ahmed ben Si Brahim," General Servière commanding the Division of Algiers to the Governor General of Algeria, Service of Native Affairs and Military Personnel, N° 2046, Algiers, March 28, 1902.

161 AGGA, 16H/6, General Grisot, Commander of the 19th Army Corps, to the Governor General, Algiers, April 9, 1901.

guilty," contending that a French administrator warned Morès that his route angered the British, who would instigate his death.[162] The accusations, though entirely groundless, nevertheless reflected larger anxieties about the Sahara, about religion, about empire. The Marquis de Morès occupied a peculiar space in colonial Algeria: French, yet opposed to the objectives of the French administration in the Sahara, Morès unsettled categories. His death at the hands of Tuareg who believed him a *representative* of the very republican government he undermined disconcerted his supporters, who resorted to bizarre conspiracy theories to preserve the illusion of his grand Franco-Muslim alliance and his status as an anti-republican hero. Even Jabārī reappeared, armed with another improbable story of a European captive among the Tuareg: Morès.[163] The anti-republican, anti-Semitic Comité du Souvenir de Morès contested the conceptions of a criminal Sahara implicit in the government's account of the death.

The death of Morès captivated a metropolitan audience fascinated by the experiences and violence of empire. Contended Pavy, "[t]he entire press occupied itself with this tragedy. The deaths were covered, with much dolorous compassion, [among] the rich of Paris, in the faubourg Saint-Antoine . . . as in the faubourg Saint-Germain and on the *grands boulevards*." All "cried over the gentleman who had had the chivalrous thought, not to tame, but to charm the African minotaur and who came . . . to be mercilessly devoured by it."[164] An expressly national mourning subverted geographic and social divisions by appealing to collective honor, national identity, and compassion. What Pavy presented as a monument to national unity represented, however, yet another emblem of the deep political, religious, and social divides of republican France.

The Comité du Souvenir de Morès and their sympathizers interpreted the death of Morès as the opening salvo in yet another battle between the intolerance and reaction of the extreme right in the metropole, and the Third Republic, which largely reserved its intolerance and more reactionary aspects for the colonies. To commemorate Morès's death, the Comité organized a "matinée artistique" on August 31, 1898, in Aix-les-Bains. The Comité, founded in July 1896, aimed "to erect at the entrance of the Bay of Algiers, a monument to our soldiers, heroes gone to die there, Savoyards and Dauphinois."[165] Never mind that Morès had died in

162 AGGA, 4H/30, Special Commissioner to the Supervisor General of the Services of Police and Security of Algeria "Rapport. Affaire de Morès. No. 634," Algiers, March 30, 1899.

163 Pavy, *Expedition*, 119–20.

164 Pavy, *Expedition*, 123. AGGA, 2H/45, Eugène Destrez, "Échos du Sud," *La Vérité*, July 13, 1896, compared Morès to Flatters.

165 AGGA, 4H/30, program for the "Matinée artistique," Aix-les-Bains, August 31, 1898.

Tunisia. Three counts and a marquis, indicative of the cause's appeal to a certain element of the decaying French nobility, attended this fundraising evening on behalf of the committee.[166] Assembled as musical entertainment for the wealthy patrons, the artistic participants included numerous entertainers and artists. Marguerite Sanlaville read the "Légende de Morès," a poem in his honor, and M. Duquesne read Victor Hugo's assuredly better, if less directly relevant, "Bataille d'Eylau." One man set the words of the Abbé Bleau to music for Flachat's performance as "L'Alliance Franco-Russe."[167] In short, the program promised an evening long on maudlin lugubrity, and short on a critical engagement with the implications of Morès's strange project.

In their commemoration, the Comité drew upon the reservoir of anti-Semitic support for Morès's hare-brained beliefs. After all, he carried with him, along with Louis Rinn's *Marabouts et khouan*, Morès's unpublished *Les Frères-mineurs, le Tiers-ordre et le Capitalisme*; *Rothschild, Ravachol et Cie*, which washed up from the ocean of sand as part of the mission's detritus.[168] His express opposition to what he portrayed as a bourgeois-British-Jewish alliance garnered attention from the more credulous elements of Algerian society. The thriving anti-Semitic media of settler Algeria avidly consumed the accounts of his death.[169] Moreover, in June of 1899, "the anti-Jewish newspapers of Constantine" organized "a meeting, at the Mairie of Constantine, of the members of the anti-Jewish league of that city, with, for the order of the day, 'Anniversary of the Assassination of the Marquis de Morès,' 'The Dreyfus Affair,'" and "'The Jewish Press of Constantine.'" To avoid the appearance of official acquiescence, the prefect demanded the eviction of the meeting from the mairie, but the meeting nonetheless took place elsewhere.[170] Commemoration facilitated the consolidation of the anti-Semitic right's conceptions of republican imperialism. In essence, they partook in the dominant tropes of ethnographic criminality; just as more mainstream

[166] AGGA, 4H/30, "Matinée artistique," and AGGA, 4H/30, Marquis de la Rochethulon, "Causerie-Préface."

[167] AGGA, 4H/30, "Matinée artistique."

[168] AGGA, 4H/29, Lieutenant Goulat, Chief of the Annex, "Procès-verbal de saisie et description de pièces [found with Morès]. Cercle de Touggourt, Annexe d'El Oued," Constantine, September 13, 1896.

[169] See the numerous press clippings in AGGA, 4H/29, from newspapers such as *La Silhouette* (its slogan: "organe anti-juif illustré. À la porte les juifs! Place aux français!") and *La Républicain de Constantine*.

[170] Fonds ministériels (FM) 80/1728, Prefect Dufoix of the Department of Constantine to the Minister of the Interior, Constantine, June 27, 1899; FM80/1728, Commissaire Central Dietz, "Extrait du Rapport du 24 au 25 Juin 1899." The next day, Dufoix banned the Cercle Républicain for its inflammatory and violent invective; FM80/1728, Prefect Dufoix, "Arrêté," Constantine, June 26, 1899.

commentators attributed responsibility to the Tuareg and Shaʿamba as collective entities, so, too, did the radical right ascribe collective responsibility to the Jews.

Ethnographic criminality permeated another meeting held to commemorate the death of the Marquis de Morès, which produced *Souvenir de Morès* (1897). Echoing the marquis's bourgeois-British-Jewish conspiracy, *Souvenir* perpetuated the conception of Morès's death as the expression of an inherently criminal population. Whereas mainstream sources blamed the Tuareg, the anti-Semitic right blamed the Jews. The preface, by an unnamed "Saint-Cyrien" (that is to say, a graduate of the military academy at Saint-Cyrien), recalled French greatness debased by bourgeois conspirators, juxtaposing contemporary French decadence with Morès as the valiant exemplar of a dying code of honor. "French society, in the past guardian of the traditions of courage and honor, inheritor of the worth and virtues of its ancestors, born protector of the national patrimony, has knuckled under the power of money." Decrying "the usurer and the speculator," the Saint-Cyrien excoriated "the bourgeoisie [who] receives, with open arms, he who presents himself with a well-filled wallet. Of little import the origin of the money. Be it the product of thefts or even assassination, little import, salute it! [i]t is His Majesty Money!"[171] Those who objected, he maintained, risked ostracism and branding as wild-eyed anarchists. "In the midst," however, "of this general debasement of character, there was found *a man*, and God desired that he be a Frenchman, who consecrated his existence to protesting against these deplorable ways."[172] This romantic view of Morès as the archetype of French masculinity drew upon the seething disaffection of various elements of French society, notably those who decried less the increasing influence of money on French politics than the decreasing stranglehold of *old* money on French politics. Morès "perished, betrayed as Abel by Cain, as Jesus by Judas . . . It is truly long, the martyrology of those who perished in the Sahara . . . it is always Frenchmen who succomb!"[173] For the anonymous Saint-Cyrien, Morès embodied a France under siege by a bourgeois-capitalist onslaught devoted to the destruction of French values.

The configuration of Morès in the "martyrology" of both the colonial Sahara *and* a reactionary conception of France drew upon longstanding tropes of the bourgeois usurer and the endemic anti-Semitism of settler Algeria. In *Souvenir*, Henri Garrot remained convinced that

171 *Souvenir de Morès: discours prononcés à la Réunion-Conférence du 9 juin 1897* (Algiers: Charles Zamith, 1897), ii.
172 *Souvenir*, ii. Italics in the original.
173 *Souvenir*, iv.

the bourgeois-British-Jewish conspiracy succeeded in bringing about his death.[174] A similar speech by one E. Feuillet identified "the financier" and "the Israelite Gambetta" as "the enemy," and compared Morès to Joan of Arc.[175] Ethnographic criminality drew sustenance from pre-existing strands of culturally assigned culpability. French anti-Semitism and the racism of empire represent but two facets of the same discriminatory coin.

Moreover, the commemoration of the death of Morès seemed to produce an insatiable appetite for truly execrable poetry. Lucien Chaze managed to include the blood libel, anti-English and anti-Russian sentiment, extremist fears of capitalism, and an intolerably saccharine romanticism into thirty-one appalling stanzas. His "Ode à Morès" surely marks some kind of nadir in the often-atrocious cultural productions of racist, imperial natterings.

> "J'ai poursuivi le Juif, vautour universel
> A travers les ghettos et les fanges des mondes;
> J'ai mis à nu l'horreur de ses lèpres immondes,
> Sur les marches de son autel
>
> "Je les ai flagellés dans leur Temple – à la Bourse –
> J'ai rugi sur leur trône aux crimes des sabbats
> Il faut frapper en haut pour enseigner en bas,
> Et noyer le mal dans sa source . . ."
>
> "La Vaillance, l'Honneur, valent quelques écus;
> Tout se vend à l'Anglais, aux Juifs . . . , même aux Cosaques;
> Le blason des Croisés, les recanches des Jacques . . .
> ". . . Et l'espérance des Vaincus!
>
> "Les peuples ni les rois n'ouvrent plus l'Evangile,
> Et la race agonise au poison du Talmud.
> J'ai tracé le chemin, j'ai désigné le but:
> Le Veau d'Or au socle d'argile."[176]

The French nation, contended Chaze, worshipped at the altar of the Golden Calf. Explicit references to the blood libel, to "the crimes of the sabbaths," its paranoiac ramblings about an Anglo-Jewish conspiracy, place "Ode à Morès" in the context of the vitriolic anti-Semitism of settler Algeria and the extreme right. Nevertheless, both the extreme right's

[174] *Souvenir*, 11–12; see also 25–7. On Morès and anti-Semitic Boulangism, see Richard D. Sonn, *Anarchism and Cultural Politics in Fin de Siècle France* (Lincoln, Nebr.: University of Nebraska Press, 1989), 37, 44–6, 130.

[175] *Souvenir*, 22. [176] *Souvenir*, 14–17.

assignment of culpability to the Jews and the more mainstream ascription of responsibility to the peoples of the Sahara as a whole conceived of crime as culturally determined, inherently anti-French, exemplified in the very identity of the purported enemies of the colonial and republican state.

Even the trial of Morès's ostensible murderers provided an opportunity for lachrymose commemoration. In 1904, the two lawyers for the marquise's civil suit, Emmanuel Joseph Augustin, Count de las Cases and Émile Broussais, published their statements as *Le Crime d'El-Ouatia*. De las Cases faced a difficult task; he had to argue for the indictment of several Saharans inculpated in the death of Morès, who, de las Cases acknowledged, "was the true artisan of his misfortune."[177] At the same time, he constructed a case against the French colonial government itself, assigning to Algiers the responsibility for the explorer's death and lambasting the perfidy of its erstwhile allies in the desert and government refusal to protect Morès.[178] De las Cases portrayed the state's indifference to the fate of Morès, not as the consequence of Morès's hostility to the Third Republic, but as national dereliction of duty.[179]

De las Cases evoked the legacy of French exploration, an appeal to geographically situated memory. "When one enters Constantine," he reminded his audience, one found a series of streets dedicated to great French explorers, including Morès, "spirits . . . fallen equally for the grandeur of France without half-seen success having consoled them." These streets of Constantine "reunited all in common memory and common apotheosis, the inhabitants of Constantine wanted to keep in their patriotic city the memory of . . . [these] glorious servants of the nation."[180] De las Cases recast the civil proceedings as a criminal trial parsing guilt, innocence, and responsibility, and contesting the conditions of colonial memory. "To honor these men, in retracing for our children their name and their traits, that is good; to honor them in retracing their life, in propagating their ideas, in glorifying their death, that is, it appears to us, still better. Such is the task that, in the name of Madame de Morès, I am going to accomplish here," de la Cases explained.[181] The trial represented not an attempt to request civil penalties for the wealthy

177 Count Emmanuel Joseph Augustin de las Cases and Émile Broussais, *Le Crime d'El-Ouatia* (Paris: Plon-Nourrit, 1904), 172. On individual guilt and betrayal, see de las Cases and Broussais, *Crime*, 68–75, 88–93, 138–49, 198–9, and *passim*. For another instance of ethnographic crime on trial, see Christopher Harrison, *France and Islam in West Africa, 1860–1960* (Cambridge: Cambridge University Press, 1988), 68–89.

178 de las Cases and Broussais, *Crime*, 94–109.

179 de las Cases and Broussais, *Crime*, 150–9, 204–7. De las Cases particularly castigated Pujat (pp. 150–9) and Rebillet (pp. 164–75), who voiced his objections at the trial).

180 de las Cases Broussais, *Crime*, 1–2.

181 de las Cases and Broussais, *Crime*, 2.

widow, but rather to offer a competing vision of colonial memory, to create a hagiographical, accusatory text perpetuating the peculiar aims of Morès.

Thus, de las Cases represented the Marquis de Morès as an emblem of empire, as the apotheosis of imperial values. A crucial part of the civil case depended on destroying the image of the feckless, conspiracy-theory addled nobleman and recasting Morès as simultaneously a politically mainstream, imperial everyman, *and* a hero, the last of a dying breed of French explorers willing to die manly imperial deaths for the values they embodied. "He was," wrote de las Cases, "a Frenchman . . . by race, by qualities, by heart." He even looked the part; "his Caesar-like profile indicated his energy and courage . . . he was powerful." For de las Cases, Morès represented the ideal French man – strong, yet a tender, loving father, filled, "not [with] that effeminate and doleful love that is the trait of weakened souls, but that virile love, acting, active, that Victor Hugo defined in one verse: 'Les vrais cœurs de lions sont les vrais cœurs de père.'"[182] The lawyer's rhetorical strategy depended on convincing his audience that with Morès died the embodiment of masculine virility and national identity.

However, de las Cases had to confront a fundamental challenge to this view of Morès as a masculine archetype of the republic. Morès represented less the embodiment of the mainstream Third Republic than the face of its inveterate enemies on the extreme right. In many ways, Morès remained an unrepentant man of the Second Empire; if Henri Duveyrier embodied the bourgeois strivings of the epoch of Napoleon III, then Morès surely marked its legacy in the reactionary elements of the Third Republic. It must have been difficult, after all, to cast as a patriot a man convinced of a sinister alliance between the bourgeoisie, the British crown, and the Jews, and whose wife, even at the trial, maintained the complicity of the French colonial government in her husband's death. A shrewd lawyer if nothing else, de las Cases appealed to anxieties about the role and future of French republicanism. "As a citizen [*citoyen*], three loves summed up [Morès's] life: the love of religion, the love of the nation [*patrie*], the love of the people [*peuple*]."[183] De las Cases wove a very fine thread: Morès was at once a republican, a *citoyen*, but also a patriot and a Catholic.[184] In using the word *citoyen*, the lawyer forestalled critiques of Morès as a reactionary zealot, a closet Boulangist, or a man out of time.

182 de las Cases and Broussais, *Crime*, 34–5.

183 de las Cases and Broussais, *Crime*, 35, 38–9. De las Cases singled out Pavy for particular opprobium and personal attacks (176–9).

184 de las Cases and Broussais, *Crime*, 35–6.

Nevertheless, the reference to the Church rooted Morès on the rightist end of the republican spectrum; "the love of nation" united love of religion and *citoyen* in one man. "Peuple," the most ambiguous word, recalled at once republican egalitarian rhetoric, and aristocratic discourse of uplift and anti-bourgeois, cross-class alliance between the born leaders and the *menu peuple*. De las Cases had to convince his readers that "Catholic and patriot were for Morès two inseparable terms."[185]

Moreover, de las Cases portrayed the voyage as Morès's duty as a man and citizen. At the heart of his civil case, the lawyer offered the mission as the rectification of the errors of the Third Republic. He even portrayed Morès's alliance between Muslims and French as a *return* to pre-existing values and policies of the French nation, implicitly the Second Empire's *Royaume arabe*.[186] "To study large social problems and to hasten the solution of them, is, in serving humanity, to do the work of a soldier . . . [Morès] wanted the material and moral amelioration of democracy . . . with all of his admirable force. But he was too proud to place himself within reach of that democracy by abasing his noble height before it; he raised to his own" level.[187] Somehow, de las Cases transformed the arrogant, anti-Semitic nobleman, obsessed with bizarre conspiracy theories, stranded by the rising tides of socioeconomic change, into a sympathetic embodiment of a moderate, masculine, imperial republicanism. De las Cases was as much magician as lawyer.

He performed similar magic with Madame de Morès. A grieving widow, she cut a more sympathetic figure than her naïve husband. Nevertheless, de las Cases demonstrated no subtlety in playing to the image of the "inconsolable yet courageous wife," pursuing her civil case not out of a sense of vengeance, but for a more collective, abstract, and patriotic notion of justice.[188] A widow marked a fundamentally individual mourning and loss; in his pursuit of assigning a culpability to the state, de las Cases needed to render her a more representative figure. Thus, as the widow, as a woman, and as a French citizen, she had particular work to do for her own case: de las Cases aimed to put on trial a republican colonial system that failed to avenge the death of Morès.

Wife, she wanted to climb back up step by step the painful calvary that her Morès had climbed, though her feet too would be torn and wounded by the stones of the road.

[185] de las Cases and Broussais, *Crime*, 37. On the Marquis de Morès and French anarchists, see Sonn, *Anarchism*, 35–7.

[186] de las Cases and Broussais, *Crime*, 217, 223–9.

[187] de las Cases and Broussais, *Crime*, 39. [188] de las Cases and Broussais, *Crime*, 3.

Mother, she wanted her children to conserve, as the harshest [part] of their patrimony, the story of the life and the last moments of their noble father.

French woman [*Française*], she wanted the French people to know in what act, in what exploit died he of whom [Maurice] Barrès so justifiably said that "he was a great educator of vigor." . . .

She has been sustained by the public opinion that in France she has always found vibrant in the memory of her hero.[189]

Wife, mother, French woman: de las Cases presented his employer in successively more general terms, invoking increasingly universal attributes and moral states. Explicitly connecting the marquise with the complicated political space he articulated for her husband, he wrote that "Madame de Morès has moreover marvelously summarized this life, in these two lines from the mortuary prayer, so noble and so French: 'My name gave me no privilege, it created for me but duties'; voilà for the gentlemen. 'Life is worth nothing but for action, too bad if this action is fatal'; voilà for the patriot."[190] Like her husband, Madame de Morès appeared as a universally applicable figure to whom anyone could relate. De la Cases wanted to offer not the American Marquise de Morès, but a grief-stricken French everywoman.

More importantly, de las Cases depicted her as the victim of a grave miscarriage of ethnographic justice. Despite the sustenance of public opinion, "what failures of support, what disillusions, what difficulties did Madame de Morès not encounter?"[191] The deft prosecutor laid those failures squarely on the colonial government.

She had believed at first in a collective vengeance, in a column going to punish the Touareg [*sic*] for the death of her husband. Was it not in the dignity of France not to allow to pass unpunished such an assassination, to in no way resume the fault commmitted in the aftermath of the death of Flatters? (1)[192] . . .

The marquise de Morès knew that the patriotism of our officers bled from the death of their unavenged comrade. She knew that they asked only to march, while on the other hand the loyal tribes waited, them too, but for an order to punish the Touareg for, at the same time as the recent crime, ancient depradations.

At El-Ouatia, it was only a question of a French expedition massacred, of the blood of the last paladin spilled by treason. Our ministers could not for so little risk a liability.[193]

No such columns. For de las Cases, the civil case avenged the colonial state's failure to punish those responsible. The lawyer preferred collective

[189] de las Cases and Broussais, *Crime*, 3.
[190] de las Cases and Broussais, *Crime*, 37.
[191] de las Cases and Broussais, *Crime*, 4.
[192] A footnote labeled (1) in the text cites the "Rapport du capitaine de Prandières, A. II, p. 351, no. 17" on the death of Flatters.
[193] de las Cases and Broussais, *Crime*, 4.

responsibility and punishment over judicial attacks on individuals; he conceived of the killing of Morès as a crime for which guilt must be apportioned among the Tuareg as a whole. Risk-averse, cowardly, the French government declined to avenge the death of Morès, irretrievably damaging their status as colonial power, wounding their national dignity.

Nevertheless, the Marquis de Morès was but one man, a free agent traveling without government approval, with an objective charitably described as contrary to official French aims. Ultimately, he bore the responsibility for the senseless end to his foolish mission. De las Cases, however, diligently portrayed Morès as the very embodiment of patriotic masculinity in order to counteract just such views. Depicting Morès as a man who had lived his life according to dying virtues and as an implicit critique of national degeneracy, the savvy lawyer transformed Morès from eccentric to national symbol; the attack on Morès became an attack on French nationhood, a declaration of war left unchallenged by the weak, decadent colonial republic. "At least, lacking a collective vengeance, will individual punishment be attempted? The assassins are known; they are not hiding; they recount everywhere their crime. They form two groups: the Chambaa [*sic*] of El-Kheïr [*sic*] and the Touareg [*sic*] of Béchaoui [*sic*]."[194]

"El-Khëir" and "Béchaoui" were not places; they were the individuals against whom Madame de Morès undertook her case. For de las Cases, they tainted entire ethnic groups with their criminal nature. The Shaʿamba and the Tuareg remained unpunished. Although de las Cases found collective punishment of these ethnic groups preferable, he would settle for a synecdoche of punishment. *Le Crime d'El-Ouatia* demonstrated the *supremacy* of notions of cultural criminality. Colonial justice took root in assumptions of a unitary resisting mind in which the guilt of one implied the guilt of all.

De las Cases explicitly referred to the collective, moralizing impulse that bound criminality and ethnography. Reiterating his preference for collective punishment, but also acknowledging the state's reluctance or impotence, de las Cases moved from the specific to the universal: the killers of Morès repesented the criminality of all Tuareg. "Be they the knights that some proclaim them [or] the faithless bandits that others maintain, I feel in myself neither the competence nor the desire to discuss here this problem of moral ethnography. Beside, what does it matter? Morès was attacked and assailed by an easily determined band, by the Touareg of Béchaoui," one of those de las Cases pursued in civil court.

194 de las Cases and Broussais, *Crime*, 5. Madame de Morès financed the search for the perpetrators; de las Cases and Broussais, *Crime*, 7–8, 14–17, 68–72, 91–3.

"Now, these Touareg, we know to which tribe and to which congregation they belong, under whose influence they live. The assassins of Morès were at once Ifoghas and Tidjania [*sic*]."[195] His protestations to the contrary, de las Cases had arrogated to himself precisely the role as moralistic ethnographer; his entire case depended on presenting as a failure of colonial statecraft the Algerian government's failure to punish the death of Morès as an ethnographic crime. In essence, he proposed the punishment of individuals as both solace to the widow and the reinforcement of collective criminality. Ethnographic crime did not function merely as a convenient fiction, a judicial fig leaf allowing the Algerian colonial government to punish faceless criminals through the censuring of recalcitrant collective groups. Rather, it represented the preferred mode of meting out colonial "justice," perpetuating colonial France's monopoly on judicial violence.

Ethnography and moral generalization

The untimely ends of the Flatters and Morès missions resonated in colonial ethnographies. Their deaths imposed criminality onto Saharan peoples and reconceptualized crime as a fundamental element of cultural identity. After all, the Tuareg and the Shaʿamba largely *succeeded* in excluding the French from the Algerian Sahara. Furthermore, the inability of the French to punish those responsible transposed collective guilt onto cultural identity. Acts of contestation, through the lens of French ethnography, functioned as *moral* markers, as synecdoches of collective ethical corruption. Incapable of subjecting desert Algerians to the disciplines of police and prison, administrators subjected them to the discipline of writing, rendering them legible, if inaccurately, for state generalizations by inscribing them as culturally predestined criminals.

Many writers simply did not or could not differentiate among the various ethnic ramifications of the Tuareg. Despite the deep political rifts that divided the Tuareg, many writers, commentators, and ethnographers aggregated all Tuareg as fundamentally, culturally, and criminally similar. Ernest Mercier left no room for doubt that he saw France's role in the Sahara as a moral one. In *La France dans le Sahara et au Soudan* (1889), the former mayor of Constantine began his section entitled "The Mores of the Saharans" with a recitation of the explorers the Tuareg had dispatched, including, of course, Flatters. In a tidy metonymy of place, he transferred his moralizing about Tuareg to the desert itself. He claimed, "the Sahara is nothing but a vast deathtrap, where

[195] de las Cases and Broussais, *Crime*, 61.

violence reigns without contest, and betrayal is the only law . . . [T]he most odious crimes have been encouraged by the most complete impunity."[196] That these deaths might have embodied acts of contestation crossed Mercier's mind, yet he subordinated political import to a rubric of indications about morality informing his conception of Saharan cultures. The entire Sahara loomed in as the essence firstly of cultural immorality, and only secondarily of anticolonial resistance. Resistance enacted yet another facet of "native" criminality.[197] In Mercier's moralized world, Tuareg opposition arose from culturally determined aggression. Republican France had no qualms about ascribing concerted political rejection to, for example, those in France who had objected to the excesses of the Revolution. However, the racist logic of ethnographic generalization prevented the acknowledgment of Algerian politics.

In contrast, when the lawyer-ethnographer G.-D. Bédier depicted the Tuareg as violent and avaricious guardians of the commercial privileges of the desert, he yolked Tuareg politics to the engine of ethnographic conceptions of identity. For Bédier, mission deaths demonstrated the inextricable ties between Saharan commerce and putative Tuareg deviance. "To arrive at their goal" of economic domination, Bédier claimed, "the Touaregs recoil at nothing: armed attacks, ruse, perfidy, poison, betrayal, all, so much importance did and do they attach to . . . their domination." Thus, he noted, "they caused to perish the unfortunate caravan of Mister Flatters of glorious memory."[198] Drawing on Flatters's infamy as anecdotal shorthand, Bédier constructed a totalizing edifice of ethnographic knowledge uniting resistance, criminality, and economic interest under the guise of what another ethnographer called "the pillaging race."[199] Understandings of Tuareg culture relied upon their denigration as criminal and deviant. Colonial ethnography reconfigured oppositional politics as, literally, identity politics: the effect of the colonial production of difference.

Similarly, the death of the Marquis de Morès catalyzed the further reification of the Tuareg as inescapably criminal. Auguste Pavy's *L'Expédition*

[196] Mercier, *La France dans le Sahara et au Soudan*, 30.

[197] Mercier, *La France dans le Sahara et au Soudan*, 31. AGGA, 1J/141, Féraud, Consul General at Tripoli, to the Governor General of Algeria, Tripoli, April 12, 1881.

[198] Bédier, *Sahara-Niger*, 9. See also AGGA, 22H/27, Rogny, "Notice sur Abderrahman ben Mekelaoui et sa famille"; Barbier, *À travers*, 52–5; H. Bissuel, *Le Sahara français: conferences sur les questions sahariennes faite les 21 et 31 mars 1891 à MM. les officiers de la garrison de Médéa* (Algiers: Adolphe Jourdan, 1891), 62–3; Philebert and Rolland, *La France en Afrique*, 48.

[199] Gustave Pérès, *L'Islam et ses anarchistes: Les Tidjanys, les Senoussii, les Berbers voilés. Conférence faite au Théâtre d'Abbeville, le 14 Janvier, 1893* (Abbeville, France: Imprimerie Fourdrinier, 1893), 12.

de Morès manifested the easy transposition of individual actions into collective generalizations. At times, the ethnography of the Sahara appears as a kind of generalizing machine, transforming the raw material of the death of the explorer into statements of culpability about a subgroup, and finally into the end product of large-scale generalizations about cultures. Pavy excoriated the Tuareg Ajjer for "not only this extreme *solidarity of race*," but also for "an *exclusivity of race*."[200] Commencing with the ostensible responsibility of the Ajjer for the death of Flatters and his companions, Pavy proceeded to juxtapose pseudo-scientific conceptions of race with a moral framework that valorized Saharan resistance as xenophobic and exclusive. From there, he rapidly progressed to statements about all Tuareg; he transmogrified Flatters's killers into a nameless, collective embodiment. "Anything that is Tuareg does not count. They believe themselves permitted anything vis-à-vis the stranger . . . and if amongst themselves they take pride in [their] word and in a certain loyalty, they estimate that they are completely emancipated of these moral rules as soon as they no longer had business with one of theirs."[201] He could not have made the moral implications of his cultural description more clear: at the heart of Tuareg identity, Pavy situated an immoral core that he first perceived in the death of Flatters. Moral judgment functioned as the engine of ethnographic generalization.

In a 1906 report, one administrator-ethnographer, Lieutenant-Colonel Laperrine, demonstrated the relationship among failed missions, representations of the Tuareg, and the moralizing mission. For Laperrine, through their orchestration of the death of Flatters, the Tuareg revealed themselves as backward and in need of empire's civilizing influence. The failure of colonial power in the desert served only to highlight its necessity. After all, ethnographic discourse contended that "the Touareg [*sic*] are inveterate looters and do not hesitate to assassinate those who try to oppose their thefts with arms."[202] "But," he continued, "like the knights of the Middle Ages . . . they have their code of honor."[203] In other words, Laperrine interpreted the structure of Tuareg society as revolving around both violence and an outdated, deviant sense of honor. For Laperrine,

[200] Pavy, *Expédition*, 65. Emphasis in the original.
[201] Pavy, *Expedition*, 66. Cf. Henri Schirmer, *Le Sahara* (Paris: Hachette, 1893), 278.
[202] AGGA, Oasis//46, Lt.-Col. Laperrine, Military Commander of the Territory of the Oases, "Rapport du Lieutenant-Colonel Laperrine, Commandant Militaire du Territoire des Oasis, sur les solutions qu'il propose, à un certain nombre de questions traitées dans le rapport de tournée de Monsieur le Capitaine Dinaux," Adrar, January 2, 1906, 8. See also pp. 13–14.
[203] Oasis//46, Laperrine, "Rapport du Lieutenant-Colonel Laperrine."

the moral state of the Tuareg rendered them primitive objects in need of colonial domination.

As late as 1911, ethnographers continued to associate the Tuareg with criminality. Captain Léopold Aymard's *Les Touareg* continued the long tradition of moralizing ethnographies. "The Touaregs [*sic*]," he explained, "are *naturally* independent, and the adventurous existence that they lead augments still their hatred of all constraint."[204] According to Aymard, the Tuareg demonstrated their independence because of a "natural" tendency in that direction. Just as in 1884, Barbier referred to their "innate hatred,"[205] so, too, could Aymard, nearly thirty years later, offer similar depictions of natural immorality. At the essence of the Tuareg, Aymard placed a resistance to authority. Even "their physiognomy," that classical ethnoscientific example of the supposed harmony between "race" and culture, "breathes insouciance and ruse." Their "wild air" cemented the association of Tuareg "nature" with immorality.[206] Aymard's ethnography remained ensconced in the moralizing tradition. The *use* of ethnography to create a criminal object for colonial moralizing depended upon the *conceiving* of ethnography as an effect of a natural science, as a kind of writing that laid bare intrinsic elements of identity.

Moreover, such representations extended to the Shaʿamba. Ethnographers often grouped the Shaʿamba with the Tuareg, subsuming both groups into a larger, pan-Saharan ethnicity. Just as the killers of Flatters stood for the Ajjer and subsequently the Tuareg as a whole, many writers failed to differentiate the Shaʿamba from others. Ernest Mercier depicted the Shaʿamba in terms redolent of both the civilizing mission and descriptions of the Tuareg. The Shaʿamba, he contended, "are veritable pirates of the land, not recognizing the rules of a sort of code that was still current in the country a few years ago."[207] Hence, Mercier even contended that their moral state had declined, presenting the Shaʿamba as brigands among brigands, incapable of abiding by rudimentary moral strictures. Although some texts categorized Shaʿamba as either "dissident" or friendly,[208] the distinction often fell out of usage in favor of a broad teleology, whereby the Tuareg inexorably drew the Shaʿamba into their orbit of criminality. Octave Depont and Xavier Coppolani presented the Shaʿamba as duplicitous agents of resistance who feigned cooperation out of self-interest. "It is moreover the same sentiment that animates the

204 Aymard, *Touareg*, 41. Emphasis added. 205 Barbier, *À travers*, 39.
206 Aymard, *Touareg*, 74–5. 207 Mercier, *La France dans le Sahara et au Soudan*, 33.
208 See, for example, AGGA, 2H/36, General La Tour d'Auvergne, commanding the Subdivision of Médéa, to the General commanding the Division of Algiers, Médéa, September 14, 1879.

Touareg [*sic*]," who feared the extension of French control and limits on movement.[209] By 1897, discursive representations of the Tuareg had so spread that Depont and Coppolani could refer to "the sentiment that animates the Touareg" with the barest explanation; the mere mention of the Tuareg implied cultural valences presumed so well known as to obviate elaboration. The association of the Sha'amba with the Tuareg essentially embodied a shortcut to ethnographic representation: the moral characteristics of the Tuareg were so familiar that ethnographers scarcely needed to enumerate them.

Perhaps the most sinister and unusual representations of the Sahara arose not out of fieldwork in the remote reaches of the desert, but rather at the corner of the rue Blanche and the boulevard de Clichy, in Montmartre. In *Les Touareg à Paris* (1910), Dr. Atgier seized the opportunity of the presence of the Tuareg in Paris to take "measurements that have not yet been published . . . by the ethnographers and the explorers of Touareg country."[210] The medical doctor's receipt of the Société d'Anthropologie's silver medal further manifested his association with physical anthropology and racial pseudoscience.[211] The "Touareg in Paris . . . such is the name given . . . to a group of . . . Arabs, Touaregs, Blacks, exhibited in the details of their normal life as much as it is possible to do so in Paris, in an encampment installed on open space making the corner of the rue Blanche and the boulevard de Clichy."[212] With the supreme confidence of a racial scientist, Atgier parsed the self-identified Tuareg into "racial" subgroupings. He used this encampment as an ethnographic field site, making recourse to the Tuareg to unite cultural description and racial pseudoscience into a totalizing edifice of knowledge.

Ethnography's emphasis on Tuareg criminality and racial pseudoscience's obsession with the physical measurement of criminal types formed a ready pairing. Throughout Atgier's text, ethnography and physical anthropology entered into a mutually reinforcing dialogue, a series of utterances and reinscriptions that consistently conflated the colonial and the criminal. Explaining the unprecedented access for study afforded by

[209] Octave Depont and Xavier Coppolani, *Confréries religieuses musulmanes: publiés sous le patronage de M. Jules Cambon, Gouveneur général de l'Algérie* (Algiers: Adolphe Jourdan, 1897), 274. On the Sha'amba, see also AGGA, 3X/2 (Personal Papers of Louis Rinn), "Le grand Sahara," *Petit Colon*, March 20, 1881.

[210] Dr. Atgier, *Les Touareg à Paris* (Paris: Société d'Anthropologie de Paris, 1910), 1; Foureau, *Une Mission au Tademayt (territoire d'In-Saleh) en 1890: rapport à M. le Ministre de l'instruction publique à M. le Sous-Secretaire d'État des Colonies* (Paris: Charles Schlaeber, 1890), 1.

[211] Atgier, *Touareg*, frontispiece.

[212] Atgier, *Touareg*, 1.

the Tuareg of Montmartre, Atgier juxtaposed racial science and cultural description. Tuareg physical characteristics

interested us all the more deeply because in 1887, we had the occasion to see in the Algerian south some brigand Touareg, taken prisoners, considered as barbarians, wild, defenders of their social liberties that linked them to no empire and which submitted them only to the customs of their tribe or group of tribes of their region.

It was then impossible for us to be able study the traits of their physiognomy that they hide jealously from the eyes of all, keeping it completely veiled, except at the level of the eyes that are seen sparkling in a slim gap in their face veil."[213]

The presence of the Tuareg allowed Atgier to compare physical characteristics with moral ones and investigate the correspondences between head shape and facial measurements and the cultural implications of belonging to a "barbarian, wild" "race." In 1881, he had "examine[d] not only [the] face after having lifted [the] veil, but also of [the] head" under the head covering, of "twenty Touareg . . . interned at Algiers, at Fort Bab-Azoun, following a raid . . . on our [erstwhile] allies, [a group of] the Chamba [*sic*]."[214] He combined these measurements to assign each individual, from Paris and elsewhere, to different "races."[215] Tuareg affiliation mattered far less to Atgier than affinities ostensibly revealed by physical characteristics. At the same time, he embedded his conclusions into two broader discourses, that of criminal phrenology, and that of Tuareg criminality. The Tuareg offered an interesting case study because of their association with criminality; they seemed, to the phrenologist, to offer a population sample composed solely of the deviant. Atgier left no doubt as to his awareness of this larger context. His references to his population samples situated them in reference to a life lived outside of the moral strictures of normative society.

The Tuareg of Paris became actors in an ethnographic theater of the absurd, engaging in various dances and performances deemed authentic by the audience. Not surprisingly, Atgier's description of these spectacles drew upon readily available stock images of bellicose and aggressive Tuareg. While the Parisian group paraded about in imitation of a Saharan caravan, some of them, "clothed in their national costume, armed for war, executed warrior dances in which they seem to provoke and excite themselves for combat."[216] At the end of the procession, "two Touareg ascended the stage in the open air and there took place a simulacrum of a duel with double-edged sabres with a large shield

[213] Atgier, *Touareg*, 2. [214] Atgier, *Touareg*, 2.
[215] Atgier, *Touareg*, 12–20. [216] Atgier, *Touareg*, 5.

that hid the body except for the head and feet."[217] The procession reinforced theatrical images of the Tuareg as pugnacious, combative, given to over-excitement precipitated by mere dancing. "The combat finished, two Ouled Naïls [*sic*] came to execute on this same stage the dance of the kerchief and the belly dance." The ostensible prostitutes, the Awlād-Nā'il, and the purported brigands, the Tuareg, ethnographic criminals all, quite literally shared the same stage, engaging in an elaborate pantomime of ethnographic generalization. The spectacle of the Tuareg in Paris physically and symbolically reenacted the totalizing creations of colonialist ethnography.

Thus did Atgier's peculiar text, this home-grown ethnography, connect Tuareg criminality with evolutionist racial pseudoscience. Hence, he concluded his Parisian ethnographic odyssey with that hoariest of French ethnographic clichés, the noble savage. After his lengthy section on anthropometry, he pleaded for a larger sample size, imploring soldiers to supply much-needed data. "A more important study of the noble and warrior cast of the Touareg, carried out on-site, would be a great aid for appreciating the origin of the numerous Touareg populations of the Sahara and to make of them the differential ethnological diagnostic by means of the most precious Anthropological Instructions of Broca."[218] He created his ethnography of the Tuareg in an intensely moralized climate, in which the Tuareg could signify only brigands or noble savages. Whether Parisian performer or implacable obstacle to the Trans-Saharan railroad, the Targui loomed as an ethnographic cautionary tale, as the culmination of the interdisciplinary edifice of colonial science: a reified identity constructed from the blueprints and measurements of racial pseudoscience and the drapings and representations of colonial ethnography.

Out of Paris and the Sahara emerged a remarkably consistent association of criminality with collective identity. Constructions of the Sahara as a place for imperial expansion demanded a moral reconfiguration of its inhabitants as collective criminals. A constitutuent part of the edifice of the civilizing mission, such cultural determinism drew upon the deaths of explorers as pretext for colonial intervention. The Sahara defied economic or political rationales for empire; in their absence, empire in the desert necessitated cultural justification. Henri Schirmer called upon a series of Algerian experts: "We will say along with Colonel Trumelet, Commanders Rinn [and] Bissuel and Capitain Frédéric Bernard and so many others: there is no possible penetration by pacific means in this part

[217] Atgier, *Touareg*, 5. [218] Atgier, *Touareg*, 21.

of the Sahara."[219] As one administrator observed, the people of the Saharan oasis of Tidikelt suspected that French contact would "attract us to their country, to study them and come to know them first and to occupy in a relatively short period of time."[220] Shrewdly, the denizens of Tidikelt had accurately identified the service ethnographic knowledge aspired to render to colonial power. Moralizing ethnographers contributed to the eventual arrival of political control. Just as ethnography provided justifications for empire's expansion, so, too, did military concerns permeate ethnographic understandings of the Tuareg, the Shaʿamba, and the Sahara as a whole. Through its association with the imperial project, through its fascination with Rinn and Morès and with the specter of violent death, the study of cultures became militant ethnography, the production of texts that facilitated and justified imperial violence under the guise of rooting out criminals.

The French colonial state acknowledged the relationship it had created between imperial power and cultural knowledge. At the Exposition Universelle in 1900, in the main gallery of the section called "Les Grands Noms de la Colonisation Française," the organizers placed busts of Paul Flatters and Henri Duveyrier.[221] Just as the teenaged explorer's voyages had inspired and abetted the ill-fated mission of the lieutenant-colonel, the death of Flatters had indelibly marked Duveyrier. In this, the empire of facts, they remained as inextricably linked in bronze and memory as they had been in life and death.

219 Schirmer, *Le Sahara*, 396.
220 AGGA, 22H/27, General Poizat, commanding the Division of Algiers, to the Governor General of Algeria, Algiers, September 29, 1898.
221 *Exposition universelle de 1900: colonies et pays de protectorats* (Imprimiene Crété de l'Arbre, [1900]), 91.

Conclusion

In the empire of facts, cultural description took on the force of creating political realities. Representations of Islam, of Algerian gender relations, and of notions of criminality emerged out of politically inflected narratives. Conducting research, asking questions, forging personal relationships, writing, all contributed to the formation of the imperial cultural politics of nineteenth-century Algeria. In the bewilderment of empire, its manifest contestations and illogics, colonial administrators, scholars, writers – in short, ethnographers – created discrete cultural depictions upon which representatives of empire could act, whether as political, moral, or legal agents. The empire of facts was an empire of words, of language, of vibrant, germinating, writhing forms made static in between the covers of a book.

Colonial ethnographers developed particular ways of researching and narrating Algerian culture, methods that attracted the interest of the state and which administrators rewarded with subventions, promotion, and attention. Nevertheless, narrators of culture took many paths through the intellectual worlds of French colonial Algeria; neither disciplined nor professionalized, ethnography offered a means of comparative intellectual freedom for aspiring intellectuals excluded from academic institutions by location, affinity, or gender. Many of the concerns that preoccupied Third Republic France intrigued colonial ethnographers in Algeria, as well. Religion, whether organized through forms of sociability or articulated through popular beliefs and practices, loomed as a discursive and at times political menace throughout the colonial period in Algeria. The redefinition of gender relations catalyzed debate over its moral consequences and social import. And, ultimately, metropolitan debates about the potential of "criminal classes" became, in the colonies, the textual reification of criminal cultures. Intellectual, political, and social debates of Third Republic France played out through the empire, as well, in dialogue and in contestation with Algerians. Ephemeral, haunting, phantasmagorical, the personal relations that constitute ethnography left their traces on deliberations about the future configurations of France, of Algeria, and of empire.

"Everything must be made real, step by step," writes Salman Rushdie. "This is a mirage, a ghost world, which becomes real only beneath our magic touch . . . We have to imagine it into being, from the ground up."[1] Empire, as a project of injustice and violence, required constant, if frequently haphazard, effort to police its oft-inchoate boundaries, to protect its interests, and to reassert its discontinuous power in the face of continuous counterclaims of its irrationality. Ethnography functioned as a kind of corpus of magical incantations, conjuring up ghostly representations that offered mere spectres of what they purported to depict, translucent imitations that never completely corresponded to the solid reality of the lived experiences of Algerians from Tilimsān to Berrouaghia to the Sahara.

France's empire of facts did not perpetuate itself through the constant repetition of static representations, but through the incessant production of new and politically inflected imagery. It produced such imagery out of expedience, out of the basic political necessity to have a cultural object upon which to act. "Act," wrote E. M. Forster in *A Passage to India*, "upon that fact until there are more facts."[2]

1 Salman Rushdie, *The Ground Beneath Her Feet* (London: Vintage Books, 2000), 268.
2 E. M. Forster, *A Passage to India* (New York: Harcourt, 1924; 1984), 204.

Bibliography

ARCHIVAL SOURCES

CENTRE DES ARCHIVES D'OUTRE-MER, AIX-EN-PROVENCE, FRANCE

Archives du Gouvernement général de l'Algérie (AGGA)
Cartothèque, F117
Series E (Justice Musulmane)
Series H (Affaires Indigènes)
Series I (Bureaux Arabes Algerois [du Département d'Alger])
Series J (Bureaux Arabes Oranais [du Département d'Oran])
Series K (Bureaux Arabes du Département de Constantine)
Series S (Instruction Publique et Beaux Arts)
Series T (Justice)
Series X (Various)

Archives du Département d'Alger (ADA)
Series U (Culte Musulmane)

Archives du Département d'Oran (ADO)
Series U (Culte Musulmane)

Archives du Territoire des Oasis
Oasis//40
Oasis//46
Oasis//54
Oasis//85
Oasis//87

Archives privées
18APOM/24 (Fonds Billaudot)
142APOM/1 (Fonds Bourlier)

Fonds ministériels (FM)
Affaires Politiques
Series F80
Series FM GEN (Généralités)

Fonds privés (FP)

65APC/1 (Papiers Paul Flatters)

ARCHIVES MILITAIRES DE VINCENNES (AMV)

Service historique de l'Armée de la Terre (SHAT)

1K/21 (Affaires sahariennes)
1M/1315 (Reconnaissances. Algérie: Province d'Alger 1843–1880)
1M/2260 (Reconnaissances [Algérie])
1M/2266 (Reconnaissances et mémoires topographiques 1877. Algérie)
1M/2279 (Reconnaissances et mémoires topographiques 1869–1879. Algérie)
5N/122 (Télégrammes concernant l'Algérie 1914–1918)

ARCHIVES NATIONALES DE FRANCE

Archives privées. Fonds Duveyrier

MUSÉE DE L'HOMME, PARIS

Fonds Topinard
Archives du Musée d'ethnographie du Trocadéro et du Musée de l'homme

PUBLISHED PRIMARY SOURCES

Abadie-Feyguine, Dr. Hélène. *De l'assistance médicale des femmes indigènes en Algérie*. Montpellier: Imprimerie Delord-Boehm et Martial, 1905.

Abou, Maurice. *Les Cérémonies rituelles de la Circoncision en Algérie: Thèse pour le Doctorat en médecine*. Paris: Imprimerie des thèses de médecine, 1914.

Abou Naddara [Shaykh Abū Naẓẓāra). *Les Conférences du Cheikh Abou Naddara. Chaër-El-Molk, à l'Exposition de 1900. 1re Conférence* [Muḥāḍarāt bi-ma'riḍ Bārīs, sana 1900, al-mumārisa al-ūlā]. Paris: n.p. [Imprimerie nationale?], 1902.

Actes du XIVe Congrès international des Orientalistes: Alger 1905. Vol. I: *Première partie: procès verbaux: Section I (Inde), Section V (Chine et Extrême-Orient), Section VI (Grèce et Orient)*. Paris: Ernest Leroux, 1906.

Actes du XIVe Congrès international des Orientalistes: Alger 1905. Vol. II: *Deuxième partie: procès verbaux: Section II (Langues sémitiques), Section IV (Égypte. Langues africaines). Section VII (Archéologie africaine et Art musulman)*. Paris: Ernest Leroux, 1907.

Actes du XIVe Congrès international des Orientalistes: Alger 1905. Vol. III: *Troisième partie: langues musulmanes (Arabe, Persan et Turc)*. Paris: Ernest Leroux, 1907.

Actes du XIVe Congrès international des Orientalistes: Alger 1905. Vol. IV: *Troisième partie (suite): langues musulmanes (Arabe, Persan et Turk)*. Paris: Ernest Leroux, 1908.

Adhémar, Count V. d'. *Mirages algériens: le voyage pratique.* Toulouse: Édouard Privat, 1900.

L'Algérie à l'Exposition Universelle de 1900: journal hebdomadaire. December 22, 1900.

Allan, C. *Conférence sur l'Algérie par M. C. Allan, publiciste. 17 septembre 1878.* Exposition universelle internationale de 1878. Paris: Imprimerie nationale, 1879.

Almand, V. *D'Alger à Ouargla.* Algiers: Adolphe Jourdan, 1890.

Amat, Dr. Charles. *Le M'zab et les M'zabites.* Paris: Challamel, 1888.

Andrews, J. B. *Les Fontaines des génies (Seba Aioun): croyances soudanaises à Alger.* Algiers: Adolphe Jourdan, 1903.

Antar, Michel. *Chevauchées d'un Futur St-Cyrien à travers les ksours et les oasis oranais.* Paris: Collection Hetzel, 1907.

L'Anthropologie. Paris XVII (1906) – XXI (1910).

Armanet, M. L. *Manuel pratique et sommaire de la Justice musulmane en Algérie.* Paris: F. Pichon. 1885.

Arripe, H. J. *Essai sur le folkore de la commune mixte de l'Aurès.* Algiers: Adolphe Jourdan, 1912.

Atgier, Dr. *Les Touareg à Paris.* Paris: Société d'anthropologie de Paris, 1910.

Auclert, Hubertine. *Les Femmes arabes en Algérie.* Paris: Société d'éditions littéraires, 1900.

Aymard, Captain Léopold. *Les Touareg.* Paris: Librairie Hachette, 1911.

Bachechacht, Mme. A. de. *Une Mission à la cour chérifienne.* Paris: Librairie Fischbacher, 1901.

Barbet, Charles. *Au pays des burnous (impressions et croquis d'Algérie).* Algiers: Ernest Mallebay, 1898.

La Perle du Maghreb (Tlemcen): visions et croquis d'Algérie. Algiers: Imprimerie algérienne, n.d. (1907).

Questions sociales et ethnographiques: France, Algérie, Maroc. Algiers: Ancienne Maison Bastide-Jourdan / Jules Carbonnel, 1921.

Barbier, J. V. *À travers le Sahara: les missions du Colonel Flatters d'après des documents absolument inédit.* Voyages et découvertes géographiques. Ed. Richard Cortambert. Paris: Libraire de la Société bibliographique, 1884.

"Géographie militante: Exploration. Les Deux Missions du Colonel Flatters." *Bulletin de la Société de Géographie de l'Est* 3 (1881): 604–23.

Barth, Dr. "Sur les expéditions scientifiques en Afrique, par le Docteur Barth," foreword by Henri Duveyrier. *Bulletin de la Société de Géographie* (1872): 133–49.

Ba Saïd, Addoun ben. *De l'indigénat: son application aux Mozabites.* Philippeville, Algeria: Imprimerie administrative et commerciale moderne, 1903.

Bassenne, Marthe. *Aurélie Tidjani, "Princesse des Sables."* Preface by Louis Bertrand. Paris: Plon, Nourrit, 1925.

Basset, Henri. "État actuel des études d'ethnographie au Maroc." *Bulletin de l'Institut des hautes-études maghrébines* 1, no. 1 (1920): 130–6.

Basset, René. *Le Chaouia de la Province de Constantine.* Paris: Imprimerie nationale, 1897.

Contes populaires berbères: recueillis, traduits et annotés par René Basset. Paris: Ernest Leroux, 1887.

Études sur les dialectes berbères. Paris: Ernest Leroux, 1894.
Étude sur la Zenatia du Mzab, de Ouargla et de l'Oued-Rir'. Publications de l'École des lettres d'Alger. Paris: Ernest Leroux, 1892.
Étude sur la Zenatia de l'Ouarsenis et du Maghreb central. Paris: Ernest Leroux, 1895.
Manuel de langue kabyle (dialecte zouaoua). Grammaire, bibliographie, chrestomathie et lexique. Paris: Maisonneuve & Ch. Leclerc, 1887.
Mélanges africains et orientaux. Paris: Libraire des cinq parties du monde / Jean Maisonneuve & Fils, 1915.
"Mission scientifique en Algérie et au Maroc," *Bulletin de la Société de Géographie de l'Est* (Nancy: 1883): 303–27.
Nédromah et les Traras. Paris: Ernest Leroux, 1901.
Nouveaux Contes berbères: recuillis traduits et annoté. Collection de contes et chansons populaires. Paris: Ernest Leroux, 1897.
Rapport sur les études berbères et Haoussa. Paris, 1902.
Rapport sur les études berbères, éthiopiennes et arabes, 1887–1891. Publications du neuvième Congrès international des Orientalistes, Londres, 1891. Woking: Oriental University Institute, 1892.
Recherches sur la religion des Berbères. Paris: Ernest Leroux, 1910.
Basset, René, trans. *Relation de Sidi Brahim de Massat: traduite sur le texte chelha et annotée par René Basset*. Paris: Ernest Leroux, 1883.
Bastide, L. *Bel-Abbès et son arrondissement*. Oran: Ad. Perrier, 1880.
Batail, Pierre. *Le Tourisme en Algérie*. République Francaise, Gouvernement général de l'Algérie. Algiers: Imprimerie algérienne for the Gouvernement général de l'Algérie, 1906.
Battandier, J.-A., and L. Trabut. *L'Algérie: le sol et les habitants: flore, faune, géologie, anthropologie, ressources agricoles et économiques*. Bibliothèque scientifique contemporaine. Paris: J.-B. Baillière et Fils, 1898.
Baudel, M.-J. *Un An à Alger: excursions et souvenirs*. Paris: Ch. Delagrave, 1887.
Beaufranchet, Baron de. *Quelques mots sur les réformes nécessaires en Algérie*. Paris: E. Dentu, 1883.
Bédier, G.-D. *Le Sahara-Niger ou transsaharien: conférence faite à Paris devant le Comité de l'Afrique du Nord*. Paris: Challamel, Librairie coloniale, 1888.
Behaghel, A. *l'Algérie: conquête et colonisation, religion et mœurs, Armée*. Paris: E. Dentu, 1870.
Béhagle, Ferdinand de. *Des Moyens de combattre la dépopulation en Afrique*. Libraire africaine et coloniale. Paris: Joseph André, 1895.
Bel, Alfred. "Bibliographie: *Les Monuments arabes de Tlemcen*, par Mm. William et Georges Marçais." *Bulletin de la Société de Géographie et d'Archéologie de la Province d'Oran* 23 (1903): 256–260.
"Bibliographie: [review of] Edmond Doutté, *Magie et religion dans l'Afrique du Nord*." *Bulletin de la Société de Géographie et d'Archéologie de la Province d'Oran* 13 (1909): 118–35.
"La Fête des sacrifices en Berbérie," in *Cinquantenaire de la Faculté des lettres d'Alger (1881-1931)*. Algiers: Société historique algérienne, 1932, 87–125.
L'Islam mystique, suivie de Es-Soût', les dires du prophète. Mayenne: Imprimerie de la Manutention, 1988 [1928].
Les Lacs d'Algérie: Chotts & Sebkhas. Oran: Paul Perrier, 1903.

La Population musulmane de Tlemcen. Paris: Paul Geuthner, 1908.

"Quelques rites pour obtenir la pluie en temps de sécheresse chez les musulmans maghribins," in *Recueils de memoires et de textes publiés en l'honneur du XIVe Congrès des Orientalistes par les professeurs de l'École superieure des lettres et des médersas*. Algiers: Imprimerie orientale Pierre Fontana, 1905, 68–71.

La Religion musulmane en Berbérie: esquisse d'histoire et de sociologie religieuse. Vol. I: *Etablissement et développement de l'Islam en Berbérie du VIIe au XXe siècle*. Paris: Libraire orientaliste Paul Geuthner, 1938.

Review of "A. van GENNEP: la formation des légendes." *Bulletin de la Société de Géographie et d'Archéologie de la Province d'Oran* 31 (1911: 1): 81–3.

"Sidi Bou Medyan et son maître Ed-Daqqâq à Fès (notes hagiographiques et épigraphiques)." *Mélanges René Basset: études nord-africaines et orientales*. 1 (1923): 31–68.

"Survivance d'une fête du printemps à Tunis signalée aux XIe siècle de l'h. (XVIIe de J.-C.[)] par l'historien musulman Ibn Abî Dînâr al-Qaîrawânî." *Revue tunisienne*, nos. 19–20 (1934): 337–45.

Bel, Alfred, and Maurice Eisenbeth. *Les Principales Races de l'Algérie: les Berbères, les Arabes, les Juifs*. L'Encyclopédie coloniale et maritime, no. 9. Paris: L'Encyclopédie coloniale et maritime, [1938].

Bel, Marguerite A. *Les Arts indigènes féminins en Algérie*. Algiers: Pierre Fontana, *c*. 1938.

Ben Cheneb, Mohammed. "Du mariage entre musulmans et non-musulmans," *Archives marocaines: publication de la Mission scientifique du Maroc* 15 (1908): 55–79.

ben Choaïb, Aboubekr Abdesselam. *De l'assimilation des indigènes Musulmans de l'Algérie aux Français*. Extrait du Compte Rendu du Congrès internationale de sociologie coloniale tenu à Paris du 6 au 11 août 1900. No additional publication information. Paris, 1900.

"Les Croyances populaires chez les indigènes de algériens." *Bulletin de la Société de Géographie et d'Archéologie de la Province d'Oran* 27, no. 29 (1906:2): 169–74.

"Les Marabouts Guériesseurs," *Revue africaine* 51 (1907): 250–5.

Benhazera, Maurice. *Six Mois chez les Touareg du Ahaggar*. Algiers: Adolphe Jourdan, 1908.

Benoist, Charles. *Enquête algérienne*. Nouvelle bibliothèque variée: sciences sociales et politiques. Paris: Lecène, Oudin, 1892.

Béraud, Hyacinthe. *La Mosquée de Sidi Abd-er-Rhaman*. Algiers: J. Gervais-Courtellemont, 1892.

Bérenger, Captain. "Notice sur la région de Beni-Abbès (avec cartes)." *Bulletin de la Société de Géographie et d'Archéologie de la Province d'Oran* 27 (December 1906): 415–74.

Bergot, Raoul. *L'Algérie telle qu'elle est*. Paris: Albert Savine, 1890.

Bernard, Augustin. *Les Confins algéro-marocains*. Paris: Emile Larose, 1911.

"Documents pour servir à l'étude du Nord-Ouest Africain" *Bulletin de la Société de Géographie et d'Archéologie de la Province d'Oran* 17 (1897): 243–52, 393–405.

Émile Masqueray. Algiers: Adolphe Jourdan, 1895.

En Oranie. Oran: L. Fouque, 1901.

Enfants abandonnés, orphelins, et orphelinats. Bel-Abbès, Algeria: Imprimerie typographique et lithographique Ch. Lavenue, 1887.

Bernard, Augustin, and N. Lacroix. *Historique de la pénétration saharienne*. Algiers: Giralt, 1900.

Bernard, F. *Deux Missions françaises chez les Touareg en 1880–1881*. Algiers: Adolphe Jourdan, 1896.

"Les Deux Missions transsahariennes du Lieutenant-Colonel Flatters," *Bulletin de la Société de Géographie d'Alger et de l'Afrique du Nord* 14 (1909:1): 42–61.

Quatre Mois dans le Sahara: journal d'un voyage chez les Touareg suivi d'un aperçu sur la deuxième mission Flatters. Paris: Ch. Delagrave, 1881.

Bernard, Dr. Marius. *L'Algérie qui s'en va*. Paris: Plon, Nourrit, 1887.

Bernard d'Attanoux, J. "Condition sociale de la femme musulmane en Afrique." *Revue de l'Islam* 2 (1897): 4–6, 21–3.

Bernard d'Attanoux, [J.?]. "Du rôle de la femme dans la société indigène." In *Congrès national des Sociétés françaises de géographie: compte rendu des travaux du Congrès. XXIIIme session. Oran. 1er – 5 avril 1902*. Oran: Paul Perrier, 1903, 144–8.

Bert, Paul. *Lettres de Kabylie: la politique algérienne*. Paris: Alphonse Lemerre, 1885.

Bertholon, Dr. L. *L'Année anthropologique nord-africaine 1902–1903*. Tunis: Société anyonym de l'Imprimerie rapide, 1903.

Bertholon, L., and E. Chantre. *Recherches anthropologiques dans la Berbérie orientale: Tripolitaine, Tunisie, Algérie*. Vol. I: *Anthropométrie, craniométrie, ethnographie*. Lyon: A. Rey, 1913.

Bertillon, Alphonse. *Les Races sauvages: les peuples de l'Afrique, les peuples de l'Amérique, les peuples de l'Océanie, quelques peuples de l'Asie et des Régions boréales*. Bibliothèque de la nature. Ethnographie moderne. Paris: G. Masson / Libraire de l'Académie de médecine, 1883.

Bertrand, Louis. *Le Jardin de la mort: le cycle africain*. New edn. Paris: Ollendorff, n.d.

Nuits d'Alger. Paris: Ernest Flammarion, 1929.

Besset, Lieutenant. *Reconnaissances au Sahara d'In Salah à Amguid et à Tikhammar*. Paris: Comité de l'Afrique française, 1904.

Bissuel, H. *Le Sahara français: conférence sur les questions sahariennes faite les 21 et 31 mars 1891 à MM. les officiers de la garnison de Médéa*. Algiers: Adolphe Jourdan, 1891.

Blochet, M. E. *Études sur l'ésotérisme musulman*. Paris, 1903.

Bloême, A. *Souvenirs d'Afrique: d'Alger à Médéa par un Français pur sang*. Algiers: Imprimerie Pézé, 1884.

de Boisroger, A. *Le Sahara algérien illustré: souvenirs de voyages, notes et croquis. 1886–1887*. Paris: G. Rolla, 1887.

Bonet-Maury, G. "La Femme musulmane dans l'Afrique septentrionale française." *Revue bleue* 5 (3 February 1906), 133–6; published separately as *La Femme musulmane dans l'Afrique septentrionale française*. N.p., 1906.

L'Islamisme et le Christianisme en Afrique. Paris: Hachette, 1906.

Bonnafont, Doctor. *Douze Ans en Algérie 1830 à 1842*. Paris: E. Dentu, 1880.

Pérégrinations en Algérie, 1830 à 1842: histoire, éthnographie, anecdotes. Paris: Challamel Aîné, 1884.

Bonsignorio, E. *Impressions de voyage d'un Parisien dans la province d'Alger*. Paris: Charles Blot, 1898.

Bordier, Dr. A. *La Colonisation scientifique et les colonies françaises*. Paris: C. Reinwald, 1884.

Bourde, Paul. *À travers l'Algérie: souvenirs de l'excursion parlementaire (septembre-octobre 1879)*. 2nd edn. Paris: G. Charpentier, 1880.

la Bourdonnaye, Lieutenant O. de. *Le Moral dans le Bled oranais*. Paris: Henri Charles-Lavauzelle, 1908.

Dans le Bled. Paris: Henri Charles-Lavauzelle (Imprimerie Librairie militare), 1904.

de Boureulle, Colonel. *Récits sur l'Algérie: province d'Alger*. Épinal: V. Collot, 1879.

Brahimi, Denise, ed. *Maupassant au Maghreb: au soleil, La vie errante d'Alger à Tunis, vers Kairouan*. Paris: Le Sycomore, 1982.

Bresnier, L.-J. *Cours pratique et théorique de langue arabe, renfermant les principes détaillés de la lecture, de la grammaire et du style, ainsi que les éléments de la prosodie, accompagné d'un traité du langage arabe universel et de ses divers dialectes en Algérie*. Preface by Adolphe Jourdan. 2nd edn. Alger: Adolphe Jourdan, 1915.

Brieux. *Les Beaux Voyages: Algérie*. Paris: Les Arts graphiques, 1912.

Brives, Abel. *Voyages au Maroc, 1901–1907*. Algiers: Adolphe Jourdan, 1909.

Brosselard, Charles. *Les Khouans: de la constitution des ordres religieux musulmans en Algérie*. Paris: Challamel Aîné, and Algiers: Tissier, 1859.

Brosselard, Henri. *Les Deux Missions Flatters au pays des Touareg Azdjer et Hoggar*. Bibliothèque instructive. Paris: Jouvet, 1889.

Voyage de la mission Flatters au pays des Touareg Azdjers. Bibliothèque instructive. Paris: Jouvet, 1883.

Brouard. "Méchéria (légende et histoire)." *Bulletin de la Société de Géographie et d'Archéologie de la Province d'Oran* 10 (1890): 215–19.

Brunel, Camille. *La Question indigène en Algérie: l'affaire de Margueritte devant la cour d'assises de l'Hérault*. Paris: Augustin Challamel, 1906.

Bulletin du Comité de l'Afrique française 15 (1905).

Bulletin de la Réunion d'Études algériennes. 1911–1914.

Bulletin de la Société de Géographie (*BSGP*). 1872–1903.

Bulletin de la Société de Géographie commerciale de Paris. 1894–5.

Bulletin de la Société de Géographie d'Alger et de l'Afrique du Nord (*BSGA*). 1898–1909.

Bulletin de la Société de Géographie et d'Archéologie de la Province d'Oran (*BSGAO*). 1883–1911.

Bulletin de la Société de Géographie de l'Est (*BSGE*). Nancy: 1881–1883.

Bulletin de la Société de Géographie de Lyon et de la Région Lyonnaise. 1911.

Calderaro. "Beni-Goumi." *Bulletin de la Société de Géographie d'Alger et de l'Afrique du Nord* 9 (1904): 307–52.

Cambon, Jules. *Le Gouvernement général de l'Algérie (1891–1897)*. Paris: Librairie H. Champion, Édouard Champion and Algiers: Librairie Ad. Jourdan / Jules Carbonel, 1918.

Instruction sur la surveillance politique et administrative des indigènes algériens et des musulmans étrangers. Algiers: Pierre Fontana, 1895.

Canal, J. *Oudjda: la frontière marocaine, 1885*. Oran: Paul Perrier, 1886.

Casset, Dr. A. *Dans le "Sud Oranais": souvenirs d'un médecin militaire*. Paris: Bureaux du Reveil Médical, 1911.

Castel, Pierre. *Tébessa: histoire et description d'un territoire algérien*. Vol. I. Paris: Henry Paulin, 1905.

Tébessa: histoire et description d'un territoire Algérien. Vol. II. Paris: Henry Paulin, 1905.

Castéran, Auguste. *L'Algérie d'aujourd'hui*. Algiers–Mustapha: Imprimerie algérienne, 1905.

Castries, Count Henry de. *L'Islam: Impressions et Études*. 6th edn. Paris: Librairie Armand Colin, 1922.

Certeux, A., and Carnoy, E. Henry. *L'Algérie traditionnelle: légendes, contes, chansons, musique, mœurs, coutumes, fêtes, croyances, superstitions, etc.* Vol. I: *Contributions au folk-lore des Arabes*. Paris: Maisonneuve et Leclerc, 1884.

Champeaux, Guillaume de. *À travers les Oasis Sahariennes: les Spahis sahariens*. Paris: R. Chapelot, 1903.

Charmetant, Le P. *Études et souvenirs d'Afrique: d'Alger à Zanzibar*. Voyages et découvertes géographiques. Ed. Richard Cortambert. Paris: Librairie de la Société bibliographique, 1882.

Charvériat, François. *Huits jours en Kabylie: à travers la Kabylie et les questions kabyles*. Paris: Plon, Nourrit, 1889.

Chatrieux, Émilien. *Études algériennes: contribution à l'enquête sénatoriale de 1892*. Paris: Augustin Challamel, 1893.

Chauvin, E. *L'Indigénat algérien devant le parlement: le projet de loi du Gouvernement et la Proposition Albin Rozet*. Algiers: Écho d'Alger, 1913.

de Chéon. *L'Algérie française et libre*. Algiers: Ernest Malleba, J. Angelini, 1899.

Chevillotte, A. *De la famille musulmane en Algérie à propos du statut personnel et des successions en droit musulman par MM. Sauterra [sic] & Cerbonneau*. Paris: Balitout, Questroy, 1873.

Cinquantenaire de la Faculté des lettres d'Alger (1881–1931). Algiers: n.p., 1932.

Cinquante-Quatrième Anniversaire de la fondation de la Société de Géographie. Paris: É. Martinet, 1875.

Clamageran, J.-J. *L'Algérie: impressions de voyage (17 mars–4 juin 1873; 14–29 avril 1881), suivies d'une étude sur les institutions kabyles et la colonisation*. Paris: Germer Baillière, 1883.

Clavel, Eugène. *Droit Musulman du statut personnel et des successions d'après les différents rites et plus particulièrement d'après le rite hanafite*. 2 vols. Paris: Librairie du recueil général des lois et des arrêts et du Journal du Palais, 1895.

Colin, Maurice. *Quelques questions algériennes: études judiciaires, administratives, économiques et sociales*. Paris: L. Larose, 1899.

"Communications: expédition de Gérard Rohlfs, lettre à M. H. Duveyrier. Ben-Ghâzi le 30 octobre 1879." *Bulletin de la Société de Géographie de Paris* 6th ser., 20 (1880): 172–9.

Congrès colonial français de 1908. Paris: Au Secrétariat général des Congrès coloniaux français, 1909.

Congrès internationale de sociologie coloniale. *Rapports et procès-verbaux des séances*. Exposition universelle internationale. Paris: Arthur Rousseau, 1901.

Congrès international des Orientalistes: compte-rendu de la première session: Paris, 1873. vols. I and II. Paris: Maisonneuve, 1874.

Congrès international des Orientalistes: XIVe session, Alger, 19–26 avril 1905. Algiers: S. Léon, 1905.

Congrès internationale des sciences anthropologiques tenu à Paris du 16 au 21 août 1878. Exposition universelle internationale de 1878, No. 17. Paris: Imprimerie nationale, 1880.

Congrès internationale des sciences ethnographiques tenu à Paris du 15 au 17 juillet 1878. Exposition universelle internationale de 1878, No. 5. Paris: Imprimerie nationale, 1881.

Congrès international des sciences ethnographiques tenu à Paris du 30 septembre au 7 octobre 1889. Procès-verbaux sommaires. Exposition universelle internationale de 1889. Paris: Imprimerie nationale, 1890.

Congrès international des traditions populaires: première session, Paris, 1889. Compte rendu des séances. Paris: Bibliothèque des annales économiques, Société d'éditions scientifiques, 1891.

Congrès international des traditions populaires (10–12 septembre 1900). Paris: Émile Lechevalier, 1902.

Congrès national des sciences historiques: deuxième congrès national des sciences historiques: Alger 14–16 avril 1930. Algiers: Jules Carbonel, 1932, 45–61.

Coppolani, X. *Confrérie religieuse musulmane de Sidi-Ammar-Bou-Senna ou l'Ammaria en 1893 de notre ère – 1311 de l'hégire*. Algiers: Adolphe Jourdan, 1894.

"Correspondance." *Bulletin de la Société de Géographie de l'Est* 3 (1881): 176–88.

Coup d'œil sur l'histoire de la colonisation en Algérie. Exposition universelle de Paris de 1878. Algiers: A. Bouyer, 1878.

Cour, A. "Le Culte du serpent dans les traditions populaires du Nord-Ouest Algérien." *Bulletin de la Société de Géographie et d'Archéologie de la Province d'Oran* 31 (1911): 57–75.

Coÿne, A. *Le Mzab*. Algiers: Adolphe Jourdan, 1879.

Daguin, Arthur, and Alphonse Dubreuil. *Le Mariage dans les pays musulmans, particulièrement en Tunisie, en Algérie et dans le Soudan*. Le Mariage indigène dans les colonies & les protectorats de la France. Paris: Lucien Dorbon, 1906.

Daumas, General E. *La Femme arabe*. Algiers: Adolphe Jourdan, 1912.

Davasse, Dr. Jules. *Les Aïssaoua ou les Charmeurs de serpents*. New edn. Paris: E. Dentu, 1862.

de las Cases, Count Emmanuel Joseph Augustin, and Émile Broussais. *Le Crime d'El-Ouatia: assassinat du Marquis de Morès, Chambre criminelle de Sousse,*

juillet 1902. Plaidoiries de M[e] de las Cases et de Me Morès. Partie Civile contre El-Kheïr, Hamma ben Cheick et autres. Paris: Plon-Nourrit, 1904.
Debanne, Odilon. "Hommage à un grand Algérien, Ernest Mercier." *Bulletin de la Société de Géographie et d'Études Coloniales de Marseille* 59 (1939): 84–9.
Delafosse, Maurice. *Les États d'ame d'un colonial*. Paris: Publication du Comité de l'Afrique française, 1909.
Delphin, G. "Les Aïssaoua," in *Oran et l'Algérie: notices historiques, scientifiques et economiques*. Vol. I (Oran: Paul Perrier, 1888), 329–39.
Depont, Octave. *L'Algérie du centénaire: l'œuvre française de libération, de conquête morale et d'évolution social des indigènes, les Berbères en France, la représentation parlementaire des indigènes*. Preface by Pierre Godin. Bordeaux: Imprimerie Cadoret, 1928.
Les Berbères en France: d'une meilleure utilisation de la main-d'œuvre des nord-africains. Paris: Publication du Comité de l'Afrique française, 1925.
Depont, Octave, and Xavier Coppolani. *Les Confréries religieuses musulmanes: publié sous le patronage de M. Jules Cambon, Gouveneur général de l'Algérie*. Algiers: Adolphe Jourdan, 1897.
Derenbourg, Hartwig. *La Science des religions et l'islamisme: deux conférences faites le 29 et 26 mars 1886, à l'École des hautes-études (section des sciences religieuses)*. Paris: Ernest Leroux, 1886.
Derrécagaix, V. *Le Sud de la province d'Oran*. Paris: Librairie de Ch. Delagrave, 1873.
"Exploration du Sahara." *Bulletin de la Société de Géographie* 7, no. 3 (1892): 131–271.
Desparmet, Joseph. *Contes populaires sur les ogres recueillis à Blida et traduits par J. Desparmet, professeur agrégé d'arabe*. Vol. I. Paris: Ernest Leroux, 1909.
Coutumes, institutions, croyances des Musulmans de l'Algérie. Vol I: *l'Enfance, le mariage et la famille*, trans Henri Pérès and G.-H. Bousquet. 2nd edn. Paris: J. Carbonel, 1948.
Desprez, Charles. *L'Hiver à Alger*. 5th edn. Paris: Augustin Challamel, 1898.
Destaing, Edmond. *L'Ennayer chez les Beni Snous (texte berbère, dialecte des Beni Snous)*. Algiers: Adolphe Jourdan, 1905.
Fêtes et coutumes saisonniers chez les Beni-Snous. Algiers: Adolphe Jourdan, 1907.
Deuxième Mission Flatters: historique & rapports rédigés au Service central des affaires indigènes. Algiers: Adolphe Jourdan, 1882.
Devoulx, Albert. *Notice sur les Corporations religieuses d'Alger; accompagnée de documents authentiques et inédits*. Algiers: Adolphe Jourdan, 1912.
Dictionnaires des sciences anthropologiques: anatomie, crâniologie, archéologie préhistorique, ethnographie (mœurs, arts, industrie), démographie, langues, religions). Paris: Octave Doin, 1889.
Documents relatifs à la mission dirigée au sud de l'Algérie par le Lieutenant-Colonel Flatters: journal de route, rapports des membres de la mission, correspondance. Ministère des travaux publics. Paris: Imprimerie nationale, 1884.
Donop, Général. *Lettres sur l'Algérie 1907–1908*. Paris: Plon-Nourrit, 1908.
Douel, Martial. *Au pays de Salammbô*. Paris: Fontemoing, 1911.

Douls, C[amille]. "Voyages dans le Sahara occidental et le sud marocain." *Bulletin de la Société normande de Géographie* 10 (1888): 1–36.

Dournaux Dupéré, Norbert. "Voyage au Sahara." Ed. Henri Duveyrier, *Bulletin de la Société de Géographie* 8 (1874): 113–70.

Doutté, Edmond. "À Rabat, chez Abdelazîz: notes prises en 1907." *Bulletin de la Société de Géographie et d'Archéologie de la Province d'Oran* 33 (1910:1): 21–68.

Les Aïssâoua à Tlemcen. Châlons-sur-Marne: Martin frères, 1900.

"Dans le sud marocain. Au pays des Anfloûs." *Revue de Paris,* 15 Mars 1913, 428–448.

"Les Djebala du Maroc, d'après les travaux de M. A. Mouliéras." *Bulletin de la Société de Géographie et d'Archéologie de la Province d'Oran* 14 (1899): 313–54.

"Figuig: notes et impressions." *Bulletin de la Société de Géographie,* 8th ser., 9 (1903): 177–202.

L'Islam algérien en l'an 1900. Exposition universelle de 1900. Algérie. Algiers-Mustapha: Giralt, 1900.

Magie et religion dans l'Afrique du Nord: la société musulmane du Maghrib. Algiers: Adolphe Jourdan, 1909.

Missions au Maroc: En Tribu. Paris: Paul Geuthner, 1914.

Merrâkech. Paris: Comité du Maroc, 1905.

"Les minarets et l'appel à la prière," Algiers, Offices de publications universitaires, [1899].

"Livres nouveaux sur l'Islam: L'Islam, par le Comte Henry de Castries." *Bulletin de la Société de Géographie et d'Archéologie de la Province d'Oran* 17 (1897): 107–28.

Notes sur l'Islâm maghribin: les Marabouts. Paris: Ernest Leroux, 1900.

"Au pays des Moûlaye Hafid." *Revue de Paris* 1 (October 1907): 481–508.

"Quatrième Voyage d'études au Maroc: rapport au Comité du Maroc. L'organisation domestique et sociale chez les H'ah'a." In *Renseignements coloniaux et documents publiés par le Comité de l'Afrique française et le Comité du Maroc* (1905): 1–16.

Doutté, Edmond, and E. F. Gautier. *Enquête sur la dispersion de la langue berbère en Algérie, faire par ordre de M. le Gouverneur Général.* Algiers: Adolphe Jourdan, 1913.

Drapier, Henry. *La Condition sociale des indigènes algériens.* Paris: Ar. Rousseau, and Algiers: Adolphe Jourdan, 1899.

Drouet, Francis. *Au nord de l'Afrique: Tunisie, Algérie, Mélilla, Gibraltar, Tanger – notes de voyage.* Illustrations by A. Douhin. Nice: Place Sasserno, 1896.

Drouët, Henri. *Alger et le Sahel.* Paris: Hachette, 1887.

Dubois, Étienne. *Les Tribunaux répressifs indigènes en Algérie.* Algiers: Adolphe Jourdan, 1904.

Duhousset, Commandant E. "Étude sur les Kabyles du Djurdjura," *Mémoires de la Société d'ethnographie* 12 (1872): 17–40.

Dumont, Henri. *Alger: ville d'Hiver, notes de voyage.* Paris: Berger-Levrault, 1878.

Dupuis, E. *Autour du monde: voyage d'un petit algérien.* 12th edn. Paris: Delagrave, 1912.

Duveyrier, Henri. "L'Afrique nécrologique." *Bulletin de la Société de Geographie* 8 (1874): 561–644.

Les "Chemins des ambassades" de Tanger à Fâs et Meknâs, en 1885. Paris: Société de géographie, 1886.

"De Telemsan à Melila en 1886." *Bulletin de la Société de Geographie*, 7th ser. 14 (1893:2).

La Dernière Partie inconnue du littoral de la Méditerranée: le Rîf. Paris: Ernest Leroux, 1888.

"Le Désastre de la mission Flatters." *Bulletin de la Société de Géographie* 7 (1881): 364–74.

"Les Explorations de Linvingstone [*sic*] dans la Région des Lacs de l'Afrique orientale." *Bulletin de la Société de Géographie* 16 (1872): 337–55.

"Historique des voyages à Timbouktou." *Bulletin de la Société de Géographie* 1 (1881): 195–8.

Journal d'un voyage dans la Province d'Alger: février, mars, avril 1857. Ed. and preface Charles Maunoir. Paris: Augustin Challamel, 1900.

Livingstone. Paris: E. Martinet, 1874.

"Livingstone." *Bulletin de la Société de Géographie,* 16th ser., 8 (1874): 291–308.

"Mission du Colonel Flatters dans le Sahara Central." *Bulletin de la Société de Géographie* 7 (1881): 250–7.

"Le Nord du Sahara central." Trans. Capt. H. Simon. *Bulletin de la Société de Géographie*. Huitième année (1903:7): 23–45.

Notes sur les Touareg et leur pays. Paris: Imprimerie de L. Martinet, 1863.

"Revues et analyses: livres et brochures. H. Brosselard. Voyage de la mission Flatters au pays des Touaregs-Azdjers." *Revue d'ethnographie* 3 (1884): 72–6.

Sahara algérien et tunisien: journal de route de Henri Duveyrier. Ed. Ch. Maunoir and H. Schirmer. Paris: Augustin Challamel, 1905.

Les Touareg du Nord: exploration du Sahara. Paris: Challamel Aîné, 1864.

"Traversée de la Zone Sud de l'Afrique équatoriale 1873–1875 par le Lieutenant Verney Lovett Cameron de la Marine anglaise." *Bulletin de la Société de Géographie* 16 (1876): 113–28.

La Tunisie. Paris: Librairie Hachete, 1881.

L'École d'anthropologie de Paris: 1876–1906. Paris: Félix Alcan, 1907.

Estournelles de Constant, Baron d'. *Les Congrégations religieuses chez les Arabes et la conquête de l'Afrique du Nord*. Bibliothèque ethnographique, no. 8 Ed. Léon de Rosny. Paris: Maisonneuve et Leclerc, 1887.

Étienne. *Le Droit de "djebr" et le mariage des impubères chez les musulmans en Algérie*. Algiers: Adolphe Jourdan, 1898.

Eudel, Paul. *Hivernage en Algérie*. Paris: Hérissey et Fils, 1909.

Exposé de la situation général des territoires du sud de l'Algérie présenté par M. Ch. Lutaud, Gouverneur Général, année 1912. Algiers: Adolphe Jourdan, 1913.

Exposition de la Bibliothèque nationale à l'occasion du Congrès des Orientalistes: choix de manuscrits d'imprimés de cartes et de médailles exposés à l'occasion du Congrès des Orientalistes septembre 1897. Paris: Ernest Leroux, 1897.

Exposition universelle de 1878: description complète et détaillée des Palais [du] Champs du Mars et du Trocadéro. Paris: Le Bailly, 1878.

Exposition universelle de 1889: colonies françaises et pays de protectorat. Catalogue officiel. Paris: J. Bell, n.d.
Exposition universelle de 1900: colonies et pays de protectorats. N.p.: Imprimerie Crété de l'Arbre, [1900].
"Extraits des procès-verbaux des séances, Séance du 6 janvier 1875." *Bulletin de la Société de Géographie* 9 (January – June 1875): 212–21
Eyssautier, L.-A. *Cours criminelles musulmanes et tribunaux répressifs indigènes.* Algiers: Adolphe Jourdan, 1903.
Fabre, Césaire. *Grande Kabylie: légendes et souvenirs.* Paris: Léon Vanier, 1901.
Faidherbe, Général and Topinard, Dr. *Instructions sur l'anthropologie de l'Algérie.* Paris: Imprimérie de A. Hennuyer, 1874.
Fallot, Ernest. *Par delà la Méditerranée: Kabylie, Aurès, Kroumirie.* Paris: Plon, Nourrit, 1887.
Fauqueux, M. *Réponse au questionnaire de la Commission sénatoriale d'études sur l'Algérie: rapport général, Département d'Oran, Conseil général, Session d'octobre-novembre 1891.* Oran: D. Heintz, 1892.
Fauvelle, G. *Traité théorique et pratique de dévolutions des successions musulmanes (rite malékite).* Sétif, Algeria: Imprimerie administrative et commerciale veuve Emile Tournier, 1902.
Feydeau, Ernest. *Alger: Étude.* New edn. Paris: Calmann Lévy, 1884.
Souna: mœurs arabes. Paris: Calmann Lévy, 1876.
Finot, Jean. *Le Préjugé des races.* Bibliothèque de philosophie contemporaine. 2nd ed. Paris: Félix Alcan, 1906.
Fontanes, J. de. *Deux Touristes en Algérie: Nedjéma.* 2nd edn. Bibliothèque contemporaine. Paris: Calmann Lévy, 1879.
Foureau, Fernand. *D'Alger au Congo par le Tchad: mission saharienne Foureau-Lamy.* Paris: Masson, 1902.
Au Sahara: mes deux missions de 1892 et 1893. Le Gassi Touil et le Grand Erg, L'Oudje sud et le Tinghert. Hassi Messegguem et Hassi Imoulay. 2nd edn. Paris: Augustin Challamel, 1897.
"Coup d'Œil sur le Sahara français: simple esquisse," *Annales de géographie* 4 (1894–1895): 61–75.
Dans le Grand Erg: mes itinéraires sahariens de décembre 1895 à mars 1896. Paris: Augustin Challamel, 1896.
Ma Mission de 1893–1894 chez les Touareg Azdjjer: le Tademayt. le Bâten et In-Salah. L'Éguélé. Le Tassili des Azdjer. L'ouad Mihero. L'Erg d'Issaouan. Paris: Impriméries réunies, 1894.
Une Mission au Tademayt (territoire d'In-Salah) en 1890: rapport à M. le Ministre de l'instruction publique et à M. le Sous-Secrétaire d'État des Colonies. Paris: Charles Schlaeber, 1890.
"Une Mission chez les Touareg." *Bulletin de la Société de Géographie de Paris,* 7th ser., 14 (1893:4): 500–44.
Mission chez les Touaregs: mes deux itinéraires sahariens d'octobre 1894 à mai 1895. Rapport adressé à Monsieur le Ministre de l'Instruction publique, à Monsieur le Gouverneur Général de l'Algérie, à l'Académie des inscriptions et belles-lettres. Paris: Augustin Challamel, 1895.

Rapport sur ma mission au Sahara et chez les Touaregs Azdjer, octobre 1893–mars 1894. Paris: Augustin Challamel, 1894.

Fraigneau, A. *L'Art arabe à Alger: la Maison Mauresque*. Collection de l'Algérie artistique et pittoresque. Algiers: J. Gervais-Courtellemont, Editeurs d'Art, 1893.

Gaël, Madame A. *En Algérie*. Paris: Librairie centrale des publications populaires, 1881.

Gaidoz, H., and Paul Sébillot. *Bibliographie des traditions et de la littérature populaire des Frances d'Outre-Mer*. Paris: Maisonneuve frères & Ch. Leclerc, 1886.

Galland, Charles de. *Renseignements sur l'Algérie: les petits cahiers algériens*. Algiers: Adolphe Jourdan, 1900.

Gaudefroy-Demombynes, Maurice. *Coutumes de mariage en Algérie*. [Paris]: Revue des traditions populaires, 1907.

Notes de sociologie maghrébine: les cérémonies du mariage chez les indigènes de l'Algérie. Paris: Maisonneuve, 1901.

Gautier, E. F. *La Conquête du Sahara: essai de psychologie politique*. 5th edition. Paris: Librairie Armand Colin, 1935.

Gautier, E. F., and René Chudeau. *Missions au Sahara*. Vol. I: *Sahara algérien*, by E. F. Gautier. Paris: Librairie Armand Colin, 1908.

Georges-Robert. *À travers l'Algérie: notes et croquis*. Paris: E. Dentu, n.d.

Girard, Henri. *Aide-Mémoire d'anthropologie et d'ethnographie*. Manuel d'histoire naturelle. Paris: J.-B. Baillière et Fils, 1898.

Giraud, Hippolyte. *Exposition internationale de Chicago: section algérienne: Rapport*. Algiers: Pierre Fontana, 1893.

Godin, Frédéric. *De l'application du Droit musulman en Algérie*. Algiers: Adolphe Jourdan, 1900.

Goldziher, I. Review of *Recueil de mémoires et textes publié en l'honneur du XIVe Congrès des Orientalistes par les professeurs de l'École supérieure des lettres et des médersas*. *Revue de l'histoire des religions* 50 (1905): 1–18.

Guiauchain, G. *Winter in Algeria*. Algiers: Imprimerie algérienne, 1901.

Guillaumet, Gustave. *Tableaux algériens*. Paris: Plon, Nourrit, 1891.

Haddon, A.C. *Les Races humaines et leur répartition géographique: édition corrigée et augmentée par l'auteur*. Trans. A. Van Gennep. Paris: Librairie Félix Alcan, 1930.

Hamet, Ismaël. *Les Musulmans français du Nord de l'Afrique*. Foreword by A. Le Chatelier. Paris: Librairie Armand Colin, 1906.

Hamy Dr. *L'Anthropologie à l'Exposition internationale des sciences géographiques: rapport présenté au Jury, au nom du Groupe III*. Paris: Imprimerie Émile Martinet, 1879.

Hanoteau, A., and A. Letourneux. *La Kabylie et les coutumes kabyles*. Vol. I. 2nd edn. Paris: Augustin Challamel, 1893.

Harmand, Dr. "Actes de la Société, extrait des procès-verbaux des séances." *Bulletin de la Société de Géographie* 7 (1881).

Hautfort, Félix. *Au Pays des palmes: Biskra*, 2nd edn. Paris: Paul Ollendorff, Éditeur, 1897.

Herbette, L. *L'Œuvre pénitentiaire. études présentées à l'occasion de l'organisation du Musée spécial et des expositions de l'administration française.* Melun: Imprimerie administrative, 1891.

Houdas, Octave. *Ethnographie de l'Algérie.* Bibliothèque ethnographique, no. 5, ed. Léon de Rosny. Paris: Maisonneuve et Leclerc, 1886.

L'Islamisme. Paris: Dujarric, 1904.

Monographie de Méquinez. Paris: Imprimerie nationale, n.d.

Humbert, Gustave, ed. *La Justice en France de 1826 à 1880 et en Algérie de 1853 à 1880: rapports, tableaux annexes, cartes et diagrammes présentés au Président de la République pour le Garde des Sceaux, Ministre de la Justice et des Cultes.* Paris: Imprimerie nationale, 1882.

Imbert, Hugues. *Quatre Mois au Sahel: lettres et notes algériennes.* Paris: Librairie Fischbacher, 1888.

al-Jazā'irī, Shaykh Sīdī Muḥammad bin Muṣṭafā bin al-Khūja. *Iqāmat al-Brāhīn al-'iẓām 'alā nafī al-ta'ṣṣub al-dīnī fī al-Islām.* Algiers: Pierre Fontana, 1902.

Joly, A. "Étude sur les Chadouliyas," *Revue africaine* 51, nos. 264-5 (1907): 5–40, 223–49.

Jourdan, Charles. *Croquis algériens.* Paris: A. Quantin, 1880.

Kiva, P. [Lt.-Col. Paul Waché]. *En Algérie (Souvenirs).* Paris: Henri Charles-Lavauzelle, 1894.

Kugener, A. *Les Congrès des Orientalistes d'Alger.* Liège, Belgium: Imprimerie La Meuse, 1905.

Lacanaud, E. *L'Algérie au point de vue de l'économie sociale.* Algiers–Mustapha: Giralt, 1900

Lacroix, N. *Les Derkaoua d'hier et d'aujourd'hui: essai historique.* Documents pour le Nord-ouest africain. Algiers: Imprimerie administrative Victor Heintz, 1902.

Laloë, Mademoiselle G. *Enquête sur le travail des femmes indigènes à Alger.* Algiers: Adolphe Jourdan, 1910.

Lambert, Abbot Edmond. *À travers l'Algérie: histoires, mœurs et légendes des Arabes.* Paris: René Haton, 1884.

Laporte, Albert. *Souvenirs d'Algérie.* Paris: Théodore Lefèvre, 1882.

Largeau, Victor. *Le Sahara algérien: les déserts de l'Erg.* 2nd edn. Paris: Hachette, 1881.

Lartigue, Lt.-Col. de. *Monographie de l'Aurès.* Constantine: Marle-Audrino, 1904.

Le Chatelier, A. *Description de l'Oasis d'In-Salah.* Algiers: Imprimerie de l'Association ouvrière, Pierre Fontana, 1886.

L'Islam dans l'Afrique Occidentale. Paris: G. Steinheil, 1899.

Le Chatelier, Jean. "Alfred Le Chatelier 1855–1929: sa carrière africaine." Unpublished ms. Centre des Archives d'Outre Mer, Aix-en-Provence, 1986.

Le Roy, Jean. *Deux Ans de séjour en petite Kabylie: un peuple de Barbares en territoire français.* Paris: Augustin Challamel, 1911.

Leclercq, Jules. *De Mogador à Biskra: Maroc & Algérie.* Paris: Challamel Aîné / Librairie algérienne, coloniale et orientale, 1881.

Legey, Doctoresse. *Essaide folklore marocain.* Preface by Maréchal Lyautey. Librairie orientaliste Paul Geuthner, 1926.

Lélu, Paul. *En Algérie: souvenirs d'un colon*. 2nd edn. Paris: A. Hennuyer, 1881.
Lestre de Rey, René G. *Guide de Philippeville (Département de Constantine) et de ses environs*. Le Tourisme en Algérie. Philippeville: Imprimerie moderne, 1904.
Liorel, Jules. "Dans Le M'zab." *Algérie artistique & pittoresque* 3 (1893:1): 1–32.
Races berbères: Kabylie du Jurjura. Paris: Ernest Leroux, n.d. [1893].
Lombay, G. de. *En Algérie: Alger, Oran, Tlemcen*. Paris: Ernest Leroux, 1893.
Lorrain, Jean [Paul Duval]. *Heures d'Afrique: chroniques du Maghreb (1893–1898)*. Ed. Fathi Glamallah. Paris: L'Harmattan, 1994.
Lourdau, E. *La Justice musulmane en Algérie*. Algiers: A. Bouyer, 1884.
Magali-Boisnard. "L'Aurès barbare." *Bulletin de la Société de Géographie d'Alger et de l'Afrique du Nord* 13 (1908:1): 33–54.
"Nos Sœurs musulmanes." *Bulletin de la Société de Géographie d'Alger et de l'Afrique du Nord* 13 (1908:4). 495–506.
Maistre, Jules. *Mœurs et coutumes kabyles*. Montpellier: Imprimerie de la Manufacture de la charité, 1905.
Notice sur le climat des pays qui entourent la Méditerranée et sur la Kabylie en 1900. Algiers: Adolphe Jourdan, 1901.
Marchand, H. *Masques carnavalesques et carnaval en Kabylie*. Extrait du quatrième Congrès de la Fédération des sociétés savantes de l'Afrique du Nord. Algiers: Société historique algérienne, n.d. [1938?].
Marin, Abbot Eugène. *Algéria-Sahara-Soudan: vie, travaux, voyages de Mgr Hacquard des Pères Blancs (1860–1901) par sa correspondance*. Paris: Berber-Levrault, 1905.
Marneur, François. *L'Indigénat en Algérie: considérations sur le régime actuel. Crique. Projet de réformes*. Colonial government pamphlets, No. 20. Paris: L. Tenin, 1914.
Martin, Alfred Georges Paul. *Précis de sociologie nord-africaine (première partie)*. Paris: Ernest Leroux, 1913.
Martinière, H.-M.-P. de la, and Lacroix, N. *Documents pour servir à l'étude du nord ouest africain*. Vol. I: *Régions limitrophes de la frontière algérienne*. Le Rif. Les Djebala. [Algiers]: Gouvernement général de l'Algérie, Service des affaires indigènes, 1894.
Documents pour servir à l'étude du nord ouest africain. Vol. IV: *Les Oasis de l'Extrême-Sud algérien*. Algiers: Gouvernment général de l'Algérie, Service des affaires indigènes, 1897.
Martino, Pierre. *L'Œuvre algérienne d'Ernest Feydeau*. Algiers: Office des publications universitaires [1909].
"L'Œuvre algérienne d'Ernest Feydeau," *Revue africaine* 274 (1909:3), 133–92.
Martinot, A. *Organisation de la justice musulmane en Algérie: recueil des lois, décrets, arrêtés, etc., en vigueur, concernant la matière*. Constantine: Imprimerie Émile Marle, 1900.
Marty, Dr. A. *Islamisme: mœurs médicales et privées. Climatologie de l'Algérie, considérations sur l'atmosphère*. Monaco: Imprimerie du "Petit Monégasque," 1903.
bin Mas'ūd, Jabārī (Djebari ben Messaoud). *Les Survivants de la mission Flatters*. Tunis: Imprimerie Brigol, 1895.

Masqueray Émile, trans. *Chronique d'Abou Zakaria*. Livres des Beni Mzab. Paris: Ch. Delagrave, Éditeur de la Société de géographie, 1879.

Masqueray Émile. *Formation des cités chez les populations sédentaires de l'Algérie (Kabyles du Djurdjura, Chaouïa de l'Aourâs, Beni Mezâb)*. Paris: Ernest Leroux, 1886. Repr., with intro by Fanny Colonna. Aix-en-Provence: Édisud, 1983.

"Henri Duveyrier." *L'Expansion coloniale* (May 23, 1892): 246–48.

Note concernant les Aoulad-Daoud de Mont-Aurès (Aourâs) Algiers: Adolphe Jourdan, 1879.

Souvenirs et visions d'Afrique. Paris: E. Dentu. Repr., ed. Michèle Salinas, Paris: La Boîte à documents, 1989.

Masqueray, Ernest. Review of Louis Rinn's *Marabouts et khouan*, *Bulletin de Correspondance Africaine* 4 (1885).

Massonié, Gilbert. *Traité théorique & pratique de la compétence et de la procédure en matière musulmane (Tell, Kabylie, Sahara)*. Législation algérienne. Paris: Librairie nouvelle de droit et de jurisprudence, 1910.

Les Tribunaux répressifs indigènes en Algérie: commentaire complet, théorique & pratique du Décret du 9 août 1903 et de la loi du 31 mars 1904. Algiers: Adolphe Jourdan, 1904.

Mathieu de Preutin, Georges. *Les Juridictions répressives indigènes en Algérie*. Nancy: A. Crépin-Leblond, 1908.

Maunier, René. *Recherches sur les échanges rituels en Afrique du Nord suivi de les groupes d'intérêt et l'idée du contrat en Afrique du Nord*. Ed. Alain Mahé. Paris: Éditions Bouchène, 1998.

Maurin, Dr. Amédée. *La Saison d'hiver en Algérie*. Paris: G. Masson, 1874.

Meilhon, Dr. *L'Aliénation mentale chez les Arabes: études de nosologie comparée*. Paris: Maisson, 1896.

Mélanges orientaux: textes et traductions publiés par les professeurs de l'École spéciale des langues orientales vivantes à l'occasion du sixième Congrès international des Orientalistes réuni à Leyde (Septembre 1883). Paris: Ernest Leroux / Libraire de la Société asiatique de l'École des langues orientales vivantes, 1883.

Mélia, Jean. *Le Drame de la mission Flatters: les pionniers du Méditerranée-Niger*. Paris: Mercure de France, 1942.

"Membres." *Bulletin de la Société de Géographie d'Alger et de l'Afrique du Nord* 7 (1902:1): lvi–lxi.

"Membres." *Bulletin de la Société de Géographie et d'Archéologie de la Province d'Oran* 23 (1903): 1–7.

Mémoires de la Société d'ethnographie, new ser., 1 (1885).

Mémoires de la Société d'ethnographie, new ser., 2 (1886).

Mémoires du Congrès international des sciences ethnographiques: session de 1889, présidée par M. J. Oppert de l'Institut. Publications de la Société d'ethnographie. Vol. VII: *Congrès des sciences ethnographiques: session de 1889*. Paris: Ernest Leroux, 1892.

Mennesson, Ch. *Organisation de la Justice et du Notariat musulmans en Algérie et législation applicable en Algérie aux Musulmans*. Paris: Challamel, 1888.

Mercier, Ernest. *L'Algérie en 1880: le cinquantenaire d'une colonie*. Paris: Challamel Aîné, 1880.

L'Algérie et les questions algériennes: étude historique, statistique et économique. Paris: Challamel Aîné, 1883.

La Condition de la femme musulmane dans l'Afrique septentrionale. Algiers: Adolphe Jourdan, 1895.

La France dans le Sahara et au Soudan. Paris: Ernest Leroux, 1889.

Histoire de Constantine (Algérie), dès origines à 1871. Constantine: J. Marle et F. Biron, 1903.

Métois, Captain Florent-Alexis. "Contes Sahariens." *Bulletin de la Société de Géographie d'Alger et de l'Afrique du Nord* 14 (1909): 509–21.

Mélanges africains et orientaux. Paris: Jean Maisonneure & Fils, 1915.

La Soumission des Touareg du Nord. Preface by F. Foureau. Paris: Augustin Challamel, 1906.

Monbrun, Th. *Conférence sur l'Algérie*. Oran: Imprimerie typographique et lithographique L. Fouque, 1904.

Morand, Marcel. *De l'abus du droit dans la législation musulmane*. Algiers: Adolphe Jourdan, 1906.

Avant-Projet de code présenté à la Commission de codification du droit musulman algérie. Algiers: Adolphe Jourdan, and Paris: Augustin Challamel, 1916.

Le Droit musulman algérien (Rite Malékite): ses origines. Algiers: Adolphe Jourdan, 1913.

Études de droit musulman et de droit coutumier berbère. Algiers: Jules Carbonel, 1931.

La Famille musulmane. Algiers: Adolphe Jourdan, 1903.

Les Kanouns du Mzab. Algiers: Adolphe Jourdan, 1903.

Motylniski, A. de C. *Notes historiques sur le Mzab: Guerrara depuis sa fondation*. Algiers: Adolphe Jourdan, 1885.

Mouliéras, Auguste. *Fez*. Paris: Augustin Challamel, 1902.

Les Fourberies de Si Djeh'a: Contes Kabyles. With an appendix by René Basset. Paris: E. Leroux, 1892. Repr. with intro by Jean Déjeux, Paris: La Boîte à documents, 1987.

"Hagiologie Mag'ribine." *Bulletin de la Société de Géographie et d'Archéologie de la Province d'Oran* 19 (1899): 374–6.

Legendes et contes merveilleux de la Grande Kabylie. Trans. Camille Lacoste. Paris: Imprimerie nationale / Librairie orientaliste Paul Geuthner, 1965.

Le Maroc inconnu: étude géographie et sociologique. Vols. I and II. Paris: Augustin Challamel, 1899.

Une Tribu Zénète anti-musulmane au Maroc (Les Zkara). Paris: Augustin Challamel, 1905.

Mulé, Antonin. *Chez les Moumenin: récits algériens*. Paris: Dujarric, 1906.

Neveu, E. de. *Les Khouan: ordres religieux*. 3rd edn. Algiers: Adolphe Jourdan, 1913 [1862].

Ney, Cdt. Napoléon. *Un Danger européen: les sociétés secrètes musulmanes*. Paris: Georges Carré, 1890.

Niel, O. *Géographie de l'Algérie*. Vol. I: *Géographie physique, agricole, industrielle et commerciale*. Bône: Legendre / Cauvy, 1876.

Géographie de l'Algérie. Vol. II: *Géographie politique et itinéraire de l'Algérie avec une grande carte de l'Algérie et de la Tunisie*. 2nd edn. Paris: Challamel Aîné, 1881.

Noëllat, le Colonel. *L'Algérie en 1882*. Paris: Libraire militaire de J. Dumaine, L. Baudoin & Ce, 1882.

"Nouvelles Géographiques." *Bulletin de la Société de Géographie de l'Est* 5 (1883): 160–76.

Oran et l'Algérie en 1887: notices historiques, scientifiques & économiques. Vol. I. *Association française pour l'avancement des sciences, Congrès d'Oran 1888*. Oral: Paul Perrier, 1888.

Oran et l'Algérie en 1887: notices historiques, scientifiques & économiques. Vol. II. *Association française pour l'avancement des sciences, Congrès d'Oran 1888*. Oran: Paul Perrier, 1888.

Pansard, E. *Histoire des Oulad Sidi Cheikh*. 1886. Centre des archives d'Outre-Mer, Archives du Gouvernement générale de l'Algérie, 22H/9.

Papier, Alexandre. *Description de Mena'a et d'un groupe de danseuses des Oulad Abdi (Aurès occidental)*. Paris: Librairie africaine et coloniale, 1895.

Parienti, Alfred. *Aux visiteurs du Rab: Tlemcen Ville Sainte*. Tlemcen, Algeria: Imprimerie du Petit Tlemcénien, 1910.

Pavy, Auguste. *L'Expédition de Morès*. Librairie africaine et coloniale. Joseph André, 1897.

Pein, Louis Auguste Théodore. *Chez les Touareg Azdjer: d'Ouargla à Tarat*. Paris: Comité de l'Afrique française, 1904

Lettres familières sur l'Algérie, un petit royaume arabe. Prefaces by A. Jourdan and H. Bissuel. 2nd edn. Algiers: Adolphe Jourdan, 1893.

Pérès, Gustave. *L'Islam et ses anarchistes: Les Tidjanys, les Senoussii, les Berbers voilés. Conférence faite au Théâtre d'Abbeville, le 14 Janvier, 1893*. Abbeville, France: Imprimerie Fourdrinier, 1893.

Petit, R. P. Louis. *Les Confréries musulmanes*. 2nd edn. Paris: B. Bloud, 1902.

Pimodan, Commandant de. *Oran, Tlemcen, Sud-Oranais (1899–1900)*. Paris: Honoré Champion, 1902.

Piquet, Victor. *Les Civilisations de l'Afrique du Nord: Berbères, Arabes, Turcs*. Paris: Armand Colin, 1909.

Philebert, Général, and Georges Rolland. *La France en Afrique et le Transsaharien*. Paris: Augustin Challamel, 1890.

Picard, Alfred. *Rapport général administratif et technique*. Exposition universelle internationale de 1900, no. 1. Paris: Imprimerie nationale, 1902.

Piesse, Louis. *Le Femme arabe: d'après les notes recueillies et classées par M. Louis Piesse: illustrations de Fromentin, Bouttet de Monvel, Rieder, etc.*. Paris: Bibliothèque de la Revue de l'Afrique française / M. Barbier, 1887.

Les Monuments historiques de l'Algérie. Deuxième étude: Le Routier archéologique de l'Algérie. Paris: Ducher, 1879.

Pomel, Auguste. *Races indigènes de l'Algérie, et du rôle que leur réservent leurs aptitudes: Arabes, Kabyles, Maures et Juifs*. Oran: Typographie et lithographie Veuve Dagorn, 1871.

Pommerol, Mme. Jean. *L'Islam africain: chez ceux qui guettent*. Paris: Fontemoing, 1910.

Pradier, John. *Notes artistiques sur Alger (1874–1875)*. 2nd edn. Tours: Rouillé-Ladevèze, 1876.

Prax, Victoriano. *Étude sur la question algérienne: à Messieurs les membres de la Commission sénatoriale*. Bône, Algeria: Imprimerie Léon Lampronti, 1892.

Pulligny, Viscount Félix Augustin de. *Six Semaines en Algérie*. New edn. Paris: Canson, 1884.

Quesnoy, Dr. F. *L'Algérie*. Paris: Librairie Furne, Jouvet, 1885.

Rabourdin, Lucien. *Algérie & Sahara*. Paris: Challamel Aîné / Guillaumin, 1882.

Rambaud, Alfred. *L'Enseignement primaire chez les indigènes musulmans d'Algérie et notamment dans la Grande Kabylie*. Paris: Librairie Ch. Delgrave, 1892.

Reclus, Élisée. *Nouvelle Géographie universelle: la terre et les hommes. XI: l'Afrique septentrionale. Deuxième Partie. Tripolitaine, Tunisie, Algérie, Maroc, Sahara*. Paris: Librairie Hachette, 1886.

Recueil de mémoires et de textes publiés en l'honneur du XIVe Congrès des Orientalistes par les professeurs de l'École supérieure des lettres et des médersas. Algiers: Imprimerie orientale Pierre Fontana, 1905.

Régis, Louis. *Constantine: voyages et séjours*. Paris: Calmann Lévy, 1880.

Renaud, Georges. *La Colonisation algérienne au Congrès d'Alger (résumé de la discussion du Congrès d'Alger)*. Bibliothèque géographique. Paris: Guillaumin, 1883.

René-Leclerc, Ch. "Bibliographie: Le Maroc connu." *Bulletin de la Société de Géographie et d'Archéologie de la Province d'Oran* 23 (1903): 359–66.

Le Maroc septentrional (été 1904). Algiers-Mustapha: Imprimerie algérienne, 1905.

Revue africaine. 1871–2. 1883. 1885–8. 1899. 1902. 1905. 1907. 1909. 1911. 1945.

Revue de l'Afrique française. 1886–1888.

Revue d'ethnographie. 1882–1889.

ben Ridouane, Cheikh Abd-el-Hadi. *Étude sur le Soufisme*. Trans. M. Arnaud. Algiers: Adolphe Jourdan, 1888.

Rinn, Louis. *Expédition du Général Solomon dans le Djebel Aourès, 539 de J.-C.* Géographie ancienne de l'Algérie. Algiers: Adolphe Jourdan, 1894.

"La Femme berbère dans l'ethnologie et l'histoire de l'Algérie." *Bulletin de la Société de Geographie d'Alger et d'Afrique du Nord* (1905:2): 461–500.

"Les Grands Tournants de l'Histoire de l'Algérie." *Bulletin de la Société de Geographie d'Alger et d'Afrique du Nord* 8 (1903): 1–24.

Histoire de l'insurrection de 1871 en Algérie. Algiers: Adolphe Jourdan, 1891.

"Lettres de Touareg." *Revue africaine* 31, no. 185 (1887): 321–41.

Marabouts et Khouan: étude sur l'Islam en Algérie. Algiers: Adolphe Jourdan, 1884.

Nos Frontières sahariennes. Algiers: A. Jourdan, 1886.

Note sur l'Instruction publique musulman en Algérie. Algiers: Pierre Fontana, 1882.

Les Origines berbères: études linguistiques et ethnologiques. Algiers: Adolphe Jourdan, 1889.

Les Premiers royaumes berbères et la Guerre de Jugurtha. Géographie ancienne de l'Algérie. Algiers: Adolphe Jourdan, 1885.

Régime pénal de l'indigénat en Algérie: les commissions disciplinaires. Algiers: Adolphe Jourdan, 1885.

Régime pénal de l'indigénat en Algérie: le séquestre et la responsabilité collective. Algiers: Adolphe Jourdan, 1890.

Le Royaume d'Alger sous le dernier dey. Algiers: Adolphe Jourdan, 1900.

Rivière, J. *Recueil de contes populaires de la Kabylie du Djurdjura recueillis et traduits par J. Rivière*. Collection de contes et de chansons populaires, 4. Paris: Ernest Leroux, 1882.

Robert, Achille. *L'Arabe tel qu'il est: études algériennes et tunisiennes*. Algiers: Imprimerie Joseph Angelini, 1900.

"Contribution au folk-lore des indigènes de l'Algérie," in *Actes du XIVe Congrès Internationale des Orientalistes. Alger, 1905*. Vol. III. Paris: Ernest Leroux, 1908, 561–78.

Métiers et types algériens. Algiers: Ernest Mallebay, 1895.

Roches, Léon. *Trente-Deux ans à travers l'Islam (1832–1864)*. Vol. I, *Algérie.–Abd el-Kader*. Paris, Librairie de Firmin-Didot, 1884.

Rosier, J. *Souvenirs d'Algérie*. Paris: Delhomme et Briguet, 1892.

Rothschild, H. de. *Notes africaines*. Paris: Calmann Lévy, 1896.

Rousselet, Louis. *Sur les confins du Maroc: d'Oudjda à Figuig*. Paris: Librairie Hachette, 1912.

Rozet and Carette. *Algérie*. L'Univers. Paris: Firman-Didot, 1885.

Ruff, Paul. "Chronique géographique." *Bulletin de la Société de Géographie et d'Archéologie de la Province d'Oran* 20 (1898): 83–295.

Ruyssen, R. *Le Code de l'indigénat en Algérie*. Congrès de l'Afrique du Nord, Paris, 1908. Algiers: Imprimerie administrative Victor Heintz, 1908.

Sabatier, Camille. "Essai sur l'ethnologie de l'Afrique du Nord." *Revue d'Anthropologie* 2nd ser., 7 (1884): 404–59.

"Essai sur l'origine, l'évolution et les conditions actuelles des Berbers sédentaires." *Revue d'anthropologie*, 2nd ser., 5 (1882): 412–42.

"La Femme kabyle." *Bulletin de la Société de Géographie et d'Archéologie d'Oran* 16 (1883): 128–36.

La Question du Sud-Ouest. Algiers: Adolphe Jourdan, 1881.

Sabatier, Germain. *Études sur les réformes algériennes*. Oran: Imprimèrie Paul Perrier, 1891.

Saint-Paul, G. *Souvenirs de Tunisie et d'Algérie*. Preface by Th. Ribot. 2nd edn. Tunis: J. Danguin, 1909.

Salmon, G. "La kherqa des Derqaoua [*sic*] et la kherq Soûfya." Archives marocaines: publication de la Mission scientifique du Maroc 2, no.1 (1904): 127–43.

Salmon, Juliette, "Visite à Beni-Ounif et à Figuig." *Bulletin de la Société de Géographie d'Alger et de l'Afrique du Nord* 10 (1905): 1–10.

"Une Visite au M'zab." *Bulletin de la Société de Géographie d'Alger et de l'Afrique du Nord* 13 (1908:3): 325–34.

Sawas Pacha, Jean. *Étude sur la théorie du droit musulman*. Paris: Marchel et Billard, 1892.
Schirmer, Henri. *Pourquoi Flatters et ses compagnons sont morts*. Paris: Augustin Challamel, 1896.
Le Sahara. Paris: Hachette, 1893.
"Séances." *Bulletin de la Société de Géographie d'Alger et de l'Afrique du Nord* 10 (1905: 3): lxx–lxxii.
"Séances: rapport des conferences." *Bulletin de la Société de Géographie d'Alger et de l'Afrique du Nord* 13 (1908:4): lxxxix–lxxxxvi.
Sébillot, Paul. *Congrès international des traditions populaires tenu à paris du 10 au 12 septembre 1900. Procès-verbaux sommaires*. Exposition universelle internationale de 1900. Direction générale de l'exploitation. Paris: Imprimerie nationale, 1901.
Senoussi, Abou Abdallah Mohammed ben Mohammed ben Youssef [Sanūsī, Abū 'Abdallah Muḥammad bin Muḥammad bin Yusuf]. *Matn al-Sanūsiyya fī al-tawḥīd: petit traité de théologie musulmane, texte arabe publié par ordre de M. Jules Cambon, Gouverneur Général de l'Algérie, avec une traduction française et des notes par J.-D. Luciani*. Algiers: Imprimerie orientale Pierre Fontana, 1896.
Sériziat, Dr. Charles Victor Émile. *Études sur l'Oasis de Biskra*. 2nd edn. Paris: Challamel, 1875.
Simian, Marcel. *Les Confréries islamiques en Algérie (Rahmanya-Tidjanya)*. Algiers: Adolphe Jourdan, 1910.
Soleillet, Paul. *L'Afrique occidentale: Algérie, Mzab, Tidikelt*. Avignon: F. Seguin Aîné, 1877.
Exploration du Sahara: avenir de la France en Afrique. Paris: Challamel Aîné, 1876.
Souvenir de Morès: discours prononcés à la Réunion-Conférence du 9 juin 1897. Algiers: Charles Zamith, 1897.
Syndicat d'initiative de Bougie. *Bougie et la Petite-Kabylie*. Imprimerie Algérienne, 1914.
Tabet, Élie. *Ethnologie arabe: notes sur l'organisation des tribus et l'étymologie des noms propres*. Oran: Imprimerie de l'Association ouvrièrie / Heintz, Chazeau, 1882.
du Taillis, Jean. *Le Maroc Pittoresque*. Preface by Marcel Saint-Germain. Paris: Ernest Flammarion, 1905.
Tchihatcheff, P. de. *Espagne, Algérie et Tunisie: lettres à Michel Chevalier*. Paris: J.-B. Baillière et Fils, Algiers: Adolphe Jourdan, and Madrid: Carlos Bailly-Baillière, 1880.
Terzualli, Jacques. *Types algériens (types arabes, juifs, maltais, etc.)*. Algiers: Imprimerie Pascal Cresecenzo, 1894.
Trenga, G. "Les Chahaouna. notes sur les Mediouna et les Oulad Zian." *Bulletin de la Société de Géographie d'Alger et de l'Afrique du Nord* 14 (1909): 1–31.
Trumelet, Colonel Corneille. *L'Algérie légendaire: en pèleriange ça et là aux tombeau des principaux Thaumaturges de l'Islam (Tell et Sahra [sic])*. Algiers: Adolphe Jourdan, 1892.

Blida: récits selon la légende, la tradition, et l'histoire. Vols. I and II. Algiers: Adolphe Jourdan, 1887.

Les Français dans le désert: journal historique, militaire et descriptif d'une expédition aux limites du Sahara algérien. 2nd edn. Paris: Challamel Aîné, 1885.

Histoire de l'insurrection dans le sud de la province d'Alger en 1864. Vol. I. Algiers: Adolphe Jourdan, 1879.

Histoire de l'insurrection dans le sud de la province d'Alger de 1864 à 1889, deuxième partie: Histoire de l'Insurrection des Oulad-Sidi-Ech-Chikh (Sud Algérien) de 1864 à 1880. Vol. II. Algiers: Adolphe Jourdan, 1884.

Vaissière, A. *Les Ouled-Rechaich.* Algiers: Adolphe Jourdan, 1893.

Van Gennep, Arnold. *En Algérie.* Paris: Mercure de France, 1914.

Études d'ethnographie algérienne: les soufflets algériens, les poteries kabyles, le tissage aux cartons, l'art décoratif. Paris: Ernest Leroux, 1911.

Verrier, Dr. E. *Études ethnographiques.* Paris: Ernest Leroux, 1906.

Vigné d'Octon, P. *Au pays des Fétiches.* Paris: Alphonse Lemerre, 1890.

Vignon, Louis. *La France dans l'Afrique du Nord: Algérie et Tunisie.* Paris: Libraire Guillaumin, 1887.

Villot, Charles. *Mœurs, coutumes et institutions des indigenes de l'Algérie.* 2nd edn. Algiers: A. Jourdan / Paris: Challamel Aîné, 1875.

Viollier, Georges. *Les Deux Algérie.* New edn. Paris: Paul Dupont, 1899.

Vivarez, Mario. *Alger. Wargla. Lac Tchad.* Algiers: Adolphe Jourdan, 1891.

Transmutations ethniques: note adressé à la Commission sénatoriale des XVIII. Algiers: Adolphe Jourdan, 1891.

Voinot, Louis "Oudjda et l'Amalat." *Bulletin de la Société de Géographie et d'Archéologie de la Province d'Oran* 31 (June 1911): 93–200.

"Le Tidikelt." *Bulletin de la Société de Géographie et d'Archéologie de la Province d'Oran* 29 (1909): 185–216, 311–66, 419–76.

Voyage du Président de la République en Algérie: notices. Algiers: Gouvernement général de l'Algérie, 1903.

Wahl, Maurice. *Cent Lectures: morceaux choisis sur l'Algérie à l'usage des lycées, collèges, écoles normales, écoles primaires, etc.* Nouvelle bibliothèque algérienne. Algiers: Adolphe Jourdan, 1879.

"Les Congrégations dans l'Islam," *Revue de l'Afrique française.* Sixième année, no. 29 (September 1887). Paris: Librairie africaine et coloniale, 1887, 286–91.

Weisgerber, Dr. *Les Chaouia.* Paris: Comité du Maroc, 1907.

Zeys, E. *Législation mozabite: son origine, ses sources, son présent, son avenir. Leçon d'ouverture faite à l'École de droit d'Alger.* Algiers: Adolphe Jourdan, 1886.

Traité élémentaire de droit musulman algérie (école malékite). Vol. I. Algiers: Adolphe Jourdan, 1885.

Traité élémentaire de droit musulman algérie (école malékite). Vol. II. Algiers: Adolphe Jourdan, 1886.

Zeys, [E.?]. *Voyage d'Alger au M'zab (1887).* Aix-en-Provence: Centre des archives d'Outre-Mer, 1971. Microfiche.

SECONDARY AND THEORETICAL SOURCES

ʿAbd al-Fatāḥ, Fu'ād. *Al-Filāsifa al-islāmiyyun wal-ṣūfiyya wa mawqif ahl al-sunna minhum.* Alexandria, Egypt: Dār al-daʿwa al-ṭabaʿ wa al-nashar wa al-tawzī, 1997.

Abun-Nasr, Jamil M. *The Tijaniyya: A Sufi Order in the Modern World.* London: Oxford University Press, 1965.

Ageron, Charles-Robert. *"L'Algérie algérienne" de Napoléon III à de Gaulle.* La Bibliothèque arabe. Ed. Pierre Bernard Paris: Éditions Sindbad, 1980.

Les Algériens musulmans et la France (1871–1919). Vol. II. Publications de la Faculté des lettres et sciences humaines de Paris-Sorbonne, Recherches, 45. Paris: Presses universitaires de France, 1968.

Histoire de l'Algérie contemporaine. Vol. II: *De l'insurrection de 1871 au déclenchement de la guerre de libération (1954).* Paris: Presses universitaires de France, 1979.

Modern Algeria: A History from 1830 to the Present. Trans. and ed. Michael Brett. London: Hurst & Co, 1991.

Aisenberg, Andrew R. *Contagion: Disease, Government, and the "Social Question" in Nineteenth-Century France.* Stanford, Calif.: Stanford University Press, 1999.

Akhmisse, Dr. Mustapha. *Médecine, magie et sorcellerie au Maroc ou l'art traditionnel de guérir.* 4th edn. Casablanca: Dar Kortoba, 2000.

Alazard, J., E. Albertini, A[lfred] Bel, *et al. Histoire et historiens de l'Algérie.* Introduction by Stéphane Gsell. Collection du centenaire de l'Algérie, 4: archéologie et histoire. Paris: Félix Alcan, 1931.

Albergoni, Gianni. "Variations italiennes sur un theme français: la Sanusiya." In *Connaissances du Maghreb*, 111–32. 1986.

Amri, Nelly and Laroussi Amri. *Les Femmes soufies ou la passion de Dieu.* St.-Jean-de-Braye, France: Éditions Dangles, 1992.

Andezian, Sossie. *Expériences du divin dans l'Algérie contemporaine: adeptes des saints dans la region de Tlemcen.* Paris: CNRS Éditions, 2001.

Asad, Talal. "The Concept of Cultural Translation in British Social Anthropology." In Clifford and Marcus, eds. *Writing Culture*, 141–64. 1986.

Asad, Talal, ed. *Anthropology and the Colonial Encounter.* New York: Humanities Press, 1973.

Azan, General Paul. *Les Grands Soldats de l'Algérie.* Cahiers du centenaire de l'Algérie, no. 4. [Algiers]: Publications du Comité national métropolitain du centenaire de l'Algérie, [1930].

Bahloul, Brahim. "La Danse en Algérie," in Henni-Chebra and Poché, eds., *Les Danses dans le monde arabe*, 157–68. 1996.

Bancel, Nicolas, Pascal Blanchard, and Laurent Gervereau, eds. *Images et colonies: iconographies et propagande coloniale sur l'Afrique française de 1880 à 1962.* Paris: Publications de l'ACHAC, 1993.

Le Bardo: Musée d'ethnographie et de préhistoire d'Alger. Algiers: Imprimiere officielle, 1949.

Behar, Ruth. *The Vulnerable Observer: Anthropology that Breaks Your Heart.* Boston: Beacon Press, 1996.

Belamri, Rabah. *L'œuvre de Louis Bertrand: miroir de l'idéologie colonialiste*. Algiers: Office des publications universitaires, 1980.

Benabdallah, Abdelaziz. *Le Soufisme afro-maghrébin aux XIXe et XXe siècles*. N.p.: Cap Tours, 1995.

La Tijânia: une voie spirituelle et sociale. Collection Hikma. Marrakech: Al Quobba Zarqua, 1999.

Bennoune, Mahfoud. *The Making of Contemporary Algeria, 1830–1987: Colonial Upheavals and Post-Independence Development*. Cambridge: Cambridge University Press, 1988.

Berque, Jacques. "Cent vingt-cinq ans de sociologie maghrébine," in Jacques Berque. *Opera Minora*, Vol. II. 2001.

L'Intérieur du Maghreb: XVe – XIXe siècle. Bibliothèque des histoires. Paris: Éditions Gallimard, 1978.

Maghreb: histoire et sociétés sociologie nouvelle: Situations. Ed. Maurice Chaumont. Algiers: J. Duculot, 1974.

Opera Minora. Vol. I: *Anthropologie juridique du Maghreb*. Ed. Alain Mahé. Paris: Éditions Bouchène, 2001.

Opera Minora. Vol. II: *Histoire et anthropologie du Maghreb*. Ed. Gianni Albergoni. Paris: Éditions Bouchène, 2001.

Opera Minora. Vol. III: *Sciences sociales et décolonisation*. Ed. François Pouillon. Paris: Éditions Bouchène, 2001.

Structures sociales du Haut-Atlas. Paris: Presses universitaires de France, 1955.

Bhabha, Homi. *The Location of Culture*. London: Routledge, 1994.

"Signs Taken for Wonders." In Bhabha, *The Location of Culture*, 102–22. 1994.

Boëtsch, Gilles, and Jean-Noël Ferrié. "L'Impossible Objet de la raciologie: prologue à une anthropologie physique du Nord de l'Afrique," *Cahiers d'études africaines* 129, no. 33 (1993:1): 5–18.

Boubakeur, Cheikh Si Hamza. *Un Soufi algérien: Sidi Cheikh*. Vol. I. Paris: Maisonneuve & Larose, 1991.

Bowlan, Jeanne M. "Civilizing Gender Relations in Algeria: The Paradoxical case of Marie Bugéja, 1919–1939." In Clancy-Smith and Gouda, eds., *Domesticating the Empire*, 175–210. 1998.

Brahimi, Denise (monographie) and Koudir Benchikou (catalogue raisonné). *La Vie et l'œuvre d'Étienne Dinet*. Les Orientalistes. Courbevoie: A.C.R. Édition, 1984.

Briat, Anne-Marie, Janine de la Hogue, André Appel, and Marc Baroli. *Des chemins et des hommes: la France en Algérie (1830–1962)*. Preface by René-Jean Clo. Hélette: Jean Curutchet, 1995.

Burke III, Edmond, and Ira M. Lapidus, eds. *Islam, Politics, and Social Movements*. London: I. B. Tauris, 1988.

Burns, Michael. *Rural Society and French Politics: Boulangism and the Dreyfus Affair, 1886–1900*. Princeton, NJ: Princeton University Press, 1984.

Cahiers d'études africaines 129, no. 33 (1993).

Camps, Gabriel. *L'Afrique du Nord au féminin: héroïnes du Maghreb et du Sahara*. Paris: Perrin, 1992.

Célérier, J. "Nécrologie: Augustin Bernard." *Revue de géographie marocaine* 32, nos. 1–3 (1948): 101–2.

Çelik, Zeynep. *Urban Forms and Colonial Confrontations: Algiers under French Rule.* Berkeley, Calif.: University of California Press, 1997.

Chbihi Moukit, Othmane. "Khamra – ivresse mystique – et pratiques religieuses au moussem de Moulay Idriss Al Akbar." Mémoire de fin d'études de deuxième cycle des sciences de l'archéologie et du patrimoine, Institut national des sciences de l'archéologie et du patrimoine (Morocco), 1992–3.

Chih, Rachida. *Le Soufisme au quotidien: confréries d'Egypte au XX*[e] *siècle.* La Bibliothèque arabe. Arles: Éditions Sindbad, 2000.

Christelow, Allan. *Muslim Law Courts and the French Colonial State in Algeria.* Princeton, NJ: Princeton University Press, 1985.

Clancy-Smith, Julia. "A Desert Civilization: The Pre-Sahara of Algeria and Tunisia. *c.* 1800–1830." In Clancy-Smith, *Rebel and Saint,* 11–33. 1997.

"L'École rue du pacha, Tunis: l'enseignement de la femme arabe et 'la plus grande France,' *c.* 1900–1914." Trans. Anne-Marie Engels-Brooks. Special issue of *Clio: histoire, femmes et sociétés* 12 (2000): 33–55.

"Envisioning Knowledge: Educating the Muslim Woman in Colonial North Africa, *c.* 1850–1918." In Matthee and Baron, eds., *Iran and Beyond,* 99–118. 2000.

"In the Eye of the Beholder: Sufi and Saint in North Africa and the Colonial Production of Knowledge, 1830–1900." *Africana Journal* 15 (1990): 220–57.

"Islam, Gender, and Identities in the Making of French Algeria 1830–1962," in Clancy-Smith and Gouda, eds., *Domesticating the Empire,* 162–72. 1998.

Rebel and Saint: Muslim Notables, Populist Protest, Colonial Encounters (Algeria and Tunisia, 1800–1904). Comparative Studies on Muslim Societies. Ed. Barbara D. Metcalf. Berkeley, Calif.: University of California Press, 1997.

"A Woman without her Distaff: Gender, Work and Handicraft Production in Colonial North Africa." In Meriwether and Tucker, eds., *A Social History of Women and Gender in the Modern Middle East,* 25–62. 1999.

Clancy-Smith, Julia, and Frances Gouda, eds. *Domesticating the Empire: Race, Gender, and Family Life in French and Dutch Colonialism.* Charlottesville, Va.: University Press of Virginia, 1998.

Clifford, James. "Introduction: Partial Truths." In Clifford and Marcus, eds., *Writing Culture,* 1–26. 1986.

"On Ethnographic Allegory." In Clifford and Marcus, eds., *Writing Culture,* 98–121. 1986.

The Predicament of Culture: Twentieth-Century Ethnography, Literature, and Art. Cambridge, Mass.: Harvard University Press, 1988.

Routes: Travel Writing and Transculturation in the Late Twentieth Century. Cambridge, Mass.: Harvard University Press, 1997.

Clifford, James, and George E. Marcus, eds. *Writing Culture: The Poetics and Politics of Ethnography.* Berkeley, Calif.: University of California Press, 1986.

Coetzee, J. M. *Waiting for the Barbarians.* Johannesburg: Ravan Press, 1981.

Colonna, Fanny. *Instituteurs algériens, 1883–1939.* Paris: Presses de la Fondation nationale des sciences politiques, 1975.

"Présence des ordres mystique dans l'Aurès aux XIXe et XXe siècles: contribution à une histoire sociale des forces religieuses en Algérie," in A. Popovic and G. Veinstein, *Les Ordres mystiques dans l'Islam: cheminements et situation actuelle* (Paris: Éditions de l'École des hautes études en sciences sociales, 1982), 245–65.

"Presentation," In Émile Masqueray, *Formation des cités chez les populations sédentaires de l'Algérie (Kabyles du Djurdjura, Chaouïa de l'Aourâss, Beni Mezâb)*. Repr. with Intro. by Fanny Colonna. Aix-en-Provence: Edisud, 1983), i–xxv.

Comaroff, John, and Jean Comaroff. *Ethnography and the Historical Imagination*. Studies in the Ethnographic Imagination. Ed. John Comaroff, Pierre Bourdieu, and Maurice Bloch. Boulder, Colo.: Westview Press, 1992.

Conklin, Alice L. *A Mission to Civilize: The Republican Idea of Empire in France and West Africa, 1895–1930*. Stanford, Calif.: Stanford University Press, 1997.

Connaissances du Maghreb: sciences sociales et colonization. Recherches sur les sociétés méditerranéennes. Paris: Éditions du Centre national de la recherche scientifique, 1984.

Cooper, Frederick. *Colonialism in Question: Theory, Knowledge, History*. Berkeley, Calif.: University of California Press, 2005.

Cooper, Frederick, and Ann Laura Stoler, eds. *Tensions of Empire: Colonial Cultures in a Bourgeois World*. Berkeley, Calif.: University of California Press, 1997.

Corbin, Alain. *Village of the Cannibals: Rage and Murder in France, 1870*. Trans. Arthur Goldhammer. Cambridge, Mass.: Harvard University Press, 1992.

Cossu d'Escamard, Pierpaolo. "L'insurrezione del 1871 in Cabilia e la confraternita Raḥmâniyya." *Atti della Accademia nationale dei Lincei*, 8th ser., 20 (1977): 87.

Coye, Noël. "Préhistoire et protohistoire en Algérie au XIXe siècle: les significations du document archéologique," *Cahiers d'études africaines* 129, no. 33 (1993:1): 99–137.

Crapanzano, Vincent. *The Hamadhsa: A Study in Moroccan Ethnopsychiatry*. Berkeley, Calif.: University of California Press, 1973.

Crosnier, Élise. *Aurélie Picard 1849–1933: première Française au Sahara*. Algiers: Éditions Baconnier, n.d.

Daughton, J. P. *An Empire Divided: Religion, Republicanism, and the Making of French Colonialism, 1880–1914*. Oxford: Oxford University Press, 2006.

Davies, Charlotte Aull. *Reflexive Ethnography: A Guide to Researching Selves and Others*. Association of Social Anthropologists Research Methods in Social Anthropology. London: Routledge, 1999.

Déjeux, Jean. *Femmes d'Algérie: légendes, traditions, histoire, littérature*. Paris: La Boîte à documents, 1987.

Dermenghem, Émile. "J'ai vu les Aissaous d'Afrique du Nord jouer mystiquement avec le fer et avec le feu." *Sciences et voyages* (February 1949): 37–41.

Des Chene, Mary. "Locating the Past." In Gupta and Ferguson, eds., *Anthropological Locations*, 66–85. 1997.

Despois, J. "Nécrologie: Augustin Bernard." *Revue africaine* 92 (1948:1–2): 217–24.

Dirks, Nicholas B. *Castes of Mind: Colonialism and the Making of Modern India*. Princeton, NJ: Princeton University Press, 2001.

Dragué, Georges. *Esquisse d'histoire religieuse du Maroc: confréries et Zaouïas*. Paris: J. Peyronnet, n.d.

Dumons, Bruno. *Catholiques en politique: un siècle de Ralliement*. Paris: Desclée de Brouwer, 1993.

Dunwoodie, Peter. *Writing French Algeria*. Oxford: Clarendon Press, 1998.

Eickelman, Dale. "New Directions in Interpreting North African Society." In *Connaissances du Maghreb*, 279–89. 1986.

Emerit, Marcel. *La Légende de Léon Roches*. Algiers: Société historique algérienne, Faculté des lettres (Institut de géographie), n.d.

Les Saint Simoniens en Algérie (Paris: Les Belles Lettres, 1941).

Ferguson, James. *The Anti-Politics Machine: "Development," Depoliticization, and Bureaucratic Power in Lesotho*. Cambridge: Cambridge University Press, 1990.

Ferrié, Jean-Noël. "La Naissance de l'aire culturelle méditerranéenne dans l'anthropologie physique de l'Afrique du Nord," *Cahiers d'études africaines* 129, no. 33 (1993:1): 139–51.

Filali, Kamel. *L'Algérie mystique: des marabouts fondateurs aux khwân insurgés XVe / XIXe siècles*. Paris: Éditions Publisud, 2002.

Fischer, Michael M. J. "Ethnicity and the Post-Modern Arts of Memory." In Clifford and Marcus, eds., *Writing Culture*, 194–233. 1986.

Forster, E[dmund] M[organ]. *A Passage to India*. New York: Harcourt, 1924 [1984].

Foucault, Michel. *The Archeology of Knowledge and the Discourse on Language*. Trans. A. M. Sheridan Smith. New York: Pantheon Books, 1972.

The Foucault Reader. Ed. Paul Rabinow. New York: Pantheon Books, 1984.

Fournier, Marcel. *Marcel Mauss*. Paris: Fayard, 1994.

Frémeaux, Jacques. *Les Bureaux arabes dans l'Algérie de la conquête*. Paris: Denoël, 1993.

Galand, Lionel, ed., *Lettres au Marabout: messages touaregs au Père de Foucauld*. Paris: Belin, 1999.

Gellner, Ernest. *Saints of the Atlas*. The Nature of Human Society. London: Weidenfeld and Nicolson, 1969.

Gellner, Ernest, and Charles Micaud, eds. *Arabs and Berbers: From Tribe to Nation in North Africa*. Lexington, Mass.: Lexington Books, 1972.

Geoffroy, Éric. *Le Soufisme en Égypte et en Syrie sous les derniers Mamelouks et les premiers Ottomans: orientations spirituelles et enjeux culturels*. Damascus: L'Institut français d'études arabes de Damas, 1995.

Ghozzi, Abdelaziz. *L'Affiche orientaliste: un siècle de publicité à travers la collection de la fondation A. Slaoui*. Ed. Abdelaziz Ghozzi. Casablanca: Malika Éditions / Fondation Abderrahman Slaoui, 1997.

Gibson, Ralph. *A Social History of French Catholicism, 1789–1914*. New York: Routledge, 1989.

Grasshoff, Malika [pseud. Makilam]. *Signes et rituels magiques des femmes kabyles*. Aix-en-Provence: Edisud, 1999.

Guilhaume, Jean-François. *Les Mythes fondateurs de l'Algérie française*. Paris: L'Harmattan, 1992.

Gupta, Akhil, and James Ferguson. "Discipline and Practice: 'The Field' as Site, Method, and Location in Anthropology." In Gupta and Ferguson, eds., *Anthropological Locations*, 1–46. 1997.

Gupta, Akhil, and James Ferguson, eds. *Anthropological Locations: Boundaries and Grounds of a Field Science*. Berkeley, Calif.: University of California Press, 1997.

Gullickson, Gay. *Unruly Women of the Paris Commune*. Ithaca, NY: Cornell University Press, 1996.

Haddour, Azzedine. *Colonial Myths: History and Narrative*. Manchester and New York: Manchester University Press, 2000.

Hagel, Charles. "Léon Carré." *Afrique du Nord illustrée* 20, no. 206 (April 11, 1925).

Halpern, Manfred, "Emile Durkheim: Analyst of Solidarity but Not of Transformation." In *Connaissances du Maghreb*, 245–7. 1984.

Hammoudi, Abdellah. *Master and Disciple: The Cultural Foundations of Moroccan Authoritarianism*. Chicago: University of Chicago Press, 1997.

The Victim and its Masks: An Essay on Sacrifice and Masquerade in the Maghreb. Trans. Paula Wissing. Chicago: University of Chicago Press, 1993.

Hannoum, Abdelhamid. "L'Auteur comme authorité en ethnographie coloniale: le cas de Robert Montagne," in François Pouillon and Daniel Rivert, eds., *La Sociologie musulmane de Robert Montagne* (Paris: Maisonneuve & Larose, 2000), 249–64.

Haoui, Karim. "Classifications linguistiques et anthropologiques de la Société d'anthropologie de Paris au XIXe siècle," *Cahiers d'études africaines* 129, no. 33 (1993:1): 51–72.

Harris, Ruth. *Lourdes: Body and Spirit in a Secular Age*. London: Allen Lane, 1999.

Harrison, Christopher. *France and Islam in West Africa, 1860–1960*. Cambridge: Cambridge University Press, 1988.

Heffernan, Michael. "The Limits of Utopia: Henri Duveyrier and the Exploration of the Sahara in the Nineteenth Century." *The Geographical Journal* 155, no. 3 (November 1989): 342–52.

Henni-Chebra, Djamila, and Christian Poché, eds. *Les Danses dans le monde arabe, ou l'héritage des almées*. Paris: L'Harmattan, 1996.

Henry, Jean-Robert, ed. *Nouveaux Enjeux culturels au Maghreb*. Centre de recherches et d'études sur les sociétés méditerranéennes, Collection «Etudes de l'Annuaire de l'Afrique du Nord.» Paris: Éditions du Centre nationale de la recherche scientifique, 1986.

Hermassi, Abdelbaki. "The Political and Religious in the Modern History of the Maghrib." In Ruedy, ed., *Islamism and Secularism in North Africa*, 87–99. 1994.

Holsinger, Donald C. "Islam and State Expansion in Algeria: Nineteenth-Century Saharan Frontiers." In Ruedy, ed., *Islamism and Secularism in North Africa*, 3–21. 1994.

Jād-Allah, Minā̄l ʿabd al-Munʿim. *al-Taṣṣawuf fī Miṣr wa al-Maghrib*. Alexandria: Munshāʾa al-Muʿārif bil-Iskandriyya jalāl ḥazī wa sharkāh, 1997.

James, Alison, Jenny Hockey, and Andrew Dawson, eds. *After Writing Culture: Epistemology and Praxis in Contemporary Anthropology*. Association of Social Anthropologists Monographs, no. 34. London: Routledge, 1997.

al-Jazzār, Aḥmad Kamāl. *Mafākhir fī ma'ārif al-Amīr 'Abd al-Qādir wa al-sāda al-awliyā' al-akābir*. Intro by Muḥammad Zakī Ibrāhīm. Cairo: Maṭba'a al-'Umrāniyya li-l Awfasat, 1997.

Julien, Charles-André. *Études maghrébines: Mélanges Charles-André Julien*. Publications de la Faculté des lettres et sciences humaines de Paris, Études et méthodes, 11. Paris: Presses universitaires de France, 1964.

Histoire de l'Algérie contemporaine. Vol. II: *La Conquête de les débuts de la colonization (1827–1871)*. Paris: Presses universitaires de France, 1964.

Knysh, Alexander. *Islamic Mysticism: A Short History*. Themes in Islamic Studies, vol. 1. Leiden: Brill, 2000.

Lacoste-Dujardin, Camille. "Génèse et evolution d'un representation géopolitique: l'imagerie kabyle à travers la production bibliographique de 1840 à 1891," *Connaissances du Maghreb*, 257–77. 1986.

Lacoste-Dujardin, Camille, and Marie Virolle, eds. *Femmes et hommes au Maghreb et en immigration: la frontière des genres en question. Études sociologiques et anthropologiques*. Paris: Éditions Publisud, 1998.

Lalouette, Jacqueline. *La République anticléricale: XIXe–XXe siècles*. Paris: Éditions du Seuil, 2002.

Larkin, Maurice. *Religion, Politics and Preferment in France since 1890: La Belle Epoque and its Legacy*. Cambridge: Cambridge University Press, 1995.

Larson, Erik. *The Devil in the White City: Murder, Magic, and Madness at the Fair that Changed America*. New York: Vintage Books, 2003.

Lartéguy, Jean. *Sahara: An I*. Paris: Gallimard, 1958.

Lazreg, Marnia. "Gender and Politics in Algeria: Unraveling the Religious Paradigm." *Signs* 15, no. 4 (Summer 1990): 755–80.

Lebovics, Herman. *True France: The Wars over Cultural Identity, 1900–1945*. The Wilder House Series in Politics, History, and Culture. Ithaca, NY: Cornell University Press, 1992.

Leimdorfer, François. "La Condition des indigènes dans l'Algérie coloniale: essai d'analyse socio-linguistique à partir des titres de theses soutenues pendant la période coloniale." In *Connaissances du Maghreb*, 185–212. 1986.

Lorcin, Patricia M. E. *Imperial Identities: Stereotyping, Prejudice and Race in Colonial Algeria*. London: I. B. Tauris, 1995.

Lucas, Philippe. "Structures dialogiques dans les ethnologies françaises de l'Algérie: hypothèses de travail." In *Connaissances du Maghreb*, 249–56. 1986.

Lucas, Philippe and Jean-Claude Vatin. *L'Algérie des anthropologues*. Textes à l'appui: sociologie. Paris: François Maspéro, 1975.

Mahé, Alain. *Histoire de la Grande Kabylie, XIXe–XXe siècles: anthropologie historique du lien social dans les communautés villageoises*. Paris: Éditions Bouchène, 2001.

al-Mahmāh, Muṣṭafā 'Abd as-Salām. *Al-mrā'a al-maghribiyya w-at-taṣawwuf fī al-qarn al-ḥādī 'ashr al-hijrī*. Casablanca: Dar al-Kitāb, 1978 /1398.

Mansouri, Driss. "Manifestations festives et expressions du sacré au Maghreb." *Prologues*, no. 1 (1993): 5–11.

Martin, Georges. *Etienne Chevalier*. Peintres Nord-Africains. Algiers: Les Éditions Fama, 1947.

Louis Fernez. Peintres Nord-Africains. Algiers: Les Éditions Fama, 1947.

Marius de Buzon. Peintres Nord-Africains. Algiers: Les Éditions Fama, 1947.

Matthee, Rudi, and Beth Baron, eds., *Iran and Beyond: Essays in Middle Eastern History in Honor of Nikki R. Keddie*. Costa Mesa, Calif.: Mazda Publishers, 2000.

McDougall, James. *History and the Culture of Nationalism in Algeria*. Cambridge: Cambridge University Press, 2006.

McGregor, Richard J. A. "A Sufi Legacy in Tunis: Prayer and the Shadhiliyya" *International Journal of Middle East Studies* 29, no. 2 (May 1997): 255–77.

McManners, John. *Church and State in France, 1870–1914*. London: Church Historical Society, 1972.

Meriwether, Margaret L., and Judith E. Tucker, eds. *A Social History of Women and Gender in the Modern Middle East*. The Social History of the Middle East, ed. Edmund Burke III. Boulder, Colo.: Westview Press, 1999.

Messaadi, Sakina. *Les Romancières coloniales et la femme colonisée: Contribution à une étude de la littérature coloniale en Algérie dans la première moitié du XXe siècle*. Algiers: Entreprise nationale du livre, 1990.

Meyer, Jean, Jean Tarrade, Annie Rey-Goldzeiguer, and Jacques Thobie. *Histoire de la France coloniale: des origines à 1914*. Paris: Armand Colin, 1991.

Miller, Christopher L. *Blank Darkness: Africanist Discourse in French*. Chicago: University of Chicago Press, 1985.

Nationalists and Nomads: Essays on Francophone African Literature and Culture. Chicago: University of Chicago Press, 1998.

Theories of Africans: Francophone Literature and Anthropology in Africa. Chicago: University of Chicago Press, 1990.

Le Monde arabe au regard des sciences sociales: conférences données au Centre de Documentation Tunisie-Maghreb. Vol. I. Tunis: Centre de Documentation Tunisie-Maghreb, 1989.

Monod, Théodore, ed. *Fous du désert: les premiers explorateurs du Sahara, 1849–1887, H. Barth, H. Duveyrier, C. Douls*. Le Tour du Monde, ed. Chantal Edel. Paris: Phébus, 1991.

Newman, Louise Michelle. *White Women's Rights: The Racial Origins of Feminism in the United States*. Oxford: Oxford University Press, 1999.

Nord, Philip. *The Republican Moment: Struggles for Democracy in Nineteenth-Century France*. Cambridge, Mass.: Harvard University Press, 1998.

Ould-Braham, Ouahmi. "Lettres inédites d'Émile Masqueray à Alfred Rambaud," *Études et documents berbères*, no. 4 (1988): 161–81.

"Émile Masqueray au Mzab à la recherche des livres ibâdites," *Études et documents berbères*, no. 9 (1992): 5–35.

Ortner, Sherry, ed. *The Fate of "Culture": Geertz and Beyond*. Berkeley, Calif.: University of California Press, 1998.

Pandolfi, Paul. "Imaginaire coloniale et littérature: Jules Verne chez les Touaregs." *Ethnologies comparées*, no. 5 (Autumn 2002): Passés recomposés.

"Les Touaregs et nous: une relation triangulaire?" *Ethnologies comparées*, no. 2 (Spring 2001): Miroirs identitaires.

Pandolfo, Stefania. *Impasse of the Angels: Scenes from a Moroccan Space of Memory*. Chicago: University of Chicago Press, 1997.

Pascon, Paul. "Le Rapport 'secret' d'Edmond Doutté: situation politique du Hoûz 1er janvier 1907." *Hérodote*, no. 11 (July-Sept. 1978): 132–59.

Pérès, Henri. *Joseph Desparmet et son Œuvre (1863–1942)*. *Revue africaine*, nos. 396–397 (1943): 251–66.

Peyronnet, le Commandant R. *Livre d'or des officiers des affaires indigènes 1830–1930*. Vol I: *Histoire et annuaire*. Gouvernement général de l'Algérie: Commissariat général du centenaire. Algiers: Imprimerie algérienne, 1930.

Livre d'or des officiers des affaires indigènes 1830–1930. Vol. II: *Notices et Biographies*. Algiers: Imprimerie algérienne, 1930.

Popovic, A., and G. Veinstein, eds. *Les Ordres mystiques dans l'Islam: cheminements et situation actuelle*. Paris: Éditions de l'École des hautes études en sciences sociales, 1982.

Pottier, René. "A propos d'un centenaire . . . Henri Duveyrier." *Notre Sahara* 3, no. 15 (25 Octobre 1960): 41–4.

"Hommage à Henry [sic] Duveyrier." *Comptes-Rendus mensuels des séances de l'Académie des sciences d'Outre-Mer* 19 (March 6, 20, and April 17, 1959): 138–45.

Laperrine, conquérant pacifique du Sahara. Paris: Bibliothèque de l'Institut maritime et colonial, 1943.

Un Prince saharien méconnu: Henri Duveyrier. Preface by Conrad Kilian. Paris: Plon, 1938.

La Vocation saharienne du Perè de Foucauld. Paris: Plon, 1939.

"Un Seigneur du désert: Duveyrier." *Sahara de demain*, no. 2 (Octobre 1958): 19–23.

Pouillon, François, and Daniel Rivet, eds. *La Sociologie musulmane de Robert Montagne (Actes du colloque EHESS & Collège de France–Paris, 5–7 juin 1997)*. Paris: Maisonneuve & Larose, 2000.

Powers, David S. "Orientalism, Colonialism, and Legal History: The Attack on Muslim Family Endowments in Algeria and India." *Comparative Studies in Society and History* 31, no. 3 (1989): 535–71.

Pratt, Mary Louise. "Fieldwork in Common Places." In Clifford and Marcus, eds., *Writing Culture*, 27–50. 1986.

Imperial Eyes: Travel Writing and Transculturation. London: Routledge, 1992.

Prochaska, David. *Making Algeria French: Colonialism in Bône, 1870–1920*. Editions de la Maison des sciences de l'homme. Cambridge: Cambridge University Press, 1990.

Rabinow, Paul. "Representations are Social Facts: Modernity and Post-Modernity in Anthropology." In Clifford and Marcus, eds., *Writing Culture*, 234–61. 1986.

Rémond, René. *L'Anticléricalisme en France de 1815 à nos jours*. New edn. Paris: Fayard, 1999.

Renda, Mary A. *Taking Haiti: Military Occupation and the Culture of U.S. Imperialism, 1915–1940*. Chapel Hill, NC: University of North Carolina Press, 2001.

Rivet, Daniel. "Exotisme et 'pénétration scientifique': l'effort de découverte du Maroc par les Français au début du XXe siècle." In *Connaissances du Maghreb*, 92–109. 1986.

Robinson, David A. "Conclusion: A Research Agenda." In Triaud and Robinson, eds., *La Tijâniyya*, 499–510. 2000.

Paths of Accommodation: Muslim Societies and French Colonial Authorities in Senegal and Mauritania, 1880–1920. Western African Studies. Athens, OH: Ohio University Press, 2000.

Rosaldo, Renato. *Culture and Truth: The Remaking of Social Analysis*. Boston: Beacon Press, 1993.

Rosen, Lawrence. *The Anthropology of Justice: Law as Culture in Islamic Society*. Cambridge: Cambridge University Press, 1989.

The Culture of Islam: Changing Aspects of Contemporary Muslim Life. Chicago: University of Chicago Press, 2003.

Roussanne, Albert. *L'Homme suiveur de nuages: Camille Douls, Saharien (1864–1889)*. Introduction by J. M. G. Le Clezio. Rodez: Éditions de Rouergue, 1991.

Ruedy, John. "Continuities and Discontinuities in the Algerian Confrontation with Europe." In Ruedy, ed., *Islamism and Secularism in North Africa*, 73–85. 1994.

Modern Algeria: The Origins and Development of a Nation. Bloomington, Ind.: Indiana University Press, 1992.

Ruedy, John, ed. *Islamism and Secularism in North Africa*. Center for Contemporary Arab Studies, Georgetown University. New York: St. Martin's Press, 1994.

Rushdie, Salman. *The Ground Beneath Her Feet*. London: Vintage Books, 2000.

Said, Edward. *Culture and Imperialism*. New York: Alfred A. Knopf, 1994.

Orientalism. New York: Vintage Books, 1978.

Scott, James C. *Domination and the Arts of Resistance: Hidden Transcripts*. New Haven, Conn.: Yale University Press, 1990.

Seeing Like a State: How Certain Schemes to Improve the Human Condition Have Failed. Yale Agrarian Studies. New Haven, Conn.: Yale University Press, 1998.

Scott, Joan Wallach. *Only Paradoxes to Offer: French Feminists and the Rights of Man*. Cambridge, Mass.: Harvard University Press, 1996.

Sibeud, Emmanuelle. *Une Science impériale pour l'Afrique?: la construction des savoirs africanistes en France 1878–1930*. Paris: Éditions de l'École des hautes études en sciences sociales, 2002.

Sonn, Richard D. *Anarchism and Cultural Politics in Fin de Siècle France*. Lincoln, Nebr.: University of Nebraska Press, 1989.

Sorrel, Christian. *La République contre les congrégations: histoire d'une passion française (1899–1914)*. Paris: Éditions du Cerf, 2003.

Stocking, Jr., George W. *Delimiting Anthropology: Occasional Essays and Reflections*. Madison, Wisc.: University of Wisconsin Press, 2001.

Stoler, Ann Laura. *Carnal Knowledge and Imperial Power: Race and the Intimate in Colonial Rule*. Berkeley, Calif.: University of California Press, 2002.

Race and the Education of Desire: Foucault's History of Sexuality *and the Colonial Order of Things*. Durham, NC: Duke University Press, 1992.

Stoler, Ann Laura, and Frederick Cooper. "Between Metropole and colony: Rethinking a Research Agenda," in Cooper and Stoler, eds., *Tensions of Empire*, 1–56. 1997.

Stora, Benjamin. *Algeria 1830–2000*. Trans. Jane Marie Todd. Ithaca, NY: Cornell University Press, 2001.

Taraud, Christelle. *La Prostitution coloniale: Algérie, Tunisie, Maroc (1830–1962)*. Paris: Éditions Payot, 2003.

Thomas, Nicholas. *Colonalism's Culture: Anthropology, Travel and Government*. Princeton, NJ: Princeton University Press, 1994.

Thomson, Ann. "La Classification raciale de l'Afrique du Nord au début du XIXe siècle," *Cahiers d'études africaines* 129, no. 33 (1993:1): 19–36.

Triaud, Jean-Louis. *La Légende noire de la Sanûsiyya: une confrérie musulmane saharienne sous le regard français (1840–1930)*. Vols. I and II. Aix-en-Provence: Institut de recherches et d'études sur le monde arabe et musulmane, and Paris: Éditions de la Maison des sciences de l'homme, 1995.

Triaud, Jean-Louis, and David A. Robinson. eds. *La Tijâniyya: une confrérie musulmane à la conquête de l'Afrique*. Paris: Karthala, 2000.

Turin, Yvonne. *Affrontements culturels dans l'Algérie coloniale: écoles, médecines, religion, 1830–1880*. 2nd edn. Algiers: Entreprise nationale du livre, 1983.

Tyler, Stephen A. "Post-Modern Ethnography: From Document of the Occult to Occult Document," in Clifford and Marcus, eds., *Writing Culture*, 122–40. 1986.

al-ʿUbūd, Ṣāliḥ bin ʿAbdallah bin ʿAbd al-Raḥmān. *ʿAqīdat al-shaykh Muḥammad bin ʿabd al-Wahhāb al-Salafiyya wa Athr-ha fī al-ʿĀlim al-Islāmī*. Vols. I and II. Al-Manūra: Maktba al-Ghurbāʾ al-Athriyya, 1996.

Valensi, Lucette, "Le Maghreb vu du centre: sa place dans l'école sociologique française." In *Connaissances du Maghreb*, 227–44. 1984.

Vatin, Jean-Claude. "Désert construit et inventé, Sahara perdu ou retrouvé: le jeu des imaginaires." *Revue de l'Occident musulman et de la Méditerranée*, no. 37 (1984): 107–31.

al-Wardānī, Ṣāliḥ. *Al-Khaṭar al-wahhābī: thalāth risāʾil ḍid al-wahhābiyya*. Al-Qāhira [Cairo]: al-Hadaf lil-Iʿlām, 1997.

Webber, Sabra J. *Romancing the Real: Folklore and Ethnographic Representation in North Africa*. Publications of the American Folklore Society, New Series. Ed. Patrick Mullen. Philadelphia, Pa.: University of Pennsylvania Press, 1991.

Westermarck, Edward. *The Belief in Spirits in Morocco*. Acta Academiae Aboensis, Humaniora I, 1. Åbo, Finland: Åbo Academi, and Helsingfors: The Finnish Literary Society, 1920.

Wilder, Gary. *The French Imperial Nation-State: Negritude and Colonial Humanism Between the Two World Wars*. Chicago: University of Chicago Press, 2005.

Yacine, Tassadit, ed. *Amour, phantasmes et sociétés en Afrique du Nord et au Sahara: Actes du colloque international des 14–15–16 juin 1898 organisé par le CERAM à la Maison des sciences de l'homme, Paris, en hommage à Mouloud Mammeri*. Paris: Awal / L'Harmattan, 1992.

Index

'Abd al-Fatāḥ Fūād 110
'Abd al-Qādir bin Ḥamīd
  and Flatters mission 216
'Alī wālid Aḥmad, rabies cure 165–6
Abadie-Feyguine, Dr Hélène 207
Abū Naẓẓāra, Shaykh, lectures for Paris General Exposition of 1900 46–8
Abun-Nasr, Jamil 117–19, 122–4
Adhémar, Comte V. d' 34
Ageron, Charles-Robert 5, 11, 88, 94–6, 103, 210
Aisenberg, Andrew R. 176
Akhmisse, Dr Mustapha 164
Albergoni, Gianni 63–4, 228
Algerian family life
  ethnographic moralizing 203
  as key to culture 203
  legitimate field for cultural research 205, 207
  moral theory of colonial relations 203–4
  see also Algerian women; Barbet
Algerian question, the inseparability of politics and anthropology 11–12
Algerian view of French 4, 180
  cooperation with occupiers 115–16
Algerian women
  dancers 190, 192–3
  "emancipation of" 206–7
  as enslaved by the veil 196
  and ethnographic moralizing 200
  and prostitution 194–6
  public accessibility of 200–1
  roles of 182
  unattainability of 204
  see also Algerian family life
Allan, C. 45, 233
Almand, V. 94
Amat, Dr. Charles 166
Andezian, Sossie 97, 134, 143
Andrews, J. B. 151
  on genies 172–4, 177, 179
anti-Semitism 96, 232–3, 247–8
  see also Chaze; Comité du Souvenir de Morès; Morès; *Souvenir de Morès*
Appel, André 215
Archives militaires de Vincennes 19
Arripe, H. J. 162
Asad, Talal 13, 14, 149
Atgier, Dr, *Les Toureg à Paris* 46
  physical anthropology and racial pseudoscience 258
    and criminal types 258–9
    and the 'noble savage' 260
    and theatrical spectacle 259–60
Auclert, Hubertine 190
  and civilizing mission 198, 207
  prostitution and immorality 198–9
Awlād-Nāīl
  artistic dancing 192–3
  colonial moralizing mission 193–4, 196–8
  moral foundation of Empire 195–6
  prostitution 194–5, 199
  Tuareg theatre in Paris 260
  see also Auclert; Hautfort
Aymard, Captain Léopold 211, 213, 215, 218–19
  association of Tuareg with criminality 219, 257
    and Duveyrier 227–8
  on genies 172, 174, 175
  voyeurism 189–90

Bachechacht, Mme A. de 207
Bahloul, Brahim, Théâtre National Algérien 193
Banque de l'Algérie, and Edme Rinn 67
Barbet, Charles 135, 194–5
  and civilizing mission 202
  invasion of homes 204–5